From Beijing to Port Moresby

From Beijing to Port Moresby
The Politics of National Identity in Cultural Policies

Edited by

Virginia R. Domínguez
University of Iowa, Iowa City, USA

and

David Y. H. Wu
Chinese University of Hong Kong

Gordon and Breach Publishers
Australia Canada China France Germany India
Japan Luxembourg Malaysia The Netherlands
Russia Singapore Switzerland

Copyright © 1998 OPA (Overseas Publishers Association) N.V. Published by license under the Gordon and Breach Publishers imprint.

All rights reserved.

No part of this book may be reproduced or utilized in any form or by any means, electronic or mechanical, including photocopying and recording, or by any information storage or retrieval system, without permission in writing from the publisher. Printed in India.

Amsteldijk 166
1st Floor
1079 LH Amsterdam
The Netherlands

Chapter 4 in this book originally appeared in the journal *Culture and Policy*, 6(1). Copyright © 1994 Griffith University, Brisbane, Queensland, Australia. Reprinted with permission.

British Library Cataloguing in Publication Data

From Beijing to Port Moresby : the politics of national
  identity in cultural policies
  1. Culture - East Asia 2. Nationalism - East Asia 3. Politics and culture - East Asia 4. East Asia - Civilization
  I. Domínguez, Virginia R. II. Wu, David Y. H.
  306'.095'09049

ISBN 90-5700-502-6

CONTENTS

Acknowledgments ix

Romanization of Chinese xiii

List of Contributors xv

1 Introduction: Cultural(ist) Articulations
of National(ist) Stakes
Virginia R. Domínguez, with Sasha Su-Ling Welland 1

I SINGAPORE

2 The Making of a New Nation: Cultural
Construction and National Identity in Singapore
Chua Beng-Huat and Eddie Kuo 35

3 A Second Look: On "The Making of a New Nation"
Allen J. Chun 69

II TAIWAN

4 The Culture Industry as National Enterprise:
The Politics of Heritage in Contemporary Taiwan
Allen J. Chun 77

5	"Invention of Taiwanese": A Second Look at Taiwan's Cultural Policy and National Identity *David Y. H. Wu*	115
6	Rejoinder to Second Look *Allen J. Chun*	133

III PAPUA NEW GUINEA

7	Pasin Tumbuna: Culture and Nationalism in Papua New Guinea *Lamont Lindstrom*	141
8	Cultural Diversity and Identity in Papua New Guinea: A Second Look *Wari Iamo and Jacob Simet*	189

IV CHINA

9	"Cultural Fever": A Cultural Discourse in China's Post-Mao Era *Haiou Yang*	207
10	The Cultural Mission of the Chinese Intelligentsia: A Second Look at Cultural Fever *David Y. H. Wu*	247

V JAPAN

11	Hegemony of Homogeneity in the Politics of Identity in Japan *Harumi Befu*	263
12	A Second Look: Anatomy of Misinterpretation *Darrell William Davis*	293

VI THAILAND

13 Buddhist Cultural Tradition and the Politics of National Identity in Thailand
Yos Santasombat — 305

14 The Politics of Cultural Citizenship: A Second Look at "Buddhist Cultural Tradition and the Politics of National Identity in Thailand"
Chaiwat Satha-Anand — 353

About the Contributors — 367

Index — 373

ACKNOWLEDGMENTS

Our thanks go, first and foremost, to the East–West Center (EWC) in Honolulu, Hawai'i, whose long-standing commitment to scientific and cultural exchange enabled David Wu, Geoffrey White, Elizabeth Buck and Larry Smith—all then at the EWC—to begin serious discussion of "cultural policy(ies)" in the late 1980s and draw a number of us both physically and intellectually into those discussions. Financing for a week-long working conference on cultural policies and national identities, in June 1990, was made possible through the generosity and support of the East–West Center. With the exception of Chaiwat Satha-Anand, Eddie Kuo and Sasha Su-Ling Welland, who were not present at that conference, all the contributors to this book participated as authors or exchanged views at the initial meeting.

Other participants at that "originary" moment provided intellectual leadership, additional perspectives, engaging questions and scholarly camaraderie and, although not all became contributors to this project, their presence, insights and knowledge at that formative time deserve special acknowledgment here. They include: Tu Wei-ming, then head of the Institute of Culture and Communication that sponsored the meeting; Wimal Dissanayake, long-time writer and editor of the *East–West Film Journal*; Princess M. L. Walwihpa Burusratanaphan, historian at Thammasat University in Bangkok; Burt Feintuch, folklore scholar from the University of New Hampshire; David Whisnant, from the University of North Carolina at Chapel Hill; Lawrence Foanaota, director of the National Museum of the Solomon Islands; and Ma Rong, sociologist from Beijing University.

In the years immediately following the 1990 East–West Center conference, talks continued and individual researchers pursued their work, but a group of us became increasingly convinced of the need to make these researchers' papers available, first through a Working Papers Series and later through a formal publication. As the desire to explore these options grew, I became more and more drawn to the issues and the project. Special conferences with related themes were happening in a number of venues very different from the EWC, including working conferences in which I participated in Ottawa, Canada (December 1991), Maribor, Slovenia (February 1992), Hong Kong (December 1992–January 1993), Santa Cruz, California (January 1993), and Mijas, Spain (June 1994).

While, arguably, they focused on different topics—from art to the political rights of official minorities in emergent small states of Europe to the variable relevance of territorial borders in collective self-definition—all addressed sociopolitical arenas in which culture is invoked, debated or highlighted and in which the persistent overlapping themes were sovereignty, freedom, collective rights to self-determination and the power to shape fields of cultural production. "Cultural" politics and "cultural" policies clearly deserved intense scrutiny and an awareness of the relevance of location. Eventually a book project drawing primarily on the expertise, disagreements and exchanges among a number of key participants in the East–West Center initiative emerged as viable and worthwhile.

Other individuals have contributed in significant ways to this project and we are duly grateful. Editor Philip Rappaport was very helpful in improving the manuscript while enthusiastically backing the project. Monica Glina, who inherited the project, exuded just the right amount of enthusiasm to get the revised final version of the book actually into production. Elizabeth (Betty) Buck, political scientist, colleague and friend at the EWC, who had originally planned to function as co-editor, helped enormously with some of the major conceptual and stylistic editing of a couple of the earlier drafts of essays now appearing in this book. Sasha Su-Ling Welland, who worked with me on a number of projects at Iowa from 1994 to 1996, made the book's mechanics manageable and its contents gel.

David Fowler and Michael Lewis, who helped with the project at different stages of the actual publishing process, improved the content and aided in its completion. Geoff White, David Wu's long-time colleague at the EWC (and by now long-standing colleague and friend of mine as well) chose not to pursue the role of co-editor with us, but continued to offer insights and feedback on essays, issues and drafts of the introduction, without which the book would have suffered greatly. More anonymously, we also wish to thank the two insightful, diligent, committed and constructively critical reviewers whose lengthy commentaries on our first full draft gave us all a boost of confidence and a great deal to chew on.

In many ways, we also want to note with appreciation the *settings* in which we as editors work and their own intense, though less individualistic, contributions to this volume. Many of this book's earlier discussions took place in Hawai'i, *formally* a state of the United States, where sovereignty is a hot issue and "culture" a key element in contemporary political life. Over the past eight years, as I have followed developments in Hawaiian cultural politics and the Hawaiian sovereignty movement, I have been interested in how, when and why culture is invoked. The 100th anniversary of the overthrow of the last Hawaiian monarch, Queen Lili'uokalani in 1893, galvanized large sectors of the Hawaiian-identified population, but a Hawaiian cultural and political renaissance neither started nor ended with the 1993 anniversary commemoration. A national(ist), culturally inflected movement for self-determination occurring within the territory of the contemporary U.S. makes it hard to downplay the role that "culture" (in multiple senses) plays in assertions and contestations over "nationhood" in myriad contemporary political settings.

Much the same can be said of Hong Kong, David Wu's current home. After a century as a British crown colony, its agreed-upon reintegration into the People's Republic of China has reportedly produced deep anxieties across wide sectors of Hong Kong society concerned not just about a feared potential decline in economic prosperity after reintegration but also, and at times most vocally, about a potential loss of "cultural identity," cultural and artistic freedoms, and a cultural public sphere.

To our colleagues in Hawai'i and Hong Kong most active in these public debates, articulations and positions of advocacy, we owe an indirect but strong vote of thanks.

Finally, special thanks to my colleague and partner Jane Desmond, co-director of the International Forum for U. S. Studies, with whom I have shared the thrills and tribulations of large edited collections and whose patience, support and intellectual insight enabled this book to become a reality—and to P. Nickle and M. Poke, for whom book manuscripts are special sources of palpable pleasure.

Virginia R. Domínguez

ROMANIZATION OF CHINESE

All transcriptions of Chinese in the essays on China and Taiwan are in *pinyin*. This has been done to increase uniformity and clarity for the reader; it can be confusing if different authors refer to the same term with different spelling.

There are three exceptions to this, however. References in the notes and citations sections of each chapter follow the forms used by the author being cited, and quotations from an original source using a different system, usually the Wade–Giles, have not been changed. Also, widely recognized names such as Sun Yat-sen (rather than Sun Zhongshan) and Kuomintang or KMT for the Nationalist Party (rather than Guomindang) have not been changed to *pinyin*. Finally, for the names of people and places in Taiwan, we use the form of romanization preferred in Taiwan, hence Chiang Kai-shek, Chiang Ching-kuo, Lee Teng-hui and the capital city Taipei.

CONTRIBUTORS

Harumi Befu, professor emeritus, Stanford University; professor, Kyoto Bunkyo University, Japan.

Chua Beng-Huat, associate professor, Department of Sociology, National University of Singapore.

Allen J. Chun, research fellow, Institute of Ethnology, Academia Sinica, Nankang, Taipei, Taiwan.

Darrell William Davis, lecturer, Kobe University of Commerce, Japan.

Virginia R. Domínguez, professor of anthropology; co-director of the International Forum for U.S. Studies, University of Iowa, Iowa City, USA.

Wari Iamo, director, Papua New Guinea National Research Institute.

Eddie C. Y. Kuo, professor; dean, School of Communication Studies at Nanyang Technological University, Singapore.

Lamont Lindstrom, professor of anthropology, University of Tulsa, Oklahoma, USA.

Yos Santasombat, professor of anthropology; faculty of social science, Chiang Mai University, Thailand.

Chaiwat Satha-Anand, president of the Social Science Association of Thailand; and director of Peace Information Center, Foundation for Democracy and Development Studies.

Jacob Simet, executive director, Papua New Guinea National Cultural Commission.

Sasha Su-Ling Welland, graduate student in anthropology, University of California, Santa Cruz, USA.

David Y. H. Wu, professor and chair, Department of Anthropology, Chinese University of Hong Kong.

Haiou Yang, research associate, Center for Occupational and Environmental Health, University of California, Irvine, USA.

1

Introduction: Cultural(ist) Articulations of National(ist) Stakes

Virginia R. Domínguez, with Sasha Su-Ling Welland

Picture these scenes. Clusters of Japanese high school students, variously clad in uniform school blazers or Raiders starter jackets, disembark from a fleet of air-conditioned buses and roam the Beijing Friendship Store shopping for souvenirs of their summer tour in China. A Tibetan cab driver in Chinese-controlled Lhasa tells a tourist he presumes to be Western that he prefers and identifies with Indian popular music and cinema and not with the Hong Kong and Taiwanese music and films that are far more popular in contemporary socialist China. And in Washington, D.C., a professional woman from the Solomon Islands, flown in by the Rural Advancement Foundation International headquartered in Ottawa, Canada, speaks critically and eloquently (and in English) at a key public session on "the Human Genome Diversity Project," sponsored by the U.S. National Academy of Sciences.

Borders are indeed being crossed with unprecedented speed and in unparalleled volume—by consumer goods, information-age images, and myriad travellers. What is equally clear, however, is that intense border crossings of this sort are not making borders disappear or even, in many cases, weaken. Side by side with the traveling, communicating, and consuming possibilities of the late twentieth century lies the seemingly paradoxical but very widespread phenomenon of assertions of sovereignty and distinctiveness formulated in terms of culture.

There is indeed a paradox at work here. Fast information technology, leisure, business, and labor travel, multinational capital investments, ever-expanding NGOs (non-governmental organizations), and the relative ease with which particular products of "popular culture" nowadays cross national boundaries all make it untenable to just assume that territorial sovereignty is the obvious and simple product of cultural distinctiveness, or that cultural difference, cultural uniqueness, and cultural identity are the inherent and only possible justifications for national sovereignty.

But people, groups, or countries insist on a cultural framing of their collective existence for a host of reasons. Some, we know, relish the new opportunities to participate in what they take to be a global culture. Some actively draw lines by identifying others they believe have crossed them. Among the examples that come to mind are (1) mainland Chinese critics, professional and popular, decrying film directors Zhang Yimou and Chen Kaige for catering to "Western" audiences and international film festival juries with their foreign-financed representations of China[1], and (2) Taiwanese students' and Taipei artists' protest against the National Palace Museum's decision to loan centuries-old "national treasures" for the 1996 "Splendors of Imperial China" exhibit at the New York

Metropolitan Museum of Art as messing "with [their] cultural patrimony" (cf. Solomon 1996).

Some see in all this culture-crossing and culture-asserting good marketing possibilities—and, hence, a strategy for subregional or national economic development—while others perceive an urgency, now more than ever, in asserting particular cultural differences for the sake of national or even regional unity. The Cultural Development Program of Papua New Guinea is an example of the former, using its Australian funding to promote, among other projects, the marketing of traditional culture for international tourist consumption. Malaysian Prime Minister Mahathir Mohammed's public position is an example of the latter—as he reportedly asserts that "by embracing shared 'Asian values,' emerging nations can achieve unity and power" (*Honolulu Advertiser*, March 31, 1996, p. B1). Still others respond to statements like Mahathir Mohammed's by arguing for the need to curb governmental impulses such as his out of fear they might lead to isolationism, xenophobia, or domestic repression of "minorities" and political dissidents.

At stake are the grounds for asserting boundedness and, through boundedness, claims to recognition, equality, privilege, or sovereignty. Fast-paced border crossings did not suddenly cause this, but they do exacerbate the problem. If boundedness cannot be taken for granted, how can it be claimed and sustained and in whose interest? It is in this light that we find the invocation and policing of cultural distinctiveness most interesting.

"A global resurgence of assertions of cultural identity," Wu and his East-West Center colleagues wrote prophetically in 1989, "has come in many forms: at the national level as state-defined national ideology; among ethnic groups as assertions of minority rights and values; and among indigenous populations as regional and even separatist nationalist movements." Artists, scholars, and grassroots activists can find moral and even financial support by joining the battle for "cultural resistance," "cultural politics," and "cultural identity." And governments respond, generate initiatives, challenge, and manage these culture claims quite often these days by making their own claims in terms of culture.

Like nineteenth century Europe, the late twentieth century seems hell-bent on invoking culture, indeed on privileging culture, in struggles to define, redefine, control, and contest the shape of sociopolitical entities. Although there is nothing in the idea of group formation that makes it necessary for a group to define itself as culturally distinct, culturally derived, or culturally motivated, it is obvious that at this historical juncture groupness often appears to demand it. Large and small institutions—national as well as international—participate in this "culturalization" of groupness at this historical juncture (cf. Domínguez 1992).

Cultural Survival, for example, seeks to save small, often peripheralized peoples around the world from total loss of resources, self-governance, and *cultural* extinction. The British, Australian, and U.S. Cultural Studies movements lend academic legitimacy to non-dominant, non-elite populations' aesthetic forms and popular practices in the former colonial metropolitan centers as well as in their ex-colonies. UNESCO encourages, even pressures, all of its member states to develop official *cultural* policies. In 1970 and again in 1982, UNESCO sponsored World Conferences of Cultural Policies, and throughout the 1970s and 1980s commissioned and published studies of "cultural policies" in well over forty different member countries. Included were countries with senses of themselves as old as well as those with only shallow histories of sovereignty, Western European countries as well as Eastern ones, countries that have never been colonies of Europe as well as those constituted as entities by the force of European colonialism (cf. Domínguez 1995).

This widespread pattern of invoking culture, which several of us increasingly refer to as culturalism, deserves attention as a cultural*ist* politics, that is, as a form of articulation of power and power claims in terms of culture, often overshadowing forms of articulation of power and power claims in terms of other things. Like culturalist politics in Europe in the nineteenth century, contemporary invocations of culture promote the naturalization of something called culture and of politics based on it. But unlike nineteenth century culturalism, contemporary culturalism is not regionally restricted, not primarily European, and not simply a case of mimicry by Europe's former colonies.

Something is definitely going on, and we have not yet linked all the parts. Indeed some of us are involved in activist grassroots politics framing claims in terms of culture. Some of us are participant observers in postcolonial governments' ministries and commissions of culture. Some of us come from social and intellectual elites but seek to undermine elitism by invoking culture; others of us come from social and intellectual elites and seek to claim privilege by invoking culture.

Wu, White, Buck, and Smith (1989) predicted that these trends would "become increasingly prominent during the 1990s due to new economic and political developments and due to intensified cultural interaction through international communication and trade, including trade in cultural commodities... and that the contemporary importance of culture in the 1990s [would lie] in its dynamic quality as an object of discussion, debate, manipulation, and struggle." Wu and his colleagues wrote this while sitting in the middle of the Pacific, not in Paris, Prague, Montreal, or New York. And their referents were Japan and its feverish *Nihonjinron* (a widespread public discourse on Japanese uniqueness), the People's Republic of China and the high-brow "culture fever" of the 1980s (following Mao's Cultural Revolution), Singapore's engineered Singaporean culture, Vanuatu's public discussion of "kastom," and Papua New Guinea's high profile "cultural policies."

Of special interest to these East-West Center scholars and the colleagues they intrigued and recruited to various meetings and discussions (of which this volume is an outgrowth) were "cultural policies." Most visible, of course, were official statements issued by specific governments, often by specific ministries formally dedicated to "culture"—sometimes in conjunction with education, sometimes in conjunction with tourism, sometimes in conjunction with majority and minority statuses. These official statements represent political articulations of unity and disunity, relations with other societies as well as between sectors of their own society, aesthetic forms to be privileged, tolerated, or silenced, all framed in terms of culture.

We noted, for example, that official cultural policies in Singapore and Papua New Guinea have openly tried to forge new national identities out of recent postcolonial situations—with Singapore developing a self-image as a model of modernity and Papua New Guinea a campaign for "unity in diversity." And we explored how in Taiwan, the official invention or revival of "traditional Chinese culture" in the post-1949 KMT (Kuomintang) era sought fairly openly to (1) suppress native Taiwanese sentiments, (2) counter the lingering influence of Japanese colonization that had just ended in 1945, and (3) define Taiwan in direct opposition to the radical visions of the Communist Party on the Mainland.

But we also noted the level of intensity in many of these countries' public discussions of "culture" among intellectuals, artists, journalists, and politicians infusing the issue of "cultural policies" with poignancy, forcefulness, and drama far beyond the apparent formality of official statements on "cultural policy." China's "Culture Fever," Japan's *Nihonjinron*, and Thailand's *Santi Asoke* movement could never really be equated with these countries' official cultural policies, but all three clearly exemplified why explorations of "cultural policies" should never limit themselves to the most visible articulations of official policy by one or more government ministries.

What may not start off as government policy at all often reflects on government policy, articulates political dissent in terms of culture, and may even acquire enough public support to insert itself in official government ranks. As Haiou Yang describes it in this book, "Culture Fever" emerged from "the underground hotspring" of political dissidents (many, but not all, intellectuals) in late 1970s China, but was later partially validated by the state when the officially-formed New Authoritarianists joined the discussion.[2] *Nihonjinron*, described by Harumi Befu as something of a "national pastime" in Japan, was indeed initially supported by a vast popular literature and is often identified with it, but it was also later officially sanctioned by a policy-making committee of *Nihonjinron* advocates appointed by the Prime Minister. And the *Santi Asoke* movement, a Buddhist fundamentalist movement often at loggerheads with the official government of Thailand over the contemporary nature of Thai society and "culture," entered and affected the political arena by actively capitalizing on the wide popular support enjoyed by its religious leaders.

"Cultural policies" *and* their sociopolitical contexts, hence, came to constitute the subject of this book. Inspired by those earlier discussions at the East-West Center in the late 1980s and early 1990s and intrigued by the debates they provoked, we chose to juxtapose papers that would reflect not only the issues but also the debates. We chose to focus less on arguing for or against the truth claims of particular narratives of history, particular calls for authenticity, or particular social movements' ideologies of culture than on what these claims, calls, and ideologies do. We are much more interested in how they function, how they are used, and what they enable, as well as what enables them to play a role in social and political life in a range of countries in the late twentieth century.

We deliberately chose countries outside Europe, not just to add to knowledge and debate about those countries or those geographic regions but also to expand our knowledge of the modalities of institutional culturalism and their spatiotemporal politics. The countries discussed and debated in this book are quite varied and have a Pacific rather than Atlantic axis. They are located in East Asia, Southeast Asia, and the Pacific, regions subjected to varying degrees of European colonization over the past few centuries (including some countries never formally colonized by European powers although over the years threatened, invaded, or colonized by neighboring regional powers). They also come from a region(s) now rich in economies that more than rival the industrial economies of Europe and North America, but also a region(s) in which poorer and richer countries articulate uncertainties about political stability, historical worth, economic competitiveness, and boundedness explicitly (and often loudly these days) in terms of "culture."

This intended expansion of the geographic bases for theorizing about cultural(ist) politics and its intersection with institutional nation-building makes sense both intellectually and historically. Recent scholarship has drawn on, and sought to apply, Hobsbawm and Ranger's *The Invention of Tradition* (1983) to societies outside Europe and time periods other than the late nineteenth century. Much of this literature on "the politics of culture" has focused on evidence that symbols, rituals, dress, dance, and historical accounts are subject to political manipulation and interpretation, indeed to invention. A number of those analyses (cf. Hanson 1989; Keesing 1989 and 1991; Levine 1991; Linnekin 1991) have sparked public controversies, some of them quite heated in the Pacific, pitting non-native intellectuals against politicized native intellectuals (e.g. Trask 1991 and 1993). Archeological sites, history textbooks, arts festivals, and ethnographic films have become hot potatoes in the process.

As *Exhibiting Cultures* (1991), *Nation and Narration* (1990), *Reading National Geographic* (1993), *Cultural Nationalism in East Asia* (1993), and *Culture, Kastom, Tradition* (1994) all vividly illustrate, this level of politicization of "cultural representation" is geographically widespread. Objects, exhibits, print matter, and audiovisual creations displayed as or consumed as representations of particular peoples' "cultures" have become such frequent targets of criticism that growing numbers of scholars refuse to get near them. To us, in this volume, this is all evidence of a wider social phenomenon not restricted to matters of representation or symbolism.

When push comes to shove, it is the very sense of "groupness" that is at stake, not just its positive or negative representation. In an era in which groups proclaiming sovereignty (or at least the right to self-determination) must articulate those claims in terms of culture, self-constituting groups whose culture claims are contested experience the contestation as a challenge to their groupness. "Groupness"—its experience, its processing, its packaging, its promotion, its insistence, and its stakes—are then the real heart and soul of contemporary invocations and formulations of "culture."

TECHNOLOGIES OF BOUNDEDNESS

Boundedness does not just happen. Which form it takes, how it relates to other forms, and how it is deployed in social relations, political struggles, and economic flows come about under particular spatial and temporal conditions. What and where is "China"? When, how, and why is there such a thing as "China"? Knowing that two competing states both claim the designation no doubt leads us to highlight the explicit political nature of the question, but the conditionality of boundedness often appears far less obvious. What and where is "Japan"? "Thailand"? "Singapore"? or "Papua New Guinea"? When, how, and why are there such "things"?

Richard Handler's thoughts on the epistemologies of "entitivity" in his 1988 analysis of nationalism in contemporary Quebec (Handler 1988), Benedict Anderson's often cited idea that the things we have come to call nations are all products of a particular way of imagining community (Anderson 1983), and Domínguez' examination in 1989 of the never-finished quality of things we call "peoples" all address a level of perception, conception, feeling, and naturalization far deeper than the explicit and blatant political struggles that bring states to the brink of war (Domínguez 1989). How these naturalizations take place, i.e. how they are promoted, institutionalized, disciplined, and contested, is best seen through the range of formulations, activities, debates, practices, and technologies we harness here under the rubric of "cultural policies."

Nihonjinron is one seemingly obvious example. Often known outside Japan as a widespread and popular discourse among Japanese people about Japanese cultural uniqueness, it is easy to depict it as a form of blatant cultural nationalism. But such labeling is just as likely to block further analysis as it is to incite Japan-bashing in particular corners of the world, at least some of them characterized by unfriendly historical, economic, or territorial relationships with Japan. In his contribution to this volume, Befu argues that, although *Nihonjinron* appears in its declarative statements to be a descriptive cultural model, its underlying premises and the positive valence it gives to Japanese culture turns it into a prescriptive model with normative implications for people and policies in Japan. Befu insists that what is important is how the Japanese perceive and, hence, construct this identity, rather than whether or not the perceptions are grounded in any objective reality.

Toward this end, Befu provides a survey of *Nihonjinron* literature which is quite large and continually growing. He estimates that approximately 1,000 books on the subject have been written in the last 43 years, and many of the most popular publications end up in numerous reprintings. Japanese uniqueness, purity, and homogeneity are asserted and praised throughout this literature, and Befu usefully notes that the objectivist rhetoric of *Nihonjinron* makes its hegemonic role all the more effective. But how hegemonic and how effective?

One survey conducted by Befu and associates in Nishinomiya showed that a significant number of people disclaim belief in certain *Nihonjinron* propositions, but Befu finds it significant

Introduction

11

that these opposing views are rarely voiced in public venues. Darrell William Davis (chapter 12), however, finds solace in the Nishinomiya survey results, which he takes to be statistical data that *Nihonjinron* is far less pervasive than its ubiquitous presence in media, education, and government would lead one to think.

One could argue that *Nihonjinron*, in fact, reveals the cracks in the presumed boundedness of "Japanese society," that its emergence and continued existence derive from a continued sensory barrage suggesting the non-uniqueness of Japanese culture, or at least pointing to the many signs that its "boundaries" are both permeable and fuzzy. If Befu is correct, an inherent ethnocentrism creeps in. If Davis is correct, what is in evidence is a defensive culturalist nationalism, far more limited in its scope and bite, blown out of proportion by outsiders with a strong stake in demonizing the Japanese.

Nihonjinron is interesting in and of itself, but it is its culturalist articulation(s) of the sociopolitical problem of boundedness that makes it central to this volume. There is an intensity to the way Davis takes on Befu's argument. This is not just an academic dispute about the nature and spread of a particular cultural ritual, regional festival, or literary formulation. Davis, an American without genealogical ties to Japan, is as concerned with American "Japan-bashing" as he is with Japanese *Nihonjinron*. Befu, a product of the Japanese diaspora who remains professionally and personally engaged with "Japan," has his own bottom line. "Herein lies the root problem," he writes, "[it is] the need to accommodate ethnic minorities in the discursive and symbolic identity of the states which have so far defined themselves in terms of the dominant group" (Befu, p. 286). *Nihonjinron* may indeed verge, as Davis claims it does, on what he calls the "flippant and frivolous" side, and it may well be, as he argues, that it is an ideology "that nearly everyone knows should be taken with a large pinch of salt" (Davis, p. 301). But it also puts in plain view, and articulates in culturalist terms that are globally very much in vogue, an argument for continued boundedness that is neither flippant nor frivolous nor inconsequential.

As the debates over *Nihonjinron* point out, the fact is that there do not appear to be too many terms in which is it "acceptable" at the close of the twentieth century to speak of boundedness. If a significant number of people want to assert a collective self-definition as Japanese, in which terms can they do so without inviting immediate local, regional, and more global criticism? "Race" may remain an ongoing discursive object in a variety of settings and countries, especially within the European diaspora, but its acceptability as a mode of self-characterization in the aftermath of World War II is highly questionable. Nationhood, or as Benedict Anderson prefers to label it "nation-ness," appears to be the continued and, hence, globally acceptable mode of political organization, but its periodic slide into aggressive nationalisms leaves it perennially suspect. In contrast, invoking "culture" as a principle of boundedness appears acceptable on the world scene.

"Culture" may have two unbeatable advantages. One is clearly its aura of positivity, the other, its referential malleability. A "culture" may well be disparaged by some but global discourses on culture tend to be egalitarian, relativistic, and often even celebratory. Even though totally unambiguous praise is unrealistic and usually unintended, there is the presumption that there is some good, something of value, something distinctive and worth preserving in each and every "culture." To articulate boundedness in terms of culture is then to articulate that there is goodness, value, and praiseworthiness associated with the bounded group. It is also to articulate that it has a distinctive contribution to make to humanity now and in the future. What group would not want such a positive twist to its existence?

But one of the most curious, less visible, and most advantageous characteristics of culturalism is the slipperiness, mutability, multidimensionality, and polysemy of its referent. What does culture refer to? There is no one set of "things" to which it must refer. There is no one level of social organization that it automatically indexes. There is no literary or anthropological consensus about what it means, where it can be found, or even how it can be researched. Even though one large branch of the field of anthropology has defined itself as "cultural anthropology" and has regularly invoked culture throughout the twentieth century, anthropologists are far from being in complete agreement on the usage of the term. The bottom line is that it can be and is invoked in many ways by many people, organizations, institutions, and social movements. Invoking culture may be a very acceptable thing to do in the late twentieth century, precisely because what it really means in any one debate, policy, exhibit, or characterization may not be altogether clear or because it can be easily invoked for multiple—even competing—uses (cf. Domínguez 1996).

What does the Singaporean government refer to when it promotes Singaporean-ness? Asserting certain sameness-es as Singaporean culture, Singaporean nationhood, and Singaporean peoplehood simultaneously means ignoring or silencing other things or treating them as less significant. Modernity, economic success, and social unity (rather than racial strife) get stressed at the expense of differences based on languages of origin, physical differences, or religious differences.

What does it mean for the government of Papua New Guinea to invoke culture and formulate a formal policy about culture in Papua New Guinea? As Lindstrom and White explained in their introduction to *Culture, Kastom, Tradition: Developing Cultural Policy in Melanesia*, "rhetorics of The Pacific Way, The Melanesian Way, Melanesian Socialism, Melanesian Kastom are all attempts to imagine national communities in culturalist terms" (1994:7). What to hook on to is the question. Values, interpersonal patterns, religious rituals, gender relations, modes of power, and bodily habits may serve as referents for culture (see Lindstrom's essay in this volume, along with Iamo and Simet's response also in this volume). Picking one or several as the key referents will result in there being larger or smaller "groups" seen as sharing a culture.

Likewise, in the cultural(ist) discourse of China's post-Mao era (mid-to-late 1980s), the various strands of "culture fever" referred to and, of course, debated Chinese "national character," the Confucian system of hierarchic and interdependent social relationships known as the rule of rites, Mao Zedong thought, and "Western cultures" (see Yang in chapter 9 of this book). As Yang notes, the discussions, which involved interactions between official and unofficial forces, intellectuals and even the general public, regularly mixed "culture" with politics as it addressed major issues of social and political order (and disorder) in China.

But David Wu, perhaps more cynically, insists (in his Second Look commentary on Yang) that it was not a movement *about* culture but, rather, one of disguised politics in which Chinese intelligentsia "acted both within the cultural tradition of intellectual soul-searching as well as within the new tradition of class struggle for recognition in a socialist system" (Wu, p. 248).[3] Whatever the actual balance, noteworthy is the choice by both Chinese intellectuals and less intellectually-rooted political dissidents of a culturalist idiom in which to debate and wage their battles in a post-Mao era. *Youhuan yishi*, or "consciousness of collective worries and sufferance" over the fate of Chinese culture in the modern world, arguably functions performatively at least as much as descriptively as a discourse about the nature of the collectivity, claims to its boundedness, and idioms for claiming boundedness.

In much more overt attempts to build a sense of "nation," Singapore and Papua New Guinea have both made particular conceptions of heterogeneity things to praise and other forms of difference things to ignore or decry. Allen Chun (chapter 3 in this volume) calls it "ethnicity à la Singapore" when referring to the government's quota-like defusing of political affiliation along "ethnic" lines, and he argues strongly that the true aim of the government is to achieve a higher level of homogeneity in a single-party state dominated by the People's Action Party. A similar critique is echoed in Lindstrom's report (in chapter 7 of this book) of suspicions in Papua New Guinea that there is an over-Westernized urban elite largely running the centralized government, and invoking the tradition of the country's many cultures merely as a way of pulling the wool over villagers' eyes.

Official policies of multiculturalism and multiracialism target sameness at the level of national societal inclusiveness and difference at an intrasocietal level they believe the society can tolerate or even benefit from. A policy of inclusiveness invoking the language of culture can function as a particularly effective technology of boundedness because "culture" and "inclusiveness" are typically processed as good and there is nothing egregious leading large numbers of people to see hegemonic underpinnings behind these agendas (cf. Domínguez 1994).

This is not to say that such agendas cannot be recognized and actively contested or resisted in everyday life through noncompliance. What form of resistance, when to resist, and how much resistance is openly debated in this book with particular regard to Taiwan. Allen Chun describes the project of the Nationalist government in Taiwan as one meant to homogenize society through policies promoting "traditional Chinese culture." Wu counters that these cultural policies were not as successful at suppressing cultural vestiges of Japanese colonization or native Taiwanese sentiment as Chun describes them to be. But Chun responds, in a special Rejoinder, that the KMT continues to enjoy broad non-ethnically based political support in spite of democratizing voting reforms and this, he argues, evinces more success on the part of the KMT government since 1949 than significant contestation to it. But is it also not arguable that the promotion (and transcendence?) of high "traditional

Chinese culture" is seriously challenged by a resurgence or reinvention of Taiwanese folk culture and the formation of the Democratic Progressive Party, which subverts the KMT model of Chinese nation-state to one of Taiwanese nation-state?

A less ardent debate about Thailand nonetheless echoes the Chun-Wu debate with respect to Taiwan. Yos asserts (in chapter 13) that the Thai state continues to promote a unitary view of Thai society that privileges Buddhism as the social glue holding it together and insists on an enduring nation-religion-king triumvirate. Explaining that Thailand's geographical proximity to the Malay cultural world of Southeast Asia and to China led "Malay Muslims" and "the Chinese" within its borders to be viewed as constant potential threats to the security of the Thai state, Yos argues that cultural policies have continually been established with the intent of erasing Malay Muslim or Chinese ethnicity, but often with the effect of causing controversy and drawing attention to differences. Chaiwat Satha-Anand, however, suggests that notions of national identity have at times moved towards a secular state more accommodating of ethnic/cultural difference. He claims (in chapter 14) that ethnic Chinese in Thailand have recently gained leeway in exhibiting cultural difference because for years they suppressed their difference and worked hard to make themselves vital to Thai economic growth. We might ask here how much these different senses of boundedness are internalized and how much they are officially handed down. For example, how can we interpret protests over Buddha images in public schools in schools with rules forbidding Islamic dress?

Gendered lenses are telling here.[4] A poem from Papua New Guinea quoted by Lindstrom, "Yupela Meri i Senis Hariap Pinis" [you women are changing too fast], evokes the changing role of women in society as emblematic of "the evil changes" brought about in society by modernization. Lindstrom suggests that men promote "traditional culture" as a basis for nationalism because it enables them both to maintain traditional power structures over women and to marginalize women's attempts at empowerment. The controversial Thai policy forbidding Malay Muslim girls to wear hijab (blouse with long sleeves, ankle length skirt, and covered head) to school was meant to create a sense of unity among students by forcing all of them to wear the same school uniform. But the Muslim community, in their protest against majority attempts at homogenization, adopted this issue of women's dress as one of utmost symbolic importance to Muslim identity.

Even the activist Singaporean state has had to contend with unexpected consequences of its explicitly gendered policies of cultural modernity. Initially concerned with high population growth rates, the state established a "two is enough" policy bolstered by a host of official incentives and disincentives. When it realized after two decades of campaigning that a significant portion of university educated women were remaining single or having one or two children, it switched to a two-tiered (actively class-ist) population policy encouraging university educated women to have "three or more if you can afford it," while continuing to encourage lower income mothers, who are largely Malays, to have two or fewer children. It is not hard to see in this example that the official government ministries of Singapore have actively sought to shape the physical and presumed cultural make-up of Singapore even with policies many readers might not automatically associate with "cultural policies."

NATION(AL)(IST) STAKES

Our primary emphasis on national cultural policies follows from our position that nation-ness and culture are widely treated in the late twentieth century as mutually implicating, even in many cases mutually constitutive. The close of the twentieth century is obviously a time in which "nations" appear to depend on "culture(s)" both to produce them and define them, and "culture(s)" appear to depend on "nations" both to (re)produce them and protect them.

This book highlights the double entendre we intended in saying so. It isn't just that a group of people might depend on something they value and cherish as their own as a way of defining themselves as a community and relating to non-community members. It is also that a group of people who insist on something to be valued as a form of collective self-definition often internalizes the effect of such an insistence to such an extent that the effect gets perceived to be the point of origin. Deciding which comes first, however, is not the point. Realizing that both "nations" and "cultures" are first and foremost objects of invocation and that there are stakes in these processes is. As Katherine Verdery has recently argued, "nationalism is a language in which much gets talked about; it can be used by those in power and those out of power, by those who would centralize a state and those who would resist state centralization" (1994:17).

Nations, then, are both producers and objects in our analyses. Unlike numerous volumes on nations and nationalism that circulate in English in predominantly English-language countries and function as theoretical interventions in contemporary discourse, this volume seeks to maintain a tension we find more productive for theorizing "nations" and the policies, policing practices, boundary-crossings, and tangible stakes that continue to make "nations" objects of value nearly two centuries since nationalist movements swept much of Europe and most of their European settler colonies in the Americas.

We are referring here to a tension between participating in the project of nationhood by caring enough to produce and reproduce its discursive space and observing the project of nationhood with an intentional critical stance that draws on non-locally, non-nationally produced lenses in order to counter its own national rootedness and that of its fellow citizen-readers.

This is not simply a tension between participating and observing, nor is this just a diplomatic way of insisting on the mutual value of insiders' and outsiders' perspectives. Observing is always a form of participating, and this includes those we might think of (or who might think of themselves) as insiders as well as those we might think of (or who might think of themselves) as outsiders. It is rather a question of the stakes we bring to our discursive interventions, our level of awareness of their rootedness, and the strategies we may adopt to enable and empower our individual and/or collective interventions.

Three examples from this volume pop out. In his response to Haiou Yang's essay on Culture Fever in late 1980s China, David Wu claims to offer an "outsider's point of view" to Yang's perspective as someone born and raised in Mainland China. While Wu, who grew up mainly in Taiwan, stands outside of the statal nationalism of the PRC and can claim to *not* be one of the Chinese intellectuals who participated in Culture Fever, is he outside the ethnonationalism of what it means to be "Chinese" in a time of populous and far-flung Chinese diaspora communities, or of what Tu Wei-ming has called "cultural China" (Tu 1994)? Yang's argument that the ever-widening Chinese diaspora and its changing sense of "being Chinese" may have had an effect on the Culture Fever debate of the Mainland makes it a relevant question.[5] After all, in his very analysis of the forces behind the Culture Fever movement, Wu joins the larger ethnic Chinese community engaged in *youhuan yishi*, "consciousness of collective worries and sufferance" over the fate of Chinese culture in the modern world.[6]

A second example illuminates different subject positions within one country, in this case Thailand. Chaiwat Satha-Anand, who identifies himself in his narrative biography as a member of a devout Muslim family, argues that until the May 1992 Uprising in Bangkok there was a growing secular sense of "being Thai" based on political citizenship in Thailand. As a minority in a largely Thai Buddhist country, his foregrounding of a nationalism based on political unity diverges from that of the other Thai essayist, Yos Santasombat, who focuses largely on the role of Thai Buddhist cultural identity, hegemonic and otherwise, in the politics of Thai national identity.

The third example contrasts Lindstrom, who is American and not Papua New Guinean, with Simet and Iamo who are Papua New Guinean. Whereas Lindstrom can engage in critical deconstructive analysis, albeit sympathetic to the issues articulated by Simet and Iamo, the latter are very much involved in advising the government of Papua New Guinea on cultural policy and, thus, in "nation-building" as well.

These positions are neither simply nor unambiguously derived. Critical stances take many forms—and nation-building, nationalism, and internationalism can all be multiply interpreted. For example, internationalism can be a state of mind, a comment about market relations, or a description of a life frequently crossing sovereign territorial borders, but it does not simply mean a life without national(ist) stakes. In what Arjun Appadurai (1990) calls the new "global ethnoscapes," the "group" that is culturalized and indexed in these ethnoscapes may not have a single territorial base but still has national(ist) positions not wholly based on actual place of residence. As Val Daniel's research on three generations of Sri Lankan Tamil refugees points out so clearly, a sense of ethnocultural nationalism, such as Tamil nationalism, may be superseded by one of "internationalism," in which the geographical non-fixity of the group becomes a defining "group" feature without the sense of Tamil groupness disappearing.[7] Groups that see themselves as diasporic and/or transnational do not become "a-national" just by crossing borders. Many in Hong Kong who hold foreign passports and are waiting to see what fate the Chinese take-over in 1997 will bring may be very internationalist but also deeply invested in the boundedness of Hong Kong as a political, economic, and cultural entity. The same goes for middle and upper income Taiwanese and Singaporeans who as a matter of habit send their children abroad to attend college (cf. Ong 1996).

This book, then, takes the position that all critical assessments of nationalist projects are both nationally and internationally positioned, as are all celebratory assessments. This includes portrayals of transnationalism (cf. Basch et al. 1994) as well as calls for postnationalism (cf. Appadurai 1993)—positioned, as they are, within the "nations" that produce them and within the international nexus of production, exchange, and consumption of goods, positions, and ideas that complicates, but does not erase, the continued relevance of national(ist) stakes. Intellectuals in this light are never just producers of theories of nationalism(s); we are just as much producers of nations (and often unintentionally of nationalisms) and products of "national" projects (see also Fox 1990).

We take the position that this is true of all scholars and not just "native scholars." Ours is not an additive argument. By internationalizing theoretical discussions of cultural policies and national(ist) stakes, we mean highlighting the national(ist) stakes in which intellectuals participate as both producers and products, and subjecting the scholarship as well as their referents to critical analysis. The very concept of "native scholar" requires just such analysis. Usually invoked by scholars firmly rooted in self-privileging intellectual circles, especially in Anglo-American societies, it is intended as a liberalizing gesture that seeks to introduce "others" to their own customary readership. The referent hyperprivileges certain individuals as those especially empowered or experienced or authorized to comment on particular contexts, but typically implies their lack of ability, experience, knowledge, and authority to comment and theorize about much else. The intellectual stratification it sets up not only disempowers those ironically hyperprivileged, i.e. those conceptualized as "native scholars," but it unproductively perpetuates the illusion that many scholars—indeed most scholars in "theory-producing" societies—are not "native scholars" (cf. also Narayan 1993; Trouillot 1991). Positioning, as much recent feminist scholarship has argued, affects, influences, and constructs all of us, not just some of us.

Hence, we have a special interest in locating the intellectuals we discuss and the intellectuals we cite within the "nations" in which they have stakes. It is also a position that leads us to argue with each other openly in private discussions and to agree to reveal our arguments, indeed to highlight them, in the framework of this book. Each of the six main essays included in this volume is followed by an essay we entitle "A Second Look," whose author extends, elucidates, debates, and/or intervenes in the argument of her/his colleague. The authors of the two essays for each country section often hail from different parts of the world, differ in their educational and professional trajectories, and usually only partially share intellectual/political agendas.

Contributors to this volume are not easily pegged, although readers are still likely to read each essay through lenses in which they have a stake. The majority of its contributors are not U.S. (or even more generally Anglophone) scholars who study these countries. Theirs are not "area-studies" or "international studies" projects as such—largely, in the United States, references to the distanced study of societies generally foreign to the scholar. All of our contributors (with the arguable exception of Lindstrom) are at least bi-national in their work lives, and most have a personal, institutional, and/or societal stake in the country about which they write.

Collectively the book takes advantage of the fact that our experiences, observations, concerns, and viewpoints as authors do not just reflect and reproduce a North Atlantic perspective, though we caution against any attempt to romanticize our "otherness" or "transnationalism" or that of others. While we do seek to unsettle the Eurocentricity of the classic literature on nations and nationalism(s), we each draw on particular works, often by Anglo/French/American scholars, whose contributions we have found illuminating. We all, after all, live in intellectual communities that root us to our home institutions but also require us to travel, fax, email, and read the works of others—a far cry from the kind of regional isolation we attribute to earlier eras. What is reflected in our volume is the simultaneous internationalization of particular kinds of scholarly discussion and the awkwardness of only partially sharing intellectual/political agendas that refract genuine political, historical, economic, and organizational differences among regions and countries.

TWO FINAL COMMENTS

Many countries outside Europe besides the six we discuss here could have been included, including other countries in the Pacific, northeast Asia and southeast Asia. Every book has its intellectual history and its practical constraints, and this one is no exception. But the six countries addressed in this volume, we believe, are sufficient to begin the intellectual shift we propose and to suggest the complexity of inter- and intra-regional connections.

Practical constraints of what could be included in this volume do not, for example, preclude the drawing of further connections both within and without these regions. In fact, several of the essays bring up important relationships with places such as Malaysia, Vanuatu, and Hong Kong, as well as with European and European-settler colonies, in the abstract and in the particular. We have intentionally chosen *not* to group the countries in cultural, subregional, or thematic sections. It is easy to see the temptation to do so. The People's Republic of China and Taiwan are often related as "Chinese" and the PRC, Taiwan, and Japan are habitually considered together as "East Asian," but such conventional groupings are not the only productive ones around.

For example, juxtaposing Papua New Guinea with China is not common but certainly not nonsensical. The citizenries of both countries have long histories of non-European control and, hence, perhaps shallower dependence on European mindsets than postcolonial scholarship assumes for large regions of the world. Within the region, both are subjected to large-scale investments on the part of other more economically prosperous Pacific players, but in different ways. Hong Kong companies build factories in China, but plunder raw materials from Papua New Guinea. This sketch of the similarities and differences in power relations and identity struggles between just these two countries hints at the multitude of others available in the configuration of this book.

The contemporary phenomenon of global culturalism and capitalist internationalism creates an atmosphere in which it behooves us to use the cases presented in this volume even more broadly as an intervention in our theorizing of both "culture" and "nation-ness." U.S. theorizing about multiculturalism might actively reflect upon government-promoted forms of multiculturalism and multiracialism in Papua New Guinea and Singapore (and not just Canada and Australia), particularly with regard to the question of hegemonic intent behind seemingly liberal policies. The conundrum surrounding simultaneous movements of centralization and resistance backed by different meanings of "nation" might be examined in all its complexity by taking the example of Eastern Europe together with that of China and its autonomous regions or Papua New Guinea.[8] As Lindstrom concludes in his contribution to this volume, in spite of the sometimes hazy notions of national community through "unity in diversity," Papua New Guinea as a country is held together by important functions of the state, particularly within multinational orders. We should take it seriously when he suggests that Papua New Guinea might serve as a model of a post-nationalist state in which the link between nation and state need not be of utmost importance, a kind of entity similar to that of the European Community or reconfigurations of once Soviet-controlled republics in Eastern Europe.

Internationalizing theoretical discussions of nationalism(s) by nationalizing the stakes of those discussions does not mean an attempt to test Ernest Gellner's (1983), Edward Said's (1978), Benedict Anderson's (1983), Eric Hobsbawm's (1990), or Paul Gilroy's (1987 and 1993) influential theoretical positions by "trying them out" in societies that were not central to these scholars' theoretical formulations, and pointing out empirical omissions. The contributions of such scholarship notwithstanding, those moves do not suffice for there remains the tacit treatment of European-centered theorizing as both historically privileged and theoretically transcendent.

This book foregrounds two intellectual moves we advocate as further and necessary steps in the de-centering and internationalization of theoretical production in general and of our scholarly understanding of cultural(ist) and national(ist) formations in particular. It insists (1) that all processes and ideas ought to be examined *through the experiences and struggles* of countries in different regions of the world (or historical/political/economic positions) and not just within one country (or region of countries), no matter how diverse or multicultural it may believe itself to be; and (2) that all processes and ideas ought to be examined *through the eyes and theoretical agendas of scholars* in different regions of the world (or historical/political/economic positions), and not just within one country (or region of countries) no matter how diverse or multicultural they may believe themselves to be.

This is a different era, after all, from the one into which most of us were born. It is an era in which the Taiwanese government, for example, lobbies for entry as an independent nation to the United Nations by launching an ad campaign in magazines and newspapers with international distribution.[9] In the transnational flow of people, labor, raw materials, artistic products, munitions, and intellectual properties across state borders, academics have likewise been swept up and are now required to travel, fax, email, and read the works of others in an atmosphere far from the kind of regional isolation attributed to earlier eras—not just in Singapore and Thailand, Taiwan and Papua New Guinea, but also in Japan, China, the U.S. and Germany.

As we hope this volume makes imperative, to truly think about the meaning of the prefixes inter-, trans-, and post- which are both glibly and seriously invoked in many intellectual circles today in a variety of Anglophone countries, we must explore, decipher, and take positions vis-a-vis different technologies of boundedness. The "culture contests," customary dress and dance competitions, sponsored by the government in Papua New Guinea as a means to revitalize interest in a unifying cultural tradition but which devolved into true contests with rival traditions questioning each other's authenticity, serve as an apt metaphor for our examination of cultural policies and their sociopolitical modalities. Enforcing unity on culturalist grounds provides separatist or resistance movements with an equally powerful rhetoric for their claims to autonomy. This delicate balance, thrown to either side by various conditions, speaks to "nations" of both sorts and to individuals such as the contributors to this volume who attempt to straddle state, intellectual, and sometimes even ethnic or racial lines.

Clearly "cultural policies" demand our attention much more than we ever imagined. They index at the very least (1) that late twentieth century culturalism is multiply situated, multiply motivated, multiply referential, but globally fostered, (2) that it is nearly always a discourse on "the nation" simultaneously presupposing and seeking to create "nations" of particular kinds, and (3) that it coexists paradoxically with a contemporary degree of internationalism, capitalist market interpenetration, and migratory transnational flows unprecedented in their scope.

NOTES

1. See, for example, investigative journalist Dai Qing's claim that "this kind of film is really shot for the casual pleasures of foreigners" in the translation of her article, "Raised Eyebrows for *Raise the Red Lantern*," published by *Public Culture* 10 (Winter 1993), pp. 333–337. For journalistic portraits of these two directors, see Chapter 4 ("Shadows on the Screen") in Jianying Zha, *China Pop: How Soap Operas, Tabloids, and Bestsellers Are Transforming a Culture* (New York: The New Press, 1995), pp. 79–104. For a reading of films by these and other Fifth Generation directors as a new type of ethnography which "other" "China," see Rey Chow, *Primitive Passions: Visuality, Sexuality and Contemporary Chinese Cinema* (New York: Columbia University Press, 1995).
2. For biographies and writings by and about four of the leading personalities of the 1970s Democracy Movement, including Wang Xizhe, one of the authors of the Li-Yi-Zhe big character poster in Guangdong (1974), and Wei Jingsheng, leading proponent of Democracy Wall in Beijing (1978–1979), see Chapter IX ("Fire Behind Bars") in Geremie Barmé and John Minford, eds., *Seeds of Fire: Chinese Voices of Conscience* (New York: The Noonday Press, 1989), pp. 271–312.
3. Complicating the picture further at this point was the additional dimension of overseas Chinese scholars who actively participated in the Culture Fever discussion. The discussion was deflected back to the larger population through a widely broadcast, six-part television series which challenged "traditional Chinese culture" as inward-looking and eventually stifling. The controversial television series, *Heshang or River Elegy* was aired in 1988. Among its many visual images, the "Yellow River," so important to traditional Chinese civilization, was pitted against the "Great Blue Sea" of reform and openness. For translation of the script by Su Xiaokang and Wang Luxiang, see Richard W. Bodman and Pin P. Wan, trans., *Deathsong of the River: A Reader's Guide to the Chinese TV Series Heshang* (Ithaca: East Asia Program, Cornell University, 1991). For a presentation of opinions and debate surrounding the series, see "*River Elegy*, a Television Miniseries" in Geremie Barmé and Linda Javin, eds., *New Ghosts, Old Dreams: Chinese Rebel Voices* (New York: Times Books, 1992), pp. 138–164.
4. For recent relevant scholarship focusing on the political construction of gender, see, for example, Andrew Parker, ed., *Nationalisms and Sexualities* (New York: Routledge, 1992) and Chandra Talpade Mohanty, Ann Russo, and Lourdes Torres, eds., *Third World Women and the Politics of Feminism* (Bloomington: Indiana University Press, 1991).

5. As guest editor of a *Public Culture* issue focusing on the public sphere, Benjamin Lee explores the idea of an emerging Chinese public sphere which transcends national boundaries; see Benjamin Lee, "Going Public," *Public Culture* 10 (Winter 1993), pp. 165–178. For a collection of essays which address the emergence of a new cultural space defined by "Chineseness," see Tu Wei-ming, ed., *The Living Tree: the Changing Meaning of Being Chinese Today* (Stanford: Stanford University Press, 1994).
6. For an extended discussion of *Youhuan yishi*, which Perry Link translates as "the worrying mentality," see Chapter 6 ("Responsibility") in Perry Link, *Evening Chats in Beijing:Probing China's Predicament* (New York: W.W. Norton Company, 1992), pp. 249–290.
7. One of his interviewees from the most recent phase of immigration even described this sense of fluidity in the economic terms of "liquid assets" which enable it: "It is even more important to be solvent than to get asylum in England... Tomorrow I might get a chance to go to Canada. Then why would I want to be stuck here or miss the chance only because I was not solvent? Even the U.S., I understand, is now giving out green cards for those who have a million dollars." E. Valentine Daniel, "Suffering Nation and Alienation" in Virginia Dominguez and Catherine Lewis, eds., *Questioning Otherness: Papers from the 1995 Distinguished International Lecture Series* (Iowa City: Center for International and Comparative Studies, 1995), p. 93.
8. China has five autonomous regions defined by ethnic minority nationalities, including Tibet.
9. There was, for example, a full page ad with the slogan "Without a Full Team, It's Uphill for the U.N." in a 1994 issue of the *Far Eastern Economic Review*. During the 50th anniversary of the signing of the U.N. Charter in 1995, similar full page ads were also carried in newpapers such as the *San Francisco Chronicle*.

REFERENCES

Anderson, Benedict (1983). *Imagined Communities: Reflections on the Origin and Spread of Nationalism*. London: Verso.

Appadurai, Arjun (1990). Disjuncture and Difference in the Global Cultural Economy. *Public Culture* 2 (spring): 1–24.

— (1993). Patriotism and Its Futures. *Public Culture* 5(3):411–429.

Barme, Geremie and Linda Javin, Eds. (1992). *New Ghosts, Old Dreams: Chinese Rebel Voices*. New York: Times Books.

Barme, Geremie and John Minford, Eds. (1989). *Seeds of Fire: Chinese Voices of Conscience*. New York: The Noonday Press.

Basch, Linda, Nina Glick-Schiller, and Cristina Szanton Blanc, Eds. (1994). *Nations Unbound: Transnational Projects, Postcolonial Predicaments, and Deterritorialized Nation-States*. Langhorne, Pennsylvania: Gordon and Breach.

Befu, Harumi, Ed. (1993). *Cultural Nationalism in East Asia*. Berkeley: Institute of East Asian Studies, University of California.

Bhabha, Homi, Ed. (1990). *Nation and Narration*. New York: Routledge.

Chow, Rey (1995). *Primitive Passions: Visuality, Sexuality and Contemporary Chinese Cinema*. New York: Columbia University Press.

Dai Qing (1993). Raised Eyebrows for "Raise the Red Lantern." *Public Culture* 10 (winter): 333–337.

Daniel, E. Valentine (1995). Suffering Nation and Alienation. In Virginia R. Dominguez and Catherine Lewis, Eds. *Questioning Otherness*. Papers from the 1995 Distinguished International Lecture Series. Iowa City: Center for International and Comparative Studies, pp. 70–101.

Dominguez, Virginia R. (1996). Disciplining Anthropology. In Cary Nelson and Dilip Parameshwar Gaonkar, Eds. *Disciplinarity and Dissent in Cultural Studies*. New York: Routledge, pp. 37–61.

— (1992). Invoking Culture: The Messy Side of "Cultural Politics." *South Atlantic Quarterly* 91(1):19–42.

— (1995). Invoking Racism in the Public Sphere: Two Takes on National Self-Criticism. *Identities* 1(4):325–346.

— (1989). *People as Subject, People as Object: Selfhood and Peoplehood in Contemporary Israel*. Madison: University of Wisconsin Press.

— (1994). A Taste for "the Other": Intellectual Complicity in Racializing Practices. *Current Anthropology* 35(4):333–348.

Fox, Richard, Ed. (1990). *Nationalist Ideologies and the Production of National Cultures*. Washington, D.C.: American Ethnological Society Monograph Series, Number 2.

Gellner, Ernest (1983). *Nations and Nationalism*. Oxford: Basil Blackwell.

Gilroy, Paul (1993). *Black Atlantic: Modernity and Double Consciousness*. Cambridge: Harvard University Press.

— (1987). *"There Ain't No Black in the Union Jack": The Cultural Politics of Race and Nation*. Chicago: University of Chicago Press.

Handler, Richard (1988). *Nationalism and the Politics of Culture in Quebec*. Madison: University of Wisconsin Press.

Hanson, Allan (1989). The Making of the Maori: Cultural Invention and Its Logic. *American Anthropologist* 91:890–902.

Hobsbawm, Eric (1990). *Nations and Nationalism since 1780: Programme, Myth, and Reality*. New York: Cambridge University Press.

Hobsbawm, Eric and Terence Ranger, Eds. (1983). *The Invention of Tradition*. New York: Cambridge University Press.

Karp, Ivan and Steven Lavine, Eds. (1991). *Exhibiting Cultures*. Washington, D.C.: Smithsonian Institution Press.
Keesing, Roger (1989). Creating the Past: Custom and Identity in the Contemporary Pacific. *The Contemporary Pacific* 1/2: 19–42.
— (1991). Reply to Trask. *The Contemporary Pacific* 3:168–171.
Lee, Benjamin (1993). Going Public. *Public Culture* 10 (winter): 165–178.
Levine, H. B. (1991). Comment on Hanson's "The Making of the Maori." *American Anthropologist* 93:444–446.
Lindstrom, Lamont and Geoffrey White, Eds. (1994). *Culture, Kastom, Tradition: Developing Cultural Policy in Melanesia*. Suva: Institute of Pacific Studies, University of the South Pacific.
Link, Perry (1992). *Evening Chats in Beijing: Probing China's Predicament*. New York: W.W. Norton Company.
Linnekin, Jocelyn (1991). Text Bites and the R-Word: The Politics of Representing Scholarship. *The Contemporary Pacific* 3:172–177.
Lutz, Catherine and Jane Collins (1993). *Reading National Geographic*. Chicago: University of Chicago Press.
Mohanty, Chandra Talpade, Ann Russo, and Lourdes Torres, Eds. (1991). *Third World Women and the Politics of Feminism*. Bloomington: Indiana University Press.
Narayan, Kirin (1993). How Native Is a "Native" Anthropologist? *American Anthropologist* 95:671–686.
Ong, Aihwa (1996). Cultural Citizenship as Subject-Making: Immigrants Negotiate Racial and Cultural Boundaries in the United States. *Current Anthropology* 37(5):737–762.
Parker, Andrew, Ed. (1992). *Nationalisms and Sexualities*. New York: Routledge.
Said, Edward (1978). *Orientalism*. New York: Pantheon Books.
Solomon, Andrew (1996). Don't Mess with Our Cultural Patrimony. *The New York Times Magazine*. March 17, p. 30.
Su Xiaokang and Wang Luxiang (1991). *Deathsong of the River: A Reader's Guide to the Chinese TV Series Heshang*. Translated by Richard W. Bodman and Pin P. Wan. Ithaca: East Asia Program, Cornell University.
Trask, Haunani-Kay (1993). *From a Native Daughter: Colonialism and Sovereignty in Hawai'i*. Monroe, Maine: Common Courage Press.
— (1991). Natives and Anthropologists: The Colonial Struggle. *The Contemporary Pacific* 3:159–167.
Trouillot, Michel-Rolph (1991). Anthropology and the Savage Slot: The Poetics and Politics of Otherness. In Richard Fox, Ed. *Recapturing Anthropology: Working in the Present*. Santa Fe, N.M.: School of American Research Press, pp. 17–44.

Tu Wei-ming, Ed. (1994). *The Living Tree: The Changing Meaning of Being Chinese Today*. Stanford: Stanford University Press.
Verdery, Katherine (1994). Beyond the Nation in Eastern Europe. *Social Text* 38:1–19.
Wu, David, Geoffrey White, Elizabeth Buck, and Larry Smith (1989). Cultural Construction and National Identity. Paper made available in 1992 through the Culture and Communication Working Papers (Working Paper #1), by the Institute of Culture and Communication, East-West Center, Honolulu, Hawai'i.
Zha, Jianying (1995). *China Pop: How Soap Operas, Tabloids, and Best Sellers Are Transforming a Culture*. New York: New Press.

PART I
Singapore

2

The Making of a New Nation: Cultural Construction and National Identity in Singapore

Chua Beng-Huat and Eddie Kuo

Having been a British colonial trading post since 1819, the island of Singapore was not without a past, with its attendant culture, economy and polity. Culturally, the population hewed from different geographical origins. These origins were embedded in the individuals' orientation to different "homelands" that did not include the island itself. Immigrants who had no intention of settling permanently formed the majority of the population in the 1960s. They, especially the Chinese, were characteristically highly adaptable and displayed shifting loyalty towards different authorities at different times (Wang 1989). However, even the local-born had anchored their cultural orientation to "imaginary" homelands, transmitted at homes and in schools financed by the respective vernacular groups. Singaporean culture as such was an "absence," was inconceivable.

The colonial economy imposed its own cultural effects on the population. The entrepot trade, the very reason for the British establishment of permanent settlement on the island, imposed an ethnically determined division of labor. At the top of the ethnic stratification structure was the White population. Then came the English educated Indians who manned a significant proportion of the junior colonial administrative jobs. The lowest colonial jobs, such as postmen and rank and file policemen, went to some Malays. The Chinese majority, excluded from the colonial service, spread through the entire spectrum of the economy, with high visibility in both trading activities and lowly paid physical labor signified by the "coolie." This was the classic "plural society," where different ethnic groups could maintain relative racial peace living side by side because crossing over racial lines was nearly impossible. Unity of the population as a "people" did not exist, and it was not conceptualized as a desired entity.

Politically, there was the legacy of approximately one hundred and fifty years of British colonialism, from 1819 to 1963. Within the colonial regime, Singaporean as a political category did not exist; an inhabitant was either an alien or a British subject. In addition to being subjected to humiliation at the hands of the colonialists, the political legacy also imparted to the population, especially the English educated, a semblance of understanding of Western democracy and other Western cultural elements such as political freedom and scientific and technological rationality. This colonial legacy might be said to be the one shared experience of the Asian population.

Finally, there was the inescapable fact of geography. The cultural elements interacted with geography to produce on the tiny island an enclave of a numerically dominant Chinese population in a region where Malay speakers, who can claim to be "indigenous," are the regional majority.

The above configuration conspires to discourage thinking of Singapore as an independent nation; it was not a possibility that the population was trying to realize. Singapore as an independent nation-state was first and foremost a political reality hoisted on a population, in 1965, under conditions beyond the latter's control. The man who subsequently would be its first Prime Minister, from then until 1990, categorically declared that the idea of an independent Singapore was "a foolish and absurd proposition" (Lee Kuan Yew quoted in Drysdale 1984:249). However, once it was a fait accompli, it was necessary to produce a "nation" and a "people." In this sense, the birth of a Singaporean national identity can be located precisely at the point of its political founding in 1965.

SINGAPOREAN CULTURE AND NATIONAL IDENTITY AS DISCURSIVE OBJECTS

Collectively, the cultural, economic, political and geographical elements constituted a field of crisscrossing concepts and conceptual relations that over-determined the formation of "Singapore" as a nation and of "Singaporeans" as its citizens. It should be noted that in the discourse of nationalism, Singapore as an "independent nation" refers not to the geographical feature of the island as such; similarly "Singaporean" national identity refers not to the biological being-as-such. They are necessarily the results of discursive practices that formulate them as objects with specific but temporally changing characters, which are "called into existence" by statements that circulate in different discourses, in different spheres of social practices. Each of the given ontological elements, singularly or inter actively, can be discursively thematized to produce specific social, cultural and political effects in the discursive formation of the new nation and its people.

Take, for example, a person's racial origin. This ontological element can be transformed into a discursive object and inscribed on an individual as his/her "true" attributes and characters in the discourse on ethnicity, the better to invoke them for various institutional disciplinary practices. Thus, ethnicity can become not only the substratum for explaining one's behavior, it can also become the reason and focus of political decisions and social control. Each time, statements are produced to bring forth different aspects of ethnicity in order to constitute it as the relevant element in the rationalization of institutional practices.

Recourse will be made to strategically redeploy the given elements for specific moves in the discursive formation of "Singapore" and "Singaporeans." In each deployment, some elements of the past will be discursively suppressed or erased, others accented and given added semiological significance. The context of each deployment is constituted by responses to changes in the social environment, and the changing purpose at hand of the individuals who are responsible for the constitution of the discursive objects. Hence, instead of taking the past as given and to be positivistically honored, all retrospective reference to "historical" reality before 1965 must be analytically treated as part of the processes of the discursive object formation in the current conjuncture.

Practically, the ontological elements have been, and will continue to be, invoked in the design and implementation of government policies which are, ostensibly, explicitly designed for specific objectives in the realms of economy, housing, population, education, and language and to deal with the immediate and ongoing concerns of management of political stability. However, in addition to these specific purposes, the policies collectively partake in the concerted and continuous effort in the construction of a new national identity. The present analysis examines how the policies and the accompanying events and discursive statements have led, in our view, to the making of a new state, a new economy, and indeed a new social order: in other words, to the formation of emergent "Singapore" and "Singaporean-ness" in the past twenty-five years.

Of course, as in all discursive formations the intentions of the state had incurred resistance, and indeed will continue to do so. Theoretically, each instance of resistance should be subjected to analysis in its own right. However, given the historical sweep of this essay, we have emphasized the successes of the policies and strategies deployed by the long standing one party dominant government. The focus will therefore be on the process of formation itself and the resistance that was generated will be briefly noted in passing; detailed analysis of the latter will have to await other occasions.[1]

The history of the Singaporean identity as a discursive object is of very recent origin and the depth of the accumulated statements that circulate within the state's ongoing attempt to construct a "nation" and a "people" is relatively shallow and thus extremely fluid and formative. The actual shapes of these discursive objects remain relatively unclear compared to other nations with thick cultural memories. Yet analysis of the Singapore case will be of particular significance precisely because we are able to map the processes of the shaping and evolution of these discursive objects from their "inconceivable" past within a short span of three decades. Under the circumstances, we are able to see most clearly the role of the state and the process of "construction," relatively free from layers of historical and cultural memories.

THE GENEALOGY OF SINGAPOREAN CULTURE

Before embarking on a detailed analysis of the processes and substance of national identity production, an overview is first provided to serve as the overarching milieu within which the detailed processes are to be understood.

As mentioned earlier, an independent Singapore was inconceivable in the late 1950s because the population firmly believed that it would be economically non-viable for serious lack of natural resources and an absence of a viable domestic market for its industrial goods. They saw their destiny as being tied to Peninsular Malaya, which would serve as the natural hinterland, as both its market and its supply of necessary resources. Consequently, for the then anti-colonialist leaders, a merger with Malaya was the clear preference. Thus, when Singapore obtained self-government in domestic affairs in 1959 under the leadership of Lee Kuan Yew's People's Action Party (PAP), Malay was made the sole national language to prepare for an eventual merger. The national identity, and hence loyalty, of the people of Singapore was to be directed towards Malaya. For different reasons of their own, the two countries did merge, along with what are now the East Malaysian states of Sabah and Sarawak, to form greater Malaysia in 1963. The partnership lasted for no more than three years before Singapore was asked to leave the Confederation and become an independent city-state.[2] A new national identity and a new loyalty had to be forged, this time to the new state of Singapore.

The perception that Singapore was economically non-viable as an independent entity was determined in part by the then prevailing wisdom in development economics which saw import substitution as the only road to economic development for newly de-colonized territories. However, once independent, Singapore immediately embarked on an even more ambitious industrialization program with an aggressive export orientation, a path blazed by South Korea, Taiwan, Hong Kong and, of course, Japan (Rodan 1989). The subsequent economic success of Singapore has brought with it a substantial injection of self-definition and national pride in the people of Singapore, boosting their sense of national identification (Willmott 1989).

Indeed, the term success has become symbolically synonymous with the history of the past three decades since independence, as reflected in the titles of two major works on contemporary Singapore (Drysdale 1984; Sandhu and Wheatley 1989).

Significantly, successful industrialization is not only a contributor to the development of national culture and identity but is itself dependent on the development of certain cultural traits. Industrialization is not merely a technological and economic phenomenon but requires as one of its necessary conditions the active transformation of a population into a disciplined work force (Offe 1987:94). It thus contributes to the emergence of a new social order characterized by instrumental rationality and a population with a strong achievement motivation. Cultural development, in other words, had to abide by the dictates of the logic of the economy.

Some of the cultural concomitants to economic development are (i) discipline at the work place and, by extension, generalized social discipline (Quah 1983), and (ii) general orientation to constant upgrading of educational qualification which embodies a deep sense of competition with others for relative advantages in consumption. These cultural features are the predominant qualities and anxieties that characterize the everyday life-world of Singaporeans today. For example, the education of children has become one of the highest anxiety-causing phenomena for parents. Structurally, these economy-dictated values are the predominant defining character of the high growth city-state, and overlay other cultural sentiments.

Significantly, these material-based values were not extant on the island at the time of political independence. Then, an economy characterized by high unemployment gave rise to a lifestyle that left an individual with a very significant degree of freedom vis-a-vis work-related activities, albeit a freedom accompanied by very substantial material deprivation (Chua 1989).[3] In Singapore, the cultural requirements of the industrial regime had, therefore, to be actively established with the interventionist hand of the government. The promotion of a disciplined work force was ideologically linked to the people's daily struggles with "making a living;" job creation became a priority in the agenda of the new nation in view of the very high population growth rate of more than 4.3% (Lim and Associates 1988:6). The two became ideologically linked to the survival of the new nation and its people. The promotion of a disciplined work force was, therefore, given precedence over the promotion of other cultural practices from the very outset of independence, and remains so today.

The above generalized picture of cultural development since political independence describes the processes that are explicitly put in place by the government. It, however, does not imply that such politically intentional cultural production is automatically or necessarily successful in the sense that the citizens unreflectively abide by the government's actions. Resistance to the policies does occur, as do policy reversals at different historical junctures. This signals that the population is often guided by its own cultural drummers, as the analysis of specific policy terrain will show.

THE MAKING OF A NEW STATE

On political independence, a "new nation" had to be formulated and produced. This was discursively achieved through the concept of "national interest" which lends substance to the abstract entity of a nation. The first strategic move for the newly formed government was to distance itself from particularistic groups including those, such as unions and Chinese-educated students, who were crucial to the success of the PAP government itself, the better to constitute itself as belonging to all. So, immediately after independence, cabinet minister Rajaratnam proclaimed that the PAP "has come to realize that the workers are a class with a vested interest, and that as a political party, the

PAP must work for the interest of the whole country and not for not one class" but to "seek[s] to represent all the interests with the state" (quoted in Pang 1971:21).

This distancing also enabled the government to redefine the political space for race through the concept of "multiracialism." The so-called "racial cultures," whose construction will be discussed later, are held in abeyance politically by an explicit recognition that Singapore is a "multiracial" society and that racial and religious tolerance is to be safeguarded in the law. In so doing, the government places itself in a position that arguably "compelled" it to act in ways that do not privilege any particular group; racial cultural practices can then be relegated to the realm of private and voluntaristic, individual or collective, practices. The result of the policy of multiracialism is thus two pronged: a high visibility of race in the social body and, concurrently, the strategic effect of pushing race out of the frontline of politics.

The latter political effect, which ostensibly demonstrates a "neutral" stance towards all racial groups preserves for the state a very high level of autonomy and insulates it from pressures that may be generated by race. First, race cannot be constituted as a "legitimate" basis of special claims on the state; to do so is to violate the norm of multiracialism. Second, by not being identified with any race, the political leadership is at its own discretion to consult the various groups without having to act in the interests of any group, minority or majority. Thus in spite of the overwhelming Chinese majority, the Singapore state has never been a Chinese state to its own political detriment (Chua 1994).

The logic of such a political move is best seen in contrast to the Malaysian model of political development of similar vintage. In contrast to adopting "multiculturalism" to bury "racialism," political parties are organized along "racial" lines; consequently, representation and protection of racial interests continue to be central to national politics. The overall result is the unavoidable identification of the interest of the ruling Malay party with the interests of the Malay majority (Ho 1994), while in Singapore, with only one exception, all political parties are multiracial in composition. Even the exclusive Malay party tried on a multiracial stance in the 1988 election.[4] In Parliament, the high visibility of race inevitably imposed additional demands on MPs from numerically minority groups to represent not only their electoral constituencies but also their highly visible racial communities; however, they are obliged to speak of so-called racial community concerns within the terms of multiracialism and national interests.[5]

Indeed, multiracialism and national interests together provide the rationality for the constitution of certain activities by some individuals as racially "chauvinistic." So construed, such activities are perceived to have the potential for destabilizing the precarious balance of the new state and, according to the government, if allowed to fester would wreck the nation from within. Alleged chauvinistic agitations are subjected to severe legal sanctions, including incarceration under the Internal Security Act, which gives the government the power to detain anyone without trial for up to two yearly renewable terms. It should be apparent that while tolerance of racial differences was given constitutional recognition, promotion of the differences was carefully circumscribed to largely privatized celebrations of festivals, dances and ornamental adornments.

An exception to the general distancing from race should be noted. The Constitution recognizes Malays as the "indigenous" population of the island although the nature of this special status is rather ambiguous. The only concrete policy that signified this status was the granting of free tuition to all Malay students in tertiary education. In 1989, allegedly due to complaints from segments of the Chinese population about the fact that while poor Chinese households had to pay fees middle income Malays were exempted, fee exemption for the Malays was subsequently tied to a means test in each case and granted only to financially deserving cases. The money so saved is transferred to a general fund, managed by the Council for the Education of Muslim Children (Mendaki) for educational purposes. The government therefore does not stand to gain financially from the policy change.[6]

In sum, the discursive formulation of a "new nation" with "national interests" provides the legitimate space for the political containment of ethnic and/or class based differences. The concept of national interest simultaneously denies ethnic and/or class differences as the rational basis for legitimate political organization and prevents them from being politically thematized in the public domain by casting them as potentially against the national interests themselves.

Taking the "national" stance opened up several possibilities for the state. The distancing from potential interest groups enabled the government to delineate its relative autonomy, which is absolutely central to its smooth functioning (Poulantzas 1978; Lewis 1981). In this case, the autonomy of the new state was secured with relative ease compared to other capitalist states because (i) the government had already formed a partnership with labor prior to coming to power, and (ii) in a declining entrepot economy under a dying colonial regime, there was an absence of both a strong industrial or intellectual bourgeoisie and of landed interest that could mount resistances to the penetration of the new political power in the social body (Rodan 1989).

Finally, having secured relative autonomy, the state acquired for itself space to define the "national interests" within the discourse of "national survival." The discourse on survival was in turn fed by the earlier mentioned conjunctural elements: namely, perceived economic non-viability; a Chinese enclave in the Malay sea; mounting domestic difficulties of unemployment, high demographic growth rate and poor public health and housing conditions; and finally, absence of political identification with the new nation by a population of different individuals, each oriented to their own respective homelands (Chan 1970). Interests in the survival of the nation under such inauspicious circumstances can then be ascribed to and implanted in every Singaporean, without exception, an implantation that facilitates the disciplining of the population through the promotion of work-related values necessitated by industrialization. It should now be apparent that the discourse of the "new nation with national interests" floated, and continues to float, above any preceding cultural practices of the different individuals or groups of the pre-independence days.

THE MAKING OF A NEW ECONOMIC ORDER

Nationally survival in economic terms meant the transformation of the entrepot economy to an industry-based economy with foreign capital (Tan 1976). In its drive for foreign industrial capital, the experiences of the domestic trading community were completely neglected in spite of representations made to the state by the indigenous small and medium enterprises. It was not until the first severe but brief recession in 1985 that the voices of indigenous capital were taken into serious economic policy considerations along with increased attention to developing the service sector economy (Chalmers 1993).

Industrialization required the transformation of the population into a disciplined industrial work force. At the individual level, it meant giving priority to "making a living," i.e. developing an interest in "rising incomes and improved standard of living," to be achieved through willingness and ability to work hard (Goh 1976:81). It meant developing concurrently the mutually supporting consumerist and productionist orientations. At the work place, the cultural ethos promoted was one of "mutual trust and cooperation" between labor, employer and the state in order to maximize production from the workers, profits for the enterprises and achievement of the "national objective" of economic growth and survival. The dovetailing of national and individual concerns, therefore, generated their own concepts regarding the type of interests and social behavior which had to be inscribed on the new "Singaporeans."

The desired productionist orientation of the worker was, however, not left to cultural promotion alone; it was secured institutionally by legislation. As successful economic transformation was deemed to require the creation of stable industrial relations, legislative regulation of the labor force was made necessary. First, control of labor unions had to be wrenched from the pro-communist leadership by deregistering their organization and detaining the radical leadership. In its place the pro-government National Trade Union Congress was installed.[7] Next, the role of trade unions in collective bargaining for better wages and working conditions was restrained by successive legislation in 1968, 1982, and 1984. Bargaining was further limited by a National Wage Council which annually recommends the level of wage increase for the work force as a whole. The working population was in turn rewarded by real improvements in the standard of living (Deyo 1981). The government's retort to criticisms that the work force has been laboring under less than desirable legal conditions is: "but had they not benefited from economic growth?"[8]

The implantation of a production orientation required further material support. An important source of support came, significantly and perhaps unexpectedly, from the government's concerted effort to improve the housing condition of the population. Active encouragement of public housing ownership had as one of its consequences the incorporation of the population into the industrial work force. Home ownership not only increases routine household expenditure but also ties an individual to a regular schedule of mortgage payments; both can be met only by a source of regular income derived from regular employment. This means of incorporating the population into the economy was not lost on the government, which declared its intention to create a "home-owning democracy" so that the citizens would have a material stake in the nation. The promotion of home ownership has social and cultural implications which will be discussed in the next section.

The fashioning of the new productive work force required other cultural prerequisites. One of these was workers' facility with the English language, given the dependency on foreign capital. From the outset, English, the colonial language, was retained as the language of the new government, law, and commerce. However, multiracialism required the languages of the different individuals formally to be given equivalent status. Here, the differences among the individuals were radically reduced by the installation of a single language each for the "Chinese," the "Malays," and the "Indians" (Clammer 1985). The three other official languages were thus Malay, Mandarin and Tamil, respectively, thereby eliminating the dialect and language differences among Chinese, Malays, and Indians.[9] The discursive act which homogenized individual differences and brought into being the presence of "three" racial groups facilitated the administration of multiracialism. From then on, the population of the island was constituted into a convenient set of ready-to-hand categories, abbreviated as "CMIO," "O" for others (Siddique 1989).[10]

In the meantime, vernacular schools continued to operate (Kuo 1980 and 1985a). However, given the overwhelming comparative economic advantage of English in an expanding civil service and an industrializing economy, vernacular schools were soon to lose their student enrollment absolutely. The language issue will be further discussed, but for now it should be noted that the predominance of English, reflecting the dominance of economic rationality, was further entrenched by making it the sole language of instruction for academically weaker students who fail in regular school examinations, just so that they, hopefully, could remain gainfully employed. Thus, ironically, the language of the residual "other" is the politically dominant.

Finally, within the productionist orientation of a capitalist economy, and with the suspension of race as a basis of resource distribution, a formal meritocracy that allegedly denies particularistic claims was discursively deployed and, by extension, the role of the market ranked supreme in consumption. Social inequalities were individualized as the result of one's own lack of "natural" intelligence or diligence or both. The insistence on individual effort was presumed necessary to maintain productivity and avoid expansion of social welfarism.

THE MAKING OF A NEW SOCIAL ORDER

Obviously, political and economic strategies have their effects on the organization of society itself; concomitant to the making of a new state and a new economic order is thus the emergence of a new pattern of social organization. Three areas of the population's everyday life have been severely affected by policies designed for economic development and the promotion of national identity: public housing provisions, education and language policies, and family planning policies. The roles of the first two in the formation of national interests have already been mentioned; we will now flesh out their effects, along with the effects of family planning in the social organization of the new state.

(1) Restructuring Education

In addition to discipline, industrialization requires the work force to be made efficient and productive through education as investments in human capital. Opportunities in education were greatly expanded from the early 1960s. However, education is not restricted to the imparting of technical knowledge; it also partakes in the inculcation of social values that support nation-building objectives. The second function was as much pursued as the first; education became a major instrument of "social engineering" from then on (Wilson 1978).

Under the colonial regime, with the exception of limited opportunities for education in English medium schools, the education needs of the bulk of the population were largely financed and staffed by the people themselves. The vernacular schools, divided along political, cultural, and linguistic orientations, had their divisive effects on the population. Both teachers and textbooks had to be imported from the respective "homelands" abroad, and the contents of the books were of little relevance, if not detrimental, to the emergence of the new nation. However, to keep potential political tensions at bay, educational policies of the early 1960s retained nominal equality among vernacular streams. In the meantime, a new national system was being devised and instituted. Common curriculum and syllabi were introduced; textbooks were locally prepared, teachers locally trained, and a common examination standard imposed (Wilson 1978:235). The possibility of forging a common political, economic, and social orientation among the population through education was in place for the first time.

Politically, nationalistic rituals were introduced. There is a weekly flag raising and lowering assembly, during which the national anthem is played and sung. A national pledge is also recited, initially in four languages but by now only in English. All of these are, of course, aimed at instilling a sense of national identity and loyalty. However, like routinized ritualistic performances, they are done with less than the requisite enthusiasm. In the case of the national anthem, it is sung without much comprehension on the part of the majority of the students as it is written in Malay, which although retained as the nominal national language is not a compulsory language requirement for all students. Yet, the repetition may have cumulative effect among the successive generations of students that now constitute a substantial part of the citizenry.

At the individual level, educational qualification has long been a deciding factor in social and economic mobility. Without established intellectual traditions in what were essentially uneducated immigrant communities but with the contemporary emphasis on making a living, the population generally maintains an instrumental orientation towards education. The stress is on passing the successive examinations so as to obtain the necessary "paper" qualifications for a better job (certificates of formal education) and a better material life. The resulting process may be conceptualized as a process of the "certification of the self" in which self-valuation and self-worth are measured through the number of educational certificates in one's possession.

The government conceives of its role as one of deciding the level of tertiary educated manpower that is required by the expanding economy and providing equal opportunity to all at the entry point, then letting meritocracy account for the inequality of results. The shrinking number of spaces at successively higher education levels results in very keen and stressful competition, for both students and their parents. Such competition intensifies the instrumental orientation itself to the exclusion of other values. This is reflected in the unbridled dominance of English as the medium of instruction and the *lingua franca* of the society. The economic and social advantages of English led to an exodus of students from vernacular schools to English medium schools. The eventual demise of the former led to the unification of all schools into a "national stream" in 1987. This completed the restructuring of the educational system.[11]

However, by the late 1970s, the success of the materialistic orientation was read as a cause for concern. The education system was reviewed, with specific reference to "moral" education. In the process, several "cultural" consequences of the dominance of English were "revealed." First, while English proficiency gave Singaporeans greater access to global economic opportunities, it also rendered them more susceptible to cultural influences from Western sources, whose effects were discursively labelled "Westernization," which was behaviorially concretized by the government as an individual

Singaporean's inclination to such acts as drug abuse, sexual permissiveness, consumerism, and political liberalism. Cultural discourse in Singapore from then on took on an increasingly disparaging portrayal of the "West" as an imaginary unitary entity, eliminating differences between the people of Europe, America, and Australia. Second, it was argued in essentialist fashion that the domination of English is emotively problematic because it remains a "superimposed" Western language, thereby lacking cultural authenticity and legitimacy. The Prime Minister stated: "English will not be emotionally acceptable as our mother tongue" (*Straits Times*, Sept. 22, 1984).

The government's perceived deficiency in moral education and the cultural entailments of "Westernization" were to be corrected by the promotion of bilingualism and moral education at both primary and secondary levels. The "mother tongue" of a child was to be acquired in school as the second language along with English as the first. It was believed that the learning of the mother tongue would facilitate acquisition of "traditional Asian values," which would in turn act to resist the creeping negative influences of Westernization. A moral discourse was thus constituted by drawing a line between the discursively constituted "Asian" culture and "Western" culture, privileging the former over the latter. In addition, retention of the different mother tongues by the respective racial communities was supposedly to satisfy the emotive attachment each group has to its identity (Kuo 1985b). Finally, a new moral education curriculum was instituted in the early 1980s which included the teaching of religious knowledge at secondary school level; this was to be abandoned in a few years, as will be discussed later.

(2) Restructuring Community

The vast improvement in the population's physical living conditions brought about by the public housing program is not to be disputed. Nor should the program's role in sustaining the diffused mass loyalty of the population to the PAP government be doubted. The social costs incurred in the process of housing a nation should be assessed against the background of such generalized benefits. One of the most obvious and immediate costs was imposed on residents of established settlements which had to be demolished in order to make land available for new housing estates. Arguably, it was the wide distribution of the benefits that rendered the social costs bearable to those who were so negatively affected (Chua 1991). After initial protests by residents who were among the very first to have their land acquired by the government for redevelopment purposes, organized resistance to the resettlement dissipated by the early 1970s (Aldrich 1985).

As the urban squatter settlements or semi-rural villages tend to be inhabited predominantly by households of similar "race," and in the case of the Chinese often of similar dialect, demolition of these settlements was tantamount to the destruction of "racial" residential areas and their attendant cultural practices. The subsequent dispersion was intensified by the first-come-first-served rule in the allocation of public housing flats, a rule which literally prevents individuals from electing to live in close proximity.

The consequences, although suffered by all affected, are nevertheless unevenly distributed. They are more severe for members of the minority populations because dispersal deprives them of certain social supports that can be provided only by their respective members. For example, in the case of Malay Muslims, strict religious observations in terms of food and gender relations make it difficult for the working parents to entrust the childcare responsibility to non-Malays. In addition, lower income also renders it difficult for them to avail themselves of paid child-care centers.

These negative consequences are justified in terms of the national interest in the physical integration of all racial groups within the new housing estates so as to increase inter-racial understanding and avoid potential group violence. Indeed, interracial mixing is now enforced not only at the estate level but down to that of the block itself. Quotas for each of the three races in each block are monitored and maintained by imposing constraints on a flat owner's freedom to sell one's house. One is constrained to sell only to a household from the race that is not already over-represented in the block.

Promotion of home ownership has also accelerated the nuclearization of families. Easy access to a home through the public housing program, combined with the economic independence that comes from wage labor, has made it relatively easy for newly-weds to move out on their own and manage their own affairs, rather than being constantly enmeshed in the complexities of an extended household. Indeed, it was argued by the Minister of Finance in the early 1960s (Goh 1972:63) that the extended family, because of its ethos of pooling resources, acts as a damper to individual initiative and productivity. Hence, the nuclear family, with its implied selfishness, was better for the promotion of industrialization. The government was to come to reassess this rate of nuclearization in the late 1970s and introduce, again through housing policies such as priority of allocation and extension of the income ceiling of eligibility, steps to attempt to slow it down by encouraging multi-family housing arrangements with uncertain results (Chong et al. 1985: 252–257).

(3) Restructuring the Family

The material problems of unemployment, a housing shortage and a declining trading economy faced by Singapore, the new state, in 1965, could be further alleviated through reduction of the then high population growth rate. A stringent population control program was therefore instituted. The "two is enough" policy consisted of aggressive and constant publicity campaigns and the granting of a set of material incentives and disincentives in housing allocations, education opportunities for children, and tax and health care benefits.

After two decades of campaigning, helped by the higher educational level and economic development, the fertility rate declined from 3.6% in 1960 to 1.6% in 1984. This apparent success was in part dependent upon the demise of certain traditional values, a demise that was encouraged by the government. Important examples of the "discredited" traditional values included the preference for a large and extended family, a preference for sons over daughters, and the dependence on children for old age care. The success also resulted in more calculative attitudes towards marriage, family life, and kinship patterns (Wong 1979).

However, it became apparent that the effects of the policy were unevenly distributed. Lower income groups continued to have larger families and, as a majority of Malays tended to be from this income stratum, they had larger families. In addition, it was found that a significant proportion of university educated women were remaining single and, when married, were more inclined to have two or fewer children. This scenario, coupled with the geneticist view of Lee Kuan Yew, then Prime Minister, led to the introduction of a two tiered population policy in 1981: financial incentives were given to the lesser educated to stop at two, or preferably one, child while university educated mothers were encouraged to have more than two children with priority of school registration for the third child (Devan and Heng 1993). At the same time, a "match making" agency, euphemistically called the Social Development Unit, was set up within the Ministry of Community Development to facilitate meetings among unmarried university graduates. The "graduate mother policy" was strongly resisted not only by those disadvantaged by it but also those who stood to gain, especially among university students. The education privilege for the third child of graduate mothers was withdrawn in the first sitting of the newly elected Parliament in 1984, immediately after the PAP suffered its most significant decline in popular support in a general election, from the common approximately 75% to about 64%.

Finally, the reduction of birth rates appeared to produce its own problems; namely, the decline in population growth rate, similar to that of advanced developed countries, raised the issue of potential shortages of able-bodied citizens for both economic and defense activities. The government projected a future scenario of a drastic increase of the dependency ratio of an expanding retired population on a shrinking economically active counterpart. This led the government to abandon the "two is enough" policy in favor of the current "three or more if you can afford it." However, the monetary incentive for the lower income mother to have two or fewer children remains in place, while generous tax incentives were given to working mothers of high income. There have been marginal annual increases in birth rates since the new policy was introduced in 1987.

THE EXCESSES OF SUCCESS

From the above analysis, it should be apparent that evidence of the successful implantation of new cultural attitudes in the new Singaporeans was abundantly clear by the late 1970s. The economy grew by double digits annually while demographic growth subsided radically; there was a shortage of labor as opposed to high unemployment, the population became one of the best housed in the world (so much so that some economists argued that there was an over-consumption in housing (Lim et al. 1986)), and the educational attainments of the population advanced with the expansion of education opportunities. In short, the material standard of living improved massively at the end of two decades of political independence. By the late 1970s, the material orientation was well entrenched as part of the "truths" of being Singaporean. In the eyes of the government, amongst others, this manifested itself behaviorally in the various forms of "excessive material consumption" and attitudinally in "excessive individualism."

The consumer service sector had expanded rapidly; up-market hotel food and beverage facilities that are supposed to cater to well-heeled tourists are patronized equally by locals. So too are the branded goods imported from the fashion centers of the world, and for those who cannot afford "the real thing" there are plenty of "fakes" that give vicarious pleasure derived from the "names." However, one should not be hasty to label this process as "excessive" or "conspicuous" consumption. Within the historical context, the rapid expansion of consumption was to a significant degree one of making up for the hitherto material deprivations of an underdeveloped nation. Secondly, limits to consumption are quite identifiable. The extremely high costs of housing and car ownership, in addition to the high rate of forced savings through the compulsory saving social security scheme, known as the Central Provident Fund, extract a very significant proportion of any wage earner's income and substantially reduces the disposable income for consumption. Nevertheless, consumption of items of self-adornment, such as clothes and accessories, will likely be less affected, and indulgence will continue.

As for individualism, the first signs read by the government were found in the work place. In the constant search for more money, workers appeared to be "job-hopping," i.e. too willing to change jobs. The government's complaint that this was symptomatic of an absence of loyalty to the employer was conceptually problematic because, under circumstances where the market is the only constraint, a worker who actively seeks better opportunities would rightfully be considered as enterprising. Indeed, the tight labor market was largely responsible for the willingness of companies to poach each other's staff, knowing well that the employees that join readily could leave just as readily. In any event, this "job-hopping" was affecting productivity and was thus duly considered a moral problem.

Elsewhere, "creeping individualism" took a different form. It was observed that single young professionals were applying for government constructed middle-income flats in increasing numbers, apparently in a hurry to leave their families of origin. It was presumed that this would lead to premature break-up of the family unit and therefore must be stopped. The government promptly returned the deposits to the applicants and shut the register, and with it the opportunity for singles to own public housing flats (Chua 1982). This effectively reduced the degree of personal freedom for the single individual who cannot afford the steep cost of private housing.

It should be noted that individualism is but a relative phenomenon and it is common enough to hear criticisms of Singaporeans, by themselves and others, as being overly passive and conformist, particularly politically. Socially, there is yet another check on individualism that arises in the very social organization of Singapore, without direct government intervention. Being a small island-nation with a relatively stable population, the density of social encounters is relatively high; the frequency of chance meetings between acquaintances, friends and relatives, near or distant, is very high. These possible meetings act as informal checks on an individual, reducing one's inclination to public misdemeanor or individualist behavior.

Qualifications on individualism and consumerism aside, the perceived "excesses" began to acquire a concreteness in public discourse and led to several interesting formulations. Among the positive images is: "Given the achievement that has been attained and the far-flung benefits that have accrued, the Singaporean has gained self-esteem, is confident—at times overly so among some—ambitious, on the make. He travels widely, carrying his lap-top computer and his confidence with him" (Thumboo 1989:766). Others are disparaging, of which the most inarticulate and unoriginal is "the ugly Singaporean;" a more intellectual label for the perceived nascent attitude of the new Singaporean is "the cult of materialism" (Ho 1989).

Conjuncturally, similar criticisms against individualism were being raised by American intellectuals as a self-critique of the post-1960s social developments in advanced capitalist nations of the West. It was one of those few occasions in recent intellectual history in which the intellectual Right and Left arrived at the same critical conclusions. For both parties (notationally the neo-Marxists and the neo-conservatives), the malaise of the West in the 1970s was an unchecked individualism seen in the ever expanding claims of subjective interests and expressions, showing no responsibility for the social sphere. The landmark intellectual works of this American self-critique were *The Culture of Narcissism* (Lasch 1979) on the Left and *The Cultural Contradiction of Capitalism* (Bell 1976) on the Right. In the latter case, the critique was accompanied by a call for a return to traditional values such as family and religion. While there is no evidence that the Singapore government was influenced by such arguments, Lasch's book did receive public endorsement by the Minister of Education as foretelling the future of things to come in Singapore if nothing were done to check the nascent individualism.

It was in part in this intellectual context that the potential threat to the continuing prosperity of the new nation was formulated as the incipient Westernization of Singaporeans. "Westernization" became a convenient holder of all the ills of capitalist developments in Singapore, against which a very loose formulation of "Asian values" (Ho 1989:688; Rajaratnam 1977) was elevated supposedly to arrest the rot that threatened. The government then proposed several society-wide campaigns for the "revitalization" of Asian values. These included the introduction of policies that reinforced the family institution, such as giving priority allocation to three generation families (mentioned earlier), reversing the earlier nuclearization of family public housing policy, intensifying the teaching of mother tongues as second languages (as in the special aided schools for Chinese children with higher than average academic performance), and renewed efforts to teach moral education in schools. The latter culminated in the introduction in 1984 in secondary schools of courses in religious knowledge, including Confucian ethics for Chinese who did not profess any book religions.

In contrast to the earlier policies that were aimed at producing an efficient and disciplined work force necessary to the economic development of a new nation and the material wellbeing of the new citizenry, the policies and programs of the mid and late 1980s had as their motivation the inscription of the reinvented and prescribed "traditional" attitudes and values as the "truths of Asians" in general and the inscription of racial cultural elements, especially in terms of the predominant religions of the administratively convenient "three" races. Such "truths" were invoked to resist the other "truths" of the Singaporeans as individuals. In this context, the revival of such "Asian values" had the additional advantage of inciting individuals to voluntarily assume responsibility for the social sphere without disturbing the hierarchical social order itself. The inscription of Asian values on the individuals, therefore, dovetailed with the prevailing ideological discourse that had a very developed vocabulary of responsibility and correspondingly a weak set of terms for individual rights.

CONCLUSION

In this essay we have examined the development of Singapore into a new nation over a period of three decades. In the first two decades of the emergence of Singapore as a new nation, very conscious discursive distinctions were maintained between "national interests" and "ethnic culture and ethnic identity." The need for survival of an island nation without natural resources and a declining trading economy had dictated the rhetoric and limited the substantive task of nation building almost exclusively to issues concerned with improving the material conditions of the population, upon which was built the legitimacy of the new government to rule. These concerns were incessantly promoted through various ideological institutions and inscribed onto the population. The ideological efforts were backed by legislative measures to police their propagation and entrenchment when necessary.

Meanwhile, racial cultures and identities, conveniently reduced to three discursively constructed units of Chinese, Malays and Indians, were given very high visibility through the concept of multiracialism but relegated to the private sphere of individuals or of voluntary groups, with the government playing a supportive role in the religious holidays and major cultural festivals of each group. However, depending on the changing political atmosphere, the government policed the limits of such cultural expression through the elastic idea of "racial chauvinism." Furthermore, it actively sought to diffuse the political potential of the constructed racial constituencies through the demolition of exclusive racial enclaves, the perhaps unintended demise of vernacular schools, and the weakening and replacement of some traditional values by those that are necessary to capitalist economic development (such as competitiveness and meritocracy). The total effect of the multiracial policy was thus the very visible display of the racial constituencies which have minimal political effects and efficacy.

Ironically, at the point in time when the economic and materialist orientations were fully established, an apparent reversal of the cultural priorities took place. By the beginning of the third decade of the new nation, the "possible" demise of racial cultures was raised in train with the apparent fear of the wholesale "Westernization" of the essentially Asian population. Within the context of successful economic development, the inculcation of so-called "Asian values" was seen as the necessary defense against the insidious encroachment of the "morally dubious" social values of the West. In such a discursive move, a cultural entailment of capitalism, namely individualism, was detached from the economic sphere and dressed up in the moral language of anti-Westernization.

Comprehensive reviews of education and language policies were conducted in the late 1970s, culminating in the announcement of the new educational policy and the Moral Education Report in 1979. The same year saw the launching of the Speak Mandarin Campaign to promote Mandarin among Chinese; this has become an annual event. Then, in 1984, moral education and religious knowledge were introduced as part of the compulsory secondary school curriculum. Furthermore, with the ascendancy of the view that Confucianism is a basic, if not the primary, explanatory element for the success of post-war Asian capitalism, the promotion of Confucianism as a way of life for the Chinese was mooted.[12] These measures represent a response of a society overtaken by economic success and its concomitant social changes.

In all the instances of apparent reversals, selective cultural elements, discursively re-categorized as "Asian" culture, were called forth and re-inscribed on the citizens to check the domination of the economic orientation in the population. The moral contest of the two sets of implanted characters was discursively rendered as that between the good/Asian and the bad/Western.

However, despite their supposed link to traditions, the programs for inscribing "Asian-ness" were ultimately aimed at shoring up production and economic growth and, perhaps more importantly, the existing political order. Where such supportive roles became tenuous or uncertain, an about turn in policy was readily taken. Thus, in 1989, the teaching of religious knowledge, and along with it Confucianism, in the secondary school was abolished and legislation to control religious activities which merge with social and political issues introduced. In the final instance, it was the demands of the existing economic order, and the political order that ensures its continuing growth, that were privileged.

Indeed, it may be argued that in the discursive formation of nations, reversals between communal/individual, traditional/modern, indigenous/foreign (Asian/Western), and ethnic/national orientations at different historical conjunctures are to be expected. What complicates the Singapore case is that traditions are embedded in different racial cultures. Revoking or reinventing traditional values, therefore, means revoking and reinventing the various racial cultures. The dilemma appears to be one of whether such moves may prove detrimental to the social integration of Singapore as a nation and hinder the evolution of a national culture and a national identity that rise above and beyond race. Yet, the formation of the nation so far shows that such issues in themselves can be used as discursive building components of a national interest; the potential presence of the issues arising from multiracialism provides the discursive ground for the conceptualization of a national interest aimed at avoiding the realization of the issues themselves.

Nevertheless, politically the state appears to be unable to live with the potential disruptions that the differences which are embodied in multiracialism may cause. Consequently, in 1989 the government initiated the process of formulating an explicit "national ideology." In 1990, the designated Parliament committee brought forth a set of five values that were supposedly shared by the Asian cultures of the Chinese, Malays, and Indians; the invented nature of this claim is too apparent to require additional comments. Nevertheless, the proposed values were accepted by Parliament, and henceforth known as Shared Values in Singaporean political and cultural discourses. However, it should be noted that the accepted Shared Values remain until now a floating signifier without any institutional site because it is constitutionally of unclear status, being neither enshrined as a preamble to the national constitution nor an actionable legislation.

NOTES

1. The conceptual stance taken in this essay is indebted to the writings of the late Michel Foucault although no explicit citation to his corpus is given.
2. As recent as in 1990, when Singapore celebrated its 25th anniversary of independence, then Prime Minister Lee Kuan Yew lamented that the greatest disappointment in his life was "the failure to make Singapore succeed as part of Malaysia" *(Straits Times,* March 13, 1990).
3. Indeed it has been suggested that the absence of a work force accustomed to the industrial regime was the prime reason why American semiconductor industries chose Hong Kong over Singapore as the first offshore base for the internationalization of semiconductor production in the early 1960s. The flight of industrial capital from mainland China because of political instabilities since the 1930s had led to the industrialization of Hong Kong for more than two decades by then; it thereby possessed the prerequisite proletarianized labor force (Henderson 1989:77-80).
4. Electoral legislation in that same year has further entrenched the multiracial composition of Parliament by instituting the Group Representative Constituency (GRC) legislation, in which political parties contesting in a GRC must field their candidates as a slate, of whom one must be from a minority population. The slate that polls the largest number of combined votes wins all the seats in the GRC.
5. In this instance, the few women MPs similarly have to carry the additional demands of the national women's constituency.
6. This is a significant instance in the post-1984 political development of Singapore where class features are beginning to make themselves felt in the body politic.
7. For details of the suppression of radical unionists and individuals of the Left generally see Bloodworth (1986).
8. This statement was made in Parliament by the then secretary general of the National Trade Union Congress and Minister without Portfolio in the Prime Minister's Office, Mr. Lim Chee Onn *(Straits Times,* March 24, 1982).
9. Reflecting the multiracialism policy, Mandarin in Singapore is known as the "language of the Chinese" (*huayu*) as opposed to the "national language" (*guoyu*) in Taiwan and "the common language" (*putonghua*) in the People's Republic of China (Chun 1994:50).
10. The government's active promotion of the "Speak Mandarin" campaign among the Chinese, aimed at eliminating their dialect differences, has caused some to suggest that there is a generalized attempt to "sinicize" the entire Singaporean population, implying a desire to produce a "Chinese" nation. However, as one of the PAP's critics points out, this would

contradict the logic of multiculturalism (Clammer 1985:112–113) which is itself useful in giving the state a high level of political autonomy, as argued earlier in this essay.
11. The so-called "national stream" is a gloss over persistent differences among schools. Differences in school "spirit" and "ethos" are noticeable and very much determined by the histories of the schools, which are in turn colored by their original language medium of instruction; the results of streaming students with different capabilities into different schools with very different standards of education also leave their effects in the social stratification of schools themselves.
12. The attempt to "Confucianize" the Chinese population has gone through a difficult trajectory in a very short period of less than a decade; for greater details see Chua (1992) and Kuo (1992).

REFERENCES

Aldrich, B.C. (1985). Habitat Defence in Southeast Asia. *Southeast Asian Journal of Social Science* 13:1–14.

Bell, Daniel (1976). *The Cultural Contradictions of Capitalism*. New York: Basic Books.

Benjamin, Geoffrey (1976). The Cultural Logic of Singapore's Multiculturalism. In Riaz Hassan (ed.) *Singapore: Society in Transition*. Kuala Lumpur: Oxford University Press, pp. 115–133.

Chalmers, Ian (1992). Loosening State Controls in Singapore: The Emergence of Local Capital as a Political Force. *Southeast Asian Journal of Social Science* 22:57–84.

Chan, Heng Chee (1970). *Singapore: The Politics of Survival, 1965–1967*. Kuala Lumpur: Oxford University Press.

Chong, Kim Chang, Tham, Yew Fang and Shium, Soon Kong (1985). Housing Schemes: Policies and Procedures. In Aline K.Wong and Stephen K.K.Yeh, Eds. *Housing a Nation: 25 Years of Public Housing in Singapore*. Singapore: Housing and Development Board, pp. 230–262.

Chua, Beng-Huat (1982). Singapore in 1981: Problems in New Beginnings. *Southeast Asian Affairs 1982*. Singapore: Institute of Southeast Asian Studies, pp. 315–335.

— (1989). The Business of Living in Singapore. In Sandhu and Wheatley, Eds. *Management of Success: The Moulding of Modern Singapore*. Singapore: Institute of Southeast Asian Studies, pp. 1003–1021.

— (1991). Not Depoliticized but Ideologically Successful: The Public Housing Program in Singapore. *International Journal of Urban and Regional Research* 18:24–41.

— (1992). Confucianization in Modernising Singapore. *Social Welt* 8:249–269.
— (1994). Veiled by High Visibility: The Strategic Production of the Politics of Race in Singapore. Paper presented at the Workshop on "Managing Diversity: Government and Ethnicity in Southeast Asia and the South Pacific." Department of Political Science and Social Change, Research School of Pacific Studies, The Australian National University, Canberra, 10–11, January.
Chun, Allen (1994). From Nationalism to Nationalizing: Cultural Imagination and State Formation in Postwar Taiwan. *The Australian Journal of Chinese Affairs* 31:49–69.
Clammer, John (1985). *Singapore: Ideology, Society and Culture*. Singapore: Chopman Publishers.
Deyo, Frederic C. (1981). *Dependent Development and Industrial Order. An Asian Case Study*. New York: Praeger.
Devan, Janadas and Heng, Geraldine (1992). State Fatherhood: The Politics of Nationalism, Sexuality, and Race in Singapore. In Andrew Parker, Mary Russo, Doris Sommer, and Patricia Yaeger, Eds. *Nationalisms and Sexualities*. New York: Routledge.
Drysdale, John (1984). *Singapore: Struggle for Success*. Singapore: Times Books International.
Goh, Keng Swee (1976). A Socialist Economy that Works. In C.V. Devan Nair, Ed. *Socialism that Works*. Singapore: Federal Press, pp. 77–85.
— (1972). Social, Political and Institutional Aspects of Development Planning. In Goh Keng Swee, Ed. *The Economic of Modernization*. Singapore: Asia Pacific Press, pp. 60–82.
Henderson, Jeffrey (1989). *The Globalization of High Technology Production*. London: Routledge.
Ho, Kah Leong (1993). Political Indigenization of the State in Peninsular Malaysia. Paper presented at the AEAN Inter-University Seminar on Social Development, Kota Kinabalu, Malaysia.
Ho, Wing Meng (1989). Values Premises Underlying the Transformation of Singapore. In Sandhu and Wheatley, Eds. *Management of Success*. Singapore: Institute of Southeast Asian Studies, pp. 671–691.
Kuo, Eddie C.Y. (1980). The Sociolinguistic Situation in Singapore: Unity in Diversity. In E. Afendras and E. Kuo, Eds. *Language and Society in Singapore*. Singapore: Singapore University Press, pp. 39–62.
— (1985a). Language and Social Mobility in Singapore. In N. Wolfson and J. Manes, Eds. *Language of Inequality*. Berlin: Mouton, pp. 337–354.
— (1985b). Language and Identity: The Case of Chinese in Singapore. In W. Tseng and D. Wu, Eds. *Chinese Culture and Mental Health*. New York: Academic Press, pp. 81–192.

— (1992). Confucianism as Political Discourse in Singapore: The Case of an Incomplete Revitalisation Movement. Working Paper 113, Department of Sociology, National University of Singapore.

Lasch, Christopher (1979). *The Culture of Narcissism*. New York: Warner Books.

Lewis, Alan (1981). Nicos Poulantzas and the autonomy of politics. *Catalyst* 14:23–44.

Lim, Chong Yah et al. (1986). Report of the Central Provident Study Group, (Special Issue) *Singapore Economic Review*, 31.

Lim, Chong Yah and Associates (1988). *Policy Options for the Singapore Economy*. Singapore: McGraw-Hill.

Pang, Cheng Lian (1971). *The Peoples' Action Party*. Kuala Lumpur: Oxford University Press.

Poulantzas, Nicos (1978). *Political Power and Social Classes*. London: Verso.

Quah, Stella (1983). Social Discipline in Singapore. *Journal of Southeast Asian Studies* 14:266–289.

Rajaratham, S. (1977). Asian Values and Modernization. In Seah Chee Meow, Ed. *Asian Values and Modernization*. Singapore: Singapore University Press, pp. 95–100.

Rodan, Garry (1989). *The Political Economy of Singapore's Industrialization*. London: Macmillan.

Sandhu, K. S. and Wheatley, Paul, Eds. (1989). *Management of Success: The Moulding of Modern Singapore*. Singapore: Institute of Southeast Asian Studies.

Thumboo, Edwin (1989). Self-Images: Contexts for Transformations. In Sandhu and Wheatley, Eds. *Management of Success*. Singapore: Institute of Southeast Asian Studies, pp. 749–768.

Wang, Gungwu (1989). The Chinese as Immigrants and Settlers. In Sandhu and Wheatley, Eds. *Management of Success*. Singapore: Institute of Southeast Asian Studies, pp. 552–562.

Willmott, William (1989). The Emergence of Nationalism. In Sandhu and Wheatley, Eds. *Management of Success*. Singapore: Institute of Southeast Asian Studies, pp. 578–598.

Wilson, H.E. (1978). *Social Engineering in Singapore*. Singapore: Singapore University Press.

Wong, Aline (1979). The National Family Planning Programme and Changing Family Life. In E. Kuo and A. Wong, Eds. *The Contemporary Family in Singapore*. Singapore: Singapore University Press, pp. 211–238.

3

A Second Look: On "The Making of a New Nation"

Allen J. Chun

What follows is a kind of meta-commentary on what I think is a superb paper. As I see it, this paper is basically an attempt to describe the socio-political construction of Singaporean national identity and to show how this particular ideological construct is reinforced by and inculcated through a whole complex of social institutions, namely the workplace, the educational system, the public housing system, and family planning.

The historical roots (or what the authors prefer to call "the genealogy") of Singapore's national identity are unique. Even at the surface level, there are many dimensions of this nationalizing experience which contrast with those characteristic of other new nations in Asia. For one thing, rather than having to fight for national independence, the "nation" as a political entity was somewhat reluctantly thrust upon Singapore. This "reluctant nationalism" per se had some crucial ramifications for the construction of a national culture, particularly with regard to the role of ethnicity and language. Simply put, not having a tradition upon which it could fall back or by which it could "invent" (or reinvent as the case may be), it necessitated the construction of a national culture that had to transcend traditional definitions of ethnic affiliation and language unity.

In other words, when we're talking about Singaporean culture or being Singaporean, we are really talking about a different kind of "imagined community." The authors are correct in pointing out that ethnic culture became objects of discourse in the sense that ethnicity became objectified in terms of language, religion, custom, etc.. Yet more significantly, the promotion of "ethnic diversity" in these terms became at the same time the precondition for its subordination to higher national values. That is to say it is really a *facade* for the promotion of a new disciplinary ethos which is really at the heart of Singaporean national identity. Not only is the *construction* of Singaporean culture a modern one, at the same time Singaporean *culture* is quite explicitly a celebration of the values of modernity. In a Singaporean context, it is okay to be Malay (or Indian or Chinese), eat Malay and speak Malay. But being Singaporean really means adopting the proper ethos of the workplace, accepting English as the lingua franca of modern society, sacrificing the traditional ethnic community in favor of the utopian visions of public housing and embracing the virtues of the two-child nuclear family. In fact, one could say here that being Singaporean means accepting the government's broader vision of the New Society, *whatever* it is and *whoever* one may be in ethnic terms.

You can probably infer from my tone of voice that I am somewhat cynical or pessimistic about this broader vision; in fact, this is precisely where the authors and I part company. As the authors have quite brilliantly shown, the construction of Singapore culture and national identity as the ethos and consciousness of modern society was made possible by many things, e.g. the historical roots of a reluctant nationalism, the survivalism of a struggling or growing economy, the need to transcend ethnic tensions of the past, etc.. But the authors fail to ask the *critical* question, namely *who* is doing the constructing and *what about* the objectivity of *their* values and *their* visions for the future?

I suppose what I am suggesting here is that you don't have to adopt the authors' Foucaultian terminology in order to appreciate the basic point they are making, namely that the construction of Singapore culture is inseparable from the making of the new socio-politico-economic order insofar as this ideology of the nation-state (or what they refer to as the discourse) is grounded in the practice of certain institutions. I would simply add here that once one begins to look at the genealogy of the institutional practices themselves in Foucaultian terms, the picture of disciplinary society that really emerges is not unlike that which can be gotten from the darkest reading of *Discipline and Punish (1977).*

In short, what is the nature of these disciplinary practices that the authors allude to in the beginning but in my opinion never really follow through upon? I refer here not to the complex of social institutions that attend the functional exercise of political power (which is really what the authors refer to in this paper). I refer rather to the various modalities of power in a Foucaultian sense attending the disciplinary "gaze" which are general not only to productivity in the workplace but also to the policing of the family, the microphysics of residential living and the normalization of the person in Singapore society.

So to re-pose my original questions, who is doing the constructing here, what kind of rational ethos is being espoused here and what is the nature of these underlying disciplinary practices? Well, obviously the government is doing the constructing. But to answer the next two questions let me raise some examples pertaining to ethnicity and language, which appear to be the two obvious dimensions of this cultural facade, to show why there might be a hidden agenda of sorts at play. Ethnic harmony and preservation of culture in terms of traditional customs, artifacts, etc., are all very nice, but in the context of Singapore it is not obvious nor immediately apparent why ethnic autonomy or ethnic consciousness should be a necessary precondition for the promotion of a Singaporean national identity.

To be sure, ethnicity a la Singapore is quite different from a melting pot ideology that is characteristic of the U.S., for example. Both in theory represent different paths toward ethnic harmony and, therefore, both should have very different sociopolitical ramifications; to be even more explicit, both should mask different kinds of hegemonies. In the case of a melting pot ideology, the core value of the system is assimilation, assimilation to a dominant set of values and lifestyles which in the end erases ethnic differences by de-signifying ethnic consciousness. In Singapore's case, on the other hand, the government goes to great lengths to maintain existing ethnic balance, not unlike a quota system. The effect of heightening ethnic consciousness thus heightens the sense of boundaries in a way which not incidentally favors the existing dominant ethnic group. I do not mean to suggest here that this is in fact the government's hidden agenda, but the possibility of reading the situation in this extreme light is certainly there. In the realm of party politics, I would say that this extreme tends not to be the case. I think the explicit defusing by the government of political affiliation along ethnic lines, easy as it may appear to be, is in fact part of an attempt to achieve an even higher level of homogeneity, a homogeneity of a single-party state dominated by the PAP. Facetiously speaking, perestroika is certainly not the vogue in Singapore politics, in spite of the facade of participatory democracy.

In the case of language, it may be the case as the authors state in the paper that an emphasis upon economic utility and achievement motivation overrode ethnic consciousness and precipitated to some degree the demise of ethnic stream education toward a more universalistic standard of education, with English being the preferred medium of instruction. Yet on the other hand, politically inspired ulterior motives were also involved here. For instance, the eventual amalgamation of the Chinese-language stream Nanyang University into the English stream National University of Singapore was just as much motivated by utilitarian rationales as by the government's need to stamp out the possible threat of communist influence inspired by Chinese ethnic nationalism. So the language issue is a very complicated political problem, with ramifications for both national unity and ethnic identity.

Shifting gears a bit, to understand how disciplinary practices come into play here, I think it is necessary to ask, "Who or what is a Singaporean as a certain kind of moral person"? The construction of national identity or national consciousness is tied very much to the construction of the moral person. Crudely stated, the conception of the Singaporean being cultivated is neither Lasch's narcissistic individual nor Louis Dumont's monad; nor is it like the Confucian gentleman or even the KMT's public citizen *(kuo-rnin tai-piao)*. For lack of a more refined characterization, I would say that being Singaporean involves in part embracing in practice the vision of a socially ordered, normalizing if not standard society or at least accepting the benevolent authority of the government in fashioning the welfare state. It is the welfare state in broad terms which represents the epitome or ultimate realization of what Foucault initially called the disciplinary society. In the case of Singapore, the welfare state is made efficient if not successful by a whole panoply of disciplinary practices which has as its end the moral regulation of the health of its individuals through the normalization of life-routines. As I said before, these moralizing if not socializing practices are evident not just in the workplace but also in the educational process, the family, the ecology of the community, etc.. For example, if a Chinese elsewhere wanted to discipline his child, he would emphasize the need to be obedient by listening to the voice of authority, otherwise something bad would happen. In Singapore, the same child might be disciplined by saying something like, "if you don't listen, Aunty (in fact, any third party person present) will write a report on you." This is a joke, but it is a uniquely Singaporean joke. Moreover, it is not funny.

I find that the construction of social life in all aspects that the authors describe in their paper is basically a system of disciplining. Conformity backed by endless levels of confidentiality and supervision characteristic of the ever-present gaze appears to be the staple of social life in the New Singapore. In my opinion, it is this system of disciplining that in the final analysis makes the ideology of Singapore culture efficacious.

REFERENCE

Foucault, Michel (1977). *Discipline and Punish: The Birth of the Prison*. New York: Pantheon.

PART II
Taiwan

4

The Culture Industry as National Enterprise: The Politics of Heritage in Contemporary Taiwan

Allen J. Chun

The modernity of China as a nation-state must be distinguished from its continued existence as a community of people, institutions, beliefs and practices with roots in custom and civilization going back to prehistoric times. In contrast to other nations of the Third World emerging out of a colonial past and struggling to cope with both the growing pains of development and the lack of a dominant tradition from which to define a national identity, it might be said, for example, that modern China is largely immune to such crises of culture by virtue of its continuity to the past.

While it may be true that crises of culture appear to be most endemic to new nations emerging out of multi-ethnic settings or decentralized local traditions, the general point I wish to make here is that the crisis of nationalism and national culture transcends ethnicity simply because, in principle, it is trying to construct a radically different kind of bounded community called the modern nation-state. In other words, one is not just dealing with new *ideologies* of boundedness; one is dealing more precisely with a new kind of *boundedness*. The same sense of boundedness that forces multi-ethnic states to recognize a common cultural *authority* also demands a sense of *totality* which is in many crucial respects incompatible with the elite culture of traditional societies. This constant need to reinforce a sense of totality in both *name* (as invoked by one's nationality as citizenship) and *spirit* (as grounded in a sense of common values, consciousness or fate) is precisely what national culture aims to reflect and protect.

Without denying the take-it-for-granted factual existence of Chinese culture in traditional times, one must explain more importantly in my opinion why culture is invoked at particular times and takes on particular meanings under certain circumstances *in spite of* its take-it-for-granted factual existence. To say that culture becomes *meaningful* at particular moments or under certain conditions is simply another way of saying that culture, as we shall understand it in the present analysis, is largely a *political* construction. In the case of modern China, as the experience of postwar Nationalist Taiwan shall illustrate, the changing meaning and practice of Chinese culture is largely a function of changing historical and political conditions associated with the construction of the modern nation-state. In this sense, the invention of traditional Chinese culture in contemporary Taiwan becomes less interesting for how it reflects upon the authenticity of its *content* than for how it takes on different *forms* and to what extent it becomes *institutionalized* in everyday life.

Before the fall of the empire which gave rise to the nation-state, China was more a kind of cultural state of mind.[1] The middle kingdom, which is China's famous rendition of itself, was not a territorially bound nation-state epitomized by rights of citizenship, a standardized national language and a uniform educational system, but more precisely a set of core values which linked persons in time and place to an all-encompassing cosmic hierarchy.[2] The terms *zhongguo* ("middle kingdom") and *huaxia* (Chinese cultural order attributed to the mythical Hsia dynasty), which are the terms most widely used to denote China and Chineseness, actually have their origins in the feudal past characterized by a confederation of states all claiming to share a common culture or civilization.[3] The sense of unity engendered by this kind of cultural order explains in part the Chinese perception of an unbroken historical continuity despite the rise and fall of dynasties, both indigenous and barbarian, the myth of a common ethnic identity stemming from the Yellow River valley, and an attachment to the languages and values of an ongoing literary tradition.

The radical vision of a modern (Nationalist) society can easily be traced back to the events of the 1911 Revolution which led to the overthrow of the Ch'ing imperial dynasty and the birth of the Republic. Prior to the Revolution of 1911, there was no cognate notion in Chinese of society or nation-state as a territorially distinct, politically bounded and ethnically identifiable group of people. Many terms had to be borrowed from Japanese (Han and Li 1984). Up until the mid-19th century, it was unnatural for Chinese to call other ethnic groups "ethnic groups," just barbarians. Only during the early years of the Republic did intellectuals begin to associate *zhonghua minzu* (Chinese as ethnic category) with *zhongguo ren* (citizens of China).[4] This association was meant to lump together the multitude of people within territorial China into a single nation. Moreover, Chineseness in terms of material culture, ethnicity, or residence was never clearly defined (Wu 1991:162). Even the Chinese rendition of nationalism (*minzu zhuyi*) as the "principle of a common people" clearly underscored the notion of a bounded citizenry as the distinctive feature of nationhood (in contrast, for example, to the purely institutional characteristics of the nation-state).[5] This point was made early on by Sun Yat-sen, the revolutionary hero and father of the Republic, who in a famous phrase criticized the traditional Chinese polity as being "a dish of loose sand" (*yi pan san sha*). This explains at least why the raising of "societal consciousness" (*minzu yishi*) and the promotion of spiritual values to that effect have been repeatedly pointed to only in the aftermath of nationalism as the primary obstacle to the maintenance of national solidarity in the face of both Communism and the modern world system.

If the radical discontinuity brought about by the emergence of the nation-state was by definition a rejection of the traditional past, one is then hard pressed to explain at first glance why tradition (or at least selective usage of it) would need to be invented or resuscitated and why culture (as a specific ideological form) need be invoked at all. In the growing literature on nations and nationalism, what James (1989) neatly called "the rise of the cultural" is already implicated in the rise of the nation-state. For Gellner (1983), for instance, neither the high literate culture of traditional societies nor ethnic traditions per se could provide the framework for the kind of horizontal, universalistic solidarity that appeared to be characteristic of the modern nation. Gellner's emphasis upon education and popular literacy as the means by which (modern) culture becomes universally attainable parallels Anderson's (1983) focus upon "print capitalism" and the emergence of a common colloquial language.[6] Yet unlike Gellner's stress on progress in educational standards, for Anderson, the construction of a colloquial language was simply a tool which enabled the allegorical imagery of the nation and the radical time-space notions of nationhood to become engrained in the popular imagination, especially via the medium of popular literature and other forms of mass culture. Thus according to Gellner and Anderson, any notion of culture associated with this new emerging nationalism had to be *reconstructed* and *forward-looking*, in spite of its origin, insofar as it had to be able to transcend forms of solidarity or what Geertz (1963) aptly termed the "primordial sentiments" associated with traditional culture.

The rise of national culture associated generally with the radical emergence of the modern nation-state is analytically distinct from the revival of tradition, which is one particular manifestation of national culture. Perhaps not unlike the invention of tradition pointed to by Hobsbawm and Ranger (1983), the discovery of custom described by Keesing and Tonkinson (1982) and the objectification of indigenous culture brought about under the guise of enlightened colonialism (Clammer 1973, Cohn 1984, Thomas 1989), the revival of tradition as an object of gazing, discourse, codification and institutionalization is essentially a local response to ongoing and changing global situations. In postwar Nationalist Taiwan, the compelling need to redefine national identity in terms of race, language and history by rallying around the defense of "traditional Chinese culture" has to be understood in the first instance in reference to its relationship to mainland China as part of those larger global concerns. Although traditional in origin, the promotion of Chinese culture in this regard more importantly had to reflect modern designs by establishing definitions of collective identity and foundations of societal consciousness that could satisfy the totalizing vision of the state in ways that primordial notions of Chineseness, strictly speaking, could not.

Yet modern as it is, the strategic call to tradition and culture in postwar Taiwan was also a specific response to the communist threat posed by mainland China. In terms of discourse, it is thus no coincidence that the invoking of tradition represented an ideologically conservative response to the radical visions of a Communist national polity. One can say then in this regard that the construction of tradition and culture had from the beginning an explicitly political agenda. At the same time, it is perhaps equally important to point out that the usages to which tradition was put and the diverse meanings invoked by culture were always changing. These changes reflected, of course, strategic positionings within a changing political order, but as *meaningful* responses these changing constructions of traditional culture throughout the postwar period had to reflect more importantly changing utopian visions of a modern Nationalist polity.

It would probably not be inappropriate here to characterize the utopian vision of "traditional Chinese culture" in postwar Nationalist Taiwan as a kind of "historical unconscious," to mimic Jameson's (1981) understanding of "the political unconscious." Given that the government in both the practice of cultural policy and the orchestration of collective action was actively engaged in the writing of culture in various forms, these various kinds of symbolic narrative thus constitute levels of "ideological investment" which serve an important hegemonic function in the overall state apparatus. In the following sections, I shall attempt to show how ideology as culture was written at many different levels, then became manifested in social practice, institutionalized as norm, and systematically commodified.

CULTURAL RENAISSANCE AS SOCIAL MOVEMENT: PEOPLEHOOD IN POLICY AND PRACTICE

I argued above that the crisis of culture in postwar Taiwan was for the most part predicated on efforts by the state to construct new foundations of social solidarity, spiritual consciousness and ideological rationality consistent with its particular vision of a just society. Why culture was invoked, in the sense that it was *perceived* to be a necessary condition for the survival of the modern polity, had to do with the apparent need to ground this new sense of societal boundedness in symbolically meaningful terms or accepted social values. In this regard, tradition represented one particular definition of culture, or at least it represented an effective means of defining itself vis-a-vis its Communist counterpart. Yet just as culture or recourse to ideology can be seen as one of many possible agendas pertinent to the continued well-being of the state, the rationality of tradition invoked here must be understood not simply by its reference to the past (as in the case of nostalgia) but more precisely by reference to its selectivity. In other words, "Chinese traditional culture" not only involved a multiplicity of *things* (markers of national identity, icons of patriotic fervor and national treasures), it also involved the authority of different kinds of rhetorical *statements* (shared myths, beliefs and values, common language, ethnicity and custom as well as codification of discursive knowledge) whose coherence and systematicity ultimately reflected the larger utopian vision of a Nationalist state.

At the simplest level, the primary problem which emerged only after the founding of the Republic in 1911 was one of constructing a bound polity drawn together by a set of master symbols, shared beliefs (or myths) and moral/spiritual consciousness, that is to say, a set of horizontally universal values that could replace the hierarchically stratified values of Heaven and divine kingship that buttressed a previous cultural order. That the Chinese perceived nationalism or *minzu yishi* literally as "the principle of a common people," rather than as the rationality of a set of socio-political institutions like the state or its bureaucracy, is significant. This meant that much ideological energy was expended to forge a new sense of national community founded upon the heightening of "societal consciousness" (*minzu yishi*), especially in reaction to the domination of Western imperialism and the corresponding sense of political humiliation and cultural degradation. Thus, the struggle of nationalism which began with the collapse of the Chinese imperial system and has continued to be fought to the present day involved essentially the construction of a set of conscious ideological or mythological beliefs which could be used to cultivate a sense of societal self-esteem as a form of resistance to the West. For the most part, this use of culture as a heightened form of societal consciousness was the underlying strategy which linked nationalist discourse on both the mainland and Taiwan. They have differed simply with regard to their choice of master symbols and master narratives.

On the mainland, the elevation of the Great Wall to the status of de facto national symbol is a case in point. Prior to the 19th century, the Chinese had little idea of it, much less a name for it. From the late 16th century, after the Ming emperors had embarked upon a program to extend the original Qin walls to ward off Mongol invasion, to the late 19th century, the Great Wall had negative connotations through its association with the excesses of despotic emperors. Yet despite its despotic connotations, nationalists like Sun Yat-sen and Lu Xun seized upon the Great Wall as a rallying point for Chinese national consciousness. This ambivalent relationship to the Wall continued throughout the Communist era, going through periods of denigration and deification (see Waldron 1989).

In Taiwan, while it is difficult to find an iconic symbol to equal the stature of the Great Wall in mainland nationalist sentiment, the KMT government has in firm contrast with the mainland consistently maintained its role as the guardian of traditional Chinese culture. This notion of guardianship is reflected not only in its conservative attitude toward the preservation of language, thought and other traits of Chinese civilization but also in its proprietary attitude toward the possession of various "national treasures" (*guobao*) which include artifacts of high culture such as those belonging to the National Palace Museum, classic texts and objects of (historical or archaeological) antiquity which were products of this civilization. Despite their choice of different national symbols, the KMT's rhetorical use of these icons was similar to that of the mainland. These were all in the first instance rallying points for common national sentiment. As long as they could be divested of their negative connotations, they could easily portray the unique achievements of the nation (vis-a-vis other nations) and in the process enhance feelings of national pride.[7]

In Taiwan, the master symbol which appears to strike closest to the essence of Chineseness or traditional Chinese identity is the concept of *huaxia*. *Hua* invokes a sense of Chineseness that is essentially cultural, that is to say, in the sense of a shared civilization, and *xia* is the name of the (mythical) first dynasty. *Huaxia* then invokes a set of primordial values which is both a source of cultural uniqueness (vis-a-vis other peoples) and a myth of historical origin. This sweeping notion of Chineseness, albeit loosely defined, has definite rhetorical functions. In opposition to the People's Republic, *huaxia* was a metaphor of belief in the traditional past which was meant to contrast with the extreme forward-looking radicalism of the communist world-view. In the context of the global system, *huaxia* was a metaphor of cultural uniqueness and, as a symbol of national pride, a metaphor of resistance as well. In the context of Taiwan, however, the same concept was meant to anchor Taiwan within the Chinese nation-state as a whole. Insofar as national consciousness in this regard was politically incompatible with Taiwanese ethnic consciousness (especially since Taiwan was ceded to Japan in 1895 prior to the founding of the Republic), then the concept of *huaxia* represented a metaphor of political domination by the state.

The writing of culture by the state, however, went beyond the strategic deployment of master symbols and the rhetoric of nostalgia, resistance or domination. Master symbols, whenever they could, tended to be encoded within master narratives of culture. By *invoking* tradition, the writing of Chinese culture in Taiwan engendered ideologies of various kinds, which included not only loose notions of civilization but also political ideology, scholarly knowledge, moral philosophies and standards of custom. By *inventing* tradition, on the other hand, the writing of Chinese culture in Taiwan had to rewrite the content of tradition in order to suit new rhetorical forms and new political agendas.

All in all, it is possible to detect three distinct phases of cultural policy or writing in postwar Taiwan, the first of which can perhaps be called the era of cultural reunification, the second the era of cultural renaissance, and the third the era of cultural reconstruction. The era of cultural reunification covers the period between 1945–67 from the return of Taiwan to China by Japan at the end of World War II until the height of the Cultural Revolution on the mainland. This period was characterized by a need to reconsolidate Chinese culture by purging Japanese influences lingering as a result of 50 years of colonial rule and by suppressing any movements toward local Taiwanese cultural expression. While it is difficult to generalize about the ongoing influence of Japanese and Taiwanese traditions in this period of transition, it is important to note that the KMT viewed them simply as threats to Chinese national identity.[8] The main tool of cultural reunification in this regard had to be the forced imposition of standard Mandarin as the official language of everyday communication and medium for disseminating social values. Colloquial Taiwanese and Japanese in all avenues of mass communication like radio, film, television and newspapers, which were government controlled, were banned along with all publications originating from Japan and mainland China. This continued to remain in effect throughout the period of martial law. The dictatorship of a unified language became in turn the precondition for the widespread inculcation of traditional Chinese history, thought and values, or culture in a broad sense. Given the explicit state of war and the emphasis upon reorganization and development of basic industries, culture here was never part of an explicit program of political reconstruction. Emphasis was rather upon accepting the myth of a shared cultural origin, as invoked by the notion of *huaxia* and the protection of national treasures.

A second phase of cultural discourse, the era of cultural renaissance, covers the period of 1967–77. During the sixties, the hysteria of war did not wane much, but the socio-political infrastructure was established enough to permit a "war of position," in Gramsci's terms, regarding the deployment of ideology in national development. In 1966, coinciding with the 100th anniversary of the birth of Sun Yat-sen but primarily to counter the Cultural Revolution on the mainland, the government launched a large-scale "cultural renaissance movement" (*wenhua fuxing yundong*). This was officially inaugurated in a speech given by Chiang Kai-shek entitled *Chung-shan-lou chung-hua wen-hua-t'ang luo-ch'eng chi-nien wen* (Chung-shan-lou Commemorative Essay), an arcane four-page essay containing no less than 86 footnotes.[9] In the following year, a committee was established at the level of the provincial government to promote the Chinese cultural renaissance movement. The provincial committee then set up smaller regional committees at the level of city district and rural township administration to carry out the work of cultural renaissance, primarily through the local agency of the elementary and middle school. That schools were called upon to serve as active nerve centers for the promotion of cultural learning and awareness, both as part of the daily curriculum and in extracurricular activities, was a central tenet of government policy to extend the level of collective consciousness to the local level. The scope of cultural renaissance was far-reaching and by the government's own design was meant to combine the work of administrative planning, media dissemination, and scholarly research as well as engage the coordinated efforts of the party, newspaper and broadcasting industry, and various other government-sponsored "people's interest groups" (political grassroots organizations). The work of tradition in these domains was motivated by four explicit guidelines: 1) allow the media to sow the seeds of public dissemination and incite education to take the initiative, 2) exemplify and actively lead through the expression of social movement, 3) use the schools as activity centers for the extension of the culture renaissance movement to the family and society-at-large, and 4) use the full network of administration to step up coordination and supervision.[10]

The promotion of the cultural renaissance movement beginning in the mid- 1960s was not a spontaneous discovery of traditional culture and values. It was a systematic effort to redefine the content of these ideas and values, to cultivate a large-scale societal consciousness through existing institutional means and to use the vehicle of social expression as the motor for national development in other domains—economic, political, even athletic. In other words, not only was there an organized effort to cultivate a spirit of national unity through recourse to tradition, but also an effort to lead people to believe that this spirit of cultural consciousness was the key to the fate of the nation in all other respects. That is to say, achievements as diverse as economic progress and athletic success were all seen as consequences of (and causes for) this spirit of national unity. That the cultivation of a spirit of cultural consciousness was also explicitly linked to the policy of cultural development in other regards, namely the extension of ties with overseas Chinese and foreign cultural agencies, financing of various grassroots cultural groups, development of the tourist industry, increased publication of the classics, preservation of historical artifacts, large-scale promotion of activities in science, ethics and social welfare, development of sports, and the use of mass media to step up cultural coverage and intensify anti-communist propaganda, was not coincidental.[11] This was simply the first step in an orchestrated program to objectify (and commodify) culture.

At the local level, cultural renaissance was a three-step process involving public dissemination, moral education and active demonstration. In the schools, courses on society and ethics as well as citizenship and morality were taught at the elementary and middle school levels, respectively. At the high school level, introduction to Chinese culture, military education, and thought and personality became a staple part of the curriculum in addition to regular courses in natural and social science. Outside the classroom, essay and oratory contests on topics pertaining to Chinese culture were regularly held as were peer-group-sponsored study sessions to discuss current speeches and writings. They were supplemented by occasional activities in all aspects of traditional culture, such as music, dance, folk art, painting, calligraphy and theater. Moral education, moreover, was not limited to the schools and children. The schools were meant to be the basis for cultural training that was to extend to the family and local community in the form of family training groups, social work teams as well as women's and neighborhood associations. Local organizations awarded prizes to model youth, model mothers, model teachers, model farmers and other deserving Samaritans on appropriate occasions like Martyr's Day, the birthdays of the famous general Yue Fei, the Qing dynasty naval hero Koxinga as well as the consummate teacher Confucius. Even teachers underwent similar moral supervision and training by having to periodically participate in study groups and various grassroots activities as well as attend talks given by scholars on topics pertaining to Chinese culture.

From the top looking down, the diffusion of the party and the military to the local level was and has continued to be an important element in the institutional promotion of cultural renaissance. Given the single party politics of the state, the line of demarcation between the party and the government was always ambiguous to begin with. All civil servants were strongly persuaded to be active members of the party. Local party units were set up in each institution, and members were not only actively engaged in recruiting more members but were constantly on the lookout, supervising the actions and thoughts of colleagues.[12] Having the right moral attitudes and political beliefs was just as important to success as having the right professional qualifications, if not more important. Indeed, the idea of one nation, one party, one family and one mind appeared to be an implicit guiding principle underlying the promotion of cultural consciousness. Likewise, the appointment of military personnel as *xiaoguan* ("school officers") or enforcers of correct moral behavior in the middle school and university was an extension of the state into the disciplinary apparatus of the school. Another important role of the *xiaoguan* in the high school and university was to oversee activities of the China Youth Corps (literally Anti-Communist China Youth for National Restoration Corps, a party-sponsored youth activities organization in which each student had to nominally participate). The presence of the military, while seen in some ways as a direct imposition of the party and state in the operation of the school, was also portrayed as part of the overall socializing, if not civilizing, environment of the school. The socializing function of military training became most evident during the two-year period of conscription to which every male was subject. Here, military training was combined with intense political indoctrination, moral reinforcement and daily discipline to mold a ritualized code of personal conduct.

In the cultural renaissance movement, there was clearly an attempt by the government to explicitly (re)write "traditional Chinese culture" in postwar Taiwan. Obviously, it was not the only attempt; it was only the most obvious attempt. Yet in order to assess its significance vis-a-vis other forms of ideological writing, one must note that the movement itself was predicated upon the need first to instill what Fox (1990:3) would call "ideologies of peoplehood," a common consciousness which persons could identify with as being of the same nation. This consciousness was not simply an esoteric and abstract sense of common identity; it had to be invoked by feelings of social solidarity which had roots in established symbols, myths and narratives. Moreover, this spiritual unity was not just something invoked for its own sake; it was presumably the key to defeating Communism as well as the cure for all problems of national development, whether they be economic, social or otherwise. Yet the way in which cultural renaissance was promoted in Taiwan, that is to say, backed by the full force of institutional power, also had ramifications for the nature of cultural authority. In this regard, it is simply not enough to say the writing of culture in Taiwan was political in origin and motivation. That the cultural renaissance movement could not be spontaneously initiated and indigenously defined but rather had to be carefully orchestrated from the above meant, of course, that the state was the sole arbiter of culture. In essence, the state defined culture by making culture (in terms of tradition) conform to the exigencies of the new polity and the "rational" ethos of the KMT world view. The orchestrated if not oppressive way that culture was promoted, defined, then disseminated or imposed upon the populace, in effect, produced two kinds of responses: conformity or resistance. In the long run, by making culture conform to the nation and, in the process, making the state the sole voice of cultural authority, the political writing of culture as patriotic fervor (combined with nostalgia of an imagined past) made responses to culture, the state, and cultural authority an all or nothing affair: an attack on one was by definition an attack on the other two as well.

Nonetheless, while the cultural renaissance movement was not the sole definition of culture in contemporary Taiwan, it was certainly the basic framework around which all other levels of public discourse revolved, especially in relation to the construction of a *national* culture. Insofar as culture in Taiwan invoked tradition, it also invoked to some degree a defense of Confucianism as the rational foundation of Chinese tradition. However, not unlike other discourses of tradition, Confucianism was invoked here not as a system in itself but as a set of stripped down ethical values which had a particular role in the service of the state. As a generalized moral philosophy or a kind of social ethics that could be easily translated into secular action, Confucianism here meant for the most part a devotion to filial piety, respect for social authority, and etiquette in everyday behavior. This was a far cry from the variations of Confucian ideology that emerged in the different schools of Confucian learning and came to influence the practice of imperial government. Thus, recourse to Confucian tradition, especially in its emphasis upon filial piety, was actually an attempt to extend feelings of family solidarity to the level of the nation.

Curiously enough, the divergent positions taken by the KMT and the PRC with regard to Confucianism split precisely over their opposing viewpoints with regard to filial piety. While the KMT opted to view national unity as an extension of primordial family ties, the mainland chose to reject Confucian filial piety by subordinating the family to the good of greater society, as defined by the state. This divergence in policy toward Confucianism was an explicit point of difference between the two regimes and clearly manifested itself at many levels of rhetoric and text.[13] In Taiwan, Confucian values were written into different levels of textbook narrative. At the primary school level, the classical text *Ershisi xiao* (24 stories of filial piety) supplemented other general readings on social etiquette and personal health. At a higher educational level, Confucian ethics was taught using selected classical works and was explicitly combined with courses on Nationalist political ideology in a way which subtly lent to KMT moral philosophy a generally Confucian flavor.

In retrospect, one can say that the writing of Chinese culture during the era of cultural renaissance, far from being just an isolated act, was instead part of a highly orchestrated program to construct elaborate representations of national identity and to inculcate their underlying images, concepts and ethos into the practice of social life and behavior. The political construction of culture in this sense involved in the first instance the promotion of an outwardly expressive societal consciousness which rallied about unifying symbols like the flag, national celebrations, songs and slogans as well as assumptions of common ethnicity, sacred origin, material civilization and traditions of thought. All these elements of patriotic fervor contributing directly to feelings of national solidarity also found a source of legitimacy in other more abstract forms of cultural (national) narrative, which took the form of political ideology, ethical world view and moral philosophy, that formed the ideological basis for other institutions in society. Thus, ideological dissemination depended upon detailed collaboration between the party, military, schools and grassroots organizations at all levels in a way that bound these institutions even more firmly under government control.

OFFICIAL CULTURE AND MASS CONSUMPTION

The activities of the Cultural Renaissance Movement led eventually to the promotion of cultural reconstruction, from about 1977 to the present. The call for cultural reconstruction was the last of twelve recommendations put forth by the then President Chiang Ching-kuo to the Legislative Yuan on September 23, 1977 as part of his plan for national development. Cultural reconstruction was seen as a development parallel to the current drive to stimulate economic progress and raise standards of living. To this end, cultural centers (*wenhua zhongxin*) were established in each of some twenty-odd townships to take charge of organizing and conducting cultural activities. A Committee for Cultural Reconstruction (*wenhua jianshe weiyuanhui*) was set up in November 1981 to be the agency responsible for the management of cultural affairs, operating directly under the aegis of the Executive Yuan. Cultural reconstruction paralleled activities undertaken by the Committee for Cultural Renaissance and tended to emphasize the "fine arts," such as music, art, theater, expressive culture and heritage conservation.

In the field of high culture, the Committee for Cultural Reconstruction not only continued to promote the preservation of "national treasures" and cultural education, broadly speaking, but also supported the production of knowledge pertaining to all aspects of the classical past. The privileging of culture as national treasure meant that not everything was cherished as forms of "traditional culture," just those things that were attributable to the *civilized* past. Thus, fine art, calligraphy, high religion and haute cuisine were considered both traditional and good, whereas things like popular religions, folk (especially "superstitious") practices, even non-scientific ideologies like Chinese medicine and spirit healing were not. This was correspondingly the side of "traditional Chinese culture" that was portrayed to the outside through assorted government subsidized publications like *Sinorama, Free China Review,* tourist leaflets and semi-scholarly journals.

Although cultural reconstruction, like the activities in the era of cultural renaissance, was concerned with promoting the importance of culture in relation to the well-being of society, it was not involved, at least in a politically explicit way, with the moral cultivation of a national culture. Cultural centers were not only active in disseminating the larger view of Chinese tradition but were also active in promoting interest in and preservation of local traditions. Yet far from indigenizing Chinese culture, this revival of interest in ethnic folk customs was an attempt to incorporate little traditions into the larger homogeneous stream of Chinese civilization. Moreover, in line with its "non-political" orientation, the Committee's sponsorship of culture and the arts was not limited to things Chinese and often included cultural interchange of all sorts. In the end, the domestication of culture during this era of "reconstruction" coincided with the development of "the culture industry" in Taiwan in other regards, e.g. tourism, public celebrations, mass media, film and popular music.[14] Concurrent with an era of unprecedented economic growth, "cultural" reconstruction was seen as a barometer for measuring social progress at a time when outside threats to national security correspondingly appeared increasingly remote to everyday life.

The promotion of cultural activities and cultural knowledge in this broad sense was tied to the dissemination of cultural ideology and everyday information within the public media, all of which was tightly regulated by the government's Bureau of Cultural Works (*wenhua gongzuo weiyuanhui*) in conjunction with the official News Agency (*xinwen ju*). Rigid political censorship continued to be enforced in all forms of public media, namely television, radio, newspaper and other printed literature, to insure the suppression of communist sentiment and views unfavorable to the government. In light of cultural policy, rigid control over the flow and content of everyday information was meant to reinforce the consensus of a unified people, harmony of an ethical world-view, continued maintenance of moral solidarity and determination of a single mind, all of which were crucial to the KMT's particular vision of a total society (i.e. nation).

In the realm of general cultural dissemination, the News Agency was also responsible for the international publication of foreign language and foreign-oriented magazines like *Free China Review* (*ziyou zhongguo pinglun*) and *Sinorama* (*kuang-hua*) as well as weekly newspapers like *Free China Journal* (*ziyou zhongguo zhishi bao*), five smaller regularly published magazines and 178 other occasional pamphlets and monographs. For the most part, such publications are gratuitously sent to public agencies and select individuals, both domestically and abroad. The function of these various publications was less to disseminate propagandistic information, in spite of its obvious pro-Taiwan sympathies, and more upon coverage of "softer" issues of cultural, artistic, folk-popular and touristic interest presented within a glossy format and written for easy consumption.

The peculiarities of the Taiwan experience shed significant

light upon the nature of the culture industry described elsewhere in the literature. In their critical essay on "the culture industry," Horkheimer and Adorno (1972) were concerned primarily with the growth of mass culture and the state of the arts in contemporary society. The emergence of a culture industry was first and foremost dominated by the large-scale commercial interests of omnipotent entrepreneurs. Culture was thus the achievement of standardization and mass production, and the consumer, rather than being treated as subject (as the culture industry led him to believe), was instead seen as object of manipulation and domination, hence the subtitle of their paper "enlightenment as mass deception." Culture was not just objectified or commodified, "through and through" as Adorno (1989:129) put it, it was something successfully and ruthlessly accomplished with the full force of productive means at the disposal of the industry. As such, the culture industry was not an aberration of society; it reflected more exactly the intrinsic irrationality and tyrannical tendencies of an unrestrained capitalism, and it was with reference to this that Horkheimer and Adorno addressed their critique, properly speaking.

The commodification of mass culture and popular arts that Horkheimer and Adorno describe in their account was not peculiar to capitalism just the ruthless efficiency with which the end product was manufactured, distributed and inculcated in the minds and actions of individuals. The culture industry in Taiwan, on the other hand, was very much a national enterprise in the sense that the state felt it necessary to construct a total ideology of culture as a means of creating national identity, sustaining the spirit of societal consciousness, guaranteeing conformity to the political order and regulating the standard of everyday behavior. The culture industry was an industry in the sense that it involved large-scale coordination between various government agencies which had to oversee the dissemination and control of information throughout various sectors of the media. Yet, the charitable rather than profit-maximizing goals of cultural publications and activities underscored the importance of redistributing cultural capital among a broad range of consumers, ultimately with the aim of cultivating in the long run a higher level of collective solidarity, namely that constitutive of society as a whole and determined by the state in the name of national interest. The aim of this kind of cultural promotion was quintessentially hegemonic. In this hegemonic scheme, commodification or objectification of culture was the inevitable result of a deliberate process of demystifying the traditional (sacred) aura of culture as a precondition for making it a tangible reality accessible to all people. In Taiwan, the writing of a national ideology as ethical world view, the cultivation of an etiquette of moral conduct and the objectification of culture and traditional custom all had to be concurrent processes of nation-state formation, whose end result was the promotion of a solidly collective conscience within the minds and actions of every citizen. It appeared that the fate of the nation depended on it.

Within the overall history of discourse and policy on national culture in Taiwan, the era of cultural reconstruction represented a significant transition in the politics of culture. Far from having "depoliticized" culture as might be interpreted from the apparent blooming of culture and the arts in the age of new-found prosperity, this *normalizing* trend in cultural reconstruction was quite consistent with the KMT's overall attempt to indigenize Nationalist ideology and defuse mainland-Taiwanese ethnic tensions which had plagued most of Taiwan's postwar history since its return to the Nationalist government. This trend can be attributed largely to the vision of President Chiang Ching-kuo, which contrasted sharply with the staunch Cold War rhetoric of his predecessor Chiang Kai-shek. In this regard, the establishment of a Chinese hegemony, rooted as it were in the origins of civilization, its sense of continuous history, Confucian ethical legitimacy, and the spiritual consciousness of one people that had been inculcated over previous decades, was an important precondition for the reconstruction of local tradition and the full-fledged development of cultural values. Instead of instilling meaning into the notion of an autonomous Taiwanese culture, it served even more firmly to anchor local folkways within the larger cultural stream of Chinese language, history and civilization. Moreover, during this period of "liberalization" of culture due to the rhetorical detour away from the patriotic fervor of national consciousness in the defense of tradition, there was little indication that the government had relinquished its *authority* over the writing and practice of culture.[15] The culture industry remained very much a state enterprise. If anything, its authority over culture (as ideological hegemony) should have been enhanced by its success in displacing the legitimacy of Chinese culture with the legitimacy of all Chinese cultures and its effort to promote an internalized sense of cultural value with relevance to everyday life to balance the overt, collective sentiments provoked by cultural renaissance.

In sum, normalization here meant that certain aspects of tradition were identified as accepted standards or valued norms. In this sense, education served to disseminate or diffuse the sacred aura associated with culture by effectively "sanitizing" it, e.g. by Confucianizing and secularizing it, as a precondition for making it an object of perceived knowledge and lived-in experience. Thus, the work of reconstruction played an important role in promoting the emergence of a full-fledged culture industry by providing the conditions under which culture became *categorized* (as an object of gazing, discourse and practice), *commodified* (as something to be appropriately packaged for public consumption), and *totalized* (as something relevant to all aspects of social life) in ways which had not previously been possible.

Strictly in terms of the "writing" of culture, it goes without saying that the historical episodes which characterize the construction of official culture in contemporary Taiwan involved many levels of ideological investment in a way which easily parallels the complexity of Jameson's (1981:30–31) account of Biblical narrative. Beginning with the nation as literal referent, master symbols like the notion of *hua-hsia*, common ethnic traits, national icons and treasures functioned perhaps as allegorical key or interpretive code for the further production of texts. The construction of narratives from symbols becomes most clearly manifested, for example, in the scripting of traditional culture prevalent during the cultural renaissance movement. That these scripts ultimately provide the moral blueprints for social or collective action mirrors the function of moral or psychological narratives in Biblical text. Lastly, it was on the basis of such moral blueprints that anagogical texts like myths of origin, collective history and political readings were generated. It was presumably at this anagogical level that the hegemonic function of ideological writing emerges.

While these levels of ideological investment epitomize the extent to which the Nationalist government set out to construct cultural ideology, orchestrate in practice collective expressions of cultural consciousness and disseminate cultural knowledge among the populace, they also reflect upon the peculiar ethical vision of the modern polity whose survival prompted the recourse to culture in the first place. The future of this culture-cum-state is the topic of the ensuing discussion.

DEMOCRACY, ETHNICITY AND TRADITION IN TAIWAN'S NATIONAL FUTURE

The contagion of democracy that has afflicted many parts of the globe in recent years has brought about significant changes in Taiwan's political climate in ways that have directly influenced official discourse and cultural policy. To say the least, the dismantling of the communist regime in Eastern Europe leading to the diminution of Cold War hostilities of the last half-century first of all altered considerably the real and imagined state of war between Taiwan and mainland China. The government's active role in fueling democratic sentiment in the midst of the Tiananmen incident of 1989 then gave birth to increased and unexpected pressure from various opposition parties and activist groups to increase the pace of democratic reform and loosen the KMT's monopoly over power.

Yet even before the dissolution of Eastern Europe began to accelerate in 1989, Taiwan under President Chiang Ching-kuo had already quietly embarked on a path of reform based upon economic growth and political indigenization. This was in large degree prompted by Taiwan's expulsion from the United Nations and the diplomatic isolation that ensued. Ironically, it was the need to forge a new path toward political and economic survival that forced a subtle change in political agenda away from a confrontational Cold War climate and increasingly toward a tacit acceptance of the territorial boundedness of the Republic of China within Taiwan. This overt relaxation of Cold War tension made possible an atmosphere of reform, economic as well as political. Economic success through the opening up of a market economy in turn provided a new basis for consolidating political power in the KMT's favor. Thus in 1986, Chiang allowed the legal existence of opposition parties as a prelude to free elections.[16] This was followed by the lifting of strict censorship over the press in 1987 and the lifting of martial law in 1988.

Economic and political liberalization was then part of an overall policy of indigenization rather than the other way around. Reformism was not precipitated by a sudden humanistic urge to bring about democracy for its own sake, as might be suggested by claims of "the end of history," but instead as a conscious effort to garner popular support for the KMT among an indigenous majority by deliberately avoiding the divisive politics (ROC vs. PRC, mainlander vs. Taiwanese) that had characterized the authoritarian style of his father Chiang Kai-shek. Moreover, it recognized the pragmatic reality of governing territorial Taiwan without having to abandon its claim of (political) legitimacy over all of China. In this regard, the younger Chiang consistently pursued a conciliatory agenda that aimed at least in theory to include all of Taiwan and its inhabitants, often to the displeasure of the KMT old guard. He even referred to himself as Taiwanese, and his choice of Lee Teng-hui, a native Taiwanese, to succeed him underscored his goal of localizing the state apparatus in a way which was meant not only to embrace all Taiwanese but also to absorb local culture into the folds of a greater Nationalist society.

This gradual indigenization of Nationalist politics within the territorial confines of Taiwan and the ensuing policy of reform definitely had important ramifications for cultural discourse and changing notions of national identity during the era of (post-1989) democratization. While the breakup of states like the Soviet Union and Yugoslavia was heavily fueled by a rise in ethnic nationalism, to an extent that led Ferenc Miszlivetz (1991), for example, to question the decline of the nation-state, such a crisis of cultural authority was in Taiwan already preempted by the effects of liberalization which gradually won support for the ruling regime among an indigenous populace. When Taiwanese nationalism was finally allowed to surface after decades of harsh suppression, it emerged at a point in time when economic progress had won over support for the KMT and after ethnic divisiveness had softened considerably. The results of the first free legislative elections of 1990 perhaps came as little surprise, as the KMT won approximately 3/4 of the popular vote as compared with that of the Democratic Progressive Party's (DPP) remaining 1/4, running on a platform of national independence for Taiwan. However, the win was surprising considering the fact that the DPP was unable to rally support for a policy of indigenous self-rule in a population 3/4 composed of ethnic Taiwanese, whose calls for self-identity in the past were brutally suppressed. This was clearly not the case of an ethnically dormant Yugoslavia or USSR. The work of cultural reconstruction, bolstered by the "success" of economic liberalization and combined with a deliberate policy of political pragmatism and ethnic conciliation, achieved in the end a hegemony which would have seemed unlikely a few decades earlier.

In sum, despite winning the people's mandate, the achievements brought about by Chiang's reformism were no liberal democracy.[17] To the contrary, through his synthesis of a Nationalist Taiwan, Chiang constructed a homogeneous nation-state in the *classic* sense understood by most social scientists where *cultural consciousness* constituted the basis for defining *national identity*. This homogeneity was achieved precisely by transcending the "primordial sentiments" that would have given rise to divisiveness such as local ethnic affiliation or religion (in other cases) and instead opting to accent seemingly "neutral" ideologies or values such as those found in a shared sense of ethics, history, and civilization that could serve as the basis of an "uncontested" national identity. National solidarity in this classic sense depended upon such homogeneity. It may have recognized differences in fact but subordinated them to a higher sense of commonality. This was surely not a consensus brought about by a plurality of voices in a civil society.

From this perspective, the Taiwanese nationalism that emerged in this era of political liberalism, while appearing to appeal to "nativist" ethnic sentiment, also constituted a post-hoc political construction which only had meaning in light of the dualistic opposition of Taiwanese (*bensheng* "insider") versus mainlander (*waisheng* "outsider"). Born out of the repression that characterized KMT rule rather than any pristine notion of Taiwanese "identity," Taiwanese nationalism in this sense had to flaunt its oppositional quality as a means of establishing its existence. Even the DPP's self-characterization as *dangwai* ("the other party") pointedly reiterated its own role within an essentially monolithic environment.

Yet one must distinguish here how Taiwanese ethnic nationalism represents a critique of the state (as societal polity)

Culture Industry as National Enterprise 103

from the way it represents a critique of the nation (as cultural imagination). Aided by the KMT's retreat from its previous insistence upon eventual recovery of the mainland, hence its gradually weakening claim of legitimacy over all of China, the Taiwanese independence movement first capitalized upon the actuality of territorial Taiwan as a politically independent entity. This prompted many in the opposition party to apply for legal recognition of Taiwan's independent status in the United Nations. This attempt to force the issue of national recognition immediately sparked debate within the KMT, whose tacit acceptance of Taiwan's unofficial status has never abandoned future claims of legitimacy over all of territorial China, if and when it were possible.

However, this drive for national independence has more often than not been fueled on the other hand by a need to accentuate in the minds of the populace Taiwan's cultural uniqueness. This has prompted some within the independence movement to justify the existence of a Taiwanese nation-state by divorcing the issue of state (as separate politico-legal apparatus) from its ethnic roots in Chinese nationhood, while prompting others to seek alternative cultural origins altogether in the imagination of an indigenous (pre-Japanese, pre-KMT) past.

While it is too early to predict the end result of such political contestation, it will in the first instance depend less on the ability of the respective parties to demonstrate the reality of Taiwan's existence as a nation-state than on the ability to unmask the hegemonic fictions of Chineseness that have been inculcated as a result of decades of cultural discourse. More importantly, it will continue to be, as it has always been, a struggle of mutual perception and adaptation.

In the history of political interaction between government and people, it is oversimplistic to say that the seemingly unshakable authoritarian domination which enthralled Taiwan during the long period of martial law had successfully eradicated local resistance, or to attribute the government's success in inculcating ideology and culture solely to the amount of force it used to demand conformity. The government's bloody massacre of thousands of Taiwanese incited by anti-KMT riots on February 28, 1947 (simply known as The 2-2-8 Incident) perhaps did more to instill a permanent sense of hostility among a generation of Taiwanese which could not be stamped out, even after decades of official suppression of the incident in the media and history textbooks.[18] Even during martial law, subtle forms of resistance often tested the limits of legal permissibility, given their inability to be manifested publicly.[19] Thus, brute force alone was never able to stamp out the possibility of resistance; it was made effective only when buttressed by claims of ideological (cultural) legitimacy or combined with other institutional tactics to co-opt potentially subversive elements.[20] Ironically, KMT authoritarianism worked best when the government was able to cultivate a facade of democracy, reform and innovation while allowing leeway for the existence of marginal groups which had to be in turn checked through various tactical maneuvers and policing strategies. The resemblance to Leninist practices is not coincidental.

At least in one respect, the trend toward reform and move away from the authoritarianism of the past introduced the possibility of new variables which could not be readily reversed. For example, the KMT's attempt to orchestrate social consciousness in support of the democracy movement on the mainland in 1989 in the style of cultural renaissance reflected in my opinion a set of gestures which eventually not only proved to be anachronistic but even accelerated popular calls for the KMT to clean up its own house and respond seriously to criticisms of its monopoly over institutional power, including above all popular election of the President. Its explicit support of democracy and its ongoing process of relaxing control over the media, reforming the legislature (many of whose original members were elected on the mainland and remained in office "for life" pending recovery of the mainland), lifting restrictions on ideological expression, etc., also constituted inevitable trends in the process of becoming. Political liberation not only allowed for the emergence of Taiwanese independence, formerly a taboo topic of discussion; it allowed for the emergence of all other forms of counterculture as well, namely the youth culture, intellectual dissidence, artistic freedom, even the flourishing of tabloids and sexual liberation. In short, democratization was not just political in nature. It had serious reverberations which penetrated all sectors of society. By multiplying the possibility of voices and giving credence to those voices, it created a situation which could not be effectively checked by previous policing tactics. Subsequently, old dualisms within the one China-Taiwanese independence political spectrum naturally broke down and gave rise inevitably to a number of middle-of-the-road positions. In the short term, it eroded the monolithic support the KMT had traditionally enjoyed, but more importantly in the long run it forced the KMT to develop new strategies to respond to a much more diverse base of criticism, all the while accelerating the process of democracy to maintain its progressive, reformist image as a basis of legitimacy for capturing majority support.

When Lee Teng-hui succeeded to the presidency following the death of Chiang Ching-kuo, he opted generally to continue the policy of indigenization and political conciliation adopted by his predecessor. Indigenization meant in essence the implementation of a Nationalist policy which catered primarily to pragmatic issues centering on Taiwan in order to focus upon Taiwan's rising economic status within a changing Asia-Pacific regional system, effectively relegating its Cold War "no-contact-with-the-Communist-bandits" policy to the backstage. In terms of cultural policy, it sought peaceful co-existence and mutual respect with the mainland on the one hand while rejecting Taiwanese national independence on the other. Globally speaking, this policy trend was based on a realization that Taiwan had done quite well for itself in spite of its diplomatic isolation. Its power in the marketplace was moreover translatable into political influence which could be accumulated by continuing to work within the existing situation. Internally speaking, the trend toward indigenization was meant to enlist the support of moderate Taiwanese who had been advocating the priority of Taiwan's tangible interests as a state while not necessarily abandoning its idealistic vision of cultural China as a nation. Given the trend toward indigenization, albeit in a sense which was directly opposed to ethnic nationalism, the indigenous faction of the KMT provided the biggest threat to the DPP's political platform and sought consistently to undercut the latter's position through co-optation, its recent decision to consider future application to the United Nations as a separate nation (largely in recognition of its economic status) being its latest effort to incorporate Taiwanese interests while at the same time rejecting extreme ethnic separatism.

The multiplicity of voices spawned by trends toward democratization also enabled dissident elements within the KMT to become a more important political force in the gradual erosion of the KMT's monopoly of power. In this regard, the second legislative elections of 1992 provided firm evidence of diversification beyond the old dualisms that dominated pre-existing political landscapes. While the DPP made substantial gains to garner about 1/3 of the popular vote, it was clear that the overwhelming winners in the election were dissident KMT legislators like Wang Chien-hsiun, the former Finance Minister and major architect of a proposed controversial economic reform package, and Jau Shao-kang, the outspoken EPA Minister and self-styled new wave technocrat. Both campaigned as independent KMT members whose nominations were initially rejected by the Party and who were ostracized by the mainstream faction for being troublemakers when they decided to enter the race as independents. The KMT's proportionate loss of seats to the DPP, along with its failure to exclude dissident Party members through its manipulation of rules to strong-arm unruly opponents (all of whom won handily), clearly represented the electorate's rejection of the KMT's monopolistic practices that had been a staple during the era of single party politics. This electoral setback then intensified pressures upon the KMT to democratize its *institutional* apparatus of state domination, while allowing the DPP and other parties to play a more mainstream role within the legislative process.

The success of dissident elements within the KMT, who have since gone on to form their own party, The New KMT Alliance, apparently suggests that the creation of a new ideology, one which explicitly represented "indigenous" ethnic interests, was not sufficient in itself to win support away from the KMT in a way which reiterates the successful absorption of local identity within the KMT's vision of a cultural China among a predominantly Taiwanese populace. It points to even more serious discontent among people regarding broadly based social issues left out of identity politics (like urban congestion and environmental pollution) indicative of the overall quality of life as well as institutional factors like corruption and an unresponsive bureaucracy, which have contributed to the total monopoly of a state apparatus in collusion with the Party and military at all levels of organization.

Meanwhile, the DPP's unwavering stand on Taiwan's independence as its prime party platform even in later years continues to reflect the importance it has attached to its advocacy of a different homogeneous ethnic nation-state to counter the KMT's own. More importantly, it also reflects the tacit importance already built into a generation of KMT cultural indoctrination which presupposed the imagination of a shared cultural (in this case ethnic) consciousness as the seminal key to national survival and societal progress in all other respects. However, it remains to be seen how the DPP will adjust to new strategic maneuverings by the government and whether it will abandon its cultural vision of a unified polity.

As long as a state of warfare over Taiwan's "identity" continues to maintain a prominent profile in ongoing political debates, it will underscore even more emphatically the significance of cultural discourse in shaping the evolution of the national polity. Clearly, in the span of a few decades the KMT has managed to inculcate the reality of an imagined cultural community, and it is in the face of this continued cultural illusion, forcefully imposed by the dictatorship of a common language and ideology, systematically orchestrated through social movement, and routinely normalized in the ritual of everyday life, that opposition forces like the Taiwanese independence movement have established alternative roots. Changes in the overall political climate will no doubt continue to force all respective parties to adopt new strategies. Just as recent trends toward democratization have introduced new variables into the political equation, effective opposition must correspondingly involve in the first instance a fundamental deconstruction and resignification of the prevailing cultural hegemony. Far from being simply a set of neutral values or matter of fact statement of one's "identity," culture has been shown to be a powerful agent for constructing new possibilities for identity where symbols of the past are constantly being reappropriated with new meanings for an ongoing present. While new cultural discourses alone are insufficient criteria for changing politics, nation-states also find meaning in culture, however constructed, from which they derive legitimacy of rule. It may be that the course of politics engenders culture, but only by contesting the mythology of culture can one then begin to contest the authority of the state to define its own existence.

NOTES

1. Eric Wolf (1988:755) remarks, for instance, "China constituted less a society than a cultural world order."
2. The implicit sinocentricism of this middle kingdom stemmed from their own perceived separation from the barbarians situated on the outside or periphery of their world (see Wang Erh-min 1985:2 for extended discussion).

3. Hu Hou-hsian (1985:368) argues that although *zhongguo* was a term coined by the Zhou, it originated from *zhong-shang* to denote the alliance of states which traced their cultural foundations to the Shang dynasty. Thus, Ts'ai Hsueh-hai (1981:139–40) maintains that both *zhongguo* and *huaxia* were interchangeable.
4. According to P'eng Ying-min (1985:9–12), full-fledged definitions of the nation as people (*minzu*) and nationalism as the principle of a common people (*minzu zhuyi*) were spelled out explicitly by Liang Qiqiao and Sun Yat-sen and were later influenced by foreign writings, like those of Joseph Stalin.
5. This is similar to what Fox (1990:3) calls "ideologies of peoplehood."
6. While the genesis of a standard colloquial Chinese (Mandarin) has had important ramifications for the spread of nationalism throughout China, it is ironic to note that the terms for Mandarin used on the mainland, Taiwan and Singapore clearly reflect the ways in which language is used to serve different kinds of national sentiment. On Taiwan, Mandarin is referred to as "the national language" (*guoyu*), following early Republican usage which is itself a replacement for *guanhua*, literally "the language of officials." On the mainland, *guoyu* has become *putong hua* ("the common language") to stress universal egalitarianism. In Singapore, the use of *huayu* for Mandarin as "the language of ethnic Chinese" on the other hand conforms with the ethnic neutrality of national politics there.
7. The promotion of the panda as a national symbol in spite of its obvious lack of political content is a similar case in point.
8. There is much documentary evidence to show that, despite the profound extent to which Taiwan had been Japanized in cultural, intellectual and institutional terms, especially toward the latter half of the colonial period, its inhabitants on the whole welcomed the return of the territory to Chinese sovereignty. In other words, there was little to indicate that people believed their ethnic customs and cultural values, heterodox as they probably were, to be inconsistent with their new national identity. It was on the other hand a basic assumption on the part of the KMT that cultural indoctrination was a prerequisite for creating national identity. This explains the great lengths to which the government attempted in policy terms to reeducate people, even at gunpoint. The emergence of a Taiwanese collective identity came about in my opinion largely as a result of the government's brutal suppression of local tradition clearly as a resistance to an "outside(r)" regime.
9. A collection of this and other essays on the topic of Chinese cultural renaissance are reproduced in Taiwan Provincial Government (1967).
10. See Taiwan Provincial Government News Agency (1970, section 18, p. 2).

11. See Taiwan Provincial Government (1978).
12. Lin Biao (1985:29) notes that brownie points were earned on their achievement report (*ch'eng-chi k'au-ho*) for these two activities.
13. At a polemic level, the anti-Confucius movement on the mainland was part of a larger anti-Confucius, anti-Lin Piao campaign destined to purge extreme rightist influences. Martin (1975:244–49) shows also that these differences in ideology were systematically written into school children's textbook narratives and fables.
14. One can perhaps argue here that Horkheimer and Adorno's (1972) notion of culture industry is more broadly characteristic of the modern state.
15. As an example of coordination between state agencies in relation to culture, Li (1992:20) notes that the head of the Bureau of Cultural Reconstruction also serves nominally as the general secretary of the Bureau of Cultural Renaissance.
16. For an analysis of recent changes in the electoral system brought about by calls for democratic reform, see Ling and Myers (1992).
17. Some, following Winckler (1984), have characterized the transition between the two Chiangs as one from hard to soft authoritarianism. Western analysts on the whole like Chou and Nathan (1987) and Jacobs (1991) have tended to view the reformist policies of the latter Chiang as indicative of a deeper liberalization in Nationalist politics, contrasting with Taiwanese scholars like Chiou (1993) who argue that such reforms were the result of power politics meant to pacify the opposition party and ultimately undermining broad support for the opposition. As Chiou (1986:27) aptly put it, "in this political game, the KMT chieftains, both old and young, are shrewd and effective performers. They will never give in unless absolutely necessary." Perhaps more to the point, it was important for them to give the impression that they were initiating change rather than responding to it.
18. For a description of these events and their significance in the founding of the Taiwanese nationalist movement, see Kerr (1965) and Mendel (1970). Archival records on this incident have been made officially available only recently, resulting in the publication of a lengthy historical analysis by Lai Tse-han *et al.* (1991).
19. Ngo (1993:9–11), for example, notes that despite tight restrictions on publishing dissident journals often evaded government prohibitions by setting up shop with new journal names but employing the same editorial membership and subscription lists. Tabooed slogans like "self-determination" were also prominently displayed even as they were deliberately crossed out, to the extent of making bans futile. For an account of other oppositional movements during the martial law era, see in particular Chen (1982), Chiou (1986) and Li (1988).

20. From the outset, friendly political parties were legally endorsed by the KMT to give the facade of democracy, but their role was severely limited (Jacobs 1981). Moreover, the party created its own grass-roots organizations by establishing labor unions, farmers' associations and chambers of commerce and industry under KMT patronage largely to preempt opportunities for the autonomous development of such institutions (Gold 1986:67 and Tien 1989:46–52). Pro-KMT civic associations like writers' unions, Buddhist associations and women's groups were also set up (Jacobs 1978:243–44). Needless to say, all these groups were closely monitored by the Party, and competing institutions outside centralized control were banned.

REFERENCES

Adorno, Theodor W. (1989). The Culture Industry Reconsidered (1967). Translated in S.E. Bronner and D.M. Kellner, Eds., *Critical Theory and Society: A Reader*. New York: Routledge.

Anderson, Benedict (1983). *Imagined Communities: Reflections on the Origins and Spread of Nationalism*. London: Verso.

Chen Guuying (1982). The Reform Movement among Intellectuals in Taiwan since 1970. *Bulletin of Concerned Asian Scholars* 14(3):32–38.

Chiou, C.L. (1986). Politics of Alienation and Polarization: Taiwan's *Tangwai* in the 1980s. *Bulletin of Concerned Asian Scholars* 18(3):16–28.

— (1993). The 1990 National Affairs Conference and the Future of Democracy in Taiwan. *Bulletin of Concerned Asian Scholars* 25(1):17–32.

Chou Yangshan and Andrew J. Nathan (1987). Democratizing Transition in Taiwan. *Asian Survey* 27(3):277–99.

Clammer, John (1973). Colonialism and the Perception of Tradition in Fiji. In T. Asad, Ed. *Anthropology and the Colonial Encounter* London: Macmillan.

Cohn, Bernard S. (1984). The Census, Social Structure and Objectification in South Asia. *Folk* 26.

Fox, Richard G. (1990). Introduction. *National Ideologies and the Production of National Cultures*. Washington: American Anthropological Association.

Geertz, Clifford (1963). The Integrative Revolution: Primordial Sentiments and Civil Politics in the New States." In C. Geertz, Ed. *Old Societies and New States*. Chicago: Aldine.

Gellner, Ernest (1983). *Nations and Nationalism*. Oxford: Basil Blackwell.

Gold, Thomas B. (1986). *State and Society in the Taiwan Miracle*. Armonk: M.E. Sharpe.

Gramsci, Antonio (1971). *Selections from the Prison Notebooks*. Hoare and Nowell Smith, Eds. and Trans. London: Lawrence and Wishart.

Han Chin-ch'un and Li Yi-fu (1984). Han-wen "min-tsu" i-tz'u te ch'u-hsien chi ch'i shih-yung ch'ing-k'uang (The appearance of the Chinese term *min-tsu* and its circumstances of usage). *Min-tsu yen-chiu* 2:36–43.

Hobsbawm, Eric and Terence Ranger, Eds. (1983). *The Invention of Tradition*. Cambridge: Cambridge University Press.

Horkheimer, Max and Theodor W. Adorno (1972). The Culture Industry. In M. Horkheimer and T.W. Adorno, Eds. *The Dialectic of Enlightenment* (1944). New York: Continuum.

Jacobs, J. Bruce (1978). Paradoxes in the Politics of Taiwan: Lessons for Comparative Politics. *Politics* 13(2):243–44.

— (1981). Political Opposition and Taiwan's Political Future. *The Australian Journal of Chinese Affairs* 6:22–44.

— (1991). Chinese Nationalist Politics in Taiwan under the Two Chiangs. In G. Klintworth, Ed. *Modern Taiwan in the 1990s*. Canberra: Strategic and Defence Studies Centre, Australian National University.

James, Paul (1989). National Formation and the "Rise of the Cultural": A Critique of Orthodoxy. *Philosophy of the Social Sciences* 19(3):273–90.

Jameson, Frederic (1981). *The Political Unconscious: Narrative as Socially Symbolic Act*. Ithaca: Cornell University Press.

Keesing, Roger M. and Robert Tonkinson, Eds. (1982). Reinventing Traditional Culture: The Politics of Kastom in Island Melanesia. *Mankind* 13(4).

Kerr, George (1965). *Formosa Betrayed*. Boston: Houghton Mifflin.

Lai Tse-han, Ramon H. Myers and Wei Wou (1991). *A Tragic Beginning: The Taiwan Uprising of February 28, 1947*. Stanford: Hoover Institution Press.

Li Hsiao-feng (1988). *Tai-wan min-chu y n-tung ssu-shih nien* (Forty Years of Democratic Movement in Taiwan). Taipei: Tzu-li wan-pao ch'u-pan-she.

Li Yih-yuan (1992). Tai-wan kuang-fu i lai wen-hua fa-chan te ching-yen y p'ing-ku (The Experience and Assessment of Cultural Development since the Restoration of Taiwan). In *Wen-hua te t'u-hsiang* (Images of Culture), Volume 1. Taipei: Y n-ch'en.

Lin Y -t'i (1985). *Tai-wan chiao-y mien-mao ssu-shih nien* (Forty Years of Education in Taiwan). Taipei: Tzu-li wan-pao.

Ling, Ts'ai and Ramon H. Myers (1992). Surviving the Rough-and-Tumble of Presidential Politics in an Emerging Democracy: The 1990 Elections in the Republic of China on Taiwan. *China Quarterly* 129:123–48.

Martin, Roberta (1975). The Socialization of Children in China and on Taiwan: An Analysis of Elementary School Textbooks. *China Quarterly* 62(2):242–62.

Miszlivetz, Ferenc (1991). The Unfinished Revolutions of 1989: The Decline of the Nation-State? *Social Research* 58(4):781–804.

Mendel, Douglas (1970). *The Politics of Formosan Nationalism*. Berkeley: University of California Press.
Ngo Tak-wing (1993). Civil Society and Political Liberalization in Taiwan. *Bulletin of Concerned Asian Scholars* 25(1):3–15.
P'eng Ying-min (1985). Kuan-y‿ wo-kuo *min-tsu* kai-nien li-shih te ch'u-pu k'ao-ch'a (A preliminary analysis of the history of the Chinese concept of *min-tsu*). *Min-tsu yen-chiu* 2:5–12.
Taiwan Provincial Government (1967). *Chung-hua wen-hua fu-hsing lun-chi* (Essays on Chinese Cultural Renaissance). Taipei: Kai-tsao ch'u-pan she.
— (1978). *Chung-hua wen-hua fu-hsing y n-tung shih nien chi-nien chuan-chi* (Commemorative Essays on the Tenth Anniversary of the Cultural Renaissance Movement). Taipei: Committee for the Promotion of the Chinese Cultural Renaissance Movement.
Taiwan Provincial Government News Agency (1970). *Tai-wan kuang-fu erh-shih-wu nien* (Twenty-Year Retrospective of the Glorious Restoration of Taiwan). Taichung: Provincial Government Printer.
Thomas, Nicholas (1989). Material Culture and Colonial Power: Ethnological Collecting and the Establishment of Colonial Rule in Fiji. *Man* 24(1): 241–56.
Tien Hung-mao (1989). *The Great Transition: Political and Social Change in the Republic of China*. Stanford: Hoover Institution Press.
Ts'ai Hsueh-hai (1981). Wan-min kuei-tsung: min-tsu te kou-ch'eng y‿ rung-ho (Back to the Roots: the Constitution and Amalgamation of [Chinese] Ethnicity). In Hsing I-t'ien, Ed. *Chung-kuo wen-hua hsin lun* (New Perspectives on Chinese Culture). Taipei: Lien-ching ch'u-pan shih-yeh kung-ssu.
Waldron, Arthur (1989). The Great Wall Myth: Its Origins and Role in Modern China. *Yale Journal of Criticism* 2(1):67–98.
Wang Erh-min (1985). Chung-kuo ming-ch'eng su-y‿an chi ch'i chin-tai ch'‿an-shih (The Origin of the Term "Middle Kingdom" and Its Modern Interpretation). *Chung-hua wen-hua fu-hsing yueh-k'an* 5(8).
Winckler, Edwin A. (1964). Institutionalization and Participation on Taiwan: From Hard to Soft Authoritarianism?. *China Quarterly* 99:482–99.
Wolf, Eric R. (1988). Inventing Society. *American Ethnologist* 15(4):752–61.
Wu, David Y.H. (1991). The Construction of Chinese and Non-Chinese Identities. *Daedalus* (Spring).

5

"Invention of Taiwanese": A Second Look at Taiwan's Cultural Policy and National Identity

David Y.H. Wu

Had the state project of culture been as successful, the political socialization as thorough, and the medicine of "traditional Chinese culture" as efficacious as Allen Chun's powerful portrayal would have us believe, the "Chinese" nation-state in Taiwan would no longer remain an imagined community. The Republic of China, as the repository of "authentic" Chinese culture and history, including "traditional" arts, music, opera and, foremost, Confucian ethics and praxis, would have become the greatest unified state of Chinese culture—the center of all Chinese people and the modern Mecca of glorious Chinese civilization.

Chun's presentation has focused on the process of modern state formation in Taiwan, the cultural politics geared to socialize the entire population to be part of an imagined nation as the successor and center of Chinese civilization. Taking a second look at Chun's presentation I wish to elaborate more on the forces that run counter to the national construction of a collective Chinese identity in Taiwan. Since 1945 the making of another collective identity of the Taiwanese has been an undercurrent, a cultural counter-discourse counter to the government's cultural policies, that the authorities have made all efforts to silence. Other than legitimizing political control through a cultural project, the Mainlander-dominated state elites have a "real" cultural reason to worry: they fear the non-Chinese aspects of the Taiwanese culture.

CONTESTED COLLECTIVE IDENTITY

Let us take a second look in 1992 at Taiwan's four decades of official efforts at cultural construction and building of national identity by standing at the corner of the widest thoroughfare facing the Presidential Office in Taipei City. One has a sense of deja vu in this Post-Chiang Ching-kuo Era (since 1988). The Presidential Hall in Taipei, symbolizing the political center of the "Chinese Republic," stands tall in front of the thoroughfare which serves as a mini Tianenmen Square. Here, year after year since the early 1950s on Double-Tenth Days, the ROC president reviews the parade of soldiers and tanks passing by and waves to hundreds of thousands of school children and college students who are shouting "long live the Republic of China! Long live President Chiang!"

The ROC's Presidential Hall in Taipei, built at the turn of the century by Japanese architects, has the same architectural style as that of the Tokyo train station and the Cultural Museum of Kyoto City (the Japanese version of Baroque or Rococo).

The Taipei Presidential Hall was the building of the governor-general's Office of the Taiwan Government-General of Imperial Japan. The grand architecture, the tallest in Taiwan from the 1920s to the 1970s, was constructed during the same period as those landmark "Western style" historical buildings in Japan, a symbol of the extension of Japan's post-Meiji era "Westernization."[1]

While the National Palace Museum (built in the mid 1960s outside of Taipei) is modeled after the "Former Palace" in Beijing, as Chun has described, the Provincial Taiwan Museum, founded by the Japanese, is housed in a building constructed by the Japanese colonial government in a Japanese-Greek architectural style. Opposite the Museum is another earlier Showa-period building of grand Roman style, which houses the Land Bank of Taiwan. Another Japanese Roman-Greek architectural example of grand style is the Bank of Taiwan, which is next to the Presidential Hall. All these architecturally mixed buildings of political, cultural (in the sense of aesthetics), and historical significance, after years of debates (and opposition), have recently been officially designated as historical sites of antiquity of ROC.

In the vicinity of the Presidential Hall in Taipei there are several new examples of architecture of a grand, "traditional" Chinese style: the Chiang Kai-shek Memorial Hall and the National (Twin) Theaters (completed in the late 1980s). The centerpiece of the National Memorial resembles the Altar of Heaven in Beijing (where the emperors of past dynasties performed worship of ancestors), although the "altar" in Taipei is in blue and white to indicate the cultural symbol of mourning. The twin towers of the National Theater resemble in style the imperial palace in Beijing, and the shining, glazed roof tiles are in the royal color yellow. One of the towers of the National Theater was constructed for the purpose of staging "Peiping" Operas.[2] On occasion, the audience, predominantly elderly and China born, is not numerous enough to fill all the seats. In contrast, however, when an indoor gymnasium in another part of the city holds Western rock concerts, whether performed by local talents such as Michael-Jackson-look-alikes or by international super-stars, such as Steven Wonder or Tina Turner (both performed in 1988), the gymnasium is packed with tens of thousands of teenagers.

Popular culture on the commercial streets of Taipei reflects little of the Chinese "tradition" promoted by the government. During the late 1980s, many posh new department stores mushroomed in the East Side of Taipei; on sale are the latest fashions (and name-brands) of Japan and Europe (though they may be manufactured in Taiwan). One of the largest department stores is the Pacific Sogo of Japan. As in Japan, the basement floor of Sogo has a supermarket, where one can find groceries imported from Japan, the United States, and Europe. Japanese supermarket chains or franchises have replaced most of the traditional bazaar style markets in the heart of Taipei. In the East Side district, people, in particular adolescents, frequent modern stores not only to shop and dine but also to dance at the basement (often unlicensed) discotheques, to sing in karaoke bars, and to watch the latest pirated Japanese TV programs or American movies in private rooms of "MTV" saloons until the wee hours of the morning. Chinese restaurants have to compete with McDonald Hamburger places and Japanese fast-food joints. Whereas the foreign fast-food eateries are increasing in number, many Chinese restaurants (serving "traditional" dishes) are going out of business. Japanese brands of electronic entertainment devices and household appliances are every family's necessities. Japanization in popular culture, as the most important part of youth fashion and music in Taiwan, happens side by side with the emergence of a linguistic vernacular movement (speaking Taiwanese rather than Mandarin) in public places, including government offices. While growing numbers of scholars seek the rediscovery of Taiwan's history and prehistory, the opposition party holds rallies on the street to urge public debate of the national identity issues—an independent Taiwanese state or unification with China.

In his construction of the image (and imagery) of Oriental Orientalism on Taiwan, Chun has not given enough voice to the contested, the silent, the unofficial, the unorthodox, the peripheral, the powerless, the minority, and the underground. He ignored the collective amnesia and sublimation. For a second look at Taiwan's cultural policy, we want to pay attention to paradox and contradiction; the acts that counter the official acts of invention; the survival and resurgence of the Japanese cultural legacy on the island state; the taking over of the folk or (reinvented) Taiwanese culture from the (imagined) China's high culture; commercialized and commodified popular culture that are the consequences of the modernizing process; and current discourse of non-Chinese identity—the evocation of the Taiwanese.

JAPANESE LEGACY: OFFICIAL AMNESIA AND COLLECTIVE NOSTALGIA

That Taiwan is a recent colony of Japan (1895 to 1945) is a contributing factor to the KMT's vigorous project of Sinicization. Like Okinawa today, Taiwan became part of Japan politically and culturally, especially following the official policy of kominka since 1931, aimed to turn Taiwanese into loyal subjects of the Japanese emperor. The Japanese assimilation project seemed to be more effective than the latter-day KMT's Sinicization project; before 1945 Taiwan was a Japanese speaking country with the elite culture emulating that of Japan. A full generation of Taiwanese in emerging towns and big cities was brought up to eat, dress, and live like any other Japanese. This was in spite of the survival of Chinese folk customs, religious beliefs, and family values that were conspicuous among the lower social class and in the rural areas of Taiwan.[3] During the Second World War, Taiwanese youths were conscripted to serve in the Japanese imperial army to fight Chinese in China as well as Western allied forces in Indochina and the Pacific. Only two years after Taiwan was returned to Chinese rule, a riot in Taipei in 1947—the February 28 incident—developed into an island-wide uprising against the corrupt Nationalist government. When the Nationalist reinforcement troops arrived in Taiwan, they massacred hundreds of thousands of Taiwanese civilians. A whole generation of educated social elites was wiped out. From then on, the deep scar of the Nationalist massacre and cultural as well as linguistic differences have laid the foundation for tension between the "mainlanders" and the "Taiwanese" and sharply divided ethnic identities and national aspirations. For thirty years, until the late 1980s, the authorities forbade any mention of the 1947 incident and references to ethnic difference; violators were subjected to police harassment, criminal prosecution, or political persecution. A change in the political atmosphere in 1991 witnessed the government, now run by a majority of Taiwanese, issuing a public apology to the countless victims of the February 28 incident and their surviving family members. An official investigation of the incident sponsored by the government involving many historians yielded five volumes of reports. As one researcher-investigator confessed, oral histories reconstructed after some forty years on a tabooed subject have created a political "myth" of ethnic rivalry (Emma Wu 1992:12).

The point I am trying to make is that the elites from mainland China, since the late 1940s, had a legitimate reason to fear the "cultural" differences in Taiwan. The Nationalists saw not just the necessity to launch the project in order to, in Allen Chun's words, resuscitate "traditional Chinese culture," but they also saw the need to replace Japanese culture and indigenous Taiwanese identity. One may argue with Chun's thesis regarding the invention of a national identity as a crisis of modernity. Chun is correct in putting the whole cultural industry in the context of modernity. But the paradox or irony in the case of Taiwan is the fact that Taiwan was arguably more modern and more Western than the rest of China. Taiwan was on the wrong side of modernity—that of the Japanese. The Nationalist project of Cultural Renaissance in a way attempted to replace Taiwanese modernity with pre-modern Chinese tradition. It was destined to yield little cultural influence in people's way of life save for satisfying the Mainlanders and serving political rhetoric. Modernization of Taiwan under the Japanese colonial rule (1895–1945) has been ignored in analyses of the antecedents of Taiwan's economic development since the 1950s; ignored too has been the history of Chinese migration and settlement in Taiwan under the Qing Dynasty (1662–1895). The new generation of Taiwan born historians now could point out these omissions after the political liberalization of the 1990s (Emma Wu 1992).

As the new economic modernization proceeded on the island in the 1960s, it was accompanied by heavy Japanese and U.S. investments and technological transfer. Then came the inevitable Japanese influence again in popular culture (popular songs, music, films), in language,[4] in food habits (including Japanese style coffee houses), and in fashion.

The nostalgia for things Japanese is particularly strong among Taiwanese elders, in the Taiwanese dominated sections of the cities, and in rural areas. On the other hand, the Americanization of popular culture is also obvious. The government stepped in to curtail Japanese influence, for instance, by banning Japanese programs on television, and by imposing a rigid quota (i.e., at one time, only five per annum) for the importing and showing of Japanese movies. This was done under the noble justification of protecting local film industries (which implies that ten or fifteen years after the Japanese had left, their cultural influence was still strong and the Japanese films were too popular). However, no protest was voiced against Hollywood films and American programs dominated television broadcasts. One can argue that the identification or association of Japanese things with a Taiwanese identity (also rural and lower class in contrast to identifying Mainlanders with the urban, high class, and American) might have been the cause of official action in setting cultural policy in the realm of popular culture.[5] Hand-in-hand with the cultural industry of Chinese tradition have been official efforts to create a national amnesia of the Japanese legacy. Both economics and politics play important roles in the structure of ethnic and class divisions in Taiwan in the past four decades. Gates (1981) holds both the state policy and official KMT political ideology responsible for fostering the Taiwanese-Mainlander dichotomy in the first three decades of KMT rule, and which in turn reinforced the development of social classes along ethnic lines.

By the 1970s, the international discourse about dependency economies of Third World countries reached Taiwan. Public expression of anti-Japanese sentiment surfaced when deficits in the trade balance with Japan mounted, and the "xiangtu literature" (village-and-soil, or return to [Taiwanese] roots literature) emerged to attack industrial exploitation including economic dependency on Japan and the United States, social injustice, and poverty. Both the anti-Japanese and anti-American feeling reached national proportions when both of these countries abandoned the Republic of China and established diplomatic ties with the People's Republic of China. These international events of diplomacy, with more countries following suit since the early 1970s, shocked the entire nation. It caused much soul searching among intellectuals and emerging Taiwanese politicians as to the meaning of a national identity constructed on a myth of an imagined Chinese nation and the reality of a small island state struggling to survive.

Since the 1980s, the discourse of a new national identity has intensified. The sense of survival or urgency, instead of blurring cultural differences, sharpened ethnic demarcations between the Taiwan-oriented and the China-oriented communities, and generated new political voices from both camps. As shall be discussed later, the Taiwanese movement translates into expressions in literature, in popular arts and music, in history studies, and in the revival of the use of the Taiwanese vernacular in public places. The surprising and continued economic success of Taiwan, and the emergence of an urban middle class, were accompanied by the irresistible reinforcement of commoditized cultures from Japan, the United States, and even Europe. The process of inventing a collective identity in Taiwan has in the past four decades shown the complexity of the rise and fall of Japan's impact in culture, industry, commerce, and way of life—all of which form part of a very undefined Taiwanese identity.

FROM WHO ARE THE CHINESE TO WHO ARE THE TAIWANESE

Whereas the official cultural project gave meaning to the state symbols, served the political rhetoric of a national existence (Taiwan is China, Taiwanese culture is Chinese civilization, etc., as Chun has described), and provided ideology for a national socialization process, not all people in Taiwan accepted the official version of cultural tradition. Many played along by participating in government sponsored activities. There have been numerous conferences, resolutions passed, slogans, exhibitions, contests and competitions in support of the renaissance of Chinese culture. Yet, the results may actually contradict the purposes of the Cultural Renaissance and Cultural Construction campaigns. These activities have often been self-contradicting in their purposes, as we shall see in the following review of history.

In 1966, according to the official documentation of the Chinese Cultural Renaissance Movement (Ku 1976), "Chiang Gong," or Grandfather Chiang Kai-shek, in a lecture given to fifteen hundred top officials and leading scholars, defined "Chinese cultural foundation" as consisting of moral codes, democracy, and science. The audience was "so moved" by his wisdom and foresight that they signed a petition to form an Association of Chinese Cultural Renaissance. They elected Chiang as the Chairperson, and Sun For, the only son of Dr. Sun Yatsen, as the vice-chairperson. The declaration, or purpose, of this movement gives little emphasis to Chinese cultural tradition. Instead, and in contradiction with its hidden agenda (of emphasizing traditional ethics, seeking authoritarian rule, and reducing individual human rights), the association launched the movement in order to: (1) catch up with Western civilization, "for 'the West' had reached the peak of material civilization.... we must not lag behind and stick to our (archaic) tradition"; (2) "to counter the communist bandits' measures in destroying Chinese civilization... to save the spiritual civilization of mankind... for the Communist had degenerated humans to beasts..."; (3) "to boost economic prosperity, to selectively incorporate tradition into modern in order to adjust to modernity..." In other words, as declared in the official documents, this movement aimed for universal humanity and civilization, modernization, and to catch up with the West. During the period of the movement one could also clearly see the inconsistency between political practices of authoritarianism and political rhetoric emphasizing human rights (renquan), human dignity (renge), and human ethics (renlun).

By 1968 the Association published the guidelines for the renaissance movement which included handbooks for teaching ethics and citizenship in primary schools, educating people in the rules for standardized customs (such as men wearing the Manchu long gowns of the Qing Dynasty in official and religious ceremonies), prizes in writing contests and conferences, sponsorship and promotion of Chinese opera and the rewriting of new plays, support for music studies in advanced Western (rather than traditional Chinese) music, and efforts to improve and renew the music and dance used in the worship of Confucius on his birthdays. Interestingly, the reason given for studying and revamping the Chinese opera and music was that foreigners demanded to see it and enjoy it. The rationale goes as follows: because foreigners enjoy Chinese operas, we must satisfy them by improving ourselves in its performance. Cultural diplomacy, or the influencing of foreign countries through cultural export, was another implicit purpose of the Chinese Cultural Renaissance movement. By 1969, the Bureau of Culture was established to promote cultural exchange with foreign countries, to promote tourism and, for the unsaid real reasons, to control and monitor film production, theatrical performances, and music and dance.

At the same time, the government's efforts to tighten its control on "culture" resulted in a counter current led by Taiwanese writers and artists. The "Battle of the Indigenous Literature" happened in 1967, the same year the Cultural Renaissance was proclaimed. Socially conscious fiction writers in a national writer's seminar promoted the idea of writing about the dark side of rural villages (poverty), of creating a literature of the factories (exploitation under capitalism), and of the colonialization of Taiwan's economy (Third World dependency). Attacked and accused of being communists, several young writers were eventually arrested and forced to serve long jail sentences.[6]

In the 1970s, related to the shock of having many countries sever their ties with the Republic of China, artists, poets, musicians, and writers launched a movement to search for alternatives to Western culture by emphasizing their indigenous roots. This included "anthropological" fieldwork in the villages and remote mountain areas to find authentic national (folk) inspiration. The question for writers, artists, and intellectuals was "what is authentic, modern Chineseness."

Answers were found in indigenous, local, down-to-earth, Taiwaneseness. Even among college students, a new "Chinese" style of "campus songs" replaced the popularity of American pop and country-western music. For the first time in four decades, many "Chinese" style folk singers profited from selling recorded songs sung in Taiwanese dialects. Despite the claim of a new Chinese or Taiwanese identity, one can, however, still trace Japanese influence in this new style of popular music (see Wang (1986) and Sha (1989), quoted in Robinson, Buck, and Guthber (1991:131–134)).

In the popular music industry, like in the television and film industries, expression in Taiwanese dialects had been taboo. During the era of political protests in the 1980s an essential part of the Taiwanese "cultural" movement was the use of Taiwanese folk ballads or popular songs; they were performed even in government sponsored festivals. Increasing numbers of television programs, especially soap operas, were shown in Taiwanese—the majority in Min-nan (or Southern Fujian) dialect. By 1989 several young rock-and-roll singers had captured the island's urban youth, creating the so-called "new wave of Taiwanese music" (Hsu and Lin 1992). However, older Taiwanese listeners who were both intellectually and politically conscious accused the composers and singers of uncritical and unsophisticated use of Taiwanese dialects (and their influence upon the young followers) and, hence, of diluting the richness of the Taiwanese language (Hsu and Lin 1992:48). We can see here people recognizing language, music, and art as representations of national identity and, therefore, as fraught with political meaning, never as pure artistic or cultural forms.

Expression in, or identification with, Taiwanese in popular culture is a manifestation and an aspect of a broader process of Taiwanese identity formation. Also, as a leading anthropologist in Taiwan, Li Yih-yuan argues (Li 1988), this is not unrelated to the governmental promotion of Taiwanese "folk tradition" through the activities since 1981 of the Commission for Cultural

Planning and Development (or what Chun calls cultural construction). The Commission is a cabinet level agency headed by an ethnic Taiwanese and senior anthropologist, Chen Chi-lu. With the blessing of Chiang Ching-kuo and as part of his political indigenization strategy, Chen's agency organizes public performances of dying arts, such as Taiwanese Opera, Taiwanese hand-puppet shows, Hakka folk songs, and reinvented folk games and plays that originated in northern China (giant tops, kites, shadow puppets, etc., that had existed in northern China before the communist revolution). What is more, the Commission initiated a system to evaluate and designate important folk artists and historical sites in Taiwan for public rewards or protection. Since Chen received his high school education and a post-graduate degree in Japan, many of his ideas were copies of the Japanese system of designating masters of rare handicrafts, artistic antiques, and historical buildings as national or local treasures. The Commission, which took over the function of the Renaisance Association in the late 1970s, generated little public participation at first. Yet, eventually it inspired young artists and intellectuals, and reinforced the growing sentiment of Taiwanese identity. Li goes so far as to remark (1988:4–5): "The Commission's efforts to revive folk tradition has as its goal the meaningful construction of a modern cultural identity for Taiwan." However, the organized movement to revive folk tradition has itself fueled an old but ambiguous conflict of cultural identity: the conflict between (local) Taiwanese identity and (Mainland) Chinese identity. This conflict is commonly referred to as Taiwan *Jie* versus *Zhongguo Jie* (Taiwanese knot versus Chinese knot). Knot in Chinese is a synonym of "psychological complex," hence a Taiwan (identity) complex versus a China (identity) complex.

The question of who are the Taiwanese was not openly debated until the late 1980s, yet different versions of theories, definitions, or even plans for offering or refusing citizenship in the future have been for many years popular subjects of daily conversations and propaganda warfare. Political activists in Taiwan independence movements (which started with exiled intellectuals based in Japan during the 1950s and the United States as of the 1960s) advocated self-determination for Taiwanese by invoking their indigenous rights and different ethnic identity. They would not consider the Mainlanders who arrived after 1949 as Taiwanese. The extreme view held that Taiwanese are of different racial, cultural, and linguistic origins as compared to the Chinese (from China after 1949). They were reported (by the authorities in Taiwan) to be seeking political control of Taiwan exclusively for the Taiwanese. They also promoted the idea of replacing Mandarin with Taiwanese as the national language as well as the teaching medium in schools. To them, Mandarin is a foreign language which has been forced upon the indigenous (Taiwanese speaking) population.

The simple question of what the Taiwanese language is has become an explosive subject and has caused further emotional debates. Although about eighty percent of the population of Taiwan is considered Taiwanese and the majority are Min-nan (or Hoklo, or Southern Fujian) speakers, an estimated ten to fifteen percent among them are Hakka speakers whose ancestors came from today's Guangdong Province (instead of southern Fujian as the majority did) during the eighteenth and nineteenth centuries (see note 1 about President Lee's ethnicity). This is not even considering the so-called genuine indigenous peoples of Taiwan, the Formosan aborigines who are of Malay stock and speak languages classified by linguists as belonging to the Malayo-Polynesian language family. The government (or Mainlanders) argue that only the true aborigines are entitled to be referred to as Taiwanese, and all other Taiwanese are but Chinese under a false identity (non-Chinese) and the wrong political intention of seceding from the Chinese ancestral nation or Zuguo.

A more inclusive definition of Taiwanese today would include all who have migrated and resided in Taiwan, regardless of their ancestral origins, and would argue that there should be room for political participation for all on a democratic basis. This view has gained popularity after the Taiwan government began to allow people from Taiwan to visit China in 1987, when they realized their differences in cultural and political values with the Chinese in China. Whatever one's ethnicity or political inclinations, when a person from Taiwan visits China, as two million actually did between 1987 and 1992, he cannot deny the sharing of Chinese language, culture, and historical sentiment with the Chinese in China. On the other hand, a Taiwanese could also realize how different his or her speech, accent, values, and aspirations are. And, above all, the majority of people from Taiwan share a distinct "Taiwanese" identity that is not shared by the Chinese on the Chinese mainland. Furthermore, people in Taiwan talk about the continuing threat of China using military force if the people in Taiwan give up the position that Taiwan is but a province of China and that all the Taiwanese people are Chinese citizens of China.

CONCLUDING REMARKS

My second look at Taiwan reveals the emergence of a national identity for the Taiwanese, in spite of some thirty years of vigorous official projects of Chinese cultural construction. Perhaps the emerging ethnic, cultural, or even political Taiwanese identity is a function of the vigorous cultural policies of the authorities in Taiwan during the past three decades, a result of using political machines to force on the people a created China-centered national identity. Today the Taiwanese who used to be marginal prevail, having taken over center stage in the political battle over culture and identity. I have tried to demonstrate the interesting interplay of history, political ideology, cultural policy, economic development, and international relations that has contributed to the process of identity formation on the island state (or province) of Taiwan. The saga and problematic of cultural nationalism continues. We will probably never see a settled Chinese or Taiwanese identity.

NOTES

1. Only four presidents have held office between 1949 and 1992. They are Chiang Kai-shek, Yen Chia-kan, Chiang Ching-kuo, and Lee Teng-hui. Lee is the first Taiwanese to hold the office since Chiang Kai-shek's son, Ching-kuo, died in 1988. When he first took office in 1988 as the President of ROC, President Lee was said to be able to speak Japanese as fluently as Mandarin, but he feels more at home (on unofficial occasions) speaking in his mother tongue, Taiwanese (Southern Min, Hokkien, or "Holowei"). And it was reported that he is not really a "Taiwanese," but an ethnic minority of Hakka (the "guest people"), a Hakka descendant who has assimilated into the ethnic majority in Taiwan—the Holo, the Minnan, or the Taiwanese (depending on whose ethnic and linguistic terms these different concepts are invoked in Taiwan today).
2. This is part of the process of myth creation and the Chinese art of make believe (that is, to pretend not to see reality). To the (mainlander) political elites in Taiwan it is important to reject the name of Beijing (or the northern capital, Peking), which is not supposed to exist since China's capital, according to KMT, is Nanjing (or Nanking, the southern capital). Chinese opera used to be known, and is still known in China, as Beijing Opera. People in Taiwan stick to the term "Peiping Opera (pingju)" rather than "Beijing Opera (jingju)" to symbolically signify that the KMT is still the legitimate ruler of all China with its capital city in Nanjing, not Beijing (or Peiping—the northern peace—according to Taiwan's official English spelling).
3. A short account of the demographic history of Taiwan may be helpful to the readers who have little background knowledge of Taiwan. Taiwan was first mentioned in Chinese historical documents in the third century A.D. as Ryukyu. During the era of European exploration and colonization in the fifteenth century, the Portuguese named the island Formosa (the beautiful island). The Dutch established a colony in southern Taiwan in the early seventeenth century, but they were soon driven away by the Ming loyalist Koxinga (a phonetic adoption of the general's honorable title "one who is bestowed the surname of the emperor") or General Cheng Chenggong, when the Manchus conquered China. Koxinga established a short lived government in Taiwan (phonetic adoption of an

aboriginal name for the island), but brought hundreds of thousands of Chinese troops and civilians from Fujian (known in English as Hokkien). Although the Manchu or Qing Dynasty rulers banned immigration to Taiwan, many political refugees, vagabonds, and poor peasants continued to arrive and settle in Taiwan during the seventeenth century. Large numbers of Chinese immigrated mainly from southern Fujian and part of Guandong (the Hakka minority) and developed the "frontier land" of Taiwan. It was offered the status of a province by the end of the nineteenth century. Taiwan was ceded to Japan after China's defeat in the Sino-Japanese War; migration from China to Taiwan then ceased. Toward the end of Japanese colonial rule, as the Second World War was approaching, a Japanization project—Kominka—to make the Taiwanese loyal subjects of the Japanese emperor—was launched by the colonial government through an effective educational system. When Taiwan was returned to China in 1945, there was an estimated population of five million people. When the KMT region was reestablished in Taiwan the population on the island grew to an estimated eight million, including two million Chinese refugees who arrived from all parts of China. Gradually two terms emerged in Taiwan: *waisheng ren* (people from outside of the province) referring to the refugee population that arrived after 1945, and *benshreng ren* (people of the indigenous province) referring to descendants of the Chinese immigrants who came through the several waves of migration from China between the sixteenth and the nineteenth centuries. There are about 300,000 aboriginal people in Taiwan, descendants of people who, according to anthropological findings, have inhabited the islands for thousands of years. The aboriginal languages have been classified under the Malayo-Polynesian language group.

4. Many Japanese words, including Japanese (foreign) borrowed words, have been incorporated into the Taiwanese (Minnan or Hakka) language. For instance, when one feels good one must use the Japanese word *kimochi* to express it; the Japanese "national" sweet rice-cake, mochi, is thought to be indigenous Taiwanese. As in Japan, a Taiwanese refers to radio as *rachivo*, truck as *toraku*, taxi as *takushi*. To the present, Taiwan continues to borrow Japanese terms to refer to non-indigenous concepts.

5. Taiwan's leading psychiatrist, Professor Lin Tsung-yih, points out (1958) that, even among juvenile delinquents, members of street gangs in the cities were categorized according to ethnicity and cultural background. Through the 1960s, Liumana or the "Taiwanese" delinquents favored Japanese attire and carried Samurai swords as weapons; while Taibao or "Mainlander" gang members wore American jeans and followed the fashions of American rock stars.

6. It was a common practice at the time to charge that all anti-government thoughts or activities were the doings of communist spies from China. Also, in this case, the government dared not admit the reality that (despite years of nationalist education) there were political activists promoting the cause of Taiwanese identity or Taiwanese independence. Some of these writers in the late 1980s joined the opposition party and successfully won election as national level legislators.

REFERENCES

Gates, Hill (1981). Ethnicity and Social Class. In E.M. Ahern and H. Gates, Eds. *The Anthropology of Taiwanese Society*. Stanford, California: Stanford University Press, pp. 241–281.

Gu, Feng-xang (1976). Tuixina Zhongiua Wenhua Fuxing Yundong Ershinian (Twenty years of the Chinese Cultural Renaissance Movement), *Zhonghua Wenhua Fuxing Yuekan* (Chinese Cultural Renaissance Monthly) 20(7): 12–14.

Hsu, Ching-yun and Ching-chieh Lin (1992). The Songs, They are A-Changin', *Free China Review* 42(3):46–51.

Li, Yih-yuan (1987). Background Paper on Cultural Identity in Taiwan. A paper presented at the Conference for Cultural Studies, Institute of Cultural Studies and Communication, East-West Center, Honolulu, August 1987.

Lin, Tsun-yih (1958). Tai-pau and Liu-maing: Two types of delinquent youths in Chinese society, *British Journal of Delinquency* 8:244–256.

Robinson, D.C., E.B. Buck, and M. Cuthbert, Eds. (1991). *Music at the Margins*. Newbery Park, California: Sage.

Sha, D. (1989). Arriving of the personality age in recording industry (February 20, 1989), *United Daily News*, p. 17.

Wang, G. (1986). "Popular Music Industry in Taiwan." Unpublished manuscript.

Wu, Emma (1992). Local scholars take a closer look at home, *Free China Review* 42(3):4–19.

6

Rejoinder to Second Look

Allen J. Chun

I believe the concerned reader should understand the dialogue between the author and commentator not only in regard to how radically their viewpoints differ but also in regard to how these differences are a function of their respective subject-positions. Dr. Wu is a native Taiwanese whose scholarly writing has been situated for the most part in a U.S. context where he has worked for many years. On the other hand, the author is a U.S. trained (non-Taiwanese) overseas Chinese who has worked in Taiwan for the past ten years. Both persons in my opinion bring to the topic of culture and identity in contemporary Taiwan roughly the same degree of familiarity with "the native's point of view" yet differ in their essential interpretation of the facts. I think this difference of interpretation can be explained in the following terms.

On the whole, I am appreciative of Dr. Wu's criticism of my neglect to examine with equal profundity Taiwanese counter-discourses that co-exist with the official state policies and cultural constructions that I focus on in my analysis. This is doubly incisive especially in light of Dr. Wu's insights as an "insider," which also accounts for the impassioned nature of this criticism. My reasons for this benign neglect are attributable simply to the fact that the subject of the original conference was cultural policy and national identity and secondly that, given the long history of authoritarian rule in Taiwan, one can really only understand the cultural outlook of indigenous Taiwanese firstly in the context of (or in juxtaposition to) the way in which the state initially framed the discourse of culture rather than *vice versa*. Correspondingly, one cannot assume there was any *a priori* Taiwanese "identity" independent of that larger (dominant) discourse. I use "identity" carefully because this denotes a sense of social collectivity which is different from culture as a set of ongoing customs, beliefs and practices (the latter being *a priori*). I do not believe there was any Taiwanese "identity" until it emerged in opposition to KMT totalitarianism. Likewise, there was no Taiwanese ethnic "nationalism" prior to KMT rule because the intrinsic relationship between ethnicity and nationhood was something introduced only as the result of the KMT's postwar cultural policies.

If one can recognize the distinction between identity and the kind of culture anthropologists usually talk about, then I can accept many of the comments made by Dr. Wu about the syncretic cultural outlook of the Taiwanese and how it is influenced by Japanese nostalgia, local ethnic custom, Chinese traditions, Western science, etc., which may, of course, be true of any society, but none of this is necessarily crucial to notions of national identity held by the Taiwanese. For example, Americans privilege French haute culture and prefer to buy Japanese high tech goods, all of which easily accounts for the syncretic nature of their material culture (i.e. where pizza and hot dogs are quintessentially American in spite of their ethnic origin). The same cannot be said for the Japanese, whose preference for things Japanese may be the result of successful marketing ploys about their quality or just plain ethnocentrism. In other words, there may be instances where the consumption of culture in one society is not tied to national identity at all and instances where the two are intertwined. In postwar Taiwan, it is acceptable to practice Christianity, buy Japanese goods from Sogo, have permanent residency in the U.S. and vote for hard-line KMT causes. Yet as one looks at how national identity is constructed, one will find that it involves notions of ethnicity in other senses in a way that makes the national future of a people and their roots in a common civilization inseparable. I doubt whether other societies share this kind of notion, at least to this extreme. Yet, this is a crucial point of the paper.

One minor clarification: one should not confuse the commentator's remarks about modernization, which is a loose code word for economic progress, with modernity. The process of state formation is essentially a project of modernity. The very processes of identity construction, cultural reconstruction through inventions of tradition and utopian ideologization are intrinsic to modern nation-states in ways that did not previously exist, even though each nation construes them in very different ways. While most of my analysis dealt with the KMT's invention of traditional Chinese culture, one should note that this "conservatism" was wholly consistent with their "progressive" policies, especially regarding the KMT's embrace of Western science and rationality. The aspect of Japanese cultural influence relevant to the postwar era of KMT nationalism can be seen in the following: at no point was the issue of Japanese *nationalism* among the Taiwanese a problem in the years immediately following Taiwan's return to China, just the influence of Japanese *cultural* sentiment upon Chinese nationalism, with culture here reflecting a broad set of intellectual values.

So, having clarified my position on national identity and ethnicity, which have always been analytically distinct (at least until the advent of the nation-state), one might ask, "How did the KMT experience affect indigenous Taiwanese perceptions of themselves and their society?" To say the least, this is a complicated question and its answer must be prefaced by the question, "Who are the Taiwanese?" Dr. Wu's impassioned remarks appear to suggest that there has always been a sense of Taiwanese collective consciousness, which I find questionable. Even Taiwanese perceptions of the KMT are varied and diverse, being influenced by political beliefs as well as class background, among other things. Clearly, one thing that Dr. Wu cannot explain is why, with the advent of free elections and the trend toward democratization, a population composed of 75% ethnic Taiwanese supported the KMT over an opposition party running explicitly on behalf of Taiwanese interests by the ratio of 75%–25%, contrary to the rise of ethnic nationalist sentiment in the former U.S.S.R. and Yugoslavia. Certainly, the reality of the people's self-perception as Taiwanese is not an issue; the relevance of (Taiwanese) ethnicity to national identity, on the other hand, is. For those Taiwanese who voted for the KMT, their local ethnic origin was apparently not a relevant *political* consideration.

So, one might ask, was the KMT "successful" in inculcating among the indigenous Taiwanese a constructed sense of Chinese national identity which subverted to some degree the influence of ethnic nationalist sentiment? The answer is yes, but it was successful *only* in a Gramscian sense, that is, in the sense that it could not rely upon domination alone (i.e. as in martial law) but also had to be grounded in ideologically neutral values (Confucianism, inclusiveness of *huaxia*, etc.). Successful hegemonic inculcation (in a Gramscian sense) was really only a product of cultural renaissance and reconstruction, but this by no means implies that these indigenous voices were correspondingly eradicated. Resistance is usually the product of excessive domination; in the Taiwan case (like the former U.S.S.R.), it simply remained dormant. Yet, on the other hand, who are the silent, minority, contested, peripheral, powerless, unofficial, unorthodox, etc., that are invoked by Dr. Wu? My suspicion is that these are diverse elements of the Taiwanese population which occupy particular economic, intellectual and other niches; they do not represent "the" Taiwanese, which Dr. Wu claims to be a real, *a priori* collective entity. To say the least, ethnic identities and boundaries are very complex and have always changed over time. Their "naturalness" is simply an illusion created by the "imagined" community of nationhood. Yet despite their imagined and constructed nature, one should never deny their "reality" in political terms.

In short, Dr. Wu seems to assume that, without this hegemonic experience of KMT official culture and socialization, indigenous Taiwanese culture would have been able to blossom, uninhibited if not "naturally," as it were. If that is what he meant to say, he should have just said so, even though this is a highly speculative argument. I find it rather ironic on the other hand that he is less critical of the anthropologists-cum-bureaucrats like Chen Chi-lu and Li Yih-yuan who have played a large role in influencing and defining the course of cultural policy when I believe that they too are part of the overall trend toward cultural objectification, especially during the most recent phase of cultural reconstruction. Instead of invoking literary criticism to criticize my lack of sensitivity to the oppressed and repressed, I believe it is a more important responsibility for scholars to reflect on their critical role as agents already intertwined within the system. It is easy perhaps to recognize our own subject-positions; it is less easy to see how our subjectivity, empassioned as it can be, is itself the product of a system which engendered it and made it seem "natural."

PART III
Papua New Guinea

7

Pasin Tumbuna: Culture and Nationalism in Papua New Guinea

Lamont Lindstrom

If nations, in Benedict Anderson's phrase, are "imagined communities" (1991), then some people have to imagine harder than others. A creative, even laborious, construction of nationality is notable in many post-colonial precincts around the globe. Here, state institutions may appear as relics, and recent relics at that, of departed European colonialists (see Larmour 1992b). The nation, such as it is, may consist of a variety of communities that had not before imagined much common identity among themselves. This is the case in the South Pacific state Papua New Guinea (PNG), which is renowned for its cultural and linguistic diversity. This country of three million people, speaking 800 or so languages from two major language families, obtained its independence from Australia in 1975.[1]

Papua New Guinea's state institutional structures are both relatively new and weak for a variety of reasons including Australian colonial practice, only moderately developed communication and transportation infrastructures, and the insulation from forces of the outer world that a viable subsistence economy provides to local communities. It is no surprise, thus, that the people who led PNG into independence, and who have served since as state functionaries, have worried about fostering sentiments of a shared national identity.

My texts, here, are the writings of PNG politicians and academics, and also scattered poems, plays, and letters to the four newspapers that were published in the capital, Port Moresby, in the late 1980s. This, then, is an elite discourse of national identity produced by a small minority of urban, Western-educated Papua New Guineans, many of whom work for the state and thus have obvious personal interests in promoting talk of national identity, unity, and stability. How, or if, the large majority of village Papua New Guineans—who did not write poetry or letters to editors in the 1970s and 1980s—might imagine their nation I am less able to assess.[2]

The challenge to imagine a national community of Papua New Guineans is more profound than that faced by Singaporeans, say, who only have to envisage how three existing ethnicities might be combined into one nation (Chua and Kuo, this volume). Former PNG Prime Minister Michael Somare admitted this challenge: "We Pacific peoples are only just emerging as individual and distinctive nations. We look forward and we strive for some sort of national identity. That yearning is deep rooted in the hearts of all peoples" (1991:3). The work of imagination in PNG is to envision a national identity that distinguishes citizens from other possible things they might be. This includes Australian, the former colonial power, but also importantly Indonesian. That much larger, neighboring nation of 160 million people absorbed the western half of New Guinea in 1964, dislodging the Dutch.

Prime Minister Somare strives and looks forward to *some* sort of national identity—and we can agree with him that national identity can be variously imagined, whether or not it springs from deeply rooted yearnings. The stuff of imagined identity is sentiment and discourse—ways of feeling and talking—and people may conceive of the "deep, horizontal comradeship" (Anderson 1991:7) of a nation in a variety of terms. A culturalist discourse is only one of a number of possible languages of identity. Nationhood might be imagined instead around identities of race (e.g., Japan, see Befu this volume), religion (Thailand, Santasombat this volume), a shared economic future (Singapore, Chua and Kuo this volume), and so on.

In Papua New Guinea, the exercise of nationalist imagination has in large part fixed upon culture. In this, national identity is located within cultural traditions (or *ol Pasin bilong ol tumbuna*—"the ways of the ancestors"—in Tok Pisin, PNG's Pidgin English lingua franca). I suggest several reasons why culture has been particularly significant within PNG's discourses of nationhood instead of shared religion, history, race, language, or geography. But Papua New Guineans are not alone in turning culture into a national resource, a weapon, and an excuse. Culture has emerged as a strategic site of debate within many communities (including the United States, where numerous colleges and universities now require a mandatory celebration of American "multicultural" diversity within their core curricula).

As more and more powerful communicative technologies link once isolated regions of the world and transmit information, images, and representations from one society to another, issues of global informational power and interpretive control become unavoidable. If people in PNG and elsewhere do not insist on the right of self-definition—the right to have the last word about who they are and about what their traditions mean—then they will find that others will have done this job for them. A catalog of alien images and interpretations of PNG and its people circulate around the world information system, and return to infiltrate local talk about culture with increasing facility. Insofar as a precariously sanitized image of shared culture contributes to sentiments of national identity and national stability, local elites must attend to the ways in which their traditions are being defined and evaluated.[3]

By most measures, PNG is a culturally diverse place and the phrasing of a common national identity in cultural terms presents certain difficulties. It is no surprise that in Papua New Guinea, and its neighboring Melanesian countries Solomon Islands and Vanuatu as well, nationalist discourse, when mapping out an identity, celebrates both shared *and* unshared culture. Or rather, cultural diversity itself is celebrated as a remarkable facet of the nation, and national rhetoric acclaims "unity in diversity" (see Iamo and Simet, this volume). The potential of a celebrated cultural diversity to wreck any unity, however, haunts this slogan; diversity must in some way be policed and domesticated for cultural difference to be useful in nationalist imagination. The toiling now underway in the United States to institutionalize "multiculturalism" in a number of arenas might be taken as this sort of domestication of difference. The nation, at one level, celebrates its cultural diversity but the unitary apparatus by which that diversity gets celebrated ensures that difference, monitored through its display, is only spoken of in common terms (cf. Sissons 1993).

Alternately, discourses of cultural diversity may be exiled to safer milieus. State leaders in Singapore, for example, proclaimed ethnic difference to be aesthetically pleasing yet proscribed the assertion of such difference within political arenas (Chua and Kua, this volume). Papua New Guinea, lacking Singapore's robust institutions of state control, including a repressive Internal Security Act, has been less successful in muting some of the oppositional implications of its cultural nationalism. Also unlike Singapore, where most people have only labor power to sell, the majority of Papua New Guineans occupy their own lands and they vigorously challenge state claims to the timber and mineral resources located thereon.

Nationalist talk about the "ways of the ancestors" can be both helpful and dangerous to the state. There are marked ambivalences in people's evaluations of PNG culture, and also disagreements over how this is to be defined. These ambiguities and disagreements, in part, relate to the several uses of an idea of culture within nationalist discourse. Constructions of tradition that work at the local village or regional level may subvert representations of culture that national elites in the capital city devise. If in PNG talk about local traditions has been harnessed to the tasks of national unity, development, and general identity-building, such talk can also serve regional claims for autonomy and disengagement from state institutions.

CULTURE AS IDENTITY

Nations have imagined their identity in a number of terms. A typical, "lowest common denominator" approach is to find (and sometimes resuscitate or create) a shared "primordial sentiment" and build upon and widen this. Some new states have relied on strongly felt religious identities (such as Islam), and others on race or ethnicity, shared language, a shared past or history, or shared traditions. Papua New Guinea is an interesting case in that there are no obvious primordial ties to which national identity can be anchored. The local intelligentsia has nonetheless surveyed a number of possible fields on which a PNG national identity might be cultivated.

First, there is religion. This, however, is stony ground. PNG's religions are localized and diverse. Still, ancestors have a widespread importance, and ancestral authority becomes a theme in talk about identity. There is also today's widespread

Christianity. Here is at least one important affiliation that most people share, and PNG's nationhood, like that of neighboring Solomon Islands and Vanuatu, stresses the fact that this is a Christian country (see Latukefu 1988): *Yumi stanap long God* (we stand/develop with God), as this is put in Vanuatu.

Christianity, however, presents certain problems. In PNG, it comprises various sects and denominations that have not always cooperated in the past. More seriously, Christianity is not native to PNG. It is an alien religion that came into the country arm-in-arm with European colonialists and businessmen—all that today's discourse of national identity strives to define itself against (see Narokobi 1980:229–233; Kros 1975). Moreover, Christianity's universal claims do not serve well to define a distinctive PNG identity. It tells people who they are like more than why they are different. Discursively, Christianity is devalued because it always must apologize for its past, as it must try to assert some local and distinctive form, such as "Melanesian" Christianity, or "our ways" of believing (see Trompf 1987).

Second, there is common history. This, too, is not very fertile. PNG has no written accounts of the pre-colonial past. Still, at least one local archaeologist has called attention to people's probable 50,000 year presence on their islands: "In order to build up Papua New Guinea as a nation, a common identity must be sought in the unwritten past ... Therefore we should talk about our identity by appreciating common unifying forces witnessed by the earliest waisted axes" (Muke 1985:65–66; see also Narokobi 1983:22–24). As a physical embodiment of shared history, however, waisted axes have serious limitations, especially when compared to the more striking songs and dances used to embody and display shared culture.

Perhaps more than archaeology, in PNG there is a discursive emphasis on oral history (including a published journal of that name) (see also Waiko 1986). Oral history is both a methodology to document and make available some of the unwritten past, and a growing body of stories and narratives than can be used in school curricula to counterbalance the literary weight of the historical opus from the outside world. Actually, PNG owes its existence and its boundaries to the happenstance of ninety years of German, Dutch, British, Australian, and Indonesian colonialism. Discursively, however, it is not very satisfying to found one's national unity and identity in this compulsory history that appears both accidental and distasteful.

Third, there is language. This too is problematic. PNG has no indigenous shared language. Rather, it has hundreds. This linguistic diversity may be discursively appreciated in principle, but not often in practice. The colonial language, English, remains the language of governmental and educational advancement (although a few pilot programs in vernacular primary education now exist.) Linguistic diversity, in fact, has become the common way to talk about regionalism and nepotism: the Pidgin English word *wantok* ("one language") refers to fellow, urban dwellers who come from the same region of the country, and who speak the same language, from whom various forms of assistance might be obtained. People both praise and condemn the "*wantok* system" that functions as an informal social security net, but that also corrupts bureaucratic rationalism in hiring practice, and in the distribution of government resources (see Mannan 1976; Centurion 1989:3). Language's symbolic functions in signifying social divisiveness rather than identity perhaps accounts for the following letter to the editor:

> I do not think that it is a good idea for people to speak their mother tongue in towns. You should understand that these towns are not your villages in which you can speak your own language in front of other people, especially those of you roaming the town of Kundiawa (the Kuman speakers) and the Wabag people, in most other provinces. I say this because it is, after all, rude. What do you think? (John 1988:11).

Two lingua francas overlay PNG's 800 or so indigenous languages—Tok Pisin (Pidgin English), and Hiri Motu. The latter is spoken around the southern, Papuan half of the country; the former, much more widespread, is spoken everywhere although it still retains connotations of its northern, New Guinea origins. Keesing has remarked on Pidgin's functions as a unificatory symbol (1982:300; 1989:26). This is perhaps more true of Vanuatu and the Solomon Islands than it is of Papua New Guinea. PNG's two lingua francas sometimes work instead to accentuate Papua vs. New Guinea divisions, especially as Papuans see Hiri Motu rapidly losing ground as Tok Pisin spreads. Some Papuans, for example, criticized PNG's only television station that ran its signature piece, and also Coca Cola commercials, in only English and Tok Pisin versions. Hiri Motu editions were then belatedly added.

Tok Pisin, moreover, retains a negative evaluative charge. In general, neither the British nor the Australians saw much good in this language. They perceived it to undermine their attempts to teach standard English. Pidgin today, for many people, still remains depreciated vis-a-vis English.[4] Pidgin retains much of its colonial negativity, as evident in this newspaper commentary written by politician Sir John Guise:

> The first announcement at the airport terminal is "Ladies and Gentlemen your flight is ready for boarding etc. etc." This is followed by the announcement of *"all man-meri balus bilong yupela* etc. etc." ... The 2 separate announcements do instill in one's mind that there are 2 separate races of people at the airport and on domestic flights; a subtle discrimination of people using the language barrier as an excuse! No thinking national person travelling with his wife on a domestic flight would want his wife, a loving companion in life, to be addressed as *"all man-meri"* ... At least the Motuan language does give one a sense of dignity and self-respect by having the words *Hahine bona latau* instead of *Man-meri!* Pidgin a master to servant language! (Guise 1989:10).

When prominent politicians are talking in this fashion, the problems of building one's national identity around a "servant language" are obvious.

Fourth, there is race. There is some sympathy in PNG's national discourse for racial statements, not surprisingly so, given the prominence of race within former colonial society. A powerful racist category, labeled "blacks," "natives," or "boongs," and its distinctiveness from "whites" returns to inform contemporary talk about identity. Section 65 of the constitution that grants automatic citizenship only to persons with at least two indigenous grandparents born in the country might be interpreted in racial terms (see Wolfers 1982:94; Larmour 1992a). Race appears more clearly in nationalist writings about "Melanesians"—the modern, positive term that labels the category—although given the contemporary low value of racist talk within global arenas, these texts have to deny that racialism: "Promoting Melanesian identity is not racist. It is not even unchristian. It is a call to develop our inherent talents, qualities and virtues as people" (Narokobi 1980:23).

Today's racist discourses have to keep their volume low, whether these are about "whites" or "Melanesians." Still, evocation of shared Melanesianness remains a part of PNG's national discourse. It is somewhat undercut, however, by people's proclivities to use physical and other presumed inherent, natural, or biological characteristics to *distinguish* among themselves (see Chowning 1986:158). The "black skins" from the secessionist island of Bougainville thus set themselves apart from the "red skins" from the rest of the country, as do tall, coastal Papuans from shorter Highlanders.[5] As a constructed race category, "Melanesian" serves pretty well to make counter claims vis-a-vis "Australians," "whites," or even "Indonesians"; but it uneasily unites peoples who inhabit a region notorious for its physical diversity, and for its diversifying.

Fifth, there is land—or what anthropologists have called shared "place." Everyone living in Papua New Guinea, at the broadest level, can be talked about as co-residents—as neighbors living on the same land. Talk like this abolishes regionalism by pretending the entire country to be a single village. Sione

Latukefu—a scholar of Tongan descent working in PNG—wrote in 1972, before independence, that:

> Personally I believe that the best way of aiding rural modernization would be to declare all land to belong to the state ... It would also be a good thing that the land should go to those who can develop it for the benefit of the whole nation, instead of allowing it to lie idle and undeveloped in the hands of traditional owners. I believe the claim that primitive people have a sort of mystical attachment to their land has been greatly exaggerated ... The realization of the value of land is itself the result of contact and progress towards the monetary economy (1972:9–10).

It is also the result of progress towards independence (see Keesing 1989:29). Nationalist discourse supercharged people's mystical connections to land, in order to legitimize claims to political autonomy and the recapture of alienated lands, to such a degree that Latukefu's statist position is no longer possible (see Samana 1988:11–17; Ghai 1985; Larmour 1992a).

Still, shared place is an effective way of presenting larger identities, and may become even more so as the country's air and road systems develop. Perhaps related to this is a curious spate of "trekking" that has broken out around the country. During the latter 1980s, at least, various church youth groups would start walking off into the bush, heading for Port Moresby hundreds of kilometers away, in order to raise money for worthy (although local village) causes from urban residents. Badly prepared and ill provisioned, these groups frequently had to be saved by police and military rescue squads. This movement across the countryside from village to capital city perhaps has the same symbolic function as the western parade—a public journey across territory that signifies shared rights and identity.[6] These cross-country journeys work to stitch together diverse regions into a symbolic national whole.

Finally, there is culture (or tradition—I will use the two synonymously). Given the various symbolic disabilities of religion, history, language and, to a lesser extent, race and shared land, one could suspect that PNG's talk of nationhood has been forced to fall back upon cultural traditions because there is nothing else suitable to the task. More than this, though, those traditions have a striking immediacy. PNG enjoys an internationally renowned set of diverse cultures. From the beginning, its national discourse has built upon this wealth of culture—on whatever shared "ancestral ways" might be profitably asserted.

The first words of PNG's 1975 constitution proclaim:
> We, the people of Papua New Guinea—united in one nation; pay homage to the memory of our ancestors—the source of our strength and origin of our combined heritage; acknowledge the worthy customs and traditional wisdoms of our people—which have come down to us from generation to generation; pledge ourselves to guard and pass on to those who come after us our noble traditions and the Christian principles that are ours now.

The constitution goes on to stress the guiding importance of sundry noble traditions in a number of its clauses.

Looking back on ten years of independence, PNG's then Minister for Culture and Tourism noted this identificatory reliance on culture: "At Independence 10 years ago, Papua New Guinea could not be compared with other more powerful countries in terms of modern technology. Instead, culture was emphasised as a means of identification and a way of expressing pride and national identity through the arts e.g., traditional dancing" (Kamod 1985:35; see Latukefu 1988:89; Crawford 1977:31; Strathern 1985:291). Others, too, advocated culture to circumscribe the new national community:

> Political self-determination could not be achieved without first of all determining cultural identity The cultural traits of the Papua New Guinean make him what he is. His cultural values and practices make him a Papua New Guinean and not a Fijian or a Solomon Islander or

even an Australian. He has to identify himself first in order to determine what he wants for his society and to define the path or direction to take in the fast changing world of today (Wari 1980:110).

Because it has these cultural traditions, PNG is special and "unique" (Kolia 1978). The Department of Culture and Tourism, not surprisingly, also stresses this uniqueness: "Papua New Guinea is one of last societies in the world today where its culture and arts are still in their original form despite of modernisation and fast development" [sic] (Beona et al. 1988:20). This cultural uniqueness sets the country apart from all others and, of course in so doing, delimits an identified, national community that—if all goes well—might be unified.

The connection between PNG identity and culture is such that a member of the Citizenship Advisory Committee suggested a "culture test" for citizenship applicants. Mr. Aloysius Nale said that he was of the opinion that many of the applicants were foreign businessmen who wanted citizenship only to use the country's rich resources and later leave: "I fear foreign businessmen are using national women not as wives but only as sleep-in partners to have members of the committee approve their applications." Rather than granting citizenship based on kinship and marriage, Nale "suggested that only those who lived and mixed with villagers and knew the country's customs and traditions will be granted citizenship" (Bengi 1988:15).

The stress on village customs, here, reminds us that tradition's presence within national political discourse also reflects the continuing importance of customary knowledge at the local level. Although connected into the world economic system and cash economy, the great majority of rural PNG people depend on subsistence production for their economic well-being. Here, cultural knowledge delineates *local* identities, and gives people rights to important resources, such as land. This level of custom, at least, still is a large part of most rural people's sense of identity.

Furthermore, tradition's weight within PNG's national discourse also relates to its importance in talk about identity within international arenas as well (see Linnekin 1989). There today is a complex apparatus of Pacific arts festivals, world expos, museums, international conferences, and cultural tourism in which those people who find themselves without practices that can be consciously displayed as authentic tradition are at a disadvantage (e.g., "deculturated" communities such as Guam's Chamorros).

PNG's surfeit of traditions makes that country a star attraction at Pacific arts and dance festivals. Locating national identity in culture, however, raises two worrisome complications that nationalist discourse must address. First, such rhetoric must assert a positive evaluation of tradition—and this, in PNG, is peculiarly problematic. Second, cultural diversity must be carefully framed so to envisage therein images of that deep, horizontal comradeship which defines nationhood.

EVALUATING CULTURE

PNG faces a serious problem in evoking tradition and culture as a foundation of the national self. A positive evaluation of island cultures to serve purposes of national identity goes against the grain of other powerful discourses that have long devalued local traditions as evil, useless, maladaptive, uneconomic, primitive, and so on. Three of the most powerful of these alien discourses include talk about development, Christianity, and a popularized version of social evolutionism. These discourses—of modernity, of religion, and of primitiveness are related and inform one another. They all discount large areas of traditional life—and occasionally go further to advocate wholesale abandonment of customary beliefs and practices. Although these discourses originated elsewhere, many people in PNG today have adopted them and use one or more of them to sort and select among their cultural traditions, determining which to keep and which to discard, which to celebrate and which to forget.

Looking toward Vanuatu, another recently independent Melanesian country, one sees custom portrayed in much better light than it often is in PNG, where darker aspects are still often admitted. Vanuatu's more troubled independence and the presence of two colonial powers generated a more clearly positive revaluation of cultural traditions in that country. Shared custom legitimated claims for independence, for the return of all alienated lands, as it also provided an important way to talk about national identity and unity (Lindstrom 1982). In PNG, on the other hand, there was perhaps less need to idealize local traditions during a smoother move to independence. Tradition, as a consequence, has not managed to shed all of its colonial negativity, despite its new functions within national political discourse. Narokobi has made this point:

> Preparation for national consciousness often takes on the form of a political struggle. In many countries, nationalism is preceded by a long and sustained struggle. The ease with which political power was transferred to Melanesian leaders via Anglo-Australian legal, political and economic institutions has given us no chance to master national consciousness (1983:71).

Apisai Enos, a PNG poet, captures the ambiguous evaluation of local culture in the first two stanza's of his poem "New Guinea"—the first stanza negative; the second positive (Powell 1987:152–153):

New Guinea, beloved New Guinea
What do they say about you?
> The rugged
> the impossible
> the broken bottle
> the hostile

>   the Saturday made
>   the waste land
>   the hot island
>   the tomb of death
>   the forgotten isle
> The land of thousand tribes and trials
> primeval forests of termites, leeches and cicadas
> hidden valleys and mountain crags of old
> deep gorges and rugged ranges
> fast rivers flowing to endless swamps
> land of killers and cannibals and sacred corpses
> of mountain raiders and mangrove snipers
> land of fevers and dreaded diseases
> molten lava and sulphurous ashes
> of coral beaches with lashing fishes
>
> New Guinea!
> Land of proud warriors of courage
> land of ancestral spirits
> entangled in myths and incarnations
> land of *haus tambaran, dukduk* and *eravo*
> land of *kovave* masks and *gope* boards
> land of *hiri, kula* ring and fire dance
> land of a thousand faces and facets
> I hardly know you!
> New Guinea, dazzling with diversity
>   wild, rugged, yet tender.

The rest of the poem goes on to evoke additional positive images of the country and its traditions. Like this poem, nationalist discourse must work hard to push positive images of local cultures that are constantly undermined by talk that accuses them of being antithetical to development.

Some of this rhetoric is a remnant of pre-independence modernism that rejects nationalists' revaluation of culture. The

Tongan Latukefu, at least in his 1971 presidential address to the Papua-New Guinea Society, endorsed this view: "A morbid preoccupation with traditional culture and a belief that it offers solutions to all one's present-day problems ... is a great stumbling block in the way of modernization" (1972:3). He went on to say that "although traditional customs are an important part of a society's inheritance and must be learned and appreciated, they must never be allowed to stand in the way of modernization" (1972:11; see also Narokobi 1980:271).

Given culture's importance in post-colonial PNG, wholesale condemnations such as this are today less common. Still, the underbelly of talk about local traditions is that preserving these customs threatens development and modernization. For example, a Member of Parliament handing out prizes at Boisen High School near Rabaul warned the gathered students: "Traditional methods ruin the proper running of modern institutions.... Some say we should remain with our customary styles. To that, I say that you can't do everything by tradition and custom. A lot of things have been tried by tradition and failed" (Post-Courier 1980:15). Despite an anthropological literature that argues that many PNG customary practices, in fact, help integrate people into the modern economic sector (e.g., Finney 1973), this discourse continues to lament tradition as economically maladaptive.[7]

People worry over what cultural practices they should keep, and what they should lose in order to achieve modernity. Narokobi, for example, gives one list of what should go:

> Self-criticism is necessary to see our pitfalls in order to avoid them or even to discard them. For indeed there are many constraints to our cultural values. These include fear, jealousy, sorcery, distrust, selfishness, stagnation, ignorance, illiteracy, malnutrition and so on. There are selfish motives in some of our cultural practices we should liberate ourselves from. These include demands for excessive bride wealth, child marriage, the

inferior role given to women in some places, marrying more than one wife for purely selfish motives, spending large sums of money on status building, feasts at the expense of proper education, health and mental growth of the people, the disintegration of village communities as viable units of life and so forth (1980:15; see also 1976b:16–17).

Other people focus on more specific customary practices they accuse of standing in the way of development—betelnut chewing, for example (Samarai Island Observer 1988:11).

Vigorous debates about brideprice payments (brilliantly analyzed in Filer 1985) have also questioned the value of tradition. Such payments affirm relations between families, and display and celebrate group abilities to produce and amass wealth. In today's cash economy, however, many people see them as getting out of hand with the record brideprice nearing K20,000 plus a couple of expensive vehicles thrown in. Newspaper readers regularly write letters to complain that brideprice threatens rational capital accumulation and the dignity of women. Young men also bemoan their inability to meet the inflated demands of their girlfriends' families. A letter to Lifeline, a lovelorn column, makes this point:

>Dear Lifeline, During the school holidays I went to my home village and through the influence of my friends I married a girl from the village. Later I discovered that the bride price was too high—K1000 in cash plus a motorbike. I am still a student and can't afford that amount. On the other hand I do not want to lose my wife because she has become very dear to me now (Poor Student 1989:26).

People accuse brideprice tradition, here, of economic irrationality and of undermining individual rights. And tradition in general is discredited every time some practice or another is held up as a barrier to a positively valued development and modernity.

Christianity is a second discourse that devalues traditional culture. National discourse emphasizing the importance of tradition contends with a very powerful, often fundamentalist Christianity in the country. It is not easy to be a good traditionalist and a good Christian at the same time.[8] Schieffelin recorded this conflict during one Christian campaign near Mt. Bosavi:

> national pastors of the ECP [Evangelical Church of Papua], particularly those from the Highlands, take the position that Bosavi traditions must be disregarded, and ceremonies, body decoration and music have almost disappeared completely in the Bosavi area ... it is not that traditional clothes, ceremonies and dances, pig festivals and food taboos are in themselves bad, rather, these traditional things are not what Christians do. If you stick to the old ways, the pastors say, it will confuse your mind so that you do not learn God's word properly and go Satan's road to the fire (1978:30).

Crawford reports similar themes from the Gogodala region: "We cannot mix spirits and witchcraft with the Lord Jesus ... To be a Christian the past was not to be allied to the present" (1976:2–3; see also Kros 1975).

Many Christian spokesmen, however, do not advocate discarding every tradition. There is a countering stance that finds commonalities between Christian and traditional beliefs and practices: "The idea is also to recognize that aspects of the people's cultures are not opposed to the Christian culture. Thus instead of playing the organ to accompany the singing of hymns, for instance, we play traditional tunes to the kundu and the garamut [drums]" (Pokawin 1987:29; see also Kadiba 1987; Latukefu 1988:92; Sowei 1988:23; Gam 1988:26). Interviews with young seminarians about local cultures revealed "a discriminating attitude. For example, they did not agree with pagan rituals for gardening or fishing but they saw no contradiction between believing in the gospel and also in traditional spirits" (Richardson 1987:15).

This more conciliatory approach states that only *some* customs are incompatible with Christianity or modernity, and should be abandoned. A letter to the editor makes this point:

> A Christian therefore uses the Bible and his Christian experience as a basis of vetting and selecting that aspect of culture as relevant ... To further argue that no effort be spared to retain all our culture is to imply that no facet of our culture is bad. Sorcery, witchcraft, cannibalism, tribal fights, head hunting, all of these must be hauled on board in the name of culture so as to give me, a Papua New Guinean, identity. I don't buy that argument (Kemba 1987:9).

A third discourse that devalues tradition is a popularized version of 19th-century social evolutionism that portrays Papua New Guinea as the land of the primitive: "the Stone Age in the Space Age." This perspective tends to depict Melanesian cultures in terms of what they *lack*: no law, no government, no economy, morals, sense of time, individuality, and so forth. National culture is thus haunted by specters of primitiveness, sorcery, cannibalism, and savage feuding. These images have been fed by a century of social theory that seized upon PNG as the epitome of The Primitive (see Narokobi 1976:12; Muke 1985:63). This renders a spectrum of traditional life unsuitable for positive images of contemporary identity.

Cannibalism is a case in point. Nowadays, who wants to be a cannibal? A PNG police superintendent wrote an angry letter to the editor after seeing Dennis O'Rourke's film *Cannibal Tours* during a study course in Britain. O'Rourke, of course, intended the tourist to be taken as the real (cultural) cannibal—but this traditionalist figure is so charged in PNG that it is not surprising that viewers overlooked his irony:

> The title really angered me. Not one bit of the documentary depicted acts of cannibalism, nor was there any evidence to suggest that such acts take place. Yet the tourists were shown pointing to a Haus Tambaran and

saying: "This is the house where cannibalism is practiced." This really hurt my feelings, especially when sitting with colleagues who would undoubtedly think that what was said was true. The following day I had to deliver a 15-minute talk on the subject of Papua New Guinea culture, and at the end I was asked if it was really true that cannibalism is practiced in Papua New Guinea. I was embarrassed, but stood my ground in denying such myths. The producer of this documentary should be condemned in the strongest possible terms. To me, he is nothing but a criminal who entered the country with sinister motives. He deliberately twisted facts to enable him to sell the documentary, no doubt at substantial monetary gain to himself (Ludwick 1989:10).

A similar dispute occurred when an Englishman, once married to a Highlands Chimbu woman, took their two children back to Britain and refused to bring them back. The case was reported in Britain's *News of the World* and subsequently picked up by PNG's *Post-Courier* in July, 1988. The *Post-Courier* quoted the British paper under the heading "Chimbus slammed as 'perverted cannibals'":

An Englishman who married a PNG woman has been reported in a London newspaper as saying that "the Chimbu indulge in repulsive sexual perversions, urinate over each other in greeting and even practice cannibalism." Bryan Hawker, 50, was reported in the sensationalist *News of the World* as having taken his two children, Clemina and Danny, into hiding "to escape torture and Stone-Age style sex rituals at the hands of perverted cannibals"... "Their mother, Katie, was a young tribal slavegirl when Bryan met her. He bought her for 10 pigs, a cow, 45 chickens and 200 pounds" ... *The News of the World* said that, according to Mr. Hawker, eight-year-old Clemina was likely to be "stretched naked on a mat for public viewing then sold off to an old tribesman," and that Danny, 4, would be corrupted as well. "Out there, ritualised homosexuality is just part of everyday life," Mr. Hawker was reported to have said. "The children would also see a bizarre ritual where the Chimbu cut off the heads of rival warriors then smear themselves with blood before eating the brains" (Senge 1988b:2).

Four days later, Chimbu residents of Port Moresby marched on the British High Commission to protest. Spokesman Paul Dage proclaimed that "The Chimbu people have never been cannibals—they have killed people in tribal fights, but they have never eaten human flesh, and never drank their blood ... The Chimbu people now regard this Mr. Hawker as a devil, because Chimbu is part of a Christian country where cannibalism does not exist" (Kili 1988:2). The demonstrators presented the High Commissioner a petition demanding 50 million kina in compensation for the damage done to their reputation, and also that Hawker be jailed. A former Chimbu Member of Parliament, John Nilkare, went further. He hired a lawyer saying "he wanted the children back, but especially to clear the name of the Chimbus. 'I will not stop until he hangs,' he said" (Senge 1988a:2). His demands were supported by a number of letters to the editor, e.g. "I want this man to be hanged" (Merimba 1988:10). British journalism, here, circulated an image—"perverted cannibals"—that the Chimbu found deceitful and distasteful and, in reaction, they attempted to silence that journalism (with the threat of a multimillion kina lawsuit) and Mr. Hawker (by hanging) in order to assert their own rights to define themselves and their culture. In this assertion, however, they too rejected cannibalism just as strongly as the British.

Talk about contemporary social problems in PNG, such as "rascal" youth gangs, "tribal" warfare, payback killings, and gang rape, are linked with notions of primitiveness and evolution. In this discourse, a genealogy of these present-day problems is traced back to customary roots, and today's evils are deemed to be evidence of a flawed culture locked in an early stage of evolutionary development. Contemporary gender relations are an example. The Women and Law Committee's pamphlet, *Wife-Beating Is A Crime* states, "Some people think that wife-beating is alright because it is custom in some parts of PNG. They are wrong. The law and the Constitution say that bad customs (like payback killings, tribal fighting and wife—beating) must be stopped" (n.d.:2). Latukefu also traces a growing urban gang rape problem back to customary roots (1988:86; see Filer 1985:166).[9]

Today's urban violence, too, is commonly traced to traditional roots. After a disturbance between police and youths in the Boroko shopping district, a letter writer observed: "They were just a group of unemployed bums hell-bent on dragging our city and our people down to the same level of degradation and lawlessness that prevails in their own tribal homelands" (Patriot 1988:10). And continuing outbreaks of violence and "tribal" warfare in rural areas are likewise attributed to cultural continuities (see Narokobi 1983:50–51; Podolefsky 1984). *Wantokism* is also given a traditional genealogy: "In Papua New Guinea one of the distinct features is the 'Wantok System' ... a system that has grown deep roots into the traditional lifestyle of Papua New Guineans" (Sedi 1988:48).[10] How can tradition be good if it bears such rotten fruit?

Nationalist discourse struggles with other powerful voices that discount the *wantok* system and other traditions. In response, it consciously associates cultural tradition with an idyllic village life, and juxtaposes this to the dangerous, modern city. A focus on the village, too, works to counter some of the negative evaluations of culture spread by developmental and religious discourses. In this approach, the tables are turned and positive custom indicts the malignant aspects of modern life. In this pastoral counter-discourse, for example, brideprice is not an irrational customary practice. Rather, as one letter writer put it, "The first important thing is that when bride price is paid this helps the married couple to stay together. Therefore you will hardly find the disease called divorce which is very common in European countries" (Filer 1985:169). Traditional/modern and customary/alien comparisons are subsumed within the rural/urban dichotomy in national discourse. The good village stands as an antidote and paragon for the evil city.

Christianity, too, is sometimes vilified in favor of positive tradition.[11] Fundamentalist Christian fears of the body, for example, collide with the national discourse's focus on dance and customary dress that typically leaves women's breasts bare. An expatriate missionary once faced "deportation over claims that he instructed students not to wear traditional clothes" telling them it was sinful (Hiambohn 1982:3). He was investigated by the Minister for Religion, Women, Youth, and Recreation who stated that "people who come to Papua New Guinea should respect its culture."[12]

In this counter-discourse of good rural village versus evil Westernized city, contemporary social ills are *not* caused by noble tradition but, in fact, are the effects of civilization and development (see Narokobi 1983:36–37). The Department of Tourism's Five Year Cultural Plan warns of the dangers of civilization: "The current threat to the nation is bad western culture and its proliferation through both print and electronic media ... Disco, beer and pornographic materials are some of the bad elements of Western Culture that seems [sic] to be seeping with ease through our cultural fabric" (Beona et al. 1988:7–8). Disco, beer, and pornographic materials are, in fact, the most powerful symbolic elements of evil urban life—partly because each is widely appreciated by young urbanites.

Given the national discourse's focus on traditional dance, disco and other forms of western dancing loom as particularly dangerous.[13] AIDS and today's gamut of sexually transmitted diseases also powerfully symbolize the dangers of pornography and Western cultural penetration. One letter to the editor makes this point:

> In the old times in PNG before Europeans came, people in the Highlands were very strict with young boys and girls ... Sexual offences were prevented. Men were taught that early marriage could make them weak ... social (sexually transmitted) diseases were few in the olden days, before the 'K2 Meris' [two dollar prostitutes]. Many of the beliefs and practices of our forefathers are still of value to us today and should not be forgotten or discarded. We need to re-adopt many of our earlier customs, beliefs and attitudes (Lisse 1989).

Simple traditional *singsings* oppose fancy disco, and safe traditional sex confronts deadly Western perversions.

People use a discourse of good tradition versus bad civilization to comment on and attempt to manage the country's new mass media. This has been a local topic of concern in that, in the 1980s, two Australian media corporations gained licenses to begin television broadcasting. (One soon pulled out of the market.) Earlier commentary had also warned of the dangers of radio and cinema in spreading alien, Western, consumerist values (e.g., Narokobi 1980:223–227; Toro 1984). The question now became what to do about foreign dominated television. Prime Minister Paias Wingti, for example, warned:

> There are few values in life that no money can buy. These are culture and language. Our cultures and languages are simply too precious for us to allow television to operate in Papua New Guinea without strict policy guidelines. We ought to be wary of its likely impact on our people, our nation ... Rather than allow foreign culture to come in and cover us like a blanket through television, we could use television to celebrate and strengthen our national culture (1986:9; see also Noga 1986).[14]

The message of evil modernity versus good custom is also common in PNG literary work, such as in two verses of Baluwe Umetrifo's poem "Yupela Meri i Senis Hariap Pinis" [you women are changing too fast] (Powell 1987:84). Like Enos' poem, "New Guinea," this too has evaluatively contrasting verses, only here it is the bad city against the good village:

> Not long ago I used to go up the Heklaka hill.
> When I looked below over the green valley
> I could see smoke popping up here and there—
> From amongst the jar trees and kunai grass,
> And I could see you young girls
> Working very hard in your gardens,
> In your traditional pulpuls
> With pig grease reflecting in the sun
> From your beautiful skin.
>
> But now
> When I go up the Heklaka hill
> And look below over the beautiful valley
> I can see grey smoke popping out of mills and factories
> From among the huge ugly lumps of metal
> And I can see you young girls
> In blue jeans and jackets
> With high heel shoes and stinky perfumes
> Purses in one hand and newspapers in the other.
> As you walk from shop to shop gardening
> With your breasts sweating in the breast bags.

The green valley is endangered by the ugly metaled city; the innocent girl by the painted hussy; and traditional gardening by the cash economy. Nationalist discourse works to sustain the positivity of shared culture by locating this within (urbanized) people's sentimental feelings about their rural, village pasts. It thus reverses the problematic of developmental discourse: the issue is not to modernize the hinterlands, but to make the city into the village.[15]

UNITY IN CULTURAL DIVERSITY

These evaluative dualities between tradition, on the one hand, and Christianity, civilization, or development, on the other, warp nationalist uses of culture. Definition of culture is especially troublesome where tradition is imprisoned within comparative relations with modernity so that it stands to the latter as either primitive forerunner or antithesis. The plurality of customary practices throughout PNG also makes shared culture slippery to define. Talk that says "we are special and unique Papua New Guineans because we all have culture" must rely on a generalized core meaning of tradition and on a vaguely defined cultural content (see Keesing 1982:299; Tonkinson 1982:304; Wolfers 1982:89). To domesticate cultural diversity, people must seek out or invent commonalities in customary lifestyles to highlight and celebrate.

While everyone in PNG has cultural traditions, these are often very different in content. It is perhaps more of a challenge here than anywhere else to put culture to work for the construction of common sentiments of shared national identity (see Chowning 1986). Traditional ways of life ranged from monogamy to polygamy; from patrilineality to matrilineality; from economies based on agriculture to those based on fishing, hunting and gathering, or trade; from chiefly polities to more egalitarian "big-man" systems; from densely populated village communities to scattered family residences; and from high mountain habitats over 16,000 feet to seaside ecologies.

Attempts have been made to domesticate PNG's cultural diversity both institutionally and rhetorically. Institutionally, upon independence, the state recognized 19 provincial governments, descending in part from the colonial administrative districts (Wolfers 1982). This decentralization, in theory, would both permit, and regulate, self-government by the country's diverse regions. Rhetorically, many have suggested making a virtue out of cultural diversity itself. Former Governor-General

Sir Kingsford Dibela tried this tack: "The last ten years of our independence have proved that 'unity is possible in diversity.' Diversity is an important tool for unity" (1985:23; see Minol 1987:165; Samana 1988:57; Narokobi 1976:14; 1983:107).

Perhaps so—but one must use this tool carefully and watch that it does not get out of hand. The provincial system, and the rhetorical frame "unity in diversity," both attempt to encompass difference so that this may play out safely within the limits of imagining the nation in culturalist terms. Neither has been entirely successful, as indicated by an ongoing rebellion of secessionists in PNG's North Solomons Province. Here, the Bougainville Republican (or Revolutionary) Army began fighting for the independence of that Province in 1989; and, as of 1994, the central government had not yet reestablished control over large areas of southern Bougainville.

One of the earliest and most influential readings of shared PNG culture is Bernard Narokobi's "The Melanesian Way" (1980). Narokobi once noted "I am often asked, 'what is the Melanesian Way?' but I refuse to define the Melanesian Way for a variety of reasons" (1980:16). In actuality, he defines this again and again in his writings as a set of unique cultural attributes that unite all Papua New Guineans. These attributes include peaceful and consensual practices of conflict resolution, a spiritual awareness of cosmic harmony, an innovative openness to social change, and an appreciation of diversity (1980:14–16); or again, close human relations, cooperation and mutual support, and self-reliance (1980:27–31); or again, "communal spirit, mass participation, food and gifts sharing, pride, dignity, proof of one's maturity, expressions of yearning for a better future ... thanksgiving to the spirits" (1977:14); and yet again, "The fundamental unity of Melanesians in PNG, for example, is rooted in a traditional non-literate, wood and stone, largely agricultural civilization centered around the family, the clan, the village or the tribe, usually from a common ancestor" (1983:105).

Other people have taken up this task, devising similar lists of positive shared cultural traits. Anthropologist Iamo (1988:7) includes kinship, reciprocity, and communal consensus and participation. Filmmaker Toro (1984:78) lists great diversity, artistic expression, spiritual energy, a strong work ethic, dance, multilingualism, and the *wantok* system. Jawodimbari, a former Secretary of the Dept. of Culture and Tourism, enumerates: "leadership through seniority, achievement and being able to provide the needy with their daily provision of food and meet, respect for the elders, communal efforts in making gardens, building houses, hunting and fishing. Everyone believed in the spirits of the dead" (1985b:27). The particular shared cultural traits that get listed, of course, are those that best serve the nationalist discourse's focus on unity and stability. The Melanesian Way purposely overlooks a lot of other cultural practices. Few would make a virtue of clan warfare, segmentary and fissiparous kinship systems, polygamy, "cargo" movements, and so on.

Furthermore, this is a *conscious* construction of shared culture. Narokobi, warning of the dangers of alien ideologies, or "isms," says "a unique Melanesian 'ISM' needs to be developed" (1983:28). Kolia lauds former Prime Minister Somare's "important point that our people must discover what they have in common, an approach sometimes very different to that of foreign anthropologists who have in the past tended to emphasise differences rather than similarities" (1978:2). Toro looks for "the gradual merger of all the peoples into a land with only minor regional differences" (1984:78; see also Talyaga 1975:39).[16] And Iamo observes:

> While Papua New Guinea might be glued together by Western social, political, legal and economic infrastructure, it is a country divided by cultural heterogeneity and political regionalism. In order to achieve a degree of social equilibrium and organic solidarity, we need a national culture which, first, will provide a measure

of consensus among diverse peoples and, second, will be capable of remaining flexible and subject to change with time and space so it does not become infinite nor indispensable (1988:5).

He goes on to recognize, however, that this task "is an arduous puzzle" that requires "defining a culture unique to Papua New Guinea, drawing from diverse cultures yet without encouraging regionalism" (1988:5).

The overt construction of a shared culture is open to local criticism. Some of this criticism has noted the contradiction in constructing an acceptable definition of shared culture applicable throughout PNG in order to promote national unity and identity, while at the same time claiming that this primordial commonality has always been there. Also, the obvious constructedness and reification of these images of shared tradition leaves them open to charges of inauthenticity (see commentary in the second half of Narokobi 1980). People working within the discourse, however, neatly sidestep this latter sort of criticism by arguing that local cultures have never been static: that there is nothing more culturally authentic in PNG than experimenting with and improving one's traditions (see Narokobi 1980:15; Jawodimbari 1985:27).

As noted above, this constructed definition of shared culture rotates around rural village life where people live together successfully. In the village, people must cooperate economically, social control procedures work most of the time, kinship and marriage conjoin families, and the ancestral spirits are a hovering presence. Almost everyone in PNG shares some village experience. They either still live in a village, or maintain at least vestigial links back to a village home. Narokobi writes "The Melanesian village must be maintained as a basic social unit from which individuals will find meaning. Towns, cities, industries must be 'villagised'" (1983:8; see also 1983:60 65; 1980: 27–31, 57–61; Waiko 1976; Samana 1988:49). The importance of the rural and village perspective within nationalist discourse is also apparent in the ubiquitous use of the term "grassroots" throughout PNG by people "who wish to place themselves in opposition to the 'elite', including some who actually belong to it" (Filer 1985:165). Many letter-to-the-editor writers sign themselves "grassroots." This is also the name of a popular newspaper comic strip character (drawn by a European), a rural migrant who uses his wits to succeed in the urban jungle.

Although nationalist discourse finds its definition of shared culture in an idealized village, not all aspects of that culture are equally useful. Complex systems of kinship, village languages, pantheons of local deities, diverse initiation rituals, and so on might all be appreciated in principle but are discursively muted. How does one embody idealized village traditions such as consensus in decision making, generosity and sharing, or reliance on ancestral spirits? PNG's stress on cultural traditions, instead, mostly reveals itself in a focus on art (cf. Chua and Kuo, this volume). This, basically, comprises singing and dancing, body decoration, and carving. Artistic cultural diversity is not threatening, as other areas of traditional life might be. In fact, the more diversity here the better. Moreover, art efficiently displays, embodies, and represents the national discourse. It is interesting to look at. The dance contests, or *singsings* that have become important parts of national ceremonial life demonstrate that people still have traditions. Citizens are unified by sharing this sort of culture in public display. Art, of course, is also a kind of traditional knowledge that is easily detached from a cultural whole, and learnable and useable by people who are part of a globalized, urban elite, as Keesing (1989:31–32) has noted.

PNG's former Minister of Culture and Tourism summarized his job along these lines: "So the years went by, stimulating and encouraging our people to understand that culture was a way of expressing our own way of life through various forms of art that we were capable of performing. These include music, theatre development, graphic and traditional designs" (Kamod

1985:35). The ministry's recent Five Year Cultural Development Plan (1988) claims:
> It is now time to embark on a campaign to recover what has been lost—to stimulate cultural development so as to allow all of us to realise full potential as human beings; but, even more so, to ensure that our identity as Papua New Guineans are safeguarded ... governments have acknowledged the crucial role of culture as the inspiration and the life blood of our nation—giving it an identity, maintaining historical continuity and providing the basis for its future (Beona et al. 1988:9).

The plan's recommendations for "cultural development" focus entirely on the arts, e.g., "Papua New Guinea's cultural identity must be displayed in public places such as parks and gardens for the enjoyment of public and tourists. The objects for permanent exhibition in public areas shall include metal sculptures, totem poles and water fountains" (1988:29). In conjunction with the plan, former Prime Minister Namaliu proposed a tax break for buildings that incorporate traditional art objects and motifs. When it comes right down to it—when talk becomes action—nationalist discourse's focus on shared culture shrinks down to public celebrations of dance, carving, and architecture (see Narokobi 1976; Strathern 1985).

It is no accident that, since independence, PNG's departments of culture and of tourism have been united in the same ministry or commission. As Eoe, head of the National Museum, noted in a newspaper article entitled "Culture: It's as Good as Having Gold Reserves": "The National Museum alone holds the National Collection which is worth between K30 million-K40 million. This can be viewed in the same light as gold bullion reserves held in the Bank of Papua New Guinea, which of course could be used in the time of financial difficulties by the government of the day" (1985:31).

The embodiment of nationalist culture in art does double duty: it reminds people of their PNG identity; and it can be sold in the international marketplace as a tourist attraction, or as primitive art. This double duty entails certain contradictions, as Keesing (1989) and others observe—contradictions that are apparent in the term "primitive art" itself (see Jawodimbari 1985:27). Is it good or bad to be identified as "primitive?" Is it good or bad to market the carvings and dances that now also serve as the cultural icons of one's national identity? An artistic focus yields positive economic and tourist benefits, and also permits nationalist discourse to ignore other areas of culture that are not shared and possibly divisive, or that have been negatively construed within powerful, alien discourses. These definitions and evaluations of culture are not fixed, however. People continue to debate and remake them, as they use them strategically and politically.

CULTURAL POLICIES

The nationalist reliance upon culture as a language of identity and unity encourages the state to support programs and institutions that curate, preserve, develop, and market tradition. In 1973, before independence, the Australians promoted a Cultural Development Program, giving five million dollars to improve the National Museum, expand the National Arts School, and establish an Institute of Papua New Guinea Studies (Crawford 1977:28). Parliament created a National Cultural Council (in 1974) to oversee these enlarged institutions. Most of PNG's provincial governments have also established departments responsible for culture and tourism.

Once a connection is drawn between culture and identity, traditions must be managed—sometimes even saved or revitalized—to protect that identity. Cultural policy, as stated in PNG's cultural development plan, is concerned to "preserve and develop the culture of our people" (Beona et al. 1988:19; see Strathern 1985). In the terms of the discourse, social change and the adoption of new ways threaten the national self.[17] A nationalist valorization of tradition makes change in that tradition worrisome. Many people lament, in a tragic mode, that some of their traditions have disappeared, and that others might soon follow. Former Prime Minister Namaliu, in an introduction to a book of high school student line drawings entitled *Taim Bipo: The Disappearing Traditions and Practices of Papua New Guinea as Seen Through The Eyes of Young Sogeri Artists*, wrote, "The arts and cultures of the Pacific region are under threat—perhaps even face extinction ... These beautiful pen and ink drawings ... show us that the young people of the country look to many of the cultural and artistic values of their tumbuna with understanding and affection. May we all hope that they will play their part in preserving our heritage" (Taylor 1988:np). Here again, traditions survive as art, if not in reality.[18] Students preserve culture by drawing pictures of local spirits, traditional fishing and hunting practices, and so on.[19]

Perhaps an authentic cultural identity, moreover, demands that abandoned practices be revived (see Wari 1980:110). Talyaga, along these lines, worried about whether or not to bring back traditional male initiation rites among the Enga—especially urbanized Enga like himself: "Should we revive our culture? How should we do it? Would it have any relevance to a changing Papua New Guinea? If we revive it, can it last? And finally, is there a danger that regional cultural revivals will promote separatism" (1975:37; see also Crawford 1976, 1981)?

To celebrate and preserve tradition, the National Culture Council and other institutions concerned with culture and tourism encourage cultural appreciation in schools (Beona et al. 1988:22). At one time, the state also proposed that everyone wear his or her customary dress (or *bilas*, "flash," i.e. decorative finery) one day of the week. "Toana Day," something along the lines of Hawaii's "Aloha Friday," however, was not a success (Latukefu 1988:92) although urbanites do wear traditional dress on special occasions, such as school graduation ceremonies. The national and provincial governments also organize cultural displays during various fairs and shows. Here, custom beauty contests select the best looking, traditionally dressed girl, and dance groups from around the nation, or the province, compete amongst themselves, attempting to out-dance, and out-*bilas* the others.

This focus on customary dress within nationalist discourse sparks disputes. Here, in a small way, people advocate rival cultural policies based on their definitions of tradition. After one dance group charged a rival Tolai team of wearing nontraditional dress, an affronted Tolai wrote:

> I would like to stress my anger on what Traditional Mangi of Hagen said on August 17. I will tell you right now on behalf of my Tolai people that since the pioneer missionaries came to our beautiful islands, only the way of dressing had been changed and even though we dress like that when we still perform our singsings. Like other people of this country, we have many traditional cultures and so on. And wearing laplaps [lavalavas] and blouses is our way of dress. Please mind your own business and stop criticising another's way of dressing and traditional cultures (Takene 1984:4).[20]

To defuse these custom contests and to underline the connection being drawn between diverse cultural traditions and nationality, the Department of Culture and Tourism's 1988 Five Year Plan demanded that public dance displays no longer be presented as competitions: "All National and Provincial festivals incorporating either traditional dancing or purely cultural show must be authentic and the costumes used must be traditional. No competitive judgement is allowed, but all groups taking part must be considered as winners" (Beona et al. 1988:31). Some people, however, still find hollow ironies in these attempts to save or revive tradition by turning this into art.[21] Others comment on the irony of university graduates, most of whom will seek work in government or commercial institutions, dressing themselves up in custom *bilas* to receive their diplomas.

Talk about culture, like any nationalist discourse, sustains a set of definitions and evaluations within a state that relate directly to questions of power. The position of ruling groups in large part depends on the popular consumption of a sense of identity that fixes the legitimacy of state powers and citizen responsibilities. Talk about culture functions to legitimize and sustain ruling groups in power within that imagined community. Nationalist tradition, in particular, has a "conservative function" in that it conveys a mandate from the past, as Linnekin notes (1989:151; see also Rodman 1987; Philibert 1986; Keesing 1989:37). The old, for example, evoke tradition in ways that work to justify their powers over the young. As urbanized youths join gangs and increasingly make serious trouble, older people talk louder about traditional values of obedience and respect (see Jawodimbari 1985:31). Men, too, talk about culture in ways that maintain their powers over women. Some of this we have heard already: gang rape is not so bad because at least it is traditional; bride price is laudatory because it prevents divorce (see Filer 1985:172–173); women's breasts must remain available to public gaze during neo-traditional events despite newer, troubling urban discourses of pornography. Cultural nationalism may assert itself against the uppity Westernized women, as Zimmer-Tamakoshi has noted: "By publicly supporting a myth of chaste and selfless village women contrasting with sexually promiscuous Westernized women living in selfish abundance in town, Papua New Guinea's male leadership has contributed to the marginalization of the national women's movement" (1993:62).

The remaining stanzas of Umetrifo's poem (Powell 1987:84) stake such claims:

> Oh *yupela i senis hariap pinis*! [Oh you are changing quickly!]
> Not long ago your names used to be Urakume, Mohoe and Ilaie

You never looked at boys nor talked to them
Always eyes were on the ground
With *bilums* [netbags] on your heads.

But now
All your names have changed
To Marys, Bettys, Jennys and Roses
And you go around hand in hand
With your *mangi poroman* [boyfriends] without *bilums*
Oh *yupela ol meri i winim*
Pinis misis Queen! [Oh you girls pretend to be the Queen!]
Na yu Goroka, yu laik winim Tokyo and New York!
[And you Goroka, you want to surpass Tokyo and New York!]

Narokobi once argued, "There's no need for women's lib here, because Melanesian women are already equal" (1980:70). In response, one young woman letter writer pointed out some of the problems that educated PNG women face, and went on to note "I am glad that Western civilization is getting deeper and deeper into our country and slowly stopping men like you dreaming of a Melanesian way of life" (Narokobi 1980:248; see also Latukefu 1988:84–85). This produced a spate of hostile responses from both men and women in defense of tradition. Such appeal to the Melanesian Way muffles and depreciates, as non-traditional, challenges to urban gender inequality—much of which, as Zimmer-Tamakoshi notes, is a recent artifact of economic and political transformation in PNG. It is no surprise that cultural nationalist rhetoric serves ruling power structures within PNG's families as well as those of the state.

But the same kind of culturalist talk, slanted a different way, can also legitimize claims vis-a-vis the state, particularly those of regional groups. If shared custom legitimizes an independent political state, smaller regional, provincial, or local groups with far more obviously common traditions can use the same discourse to imagine their own autonomy. The state's acceptance of decentralization of authority in the form of regional provinces, moreover, can have untoward consequences, insofar as political and administrative decentralization "provide[s] the infrastructure for effective secession" (Wolfers 1982:91).

When nationalist discourse fails to generate unificatory national sentiments, talk about separatism and regional differences may slip through. People may adopt culturalist language of nationality generated in Port Moresby, and bend this to different ends. For example, when politician Josephine Abaijah was not elected as PNG's new Governor-General in 1988 by the Parliament, she voiced her disappointment in regionalist terms: "She said that as Far as the Papuans are concerned, the whole country is ruled by the Niuginians. 'In the past, I used to say that one day we would be over-run and now the day has come. Today our unity has been killed'" (Tannos 1988:1).

Others cite tradition to slow or prevent development of their lands, and to claim a greater compensation or share of development profits from a state government that is desperate for funds. In the most extreme case, they may cite tradition to withdraw from the state itself. That state cannot deny their customary claims without undermining its own discursive reliance on culture for purposes of national identity and unity. The state would not have to face this problem, at least in these terms, if its nationalist discourse had focused instead on modernization and discounted tradition as worthless and old-fashioned.

Separatist discourse, like nationalist discourse, builds on talk of land, shared place, and cultural traditions. PNG is experiencing a boom in mining and oil exploration, and local people invoke their own readings of culture in troublesome disputes over the distribution of royalty and lease payments. For example, regionalist claims and armed attacks by determined local land owners have terminated the operation of the country's largest copper and gold mine on Bougainville Island which once provided 17 percent of the state's budget. Bougainville Islanders invoked traditional compensation practices to justify their rebellion: "The custom here is that when I or my animals (pigs, dogs, etc.) damage something I must restore or compensate the person(s) who suffer as a result" (Aksilly 1988:10). They criticized the mine and the state for violating "the Melanesian style of friendship" (True National 1988:10). Given the widespread culturalist language of nationality, people in PNG can adopt the discourse, turn it, and use it strategically against state elites by accusing them of nontraditionalism. The letter writer, above, is the "true" national—not state functionaries. If an authentic PNG identity requires one to appreciate custom, then the position of ruling elites is undermined if they can be talked about as being deculturated.

This slippage within nationalist discourse allows criticism of an over-Westernized urban elite. Such complaints took an interesting form in late 1988 when rumors of a locally produced pornographic movie swept through Port Moresby. A police constable, charged with having a copy of *Yokohama Mama* in his desk drawer, claimed in Magistrate's Court that he also had a second pornographic video called *Lakatoi* (a traditional Motu sailing canoe). Although this had mysteriously disappeared during his arrest, the constable nonetheless listed a number of male and female police officials, other civil servants, and prominent politicians as starring in the video. As is typical of urban folklore elsewhere in the world, many people claimed relatives and acquaintances who they were sure had seen the video, although no one admitted to have seen it personally. One letter writer observed:

> It is true that "blue" movies have been made of some national leaders taking part in explicit sex acts. These tapes have been circulated among a lot of people yet no one has been brave enough to stand up and challenge the makers and the actors and actresses in these stupid videos... How can the leaders who acted in blue movies preach to the grass roots about moral ethics when they themselves are the promoters of evil acts?

... The leaders concerned know who they are and should be ashamed of themselves (Kuro 1988:10).

The rumored list of participants reached truly orgiastic proportions. Prime Minister Namaliu suspended the five civil servants the constable named in court, although these later were quietly reinstated when no video surfaced. The likelihood is that a desperate police constable spun out a story of sex in high places to distract the court from his own charge. The nationalist discourse that valorizes culture to imagine the community, however, made these charges believable, exciting, and strategically useful. A mob of youths and rascal gang members, carrying signs demanding customary sexual purity, marched on the Boroko police station besieging the men inside. A teargas barrage and police charge sparked a small riot, as young demonstrators scattered through the shopping district throwing stones and breaking windows. Other sporadic damage and attacks on stores and vehicles occurred in downtown Port Moresby.

Political elites who evoke traditional values may suffer the consequences of their sermons. This becomes also the discourse in which their position is impeached. If the elite can be talked about as engaged in videotaped and perverted Westernized sex, then their claims to lead the nation are undermined. They lose the right to "preach to the grass roots." People's own reconstructions of tradition here both extend and subvert the official nationalist discourse. Culturalist discourse in PNG, thus, delimits multiple identities. Talk of shared culture can identify at once the villager, the provincial, and the citizen. Where culture bounds the nation, moreover, alternative definitions and evaluations of that culture can either argue for, or undermine, the legitimacy of the state.

Despite Papua New Guinea's provisory and not always successful attempts since 1975 to imagine a national community emerging from its inconstant, plural, and variable cultures, the state still endures having lost, perhaps, only parts of one of its original provinces. Although notions of a national community within PNG may be hazy, the country may nonetheless maintain its integrity without a convincing or pervasive rhetoric of common national identity for several reasons. These include the state's function as a conduit of international aid; the lack of significant competition from other political groups, except for the Bougainville Revolutionary Army; its minor demands on citizens, by way of taxes, national services, or the like; and plain institutional inertia. Multinational attempts in the 1990s to put back together Bosnia and Somalia suggest that states retain important external and internal functions despite the fact that the imagined national community has mostly evaporated.

These instances hint that the link between nation and state is here and there disintegrating. A state may now be legitimated less by the deep yearnings in the hearts of some people, and more by its position within multinational orders and its political and economic functions therein. Papua New Guinea's difficulties with a culturalist (or any other) discourse of nationality might suggest that it is a post-nationalist state (see Larmour 1992b). As volatile relations between state and nation erupt in Eastern Europe, one might look to Papua New Guinea and other excolonial, perhaps post-nationalist states. The multiple nations and identities within a new United States of Europe, should this really now fully develop, and reconfigurations of the confederated nations once controlled by the U.S.S.R., will share Papua New Guinea's challenge to imagine national identity from amidst a diverse and sometimes devalued assortment of ancestral cultural fashions.

NOTES

1. An earlier version of this paper was presented to an East-West Center conference on Cultural Policy and National Identity, in June of 1990. I would like to thank the participants at the conference and others, including Amy Burce, Virginia Dominguez, Wari Iamo, Jacob Simet, Lynn Thomas, Geoffrey White, and several anonymous readers for helpful criticism of the paper.

2. See Foster (1992) and Schwartz (1993) for analyses of village-level understandings of tradition in Papua New Guinea.
3. This explains some of the conflict that national elites have with anthropology and journalism in particular. Anthropology and journalism offer alternative pictures of PNG culture that may threaten its functions and place within nationalist discourse.
4. Tok Pisin is much less valued, for example, than Vanuatu's Bislama. Despite British hostility, the joint French presence in that country expanded Pidgin's range of utility and maintained some of its linguistic value, particularly in that many of the French delighted in using Bislama when speaking to their fellow British colonialists.
5. Letters to the editor that evoke regional character are not uncommon. For example:
> Highlanders are indeed a pain. They seem to be the most senseless of all the ethnic groups in PNG. It is a relief to be able to board a PMV [public motor vehicle, i.e., bus] in Port Moresby crewed by Momase or Papuan people. They have a great sense of responsibility towards passengers (we do value life, don't we!), are more courteous and polite and above all have a lot of common sense about their conduct in public ... I have heard some of the dirtiest things said to teenage schoolgirls by Highlands PMV drivers who disputed the normal children's fare the girls tried to pay. One is led to wonder if they have a sense of decency or any moral standards (Civilised 1988:8).
6. Meg Taylor, PNG's new ambassador to the United States, has also completed a trek, tracing her Australian father's pioneering patrol of colonially unexplored Highlands regions. This trek was filmed and the film exhibited in PNG.
7. To a university class I assigned the essay topic, "Comment on the role of tradition in Papua New Guinea society today. Do you think that *ol Pasin bilong ol tumbuna* can help economic and political development or do they slow it down?" The students had as many negative as positive things to say about their cultural traditions.
8. By way of comparison, in Vanuatu people have talked away most contradictions between custom and Christianity (see Tonkinson 1982; Lindstrom 1982). These are now deemed to be basically compatible.
9. The same genealogy is apparent in outraged letters to the editor that followed the Secretary for the Department of Culture and Tourism's use of an unfortunate metaphor to describe tourism development. The spokesman's comment was "The tourism industry in this country is still a virgin. It needs to be raped" (Smith 1988:10).

10. Sedi interviewed a number of Port Moresby residents who both appreciated and condemned the system, as does this letter: "The wantok system and favoritism in approving and paying out loan, refund and/or withdrawal applications is deeply rooted in this office. All applications should be treated on a first-come first-served basis" (Disgruntled Didiman 1988:10).
11. A letter to the editor complains: "Churches have a lot to answer for the dying culture and beliefs of PNG society. These churches should bow and confess to the people of PNG for the damage they have caused" (Manang 1980:4).
12. This dispute presented the newspapers a chance to write creative headlines ("Make A Clean Breast Of Our Culture Says Expert"; "Ban Pornography But Hands Off Our Bare Breasts"). The opposition education spokesman, however, suggested that the missionary had a point: "If the mission worker refers to his feelings that young girls bare-breasted will attract immoral attentions rather than cultural ones, then I am afraid I have to agree ... foreign lifestyle has changed our thinking, permeated our society and distorted our former cultural perspectives" (*Post-Courier* 1982:2).
13. One letter writer observes: "Every weekend the village leaders put on a hot disco for the public. Everybody, especially the youngsters, go in and start dancing with a bottle in one hand. I think they are setting a very bad example to the younger ones by putting on these fancy discos rather than our simple traditional singsing" (Watts T. 1984:4).
14. However, when Em-TV, the remaining station, did try to incorporate a few "traditionalist" elements in its presentation, it encountered criticism for "looking down" on local culture:
> the programmes are mostly from the Western countries ... the only time when PNG is reflected is through every intervals when the song called, Lukim Em TV i Namba Wan" is telecasted. But ... telecasting a mudman dancing in a ceremonial rite does not really suit [the] times. It presumably gives a wrong image of PNG to other countries ... PNG has developed this far and we should be proud to reflect the image of our contemporary society as much as possible in any media. Our traditional arts and cultures are only remnants of our past and they are preserved by the cultural authorities in the right way and on right occasions (Sebea 1988:12).
15. This, however, does not play as well back in the villages themselves, where many spokesmen say they would be happy to put up with some of the evils of modernity—asking only that more development please be sent their way.

16. Other critics, however, fear a hegemonic Melanesian Way should this ever take off, and its effects on cultural diversity. Minol argues:
    > Personally I believe there is no urgency to create a new ideology or philosophy or Melanesian way. I would rather allow the present trend to continue where diverse Melanesian cultures change, evolve, develop as they have been doing all along. What the prophets of Melanesia should be doing is encouraging unity from this diversity and not forging a new composite philosophy of the Melanesian way. Who am I to tell the rest of Melanesia what is Melanesian or not Melanesian? (1987:164–165).
17. Justifying a proposal to support local filmmaking, for example, Toro writes: "With this progress, Papua New Guineans gradually and systematically began to disregard the old ways; unknowingly accepting his master's strange culture and tradition, and hence Papua New Guinea started losing its identity and its image became twisted internally and abroad" (1984:76; see also Kolia 1978).
18. Significantly, forwarding the discourse's claims of unity in art, a newspaper account of the book's launching describes its cover: "The figures have been cleverly drawn so that they are immediately recognisable as Papua New Guinean, but not from any particular area" (Senge 1988c:22).
19. Similar concerns were expressed in the University of Papua New Guinea's 18th Waigani Seminar, which met in September, 1988. This seminar, named The State of the Arts in the Pacific, "was organised for Pacific Islanders to discuss the fate of their artistic culture and the composite vitality of their local, national and regional cultures in face of the advanced scientific and technological invasion" (Sukwianomb 1988:2). Again, tradition is largely synonymous with art.
20. Another letter writer, in similar vein, blasted money-raising activities during the 1988 Morobe Province Show:
    > I want to share my concern about something that happens every year at the Morobe Show. I'm not happy about some Buang groups because they don't present their ancestral ways at the Show. They only put on games from overseas countries, like ring tossing games and bursting balloons. You people use this kind of game just to take away other people's money. Can you tell me that this kind of game comes from your ancestors or not? I think you should be very ashamed ... What's the purpose of a show? Is a show supposed to exhibit foreign ways? I think you should abandon this rubbish practice and give up your display space to other people who can exhibit proper kinds of business and the ways of the ancestors (Kole 1988:10 [my translation]).

21. One letter to the editor complained:
    On the subject of deteriorating traditional customs, I think politicians and concerned Papua New Guineans are wasting worthwhile time grumbling over spilt milk. What is there to be done about the traditional lifestyle of a society that is fast westernising? What is there to be done about leaders of such societies voting to talk, eat and act western? For the delight of those PNG leaders trying to preserve traditional lifestyle and culture, by decorating buildings with carvings and organising once a year traditional shows, my congratulations. But what more is there to the carvings and Mekeo dances? Nothing (Mas 1984:4).

REFERENCES

Anderson, Benedict (1991). *Imagined Communities: Reflections on the Origin and Spread of Nationalism* (Revised edition). London: Verso.
Askilly, Luke (1988). People's Cause is Just. *Post-Courier* (December 7):10.
Bengi, Manga (1988). Word of Advice for "Judges." *Post-Courier* (December 28):15.
Beona, Gerald, et al. (1988). *Five Year Cultural Development Plan. 1990–1994.* Port Moresby: Papua New Guinea Department of Culture and Tourism.
Centurion, Diosnel (1989). A Missionary's Battle for Peace Amongst Warring Tribes. *The Times of PNG* (January 12–18):3.
Chowning, Ann (1986). The Development of Ethnic Identity and Ethnic Stereotypes on Papua New Guinea Plantations. *Journal de la Société des Océanistes* 82/83:153–162.
Civilised (1988). Highlander Road Hogs. *Post-Courier* (November 28):8.
Crawford, A. L. (1976). *Artistic Revival Among the Gogodala.* Discussion Paper No. 14. Port Moresby: Institute of Papua New Guinea Studies.
— (1977). *The National Cultural Council: Its Aims and Functions, with Guidelines for Establishing and Operating Cultural Centres within Papua New Guinea.* Port Moresby: National Cultural Council.
— (1981). *AIDA: Life and Ceremony of Gogodala.* Bathurst (AUS): Robert Brown and Associates with the National Cultural Council of Papua New Guinea.
Dibela, Sir Kingsford (1985). Many Cultures Forming One Nation. *Post-Courier* (September 11):23.
Disgruntled Didiman (1988). Improve Services. *Post-Courier* (December 1):10.
Eoe, Soroi Marepo (1985). Culture: It's As Good As Having Gold Reserves, So Funds Should Not Be Cut Back. *Post-Courier* (September 11):31.
Filer, Colin (1985). What is This Thing Called "Brideprice"? *Mankind* 15:163–183.

Finney, Ben, R. (1973). *Big-Men and Business: Entrepreneurship and Economic Growth in the New Guinea Highlands*. Honolulu: University Press of Hawaii.
Foster, Robert (1992). Commoditization and the Emergence of Kastom as a Cultural Category: A New Ireland Case in Comparative Perspective. *Oceania* 62:284–294.
Gam, Getake, S. (1988). A Chance for Reconciliation. *Post-Courier* (December 23):26.
Ghai, Yash (1985). Land Regimes and Paradigms of Development: Reflections on Melanesian Constitutions. *International Journal of the Sociology of Law* 13:393–405.
Guise, John (1989). Air Niugini Announcements Need a Change. *The Times of PNG* (January 12–18):10.
Hiambohn, Wally (1982). Preacher Is Facing Sack: Row Over Costumes. *Post-Courier* (November 25):3.
Iamo, Wari (1988). Culture in Papua New Guinea Nationalism. Unpublished ms.
Jawodimbari, Arthur (1985). How To Encourage Cultural Growth. *Post-Courier* (September 11):27, 31.
John, Charlie, E. K. (1988). Speaking Language. *New Nation* (Dec./Jan.):11.
Kadiba, John (1987). In Search of a Melanesian Theology. In G. W. Trompf, Ed. *The Gospel Is Not Western*. Maryknoll: Orbis Books, pp. 139–147.
Kamod, Paul (1985). Our Way of Life! We Can Be Proud of Our Own Identity. *Post-Courier* (September 11):35.
Keesing, Roger, M. (1982). Kastom in Melanesia: An Overview. *Mankind* 13:297–301.
— (1989). Creating the Past: Custom and Identity in the Contemporary Pacific. *Contemporary Pacific* 1:19–42.
Kemba, B. (1987). Culture Prevails. *The Times of PNG* (August 27–September 2):9.
Kili, Peter (1988). "Cannibals" Claim Angers Chimbus. *Post-Courier* (July 18):2.
Kole, Marsem (1988). So Bilong Olgeta Pipel. *Wantok* (December 8–14):10.
Kolia, John (1978). *Preservation and Further Development of Cultural Values in Papua New Guinea*. Discussion Paper No. 40. Port Moresby: Institute of Papua New Guinea Studies.
Kros, Peter (1975). *"A Certain Foreign Cult Called Christianity": Do We Need It?* Discussion Paper No. 3. Port Moresby: Institute of Papua New Guinea Studies.
Kuro, Renata (1988). Confront The Porn-Brokers. *Post-Courier* (December 7):10.

Larmour, Peter (1992a). The Politics of Race and Ethnicity: Theoretical Perspectives on Papua New Guinea. *Pacific Studies* 15:87–108.
— (1992b). States and Societies in the Pacific Islands. *Pacific Studies* 15:99–121.
Latukefu, Sione (1972). The Place of Tradition in Modernization: An Islander's View. *Journal of the Papua New Guinea Society* 6(2):3–12.
— (1988). Noble Traditions and Christian Principles as National Ideology in Papua New Guinea: Do Their Philosophies Complement or Contradict Each Other? *Pacific Studies* 11:83–96.
Lindstrom, Lamont (1982). Leftamap Kastom: The Political History of Tradition on Tanna (Vanuatu). *Mankind* 13:316–329.
Linnekin, Jocelyn (1989). The Politics of Culture in the Pacific. In J. Linnekin and L. Poyer, Eds. *Cultural Identity and Ethnicity in the Pacific*. Honolulu: University of Hawaii Press, pp. 149–174.
Lisse, Yamiwe (1989). Strict Customs in Traditional Society. *Niugini Nius*.
Ludwick, K. K. (1989). Where Were the Cannibals? *Post-Courier* (January 6):10.
Manang, A. (1980). A Religion of Ethnic Origin? *Post-Courier* (September 2):4.
Mannan, M. A. (1976). *The Wantok System: Its Implications for Development in Papua New Guinea: Reinterpreting an Old Value for a New Development*. Discussion Paper No. 16. Port Moresby: Institute of Papua New Guinea Studies.
Mas, S. (1984). Modern PNG Life. *Post-Courier* (August 7):4.
Merimba, Iagai (1988). Official Protest. *Post-Courier* (July 25):10.
Minol, Bernard (1987). Melanesian Way? In Ganga Powell, Ed. *Through Melanesian Eyes*. Melbourne: Macmillan, pp. 164–166.
Muke, John (1985). Access and Identity or Axes of Identity. *Yagl-Ambu* 12(2):61–66.
Narokobi, Bernard (1976). Art and Nationalism. *Gigibori: A Magazine of Papua New Guinea Cultures* 3(1):12–15.
— (1977). Our Melanesian Identity: Forward. In A. L. Crawford, Ed. *The National Cultural Council*. Port Moresby: National Cultural Council, pp. 14–16.
— (1980). *The Melanesian Way: Total Cosmic Vision of Life*. Boroko: Institute of Papua New Guinea Studies.
— (1983). *Life and Leadership in Melanesia*. Suva: Institute of Pacific Studies.
Noga, Bedero G. (1986). Keeping Culture at the Expense of Freedom? *Times of PNG* (July 4):8.
Patriot (1988). Rioters. *Post-Courier* (December 16):10.
Philibert, Jean-Marc (1986). The Politics of Tradition: Toward A Generic Culture in Vanuatu. *Mankind* 16:1–12.
Podolefsky, Aaron (1984). Contemporary Warfare in the New Guinea Highlands. *Ethnology* 23:73–87.

Pokawin, Polonhou S. (1987). Interaction between Indigenous and Christian Traditions. In G. W. Trompf, Ed. *The Gospel is Not Western*. Maryknoll: Orbis Books, pp. 23–31.

Poor Student (1989). Paying the Price of a Holiday Romance. *Post-Courier* (January 6):26.

Post-Courier (Port Moresby)

— (1980). Tradition "Harmful." (December 16):15.

— (1982). Make A Clean Breast Of Our Culture Says Expert. (November 5):2.

Powell, Ganga (1987). *Through Melanesian Eyes: An Anthropology of Papua New Guinea Writing*. Melbourne: Macmillan.

Richardson, Paul (1987). Traditional Religion Makes Impact. *The Times of PNG* (August 27–September 2):15.

Rodman, Margaret (1987). *Masters of Tradition: Consequences of Customary Land Tenure in Longana, Vanuatu*. Vancouver: University of British Columbia Press.

Samana, Utula (1988). *Papua New Guinea: Which Way? Essays on Identity and Development*. North Carlton (AUS): Arena Publications.

Samarai Island Observer (1988). Chuck Out Chewers! *Post-Courier* (November 29):11.

Schieffelin, Edward, L. (1978). *The End of Traditional Music, Dance, and Body Decoration in Bosavi Papua New Guinea*. Discussion Paper Nos. 30–32. Port Moresby: Institute of Papua New Guinea Studies.

Sebea, Seri (1988). What's TV For? *Niugini Nius* (December 3):12.

Sedi, Johannez (1988). Wantok System: What Do They Say About It? *Niugini Nius* (December 20):48.

Senge, Frank (1988a). Bring Back Hawker: EX-MP. *Post-Courier* (July 18):2.

— (1988b). Chimbus Slammed As "Perverted Cannibals": Wild Claims in Child Custody Battle. *Post-Courier* (July 14):2.

— (1988c). Taim Bipo. *Post-Courier* (November 25):21–22.

Sissons, Jeffrey (1993). The Systematisation of Tradition: Maori Culture as a Strategic Resource. *Oceania* 64:97–116.

Smith, John, M. (1988). Sickening Statement. *Post-Courier* (July 25):10.

Somare, Michael (1991). Address to Pacific Sciences Congress, Honolulu, HI, May 1991.

Sowei, Elizabeth (1988). Christmas, PNG Style. *Post-Courier* (December 23):23.

Strathern, Andrew (1985). Cultural Development Since 1972. In P. King, W. Lee, and V. Warakai, Eds. *From Rhetoric to Reality?: Papua New Guinea's Eight Point Plan and National Goals After A Decade*. Waigani: University of Papua New Guinea Press, pp. 289–293.

Sukwianomb, Joseph (1988). *The State of the Arts in the Pacific.* Program of the 18th Waigani Seminar. Waigani: University of Papua New Guinea.
Schwartz, Theodore (1993). Kastom, Custom, and Culture: Conspicuous Culture and Culture-Constructs. *Anthropological Forum* 6:515–540.
Takene, Agu (1984). Tolai Way. *Post-Courier* (August 28):4.
Talyaga, Kundapen (1975). Should We Revive Initiation Rites in Enga Society? *Gigibori: A Magazine of Papua New Guinea Cultures* 2(2):37–41.
Tannos, Jonathan (1988). Our New Governor-General: It's Ignatius Kilage. *Niugini Nius* (December 3):1.
Taylor, Lance (1988). *Taim Bipo: The Disappearing Traditions and Practices of Papua New Guinea as Seen through the Eyes of Young Sogeri Artists.* Sogeri (PNG): Sogeri National High School.
Tonkinson, Robert (1982). Vanuatu Values: A Changing Symbiosis. *Pacific Studies* 5(2):44–63.
Toro, Albert (1984). Film and National Identity in PNG. *Bikmaus* 5(2):77–79.
Trompf, Garry, W. (1987). *The Gospel Is Not Western: Black Theologies and Reflections from the Southwest Pacific.* Maryknoll, NY: Orbis Books.
True National (1988). Consult the People. *Post-Courier* (December 21):10.
Waiko, John (1976). Komge Oro: Land and Culture or Nothing. *Gigibori: A Magazine of Papua New Guinea Cultures* 3(1):16–19.
— (1986). Oral Traditions Among the Binandere: Problems of Method in a Melanesian Society. *Journal of Pacific History* 21:21–38.
Wari, Kensak, R. (1980). The Function of the National Cultural Council in Co-ordinating Cultural Development in Papua New Guinea. In R. Edwards and J. Stewart, Eds. *Preserving Indigenous Cultures: A New Role for Museums.* Canberra: Australian Government Publication Service, pp. 110–117.
Watts T. (1984). Kiunga Disco. *Post-Courier* (August 28):4.
Wingti, Paias (1986). TV Must Be Used To Serve The Nation: No Money Can Buy Our Cultures and Languages. *Times of PNG* (August 8):9.
Wolfers, Edward, P. (1982). Aspects of Political Culture and Institution-Building in Melanesia: Constitutional Planning in Papua New Guinea and the Special Committee on Provincial Government in Solomon Islands. *Pacific Studies* 6(1):85–105.
Women and Law Committee (n.d.) *Wife-Beating is a Crime.* Public Information Leaflet No. 1. Boroko: Women and Law Committee.
Zimmer-Tamakoshi, Laura (1993). Nationalism and Sexuality in Papua New Guinea. *Pacific Studies* 16:61–98.

8

Cultural Diversity and Identity in Papua New Guinea: A Second Look

Wari Iamo and Jacob Simet

Lindstrom's chapter in this volume is representative of recent literature on nations and ethnic groups in the Pacific. The construction and maintenance of national identities and cultural policies has recently received considerable attention by Pacific scholars (Crocombe 1976; Foster 1991; Howard 1989; Keesing 1982, 1989; Lindstrom 1982 and 1994, current volume; Loiskandl 1988). In this essay, we note such attention but also seek to comment on it.

Roger Keesing argued in 1982 that the process of colonialism was crucial in forcing a new sort of self-conscious reflection about their cultures on the part of colonized peoples. He wrote that it was perhaps "only the circumstances of colonial invasion, where people have had to come to terms with their powerlessness and peripherality, that allow such externalization of culture as symbol" (1982:301).

Indeed this process can be evidenced in many cases from the colonial and postcolonial experiences of Pacific nations. The effects of this externalization of culture as symbol have been manifested in several cases in the usage of native customs as organizing principles in the formation of national governments. In Vanuatu, the Solomon Islands, and Fiji, notions of "kastom" and "tradition" have been incorporated into the political and administrative structure of the nation-state where they are used with hegemonic force in dealings with local communities (Lindstrom 1990, White 1992). Although the Melanesian nations of Papua New Guinea, the Solomon Islands, and Vanuatu have no dominant cultural groups, elites in these nations have employed overarching notions of custom and tradition in attempts to unite diverse peoples.

The specific characteristics of Papua New Guinea as it exists today make the construction of a national cultural identity a challenging task. Its small population of 3.5 million is the most culturally and linguistically diverse in the world. If one arrives at the number of different ethnic groups solely on the basis of language, Papua New Guinea could be estimated to have 700 to 1000 such groups. If groups that share linguistic traits yet are differentiated by other cultural factors were enumerated, one could arrive at a figure approaching tens of thousands of distinct groups. Many geopolitical boundaries were demarcated by the colonial administration and were either redesigned, continued or eliminated by the nation's governments in ways that further complicate any attempt to enumerate the nation's peoples.

COLONIALISM AND CULTURAL AWARENESS

The years of colonial rule prior to political independence saw Papua New Guineans becoming aware of their diverse cultures on a wider scale due to labor migration and the effects of electronic and print media that increased communication and interaction between the coastal regions and the highlands as well as between the mainland and the islands. Many early nationalists, like Bernard Narakobi, student activists John Kasaipwalova, John Waiko, Arthur Jowardimbari, Leo Hannet, and Kumalau Tawali began a literary campaign juxtaposing Melanesian nationalism against everything colonial and Western. More than anyone, Narakobi, in *Melanesian Voice*—a weekly forum in the *Post Courier* in the 1970's—and in other commentaries later incorporated in his book *The Melanesian Way* (1980, 1983) saw his mission as a philosopher and critic of colonialism. He sought to influence the thoughts of many peoples, including those of Papua New Guinea, the Solomon Islands, Vanuatu, Fiji and New Caledonia. He wrote:

> Some people say this nation of ours will be united through parliament, public service, roads, bridges, armed forces and the like. I say maybe, maybe not. The one thing that can unite us is ideology or philosophy. My writing may be no more than meandering. They may be romantic or even apologetic. But I make no apology. Every race, every nation needs an ideology or a philosophy. What I say wrongly today let the learned of tomorrow, or even this day, set right. But if I do not say something today, those of tomorrow will have nothing to go from, even to correct (Narokobi 1980:v).

Even the pioneer professor of anthropology and sociology at the University of Papua New Guinea, Ralph Bulmer, saw diversity as a responsibility of the discipline of anthropology, arguing that anthropology should facilitate nation-building in Papua New Guinea. In his inaugural lecture at the University of Papua New Guinea he proposed that "problems of communication and translation between peoples of different cultural background provide the central reason why social anthropologists have a necessary future here, in studies of change as much as in studies of tradition." In fact, anthropologists were just as concerned with fostering cultural diversity as the pioneer political leaders who began to develop interest in "cultural unity" for Papua New Guinea.

"Cultural Unity" as the basis for national unity became the slogan of early politicians and nationalists. In the first and second House of Assembly, leaders like Oala Oala Rurua, Lepani Watson and the late Dr. John Guise wanted early independence and a united Papua New Guinea. In the 1970s it became a famous slogan for the United Party, following the lead of Mathias Toilman who echoed U.S. history in saying "United we stand, divided we fall." More forcefully, Narokobi reechoed this at independence and then went on to proclaim that the people of Papua New Guinea had always been culturally united. "Without the wheel, gun powder and kings, queens, emperors or high chiefs," he wrote,

> PNG maintained a fine sociological balance based not on large nation states, but on small communal autonomy. Some people call this disunity anarchy, even chaos. I say it is an aspect of unity, because no one group can claim on the basis of its technology that it is better or superior to another. All of us had a common belief in the living reality of our ancestors. We believed even the trees, the rocks and the natural life had souls or entities to which life can be attributed (1980:24–25).

Culture was seen as a possible source of national identity and pride. Michael Somare, another early nationalist, spoke of the need to develop a national identity out of the diversity of cultures, arguing that: "The task cannot be achieved merely with goodwill or sensible legislation ... it requires, above all, knowledge. We must know who we are, we must understand our past, appreciate our traditions. We must discover how much we have in common (far more than most of us think we have) but at the same time we must be aware of, but tolerant of our differences" (IPNGS Annual Report 1974–75:2). Note that at the heart of this interest in "cultural unity" was a belief that there were elements common to Papua New Guinea traditional cultures that could be used in modern-day developments. Narokobi was direct. "We should spring from our cultural values," he wrote, "to forge ahead in a world that is moving more and more towards a confused uniformity, monotony and insensitivity to the fine, subtle and sublime beauty of diversity. It is the simplistic imperialist who seeks uniformity as a technique to command obedience in a land of division, of disunity, of 700 languages and thousands of cultures" (Narokobi 1980:11).

In fact, beginning around 1974, during the years of decolonization, Papua New Guinea went through a rigorous period of soul-searching. National identity had become a major issue of discussion, with a focus on culture as one of its bases. At this time PNG had an influx of Africans, South Americans (mainly from Caribbean countries), South and Southeast Asians along with many liberal academics from the Western developed countries. These people converged primarily on the University of Papua New Guinea and became very influential shaping the thinking of the early leaders of the PNG. Perhaps because of these people's experiences in their respective countries, which appeared to be similar to those of the PNG, the leaders preferred their advice to that of the colonialists.

From the experiences of such foreigners, a body of ideas developed arguing that the emerging new PNG state should not emulate any foreign definition of "national identity"—that foreign concepts of identity should not be adopted too quickly, and that a "national identity" should instead be allowed to develop out of the diversity of cultures in the PNG. The founding Director of the Institute of Papua New Guinea Studies argued that,

> arising from this is the desire and the need to make Papua New Guinea a unique nation, not merely a blueprint of Australia or the Western world. But how can people assert this uniqueness, when every day the economic, social and political changes force them to

conform more to the rest of the world? An easy answer is to create rhetoric without bothering to define the core of the problem. It is a problem common to the Third World. "Negritude," the "African personality" and now the "Melanesian Way" are such phrases. They serve a useful function, in that they create much-needed enthusiasm, pride and they act as temporary morale boosters. But they fail to define the identity which the users of such phrases are actually seeking. To create a sense of identity then is a task of the utmost importance. For it involves the complicated way of welding a new, a NATIONAL identity of the hundreds of local identities that have existed in this country in the past (IPNGS Annual Report 1974–75:2).

Through its institutional infrastructure, colonialism had criss-crossed geographical cleavages and sociopolitical boundaries to bring the nation's diverse peoples into increased interaction—conditions crucial in setting the stage for modern cultural interaction. But this increased interaction did not automatically produce a common "superculture" based on shared cultural characteristics. Instead such interactions became the basis for an awareness and comparison of different groups' customs, traditions, and physical characteristics.

At issue here is how to interpret both the past and the present. Two characterizations of pre-contact life on the island have been offered in the literature on the PNG. In a first model (Hughes 1973), the peoples of Papua New Guinea, prior to colonization, lived in small isolated communities whose interactions with one another were dependent on the level of friendliness or animosity between them, as well as on geographical proximity. Hughes characterizes these units as societies in which settlements ranged from hamlets of not more than thirty people to villages of several hundred. Their political organization was termed the Melanesian Big-Man system (Sahlins 1963; Harding 1965), noting that chieftainships such as those found in Madang, Mekeo, and the Trobriand Islands were the exception rather than the rule. In this model, political groupings typically consisted of a few hundred or a few thousand people. Because these peoples lived on over 400 separate islands and spoke more than 700 languages, they were seen as micro-nations unto themselves. According to this model, isolation was broken through the process of colonial pacification and the different modes of transportation and communication introduced in the process.

We favor a second model, one that characterizes contact, communication, and exchange as relatively intense among some groups. Indeed it is our argument that despite the linguistic and cultural differences enhanced by geographical and sociopolitical conditions, Papua New Guinea was like a spider web that connected its main cultural groups through trade, with peripheral groups indirectly brought into loosely fragmented confederacies. These confederacies and trade groups, we believe, took the form of social systems larger than the Hughes model envisions.

Malinowski's (1915) Kula ring, for example, was connected to Seligman's (1910) Malu-Aroma trade, and this was further connected to the larger Hiri trade between the Central Mountains and their hinterland neighbors, the Koitas and the Goialas and the mainlanders and island peoples of Mailu and Southern Massim. Similar patterns of trade relations also existed among the highland peoples and between these peoples and those of the coastal regions. Despite the relative isolation of these pre-contact societies, there were some areas that should properly be recognized as "culture areas" based on ties forged through communication and trade, which shared many material, cultural and expressive forms. The sharing of such features was broader than could be evidenced by the workings of one constricted "network" of trade, for even these larger groups were not mutually exclusive in operation. In essence, while there did not develop a homogeneous Papua New Guinean culture as a result of such networks, their existence works against the model of precolonial Papua New Guinea as a collection of irreparably heterogeneous cultures existing in isolation.

Colonially bequeathed institutions were fundamental in the emergence of statehood, but we must be clear about their effects. Previously independent and self-evolving cultural groups were, during colonialism and statehood, influenced or otherwise coerced into increased communication with one another, resulting in the proliferation of national economic and political discourses aimed at integrating small-scale kinship based societies into a state system based on a Western paradigm.

These discourses began to proliferate as a result of a system of indentured labor set up by the plantation economy, which forced young men to leave their natal village communities to work for foreign plantation owners. In plantations, workers were thrown together and this promoted consciousness of their cultural differences. As the pacification process developed, colonial administrations were established and government institutions and services permeated the cultures and societies of the islands, further bringing diverse Papuan and New Guinean people together and enhancing awareness of cultural similarities and differences.

During the decades-long process of achieving national independence, culminating on September 16, 1975, however, there was an emphasis on economic development. It was not until 1974 that cultural development was perceived as a cornerstone of nation-building. An Australian grant of $3 million set up a process for making and administering cultural policy. A cultural policy was intended to establish national cultural institutions to preserve, revive, maintain, and disseminate cultural identities and practices of diverse groups of people in Papua New Guinea. This act was presumed by many leaders to represent the general will and to serve the interests of all parts of the national community.

Cultural Diversity understandably became the conscious and unconscious policy-making goal of the governments of Papua New Guinea since independence. Our national and regional governments have deliberately pursued this policy so that there is not just diversity but "greater diversity." This calls into question the function of culture at different levels of society in Papua New Guinea and the extent to which national level culture should have an integrating effect. Successive governments have promoted a culturally diverse, pluralistic model for New Guinean society.

Lindstrom presents a detached and analytic view of these issues and processes. He argues that there is no common cultural denominator for there is "greater diversity." But we do not believe that diversity necessarily produces disintegration, although it can. We argue that diversity can be maintained without necessarily having debilitating effects, and that in Papua New Guinea both educated elites and village dwellers realize that they have a national culture at the same time that they have pride and respect for the localized identities whose maintenance is sought.

Contra Lindstrom, our view is not that Papua New Guinea is having problems developing a national identity, but that its extraordinary diversity in cultures and linguistic groups warrants the creation of a new model for national identity and culture in the making. Regional claims to cultural and national identity indeed abound, making it all the more important that the country develop a national culture fostered by a cultural policy that can exert influence over the nation's diverse groups while simultaneously allowing all groups to maintain their cultural autonomy. The province of North Solomons has, after all, successfully opposed Papua New Guinea's Security forces for several years, claiming independence on the basis of cultural and physical attributes (Filer 1990; May 1982; Spriggs 1992). Bougainville has witnessed a resurgence of nationalism based on their perception of being racially, culturally and economically distinct from other Papua New Guineans (Filer 1990). Similarly, cultural nationalism is currently being asserted by other regional and cultural groups claiming political autonomy (cf. Badu 1982; Griffin 1975; May 1982; Nelson 1976).

INSTITUTING CULTURAL DIVERSITY

In light of such movements, Papua New Guinea must construct a national culture that also allows local and regional cultures to exist without being suppressed or otherwise imposed upon. The government has taken several tacks. Institutionally it created a system of provincial governments, giving autonomy to 19 provinces while maintaining a unitary state with a parliamentary system of government. Under this decentralization scheme, many powers and functions were shared. This was reflected in cultural policy when provinces and lower level communities were given the opportunity to establish cultural centers with the aid of the National Cultural Council, which served as the coordinating body. This made possible the fostering and nurturing of cultural policies and identities at the regional and community levels.

The government has also long fostered the policy of Cultural Diversity through education. We have already discussed how, in the colonial era, Papuans and New Guineans were directly or indirectly forced to work together in plantations through the indentured labor system, or conscripted as war carriers and fighters and how, in these varying social settings, they interacted and learned each other's cultures in order to communicate, or devised and used Police Motu and Pidgin to communicate across cultural barriers. Communication and interaction expanded significantly through educational institutions provided by the colonial government and Christian Missions. At schools, colleges, and later universities, students exhibited ethnic regionalism in sports, mutual associations, festivities, and other venues in which they could compete and display their cultural artifacts through dances and festivities.

The national government has frequently taken the initiative and become quite proactive. An example was the government's declaration on April 28, 1976, that Friday would be National Dress Day, known as *Toana* Day, and the directive for all schools to set aside one day of the week to be known as Culture Day. The *Post Courier* reported that the Prime Minister, Michael Somare, was reported to have said that it was not compulsory to wear "national dress" and that there were no rules about what constituted national dress. But, in the same article, Mr. Somare was quoted as saying that he was "hopeful that in time a style will emerge which can be identified as Papua New Guinean" (Cf. Lindstrom this volume). As Lindstrom noted, it was not the intent of Culture Day activities or those of other national and provincial festivals to judge the content of one culture against that of another. The working assumption was that all cultures of Papua New Guinea are excellent in their own ways, and that the identity of our nation and the potential for its survival are anchored in its diverse cultures.

PNG's National Constitution actually legitimates and inspires our cultural policy-making. Knowing that diversity is a factor to be accounted for, the Preamble states the following: "We, the people of Papua New Guinea...pay homage to the memory of our ancestors...the source of our strength and origin of our common heritage. [We] acknowledge the worthy customs and traditional customs of our people...which have come down to us from generation to generation [and we] pledge ourselves to guard and pass on [to those] who come after us our noble traditions that are ours now." Devising deliberate flexibility was to be a priority.

The first government legislation ever relating to cultural policy was passed by Parliament in 1974, following a grant of $3 million for the Cultural Service from the Australian

Government (cf. Voi 1994). This led to the passing of the National Cultural Development Act of 1974, which legitimized the establishment of the National Cultural Council and three other cultural institutions, with the Council as the central coordinating body. The three other cultural institutions were the Center for Creative Arts, the Institute of Papua New Guinea Studies, and the National Museum.

In the adoption of the Cultural Development Act of 1974, the diversity of cultures in Papua New Guinea was taken into consideration along with the recognition of the need for the creation and promotion of a national culture. This is clear in the functions of the Council, as stated in sub-sections (c), (d), (e) and (g):

- (c) to establish National, District and Local cultural institutions and cultural centers;
- (d) to control and regulate a National Cultural Development Service;
- (e) to promote and encourage the development of preservation of national and local culture; and
- (g) to foster the expression of a national identity by means of the arts (Cultural Development Act 1974).

In subsections (a) and (c), the act stated that the Center for Creative Arts was responsible to the Council: (a) for the development of contemporary cultural forms in the fields of expressive, visual and fine arts and designs; and (c) for encouraging persons talented in any of the Arts to draw on the culture of the past to develop distinctive contemporary art forms.

From 1974 to 1990, the National Cultural Development Act was amended numerous times for various reasons, including the need to accommodate the creation of other national institutions, such as the National Theatre Company, Raun Raun Theatre, and Skul Bilong Wokim Piksa. These amendments gave these new national cultural institutions functions that took into account the diversity of Papua New Guinean cultures while being geared towards the development of a national culture. The

National Cultural Development Act existed, in many amended forms, until 1990 when it was repealed to make way for the Tourism Development Act, which resulted in the creation of the National Tourism Corporation. The culture service was, until 1993, subsumed under this corporation and its functions were stipulated in the above-mentioned act.

Prior to the establishment of the National Tourism Corporation, the National Culture Service was a division within the department of Culture and Tourism. In 1988, and prior to the establishment of the Corporation, the Department of Culture and Tourism produced a "Five Year Cultural Development Plan" (cf. Lindstrom and White 1994, Appendix 3). Among the list of fourteen objectives listed in the plan, two relevant ones were:

1.4 To assist the Provincial Governments in their efforts to develop and preserve their indigenous cultures.

1.5 To create an incentive amongst the people in order to ensure continuous survival of Papua New Guinea Cultures and traditions.

This plan, in addition to the "Five Year Tourism Development Plan" of 1990, partly formed the basis for the national Tourism Development Act of 1990. In this act there are 14 functions which are listed as the functions of the corporation. Two of these functions are: (b) to take measures to protect cultural rights and identities of individual ethnic groups; and (c) to provide effective support towards conservation, preservation and promotion of cultural heritage as an obligation to maintaining national identity.

Much has changed since culture came under a commercially-oriented entity—the Tourism Corporation—which identifies culture as performing arts, visual arts, crafts, and national heritage, and omits a wide variety of areas, such as religious systems, rituals and magic, architecture, prehistoric sites, food/agriculture, customs and traditions, laws and social organization. It only identifies two cultures—urban and rural—as if they are already neatly given.

This policy is well intentioned but calls for a wholesale marketing of culture intended to provide economic opportunities for village people in regions which are deemed scenic but backward and where there is a desired intermingling of human life with nature, fauna and flora, and marine life. This might well create an inappropriate climate for discussions of culture. A troubling example was the comment once made by the First Secretary of the Corporation in passing (and perhaps jokingly) in a public address that "Our culture is still virgin and needs to be raped" (see Lindstrom, this volume). A public outcry, especially by a women's liberation group in Port Moresby, forced him to apologize to the female population for drawing such a parallel with rape, when rape and violence against women had recently become pressing topics of debate.

FINAL THOUGHTS

Papua New Guinean and other Melanesian Cultures are now observing how local cultures are constructed, valorized and maintained, and continually mediate their relationships with other cultural groups, outside influences, and the larger nation-state. This is the goal of policy in Papua New Guinea. To achieve this goal, political and administrative systems must be redrawn and policies implemented in order to achieve national cultural unity while not sacrificing local-level cultural identities.

Unlike detached analytic observers, we are interested in developing conceptions, policies, and institutions of Papua New Guinea as a nation. We do not discount other models, but we are in the midst of exploring models we might develop that would be especially appropriate for PNG, given its marked diversity. Our questions have broader analytic implications as well. In the final analysis, we are asking (1) if diversity in cultural forms and images need be thought of as incompatible with nation building; (2) if all countries need to live in the shadows of 19th and 20th century European ideologies of nationhood that have long privileged homogeneity; and (3) if nation-states are not, in fact, better off when they have plural cultures and ethnicities, and each is given the opportunity to prosper and propagate without being mutually exclusive, expansionist, or hostile.

REFERENCES

Badu, N. (1982). *Papua Benesa: Case Study of a Separatist Movement.* Unpublished MA thesis, University of Sydney.

Crocombe, R. (1976). *The Pacific Way: An Emerging Identity.* Suva: Lotu Pacifica.

Filer, C. (1990). The Bougainville Rebellion: The Mining Industry and the Process of Social Integration in Papua New Guinea. *Anthropology* 13(1).

Foster, R. J. (1991). Making National Cultures in the Global Ecumene. *Annual Review of Anthropology* 20:235–260.

Griffin, J. (1975). Ethnonationalism and Integration: An Optimistic View. *Meanjin Quarterly* 34(3):240–249.

Harding, T. (1965). *The Trade System of Vitiaz Strait.* Ph.D. dissertation, University of Michigan.

Howard, M. C. (1989). *Ethnicity and Nation Building in the Pacific.* Japan: The United Nations University.

Hughes, L. (1973). Stone Age Trade in the New Guinea Inland. In H. Chillingworth-Brookfield, Ed., *The Pacific in Transition.* Canberra: Australian National University.

IPNGS *Annual Report, 1974–76.* Boroko: Institute of Papua New Guinea Studies.

Keesing, R. M. (1982). Kastom and Anticolonialism on Malatia: "Culture as Political Symbol." *Mankind* 12(4):357–373.

— (1982). Kastom in Melanesia: An Overview. *Mankind* 13(4):297–301.

— (1989). Creating the Past: Custom Identity in the Contemporary Pacific. *The Contemporary Pacific: A Journal of Island Affairs* 1(1, 2):19–42.

Keesing, R. M. and Tokinson, R. (1982). Reinventing Traditional Culture: The Politics of Kastom in Island Melanesia. *Mankind* 13(4).

Lindstrom, L. (1982). Leftamap Kastom: The Political History of Tradition on Tanna (Vanuatu). *Mankind* 13(4):316–329.

— (1990). Pasin Tumbuna: Cultural Traditions and National Identity in Papua Identity, 19–22 June, Institute of Culture and Communication, East-West Center, Honolulu.

Lindstrom, L. and G. White, Eds. (1994). *Culture, Kastom, Tradition: Developing Cultural Policy in Melanesia*. Suva: Institute of Pacific Studies.

Loiskandl, H. (1988). Melanesian Identity as Liberation: Ideologies of a Religious Elite. *Man and Culture in Oceania* 4:111–128.

Malinowski, B. (1915). The Natives of Malu. *Proceedings of the Royal Anthropology Society of South Australia*, 39:494–706.

May, R. J., Ed. (1982). *Micronationalist Movements in Papua New Guinea*. Canberra: Australian National University.

Narokobi, B. (1980). *The Melanesian Way*. Boroko: Institute of Papua New Guinea Studies.

Nelson, H. (1976). *Black, White and Gold*. Canberra: Australian National University.

Sahlins, M. D. (1963). Poor Man, Rich Man, Big Man, Chief: Political Types in Melanesia and Polynesia. *Comparative Studies in Society and History* 5:285–303.

Seligman, C. G. (1910). *The Melanesian of British New Guinea*. London: Cambridge University Press.

Spriggs, M. (1992). *Contemporary Pacific*. Special Issue on Bougainville.

Voi, Mali (1994). An Overview of Cultural Policy in Papua New Guinea since 1974. In L. Lindstrom and G. White, Eds. *Culture, Kastom, Tradition: Developing Cultural Policy in Melanesia*. Suva: Institute of Pacific Studies.

White, G. (1992). The Discourse of Chiefs: Notes on a Melanesian Society. *The Contemporary Pacific* 4(1):65–95.

PART IV
China

9

"Cultural Fever": A Cultural Discourse in China's Post-Mao Era[1]

Haiou Yang

During the period between the mid-1980s and the spring of 1989 in China, an unusual wave of interest in discussing cultural issues engulfed the intellectual arena.[2] Certain questions produced feverish discussion. These included: What is the deep structure of Chinese traditional culture? What are the features of the Chinese national character? What is the relationship between sinicized Marxism and Chinese traditional culture? This period was termed the "Cultural Fever."[3] Discussions in the academic arena involved scholars from the social sciences, humanities, and the natural sciences. The scope of the discussion was further extended to the general public when "River

Elegy" (*Heshang*), a television documentary series, was shown throughout the country in mid-1988. Furthermore, overseas Chinese sinologists were also attracted by this cultural discourse.

Before the Post-Mao era,[4] China had never experienced such a cultural discourse in terms of its range of participants and depth of discussions. Since 1949, what China had experienced was an official "cultural hegemony." "Culture" was an area that Chinese intellectuals rarely touched upon during the Mao era. Pang Pu (1988b), a participant in the Cultural Fever, observed that during the period between 1949 and 1979, *A Brief History of Chinese Culture* by Cai Shangxi (1979) was the only book to have been published that was related to "culture" in China. Chinese traditional culture had been frequently attacked by the Chinese Communist Party (CCP) during the Mao era. During the 1950s, old rituals such as funeral rites and old values, such as prejudice against women, were targets of criticism. During the Cultural Revolution, Chinese traditional culture experienced total destruction and condemnation. "Four Olds"—old ideas, culture, customs, and habits—were targets of elimination; numerous historical monuments and temples were destroyed; traditional operas and other performing arts were banned. In addition, historical analogies and symbolisms in Chinese traditional culture were frequently used in political disputes among the top level Party leaders during the past few decades.

The development of this cultural discourse was closely related to the political atmosphere since the end of the 1970s, especially the mid 1980s. In 1978, the Third Plenary Session of the Eleventh Central Committee of the CCP encouraged intellectuals to "liberate their thoughts" and to "make a hundred flowers bloom." Since then, numerous "forbidden zones" in many areas of social sciences and humanities had been opened up. However, the tide of liberal thinking had often been hindered by continuing official controls and domination. In June 1989, this Cultural Fever was abruptly and suddenly terminated by official political force. Since the June 1989 crackdown, much of the liberal discussion on cultural issues has been suppressed and refuted.

At a time when history seems to have taken China back to the age of "cultural hegemony," this study attempts to unfold the picture of the Cultural Fever by focusing on two questions: What is this cultural discourse all about? Why did "culture" suddenly become so feverish during the period between the mid 1980s and the spring of 1989? However, the purpose of this study is not to document every episode of this discourse in great detail, nor to critique different viewpoints of the discourse with other perspectives. Two specific purposes of this study are: first, to provide an overall review of the main domains of discourse in the Cultural Fever and, second, to examine the socioeconomic and political causes of the Cultural Fever. The materials reviewed in this study are non-fiction essays, instead of fiction and poetry.[5]

MAIN DIMENSIONS OF THE CULTURAL DISCOURSE DURING THE CULTURAL FEVER

This study defines the cultural discourse of the Cultural Fever as a debate over issues on Chinese and Western cultural traditions—issues which are themselves closely related to those concerning political and socioeconomic order in China. The Cultural Fever was an activity among intellectuals, rather than a popular religion such as Taoism. It was a debate about how intellectuals would have liked to see China's contemporary history and the role that they would have liked to play in it. It was also a debate that went far beyond conventional boundaries of "culture" (as frequently understood), for in the past few decades, the term "culture" in China had only been used in connection with either education or arts (*wenhua jiaoyu* or *wenhua yishu*).[6]

For the sake of analysis, I categorize issues discussed in the Cultural Fever through three dimensions they focused on: (a) Chinese traditional culture, (b) Marxism/Mao Zedong Thought, and (c) Western cultures. These three domains parallel the three contending elements in Whyte's classification scheme on China's political culture,[7] since the development of each discussion was closely connected to the evolution of the official control and domination entering the 1980s. This section will outline the main issues discussed during the Cultural Fever.

THE EXAMINATION OF CHINESE TRADITIONAL CULTURE

During the Cultural Fever, much of the discussion on Chinese traditional culture among intellectuals was related to an effort to find solutions to problems within present political and socioeconomic orders, and people's outlook in the society. In general, a critical attitude towards Chinese traditional culture was common among the majority of the participants, except for a small group of intellectuals who were closely connected with the faction operating in the official arena. However, the degree of criticism of Chinese traditional culture varied.

A group of moderate and conservative intellectuals, represented by Li Zehou, Pang Pu, and Tang Yijie, argued that it was important to totally discard the "rubbish" in Chinese traditional culture and reserve the cream, so that a new value system that could unite the spirit of the Chinese nation could be constructed (Li Zehou 1989; Pang Pu 1988). A group of radical intellectuals, represented by Liu Xiaobo, Jin Guantao, and Liu Zehua, asserted that culture was an indivisible entity and that the examination of Chinese traditional culture required a holistic approach. There was a tendency among the radical scholars, such as Liu Xiaobo, to simply use Western culture as the sole reference system from which to criticize Chinese traditional culture. Scapegoating Chinese traditional culture, they seemed to naively believe that China could solve its economic problems by "correcting drawbacks" in Chinese traditional culture.

In addition, the discussion of Chinese traditional culture seemed to have been influenced by studies carried out by overseas Chinese scholars. Commonalities clearly existed in the shared concern about the future of Chinese traditional culture and the written language evident among overseas and domestic intellectuals. However, this situation may ironically indicate that the criticism of traditional Chinese culture during the Cultural Fever was partially imported from overseas Chinese scholars. Moreover, the discussion of Chinese traditional culture also inherited the tradition of the 1919 May Fourth Movement, especially the spirit of Lu Xun.

One of the three major questions asked by the participants in the Cultural Fever focused on the presumption that there is a "deep structure" in Chinese traditional culture and postulated that it has hindered the development of Chinese society for a long time.[8] Scholars, of course, differed. Wang He argued in 1986 that there were three major points of view : (1) one that viewed "the rule of rites" as the basic characteristic of Chinese traditional culture, (2) another that considered the center of traditional Chinese culture to be a type of "humanism," and (c) a third that regarded the main stream of Chinese traditional culture to be a type of "monarchism."

The first group represented a point of view I regard as conventional with respect to "the deep structure of Chinese traditional culture." They portrayed "the rule of rites" as the basic characteristic of Chinese traditional culture. "Rites," they argued, are embodied in a system of hierarchic and interdependent relationships in a society. "Rites" could be expressed in "the three cardinal guides and the five constant virtues," *sangang wuchang*, which defines how individuals should treat their parents, children, husband, wife, subordinates, and superiors. Some scholars argued that the system of hierarchic and interdependent relationships defined by Chinese traditional culture constituted a vision of harmonious brotherhood and principles of duties. But the "rule of rites" argument was challenged by other scholars for, under the rule of rites, an individual is only an object to be defined and he or she only exists in a network of hierarchic relationships (Wang He 1986; Liu Zehua 1986).

The second group represented a moderate but new perspective on the deep structure of Chinese traditional culture. These intellectuals considered the center of traditional Chinese culture to be a type of "humanism." They believed that, in comparison with the cultural traditions of other nationalities strongly influenced by the Greek tradition of realism, Chinese humanism is more concerned with the present world and human relations. One element in Chinese humanism that they pointed to as significant is "the attitude towards life," *rushi* (active participation). Chinese humanism, they insisted, also stresses harmony, obligations, and contributions. On the negative side, as Pang Pu pointed out in 1988, it can also be argued that Chinese humanism has been deficient in neglecting the natural rights of human beings (Pang Pu 1988a).

The third group of scholars viewed the deep structure of Chinese traditional culture as "monarchism," *wangquan zhuyi*, instead of humanism. In 1986, Liu Zhehua (1986) defined monarchism as the unlimited power of the emperor in the traditional society. He argued that the emperor in "the traditional society" had four types of unlimited power: control over Heaven and the earth, the ability to create order or chaos, the total ownership of all, and the absolute authority on matters of knowledge.

A second, though clearly not unrelated, thread in the discussion of Chinese traditional culture centered on the idea of a Chinese national character. During this period of Cultural Fever, references were often made to "deep-rooted bad habits" and these were equated with "the national character." Typically these would be negative characterizations of aspects of Chinese "mentality" described as passive, backward, closed, and narrow. There is an interesting history here. The first inklings of a national character discussion can be traced back to the period around the May Fourth Movement of 1919, and the 1930s in particular. But Mao's articulation and insistence—that "Chinese people are hardworking, brave and wise" (Mao Zedong 1952)—had curtailed studies on "the national character" for a few decades. The Cultural Fever, then, marked a turning point in the stagnant state of the long-standing discussion about "the national character." An active proponent of discussions on reforming the national character in the 1930s, Lu Xun came to be officially recognized as one of the significant figures in the literary forum of the past few decades—and his influence on China's intellectuals is incalculable.

The discourse on Chinese traditional culture has not only a long lasting historical heritage, but also some contemporary outside connections through the influence of overseas Chinese scholars. During the Cultural Fever, numerous overseas Chinese scholars in the area of Chinese traditional culture were invited to China to attend conferences and to give lectures.[9] In addition, many of their works, especially those which had a critical attitude towards Chinese traditional culture, were also introduced to Chinese domestic readers for the first time. Some of them, such as Qiu Chuiliang's *The Deep Structure of Chinese Culture*, were best sellers in China's book market. In this atmosphere, it was likely that some of the terms and arguments used by domestic Chinese scholars during the Cultural Fever were often directly borrowed from some of the works by overseas Chinese scholars.

Perhaps the scholar who held the most negative attitude towards Chinese "national character" during the Cultural Fever was Liu Xiaobo.[10] Inheriting the critical spirit of Lu Xun, Liu Xiaobo totally condemned the Chinese "national character" without reservation. He saw criticizing "deeply-rooted bad national character" as the most pressing task in criticizing Chinese traditional culture. For Liu Xiaobo, the three main pillars of Chinese traditional culture reflected in "the national character" were "populism" (*minben sixiang*), "the moral quality of Confucius and Yan Hui"[11] (*kongyan renge*), and "the unity of Heaven and man" (*tian ren heyi*). In Liu Xiaobo's criticism of Chinese national character, "Western culture" was frequently used as a reference system. For him, China's underdevelopment in modern history could be attributed to the simple fact that "Chinese traditional culture" was different from "Western culture."

Liu Xiaobo's arguments are worth exploring further because of the force and the nature of the criticism. In 1989, for example, he argued that "populism" was an illusory collective consciousness in China (1989a)—and that "People" and "individual" (*min* and *ren*) are, in contrast, two different concepts in "Western Cultures." In China, he insisted, the concept of "people" is meaningless since it does not focus on the rights of individuals. "Populism" (*minben sixiang*), to him, was an extension of the theory of the hierarchic structure that defines people as the ruled but not the ruler; hence, paying attention to, and protecting, the people should be seen as nothing but a strategy used by the rulers. Not mincing words, he wrote that the Kong-Yan moral quality (*kongyan renge*) is the personality of a conscious slave, and that when an individual is born (in such a system), he or she is born as a slave, a member of a feudalistic system and that individual's life does not belong to him or her but to the rituals of the system. In this context, the extreme of this type of personality is one who develops a strong sense of social responsibility even at the expense of his or her life. Hence, according to Liu Xiaobo, the purpose of the "populism" and "Kong-Yan moral quality" is to strangle individualism and independent consciousness, and to produce obedient slaves to protect the stability of the despotism.

Moreover, Liu Xiaobo defined "the unity of Heaven and man" as a function of "the illusory collective consciousness" and "the moral quality of a conscious slave," and argued that what "the unity of Heaven and man" has brought to Chinese people is, in fact, stagnation and retrogression. Many things were presented by Liu Xiaobo as interconnected, among them, for example, that the unity of Heaven and man had led to the "crude" and "unsystematic" development of natural sciences in China. The argument was that this idea of "the unity of Heaven and man" has hindered the Chinese people's creativity and initiative, and has intoxicated the Chinese people with an illusory harmony—that it has created a "soft bone disease" in Chinese moral values, which he identified as the problem of dependency. "The unity of Heaven and man" becomes in this analysis the rationale for the perpetuation of hierarchic despotism, since to follow the will of Heaven is equivalent to being absolutely obedient to the monarchy.

A variant of this view appears in the writings of Liu Zaifu, a scholar who follows in the footsteps of Lu Xun.[12] For him, the leaders of the May Fourth Movement, such as Lu Xun, made two important contributions in criticizing "Chinese traditional culture." The first contribution is related to the "old civilization" of China and the second to "the national character" of the Chinese people. Lu Xun had argued that the "old civilization" was nothing but a "banquet of eating human flesh" (*chiren de yanxi*), and that the most important characteristic of the Chinese "national character" was "the spirit of Ah Q" (*Ah Q jingsheng shenglifa*), "spiritual escapism" (Liu Zaifu 1988). Liu Zaifu wrote that "spiritual escapism" was a special contribution made by Lu Xun toward an understanding of "Chinese traditional culture," for he viewed the idea of "spiritual escapism" as a special way of observing the world. Implying that one's view of the world has nothing to do with what is happening in the real world but is, rather, dependent on a psychological contract one makes with one's self, this kind of portrayal suggested that people can avoid a troublesome reality and transform each actual failure into a spiritual victory. Liu Zaifu saw potential explanatory value in this argument.

Likewise, Liu Zaifu drew on Lu Xun's definition of "eating human beings" (*chiren*) in "Chinese traditional culture" and his articulation of three different levels of meaning: (a) that implying the weak being oppressed by the strong; (b) that implying the weak, who are themselves being oppressed, oppressing those who are weaker; and (c) that implying self-suppression and self-throttling (Liu Zaifu 1988; Lu Xun 1956). Based on Lu Xun's notions of "spiritual escapism" and "eating human beings," Liu Zaifu argued that "the dual personality of the master-servant" represented the core of the Chinese "national character." According to him, traditional Chinese society in history was perpetuated through this "dual personality of the master-servant," since it has become fully realized in cycles of order and disorder for over two thousand years in China. Note that this is an argument many scholars (in various parts of the world) might consider a flattened view of history. It is an argument that says that, in the history of China, there have been no substantial changes in the social system—an argument that in each large scale revolution the old master is replaced by the new master and, when the old servant becomes the master by chance, new servants are reproduced.

Compared with the above mentioned scholars, Jin Guantao wielded the most innovative tool in the context of the Cultural Fever by bringing in cybernetics and information theory.[13] Jin Guantao (1983) argued that Chinese feudalism[14] had persisted for more than two thousand years because of a "structural ultrastability" in the Confucian system. By "ultrastability," he did not mean, contrary to Liu Zaifu, that Chinese society had effectively been motionless. Indeed he noted a pattern of disruption and restoration, but still argued that the society had failed to develop a new type of structure qualitatively different from its predecessors. China, he contended, has never been free from its historical constraints. It was this framework—his framework—that later greatly influenced the TV series, "River

Elegy" (*Heshang*), extending the scale of the cultural discourse to the general public.

A final group worth mentioning, the self-proclaimed New Authoritarianists, are interesting because the discussion they generated represented a different type of debate between the official and unofficial arenas with respect to "Chinese traditional culture" during the Cultural Fever. Although a critical attitude towards "Chinese traditional culture" was common among most intellectuals at the time, a small group of intellectuals from the official arena—namely those from Zhao Ziyang's think tank—went against the tide and proclaimed themselves the New Authoritarianists. Significantly, they argued that a market economy system in the current stage of the modernization process of China can only be achieved under a system in which authority is coupled with strong and highly centralized political power. Ideologically, New Authoritarianists held a positive attitude towards the Chinese "traditional value system" and treated it as the basis for uniting and consolidating "the national spirit" (Xiao Gongqin and Zhu Wei 1989; Wu Jiaxiang 1989). Not surprisingly, they met with a great deal of criticism from intellectuals such as Yu Haocheng, Rong Jian, and Huang Wuangsheng (Wu Jiaxiang 1989; Zhang Weigo 1989). They and others argued rather directly that the fact that the ideology of New Authoritarianism was based on the traditional Confucian value system indicated a strong propensity to autocracy, a concentration of power, and the worship of political idols.[15]

THE EVALUATION OF MARXISM AND MAO ZEDONG THOUGHT

A series of discussions about various elements of Marxism and Mao Zedong's thoughts almost paralleled the discussion on traditional Chinese culture that I have just described.[16]

Covering developments of these discussions, however, would be beyond the scope of this essay and is, hence, not my central concern here. But I do want to highlight a special segment of the discussion on Marxism as it related to culture in the later stages of the Cultural Fever. That is the discussion on sinicized Marxism and relations between Marxism/Mao Zedong Thought and Chinese traditional culture.

It is important to note that the evaluation of Marxism and Mao Zedong Thought during the Cultural Fever was relatively preliminary and pedestrian, since the "complete," "original," and "true" Marxist theoretical system was often used as a reference system. In addition, scholars who used Western theories as a reference system to examine Marxism and Maoism were rarely found. It is clear that most of the scholars of the Cultural Fever intended to reconstruct a new, "flawless," and "unabridged" Marxist system instead of abandoning the existing system completely and turning to other types of Western theories. Nevertheless, the most interesting (and relevant) point, for my purposes, was that sinicized Marxism and Mao Zedong Thought were examined in the context of their connections with Chinese traditional culture. Here, too, we see the inseparability of culture and politics in China.

During the Cultural Fever, the evaluation of sinicized Marxism and Mao Zedong Thought was developed through the following two lines: (a) using the "complete" and "true" Marxist theoretical framework as a reference system to evaluate sinicized Marxism and Mao Zedong Thought, and (b) focusing on the interrelations and reinforcements between Chinese traditional culture and sinicized Marxism/Mao Zedong Thought.

The group of intellectuals who worked within the grand framework of the "true Marxism" included Li Honglin, Wang Ruoshui, and Su Shaozhi. It is important to note that they believed that there really are different genres in the Marxist theoretical system—that Lenin's, Stalin's, and Mao's theories, for example, are different types of Marxist theories—and that it was within that perspective that they forged ahead with their own critical formulations. Su Shaozhi argued that it was important to rethink socialism and relearn Marxism,[17] while Wang Ruoshui became famous for his interpretation of Marxist concepts of alienation and humanism.[18] More specifically, Wang called for the reexamination of the current Marxist framework employed in China arguing that some important concepts, such as humanism and alienation, have been neglected in the past few decades. According to him, Marx argued in his works that in order to realize the liberation of human beings alienation must be overcome, and he (Wang Ruoshui) stressed that the phenomenon of alienation exists not only in capitalist countries but in socialist countries as well.

Wang Ruoshui suggested that three aspects of Chinese contemporary society display (or are signs of) alienation. These include the extreme development of the personality cult of Mao during the Cultural Revolution, the transformation of the "public servants" of the people into the "masters" of the people, and the tendency in making economic policies to overemphasize the development of heavy industry and neglect light industry whose products are arguably more closely related to people's living standards. Since the purpose of socialist production is supposed to be to raise people's living standards, Wang Ruoshui (1989) argued that these economic policies showed and produced a type of alienation themselves.

A few extraordinarily audacious scholars, such as Liu Xiaobo and Fang Lizhi, displayed a totally different attitude toward Marxism than the group of scholars like Wang Ruoshui. Liu Xiaobo, as we have already seen, totally rejected Marxism referring to Marxism as the "tool of the ruling class" in China. Strongly against criticism of sinicized Marxism conducted within a Marxist domain, Liu insisted that as "the tool of the ruling class" in contemporary China Marxism has no theoretical meaning. Moreover, he argued that if one believes in Marxism one believes in autocracy (Liu Xiaobo 1989), and that since Marxism was apparently accepted by Chinese people, it had become part of Chinese traditional culture—thereby functioning as an idolized theory and "the absolute truth." Extending his argument further, he likened the respect, submission, and fear of contemporary Chinese intellectuals towards Marxism to attitudes of scholars in the Song and Han Dynasties toward Confucianism. To Liu Xiaobo (unlike scholars like Wang Ruoshui), Marxism in China was not only an idol but also a symbol of authority (Liu Xiaobo 1989).

At the peak of the heated cultural discourse, a group of scholars discarded "the original Marxist system" as a reference system and concentrated on the interrelations and reinforcements between Chinese traditional culture and sinicized Marxism/Mao Zedong Thought. This group of scholars was represented by Chen Yang, Li Zehou, Wang Shubai, and Xiao Yanzhong. Their discussion on the relationship between Chinese traditional culture and sinicized Marxism/Mao Zedong Thought was actually the most exciting aspect I encountered in the discourse of Marxism and Maoism in the Cultural Fever.

For example, some scholars attempted to identify components of Chinese traditional culture which made some elements of Marxism easy to accept and caused others to be rejected in China (Wang He 1986). According to Li Zehou, Marxism became sinicized through a peasant revolution and, since the arrival of Marxism in China, actually became "assimilated" into the system of traditional Chinese culture. Many elements of traditional Chinese culture, he argued, were brought into sinicized Marxism (Li Zehou 1989b), among these (and perhaps especially) Confucianism emphasizing the importance of the stability of the society and the harmony between collective and individual interests. Li Zehou interestingly proposed that Marx's theoretical framework, the ideal of communism, the theory of class struggles, and the principle of collectivism were fairly easily accepted because they have a high degree of consistency with "the cultural psychology of Chinese tradition."

Wang Shubai, together with Li Zehou, also argued that there was a component of utilitarian pragmatism in Chinese traditional culture (presumably making a certain form of Marxism palatable and acceptable) and that the acceptance and understanding of Marxism in China have undoubtedly been influenced by these "traditional values" (Wang Shubai 1987; Li Zehou 1989b).

In reexamining Mao Zedong Thought, in fact, a number of scholars also looked at interrelationships between Mao Zedong Thought and "Chinese traditional culture" with some insisting on treating Mao's theoretical framework as an independent "cultural system." Note the framing in terms of culture here. To Chen Yang and others, for instance, the key to understanding Maoism was paying special attention to symbolic terms employed in Mao's theoretical framework. Terms such as "Marxism," "bourgeois," "proletarian," "revisionism," "socialist," "capitalist," and "class struggle," they argued, were symbols with unusual meanings in Mao's cultural system (Chen Yang 1989; Li Zehou 1989a). Li Zehou (1989a) argued that these concepts imply a polarized model of cultural construction in contemporary China,[19] and that one reason why Mao Zedong Thought was so easily accepted by the people in China was that this kind of moralism was deeply rooted in Chinese cultural psychology. Note once again the implicit and explicit reliance on a notion of Chinese (traditional) culture in these formulations.

Not everyone, of course, agreed, though it is important to note that disagreements still employed a notion of Chinese traditional culture and sought explanations that had a bearing on it. Xiao Yanzhong was a good example. Attempting to explore Mao's logic for the Cultural Revolution that created the ten years of chaos in China, he argued in 1989 that Mao's logic was embedded in a contradiction between Marxism and Chinese traditional culture. This he saw in Mao's frequent use of the concepts of "People" and "the masses"—concepts always connected with notions such as "the ruled" and "the exploited." Clearly the conflict between the bureaucrats and the people was one of Mao's major concerns, and the concept of "the servants of people" undoubtedly comes from a Marxist framework. But the concepts of the master and the slave Xiao believed stemmed from the "populism" in Chinese traditional culture.

Xiao Yanzhong (1989) sought and found an underlying logic for all this in Mao's theory in his late years—in Mao's ideas (1) that in a socialist society people become the master of the society and that the bureaucrats as public servants gradually (unintentionally?) become the "master of the master," and people again become the "slave," and (2) that, if the "slaves" want to become the master of the country again, it is indispensable to have someone functioning as an "agent" who can lead the people back to power. Mao, of course, considered himself to be such an agent seeing himself unconsciously, Xiao argued, as the source and the center of people's power. This Xiao Yanzhong (1989) believed might explain theoretically why Mao initiated the Cultural Revolution.

THE DISCUSSION ON "WESTERN CULTURES"

In comparison with the extensive attention paid to Chinese traditional culture in relation to Marxism/Mao Zedong Thought, the discussion on "Western ideas" seems relatively superficial. This could largely be attributed to an unfavorable political environment at the time, especially the inconsistent and ambivalent attitude towards Western influence in the official arena. In general, systematic research on "Western culture" was still limited, although scholars flirted with many types of Western ideas and philosophies. The exploration of the relationship between the West and Chinese tradition had created an emotional entanglement between the official and unofficial scholarly arenas and it is possible that this constant emotional entanglement had, in turn, hindered further studies on "the Western Cultures." A difference between scholars in and out of the official arena, nonetheless, existed. While those in the official arena had a generally antagonistic attitude towards "Western culture," some scholars in the unofficial arena tended to hold a respectful attitude toward "Western culture." Note here, too, that "culture"—in this case something deemed a foreign culture—was a thing of some importance warranting identification and discussion in both official and unofficial circles.

Let us put this in historical perspective. The debate about the relationship between Chinese traditional culture and Western culture during the Cultural Fever can be traced back to early in the twentieth century and the May Fourth period in particular.[20] The May Fourth Movement in 1919 has been one of the most controversial and frequently discussed events in modern Chinese history and the year 1989 was the 70th anniversary of the 1919 May Fourth Movement. Not surprisingly, the participants of the Cultural Fever were reinspired by the spirit of the May Fourth Movement. Many issues discussed in the May Fourth Movement were raised again during the Cultural Fever. Discussing the meanings and implications of the 1919 May Fourth Movement to contemporary China, in fact, became a part of the Cultural Fever.

Consider some examples. Contra the old slogan in the late twentieth century, *"zhongxue wei ti, xixue wei yong"* (Chinese learning as the foundation, Western learning for its practical applications), Li Zehou coined the slogan, *xi ti* (Western essential principle) *zhong yong* (application in China). Li Zehou interpreted Western learning to be "modernization," instead of "Westernization," and meant modern civilization and modern scientific management of production. Shu Zhan (1989) argued that politically, economically, and ideologically China had no proper conditions for being "totally Westernized," and that, in fact, the path of Chinese socialist practice of the past four decades followed the Soviet model, not "the Western model." This enabled him to argue that many problems in contemporary China were really closely associated with "total Sovietization" rather than "total Westernization" (Shu Zhan 1989).

Alternatively, Yan Jiaqi avoided using the sensitive term, "Western." He (1988) wrote, instead, of "the common cultural elements" through which he suggested that there are usually two types of cultures in a country. The first type, he argued, is "the traditional culture" shared by people who live in a particular country, and the second type is "a culture" shared by people in different countries. To define the second type of culture he envisioned—the common cultural elements shared by people in different countries—he employed terms such as "democracy," "freedom," "human rights," "the rule of law," "social justice," and "humanism." Yan Jiaqi (1988) also pointed out that the main reason for the prolongation of China's "backwardness" in science and technology was that these concepts had been criticized in modern China. As he visualized it, the common cultural elements shared by all nations resulted from "the World civilization and human development." His view, however, was still labeled as "promoting Bourgeois liberalism" by the conservatives in the official arena during the Anti-Bourgeois Liberalism Campaign in 1987.

Liu Xiaobo understood "Westernization" as "modernization" or "internationalization," and proposed that this included the following elements: private ownership, freedom of speech, political participation by the general public, and rule of law. Like many Chinese writers who tend to be succinct in their writing, Liu Xiaobo used one word—"humanized" (*renhua*)—to summarize his understanding of "Westernization." For him, to be "westernized" was to have a life of "real human beings."[21]

It is interesting to see how this was portrayed beyond intellectual circles by the scriptwriters of "River Elegy" (*Heshang*), the television documentary series I mentioned earlier. Their script stressed how important it was to transform "the yellow culture," an allegedly isolated, land-based Chinese culture originating from the Yellow River, into a "blue culture," an open, ocean-based culture treated as an analogy to modern culture. According to the scriptwriters, directors and others involved in the making of "River Elegy," Chinese traditional culture is deeply rooted in the agricultural economy and has constructed a national identity which is characterized by "submitting to the will of Heaven" and "closing the country to international intercourse." "River Elegy" presented this traditional culture as on the wane because it cannot allegedly generate a spirit of progress for the Chinese nation, nor promote democracy and a legal system. The only way out for this declining culture in this representation is to learn from "the West" (Cai Zhenchan 1988).

Not surprisingly, in the official arena, the makers of "River Elegy" were identified as openly advocating "total Westernization" and vilifying Chinese traditional culture (Yi Jiayan 1989). However, "River Elegy" had by and large been accepted by scholars in the unofficial arena, although it was criticized for advocating cultural superiority and being unscientific (some of the data used have no historical evidence) (Cai Zhenchan 1988). Nevertheless, the influence generated by "River Elegy" went far beyond the political and academic arenas. It had given the general public a message that Chinese traditional culture should be reexamined with Western culture as a reference system. In this regard, "River Elegy" was highly evaluated by overseas China scholars such as Tu Wei-ming (Yu Lina 1989).

FACTORS CONTRIBUTING TO THE EMERGENCE OF THE CULTURAL FEVER

I have written in some detail about the arguments, the nuances, and the debates in order to convey the intensity and form of this phenomenon of "Cultural Fever." But the obvious question that needs addressing is why culture suddenly became so feverish during the period between the mid-1980s and the spring of 1989, and what factors contributed to the emergence of the Cultural Fever.

I view cultural construction as an interactive process between contending power groups expressing their views toward the traditions of the past and the social and political order of the present (Wu et al. 1989). In the case of Cultural Fever of China, we see that "the underground hot spring," the cultural discourse of political dissidents, had a significant impact on a group of intellectuals within the official arena who later developed an independent voice. The official force also played a key role. The changes in official political control and domination since the end of the 1970s facilitated and at the same time inhibited the development of the Cultural Fever.

"THE UNDERGROUND HOT SPRING"

Questions raised by the activists from the unofficial arena during the second half of the 1970s could be found in the later discussion of the political reform and the debates during the Cultural Fever (Chen Xiaoya and Li Qin 1988). Those activists and their works from the unofficial arena were later referred to as "the underground hot spring" by participants in the Cultural Fever (Chen Xiaoya and Li Qin 1988). Li-Yi-Zhe's big-character poster in the mid 1970s and the Democracy Wall Movement represented by Wei Jingsheng at the end of the 1970s could be treated as two of the major "spring heads." Li-Yi-Zhe was the first group to openly criticize Chinese traditional culture and to attempt to uncover the roots of traditional culture in the existing social order.[22] Wei Jingsheng was among the first to reexamine sinicized Marxism.[23] Li-Yi-Zhe, Wei Jingsheng, and other activists who engaged in the political cultural discourse during the period between the mid-1970s and the late 1970s were identified as counterrevolutionary and were politically persecuted.

It took about ten years for intellectuals collectively to generate and to express understanding and sympathy for this group of political dissidents. There was little sympathy and support toward this group of political dissidents among ordinary intellectuals partly because of extremely limited publicity through official channels, and partly because of relatively high expectations for Deng's blueprint of the "Four Modernizations" after the ten years of chaos. Chinese intellectuals had identified with the Party lines during the past four decades. A few who had their own ways of thinking had often been purged in numerous political movements and tossed to the bottom of the society. Since 1978, official control on intellectual thinking had been relaxed, although the basic structure of the official domination still existed.

The inconsistent control of the Party since the end of the 1970s provided conditions for intellectuals to form an independent force. During the Cultural Fever, a number of non-official research institutions and communication organizations were established. There were academic journals and book series, such as *Towards the Future, New Enlightenment, The Thinker, Du shu* (Reading), and *Culture: China and the World*. There were also non-official research centers, such as the Chinese Culture Study Society and the *"Heshang"* project. In addition, intellectual salons were formed on many university campuses. Thus, through various forms of organization, a "public sphere" was gradually created among intellectuals. Moreover, through a series of "civil discourses," a group of non-official intellectual elites emerged entering the 1980s which included the philosopher Wang Ruoshui, the theoretical historian Jin Guantao, the political scientist Yan Jiaqi, and the physicist Fang Lizhi (Kelly 1990)

At the beginning of 1989, there was a wave of writing open letters demanding freedom of speech and the release of political prisoners, such as Wei Jingsheng, and advocating democracy and human rights.[24] This upsurge of writing open letters indicated that an unprecedented "independence consciousness" had emerged among intellectuals in the official arena. This independent consciousness among intellectuals was best described by Yan Jiaqi (1988) as a desire to have "a scientific research world without forbidden zones, peaks, and idols."

CHANGES IN THE PARTY AND STATE POLITICAL CONTROL AND DOMINATION

Support from factions of the top officials, and the participation of the intellectuals representing the official arena, unquestionably contributed to the formation and development of the Cultural Fever. Since the late 1970s, the relaxed political atmosphere created by the reform program after Mao had provided opportunities for intellectuals to develop diversified views on socioeconomic, political, and cultural issues. The Third Plenary Session of the Eleventh Central Committee of the CCP in 1978 was a significant turning point in China's political history. It denounced the Cultural Revolution, including the Campaign of Criticizing Lin Biao and Confucius.[25]

The Third Plenary Session of the Eleventh Central Committee of the CCP, which officially "rehabilitated" Confucius, provided a possibility for reevaluating Confucianism in the academic arena at the beginning of 1980. Soon five nationwide conferences on Confucianism were held.[26] Entering the mid-1980s, the research on Confucianism expanded to an examination of Chinese traditional culture. Conferences and seminars on cultural issues were frequently organized. For example, Fudan University organized the first International Conference on Chinese traditional culture at the beginning of 1986.[27] In addition to conferences and seminars, numerous book series, monographs, and countless papers on modernization and Chinese traditional culture were published. Many newspapers and journals added a special column on culture. Moreover, a nongovernmental research institution, the Chinese Culture Study Society (*Zhongguo wenhua shuyuan*), organized seminars on comparative studies of Chinese and Western cultures.[28]

Entering the later 1980s, however, the official force itself became an inseparable part of the Cultural Fever. The debate on New Authoritarianism discussed above is an example. This debate was initiated by Zhao Ziyang's think tank, a group of intellectuals who advocated New Authoritarianism which was molded after a Confucian value system. Moreover, Zhao Ziyang, who represented a faction of the official Party line at that moment, also actively supported the documentary film *Heshang* (River Elegy) which extended the cultural discourse to the general public.

Another crucial historical event that facilitated drastic political change in the political cultural arena after the death of Mao Zedong was the Great Debate on the Criterion of Truth in the last quarter of the 1970s.[29] It enabled a group of elite intellectuals to separate from the official arena and to develop an independent voice. The Great Debate on the Criterion of Truth was initiated by a number of ordinary intellectuals. This group of intellectuals later was supported by the internal faction of the CCP headed by Deng Xiaoping.[30] During the period between the end of the 1970s and the mid-1980s, research on Mao Zedong Thought and the reevaluation of the CCP history had mushroomed. National and local research associations were established, special seminars were organized, and special journals were published.

The interruptions of the cultural discourse were also closely paralleled by changes in official controls and domination. Brugger and Kelly (1990) characterized the period 1978 to 1981 as a period of stress on the liberalization of thought after ten years of domination by dogmatism. In 1981, the CCP realized that some limits needed to be imposed on intellectual freedom. Deng Xiaoping put out his four cardinal principles: Marxism/Mao Zedong Thought, socialist path, leadership of the CCP, and proletarian dictatorship. The dominant ideological theme then switched to "creating a socialist civilization." In 1983, the Anti-Spiritual Pollution Campaign was launched to criticize intellectual freedom. This campaign was soon terminated, since the Party leaders were afraid it might stifle the reforms. In 1987, partially in response to the student demonstrations that started from the end of 1986, another political campaign, the Anti-Bourgeois Liberalization Campaign was launched to criticize intellectual freedom. Several leading intellectuals, such as Su Shaozhi, Li Honglin, Wang Ruoshui, and Wang Ruowang, were purged in these two political campaigns.

The discussion on Westernization could also be viewed as an interactive process between the official and unofficial arenas. Entering the 1980s, a broader liberalization of thought had been encouraged under the relatively relaxed political atmosphere. Facing an irreversible tide of liberal thinking among intellectuals, in 1983 and 1987, conservatives in the CCP launched two campaigns which aimed at punishing those intellectuals who were involved in spreading "unhealthy" Western influence. The inconsistent and ambivalent attitudes toward Western ideas and philosophies in the official arena provided opportunities for the emergence of discourse on Western thoughts among intellectuals. A series of both classic and modern works by Western authors were translated. The names of Friedrich Nietzche, Sigmund Freud, and Jean Paul Sartre were very fashionable among young scholars (Liu Xiaobo 1989a). Suffering from official restrictions, however, discussion on Western culture was relatively underdeveloped and systematic research on Western culture was limited. Scholars flirted with many types of classic and modern ideas and philosophies from the West, but their understanding of Western culture seemed to have been superficial. In contrast to the hostile attitude towards

"Cultural Fever" 231

Western culture on the part of the official arena, certain scholars tended to treat Western culture as the most ideal cultural system in the world.

CONCLUSION AND DISCUSSION

Understanding the Cultural Fever, an important episode of the Post-Mao era, is helpful for us in understanding politics in China. Since the spring of 1989, the popularity of "culture" has disappeared in the academic arena and in the general public. Moreover, many active participants in the Cultural Fever were in prison, in exile, in silence.[31] Examining China's cultural policies after the spring of 1989, we saw an unexpectedly large setback in cultural construction. The Chinese government launched a new campaign to criticize "bourgeois liberalization" (Zhang Jianxin 1989; Li Ruihuan 1989). "Bourgeois liberalization" was labeled as a political concept which aims at transforming China into a vassal of capitalist countries and abandoning the leadership of the Communist Party and Socialist Road. The criticism of Chinese traditional culture during the Cultural Fever was considered a demand for "bourgeois liberalization" and labeled as "national nihilism." Marxism and Mao Zedong Thought were again given the foremost position, treated as the theoretical basis for the ideology of the CCP. The discussion of non-Marxist Western culture during the Cultural Fever was again labeled as "bourgeois liberalization."[32]

Understanding the Cultural Fever will also help us to anticipate future significant changes and the role intellectuals might play in these changes in China. Cultural Fever was a debate about how Chinese intellectuals would like to see China's contemporary history and the role they would like to play in it. This cultural discourse was remarkable in many ways. It was unprecedented in its scale and range of participants. It was a dynamic process of interaction between the official and unofficial forces. The discourse involved both young and old scholars from the social sciences and humanities, as well as from the natural sciences in the academic arena. It was not merely a cultural discourse among intellectuals from the official arena. It had a broad participation of intellectuals from a wide spectrum. Because of the public ownership system established since 1949, almost all the intellectuals worked for State-owned institutions. However, the official "color" of Chinese intellectuals started to change in the Post-Mao era. During the latter half of the 1970s, many conventional intellectuals within the official arena were inspired by unofficial voices, "the underground hot spring." From the beginning to the end, this cultural discourse was partially confirmed and supported by factions of the top officials.

The Cultural Fever was also exceptional in terms of the scope of "culture" discussed during this period. It was extraordinary because it was not merely a cultural discourse. It was a cultural discourse that mixed "culture" with politics, a discourse on politics and ideology. Going far beyond conventional definitions of "culture," it focused on three major dimensions related to issues of social and political order in China. Among these three dimensions, as I have shown, the discourse on Chinese traditional culture and the evaluation of Marxism/Mao Zedong Thought were relatively more extensive than the discourse on "Western" ideas due to lack of understanding and constraints in the official arena. The interconnections and reinforcements between Chinese traditional culture and sinicized Marxism constitute one of the heated areas of the cultural discourse.

Although there is no doubt that the Cultural Fever was an unprecedented cultural discourse, it is important to note that there seems to have been a disturbing tendency among some participants in Cultural Fever to believe in and advocate cultural superiority. After the open-door policy, the central issue in the agenda of the policy makers and in the minds of intellectuals has been how to speed up economic development. Driven by deep concerns over the future of China, much of the discussion among Chinese intellectuals was directly connected to the search for solutions to problems of economic development in China. In the process of speeding up economic development, people took a distant reference group—"Western developed countries"—as models. After focusing on the economic issues, Chinese intellectuals naturally started to look at cultural issues since the distant reference group had different value systems. Especially after seeing serious problems that occurred in the Economic Reform, they attempted to find a noneconomic alternative for improving economic development in China. A group of intellectuals blamed Chinese traditional culture for China's economic underdevelopment in the past. They naively treated Western culture as a panacea and Chinese traditional "habits of the heart" as the greatest barrier to current economic development. But, as I have shown, this view is ironically similar to Mao Zedong's practice of regarding reforming people's souls as the ultimate mechanism for improving the society. Reviewing the political and economic contexts of the Cultural Fever, it is not hard to see that the negative attitudes toward Chinese traditional culture and the favorable attitudes toward Western cultures exhibited by most participants were closely related to the sagging economy in China during that time period. We can see the linkage between cultural constructions and stages of economic development from the case of the Cultural Fever in China. As cycling changes of *Nihonjinron* are seen in Japan (as described by Befu in this volume), so can we anticipate a major change in cultural construction in China with the increasing development of its economy.

NOTES

1. The research for this paper was carried out at the Institute of Culture and Communication of the East-West Center and supported by a

post-doctoral fellowship from the Rockefeller Foundation. An earlier draft of this paper was presented in the Workshop on Cultural Construction and National Identity, at the Institute of Culture and Communication, East-West Center, Honolulu, June 19–22, 1990. I am indebted to Lewis Mayo, Pan Zhongdang, Alvin So, Wang Feng, Andrew Weintraub, Geoffrey White, and David Wu, all who read earlier drafts of this paper and offered many useful comments and suggestions.

2. EDITOR'S NOTE: This essay concentrates on the period known as the "Cultural Fever" because of the obvious importance attributed to "culture" during this period and the refraction of myriad discussions about "China" and "Chinese society" through the invocation of culture. For further reading, please turn to Haiou Yang's extensive bibliography. In addition, there are a few books available in English at major U.S. research libraries that could serve as useful references, especially with regard to official articulations of "cultural policy" and the unofficial range of phenomena that fall under the rubric of "popular culture." Among these are Liu Bai's *Cultural Policy in the People's Republic of China: Letting a Hundred Flowers Bloom* (Paris: UNESCO, 1983), Richard Curt Kraus' *Pianos and Politics in China: Middle-Class Ambitions and the Struggle over Western Music* (New York: Oxford University Press, 1989) and his *Brushes with Power: Modern Politics and the Chinese Art of Calligraphy* (Berkeley: University of California Press, 1991), Shih Chih-yu's *State and Society in China's Political Economy: The Cultural Dynamics of Socialist Reform* (Boulder: Lynne Rienner, 1995), David Holm's *Art and Ideology in Revolutionary China* (Oxford: Clarendon Press, 1991), and Zha Jianying's *China Pop: How Soap Operas, Tabloids, and Best Sellers Are Transforming a Culture* (New York: New Press, 1995).

3. The term "cultural fever," *wenhuare*, appears in several review articles in Chinese about the cultural discourse since the mid 1980s. In Wang He's review article (1986) on the culture discourse *wenhuare* is translated as "cultural fever" in English, and it is translated as "culture mania" in Barme's paper (1989).

4. Barme (1989) refers to the Post-Mao Reform Era as the New Age. In China, this period is officially termed the Socialist New Age, *shehuizhuyi xinshiqi*.

5. Because of the strong political pressure of the past few decades, poetry and fiction have been treated as the sole forms of airing unofficial opinions. Thus, poetry and fiction in China have been constantly mixed with politics, and thus they are the main materials for sinologists to use in studying voices from the unofficial arena. Geremie Barme and John Minford's (1986) work is a typical example of such studies. During the Cultural Fever, because of the relatively relaxed atmosphere, Chinese

scholars did not have to limit themselves to using poetry and fiction to express their views. They started to express their opinions directly by using the medium of non-fiction. By the medium of non-fiction, the author means essay style articles. All the Cultural Fever participants' names in this study are presented in the Chinese order of family name followed by given name.
6. In people's daily life in China during the past decades, "culture" has been defined as knowledge, education, literature and the arts. Culture is also defined as *wenzhijiaohua*, "the art of ruling" in classical Chinese literature. In the modern Chinese language dictionary, culture is defined as "the sum of material and spiritual wealth produced in the historical process of human development." See the definition of *wenhua*, culture, in Cihai (dictionary) 1965, China Publishing House, Hong Kong Branch: Hong Kong. Also see Kwok's definition of culture (1989a).
7. Whyte (1989) asserts that traditional Chinese, Marxist/Mao, and Western are the three distinct cultural elements that have been constantly under contention in the post-Mao reform era in the official arena. Since the 1850s and the May Fourth Movement in 1919 in particular, China has been undergoing struggles between *Zhong* and *Xi*, the tradition of the past and the influence of the modern world. However, since the 1949 revolution guided by Marxism-Leninism, cultural policies in contemporary China have involved not only tradition and the influence of the modern world, but also Marxism-Leninism and Mao Zedong Thought. After 1949, Mao attempted to forge a new national identity and a cultural orthodoxy that would both eliminate parts of Chinese traditional inheritance and exclude non-Marxist Western cultural influence. After Mao's death in 1976, China has entered a new era which is characterized by a reconsideration of Maoist orders in all fronts. In general, a broad cultural liberation is encouraged during this new era. The shift from a negative to a positive attitude towards Chinese traditional culture is a major characteristic of the cultural construction in this new era. A new infusion of Western cultural influences is another characteristic of the cultural construction. However, how large the "door" should be opened for liberation of thoughts has always been a controversial issue in the official arena.
8. Related questions included: What is the Chinese national character, and is Chinese traditional culture a hindrance or an asset in China's modernization process?
9. Also see Footnote 25 and 26.
10. Barme (1990) gives a very detailed account of Liu Xiaobo and his relationship to the 1989 Protest Movement in Beijing. But for more detail on

Chinese traditional culture, see Liu Xiaobo's *Selected Criticism: A Dialogue with An Intellectual Elite* (*Xuanze De Pipan*). When this book was published internally in China, the original title was *A Dialogue with Li Zehou*. This book is actually an acerbic criticism of Li Zehou's two books on Chinese traditional culture, in which he emphasizes that the cream of traditional Chinese culture should be upheld.

11. Yan Hui was one of the favorite students of Confucius.
12. This perhaps is Liu Zaifu's strategy, since Lu Xun has been one of the orthodox theorists along with Marx, Engels, and Mao in China in the past four decades.
13. Also see Brugger and Kelly (1990). They comment on Jin's philosophy and its relationship with Marx's philosophy.
14. "Feudalism" in the minds of Chinese intellectuals is deeply embedded in a five-stage societal evolution viewpoint offered by orthodox Marxist historians, which defines slave, feudal, capital, socialist and communist as the five key stages of societal development that cannot deviate. According to this deterministic model, China was a slave society before the Zhou Dynasty and a feudal society for over two thousand years since the Zhou Dynasty, until a brief interlude of capitalism interceded before the socialist transformation starting in 1949. The meaning of "feudalism" here is totally different from the classic definition of the type of society that existed in medieval Europe offered by Marc Bloch (1961).
15. The other criticism is that New Authoritarianism overemphasizes the power of elites and neglects the rule of law and democracy. Critics argue that what China needs is the authority of law and a democratic system, not the authority of autocracy. Moreover, the theory of New Authoritarianism, which is based on the experience of the newly industrial countries such as Singapore, Taiwan and South Korea, is an inappropriate transplant to China's situation. Those countries have particular historical conditions that China does not possess, such as a legal system left by colonial governments, a homogeneous labor force, and an export economy. See Lin Yanwen (1989) and Zhang Weiguo (1989).
16. Brugger and Kelly (1990) divide these discussions into the following categories: stage of development, dialectics, objective economic law, praxis and pragmatism, and humanism.
17. Su Shaozhi was one of the leading intellectuals in the discussion of socialism. During the period between the late 1970s and the beginning of the 1980s, Su Shaozhi was sent to Yugoslavia and Hungary to study their economic reforms. After returning from Eastern Europe, he developed new views on socialism. He suggested that China was just entering the primary period of socialism.

"Cultural Fever"

18. Brugger and Kelly (1990) give a detail discussion of the evolution of Wang Ruoshui's theory.
19. On the one hand, people tend to associate all the bad phenomena with "capitalist," "bourgeois," and "exploitation." On the other hand, people tend to associate all the good phenomena with "proletarian" and "socialist."
20. On May 4, 1919, students in Peking protested against the Chinese government's humiliating policy toward Japan. There resulted a series of strikes and intellectual discourse. One of the goals for the participants of the 1919 May Fourth Movement was to create a new China and the major method used was to substitute the old thoughts with new thoughts. Confucianism was considered the hard core of the old thoughts and thus Confucianism and its followers were under attack. New thoughts were Western ideas stemming from the French and American Revolutions, such as realism, utilitarianism, liberalism, individualism, socialism, and Darwinism. See (Chow 1960).
21. See Jin Zhong's interview report with Liu Xiaobo (1989).
22. Li-Yi-Zhe, a writing group in Guangdong province, was composed of three persons: Wang Xizhe, Li Zhenting, and Chen Yiyang. Li-Yi-Zhe was known as the authors of Guangdong's famous Li-Yi-Zhe big-character posters in 1974, the beginning of the Campaign of Criticizing Confucianism and Criticizing Lin Biao. They focused on the following three issues: "the feudal and fascist despotism of Lin Biao," "the privileged class under socialist system," and "socialist democracy and rule of law" (Li-Yi-Zhe 1982).
23. Wei Jingsheng was another figure of "the underground hot spring." He was famous for a series of articles collectively called "the fifth Modernization—the Democratization" during the Democracy Wall Movement. He raised the question of the direction in which China was heading in the post-Mao era: "Will China continue Mao's despotic dictatorship after Mao's death?" He coined the term "the fifth Modernization," and he argued that Deng Xiaoping's Four Modernizations was insufficient and that China needed a fifth modernization which was human rights and democracy.
24. Led by Fang Lizhi, a group of established scholars petitioned the leaders of the CCP or the People's Congress to demand freedom of speech and the release of political prisoners, such as Wei Jingsheng, and to advocate democracy and human rights. Among those who joined the petition, many were active participants of the cultural discourse entering the mid-1980s, including Bao Zhunxin, Jing Guantao, Li Zehou, Liu Qingfen, Pang Pu, Su Shaozhi, Su Xiaokang, Tang Yijie, and Wang Ruoshui.

25. In the mid 1970s, the Campaign of "Criticizing Confucius and Lin Biao" was launched. It confused the masses as to whom it was addressed, compared with the previous attacks. On the surface, it called for rejection of the Confucian values of humanism, conservatism, contempt for physical labor and the inferior position of women. However, the campaign was actually a concealed attack on Zhou Enlai, who attempted to restore stability and modernize the economy. It was launched by Mao's radical trustees who were later referred to as "the Gang of Four." By means of historical analogy and symbolism, they attempted to regain their power in the CCP.
26. The research on Confucius started at the end of the 1970s and entered a new phase in the mid 1980s. On September 6, 1984, the 2535th anniversary of Confucius' birthday, the fourth nationwide conference on Confucianism was held again in Qufu. "China's Confucian Foundation" was established in this conference. In June 1985, the fifth conference on Confucius was held in Beijing. Participants not only came from different provinces within China, but also came from outside of China.
27. The main theme of this international conference was the reevaluation of essential features of Chinese traditional culture and the relationship between Chinese traditional culture and Western cultures. Participants included scholars from Australia, Canada, China, Germany, Japan, and the United States. See the two volume collection of papers presented in that conference edited by the History Department of Fudan University.
28. During the period between 1985 and 1986, the Chinese Culture Study Society organized two important seminars under the titles of "Chinese culture" and "Comparative studies of Chinese and Western cultures." Lecturers of these two training classes included senior Chinese scholars such as Zhou Gucheng and Liang Shuming, middle aged Chinese scholars, such as Li Zehou, as well as foreign scholars coming from countries such as Australia, Canada, France, Hong Kong, Taiwan, and the United States. The number of students participating in the second training class was over 800.
29. The Great Debate on the Criterion of Truth during the period between 1977–78 was a dispute between the majority faction around Deng Xiaoping and the Maoist minority faction led by Hua Goufeng over how far the criticism of Mao Zedong and the redefinition of the ideological system should or could be permitted to go. The Maoist faction was opposed by Deng's majority faction in terms of a slogan saying "the practice is sole criterion for gauging the truth."
30. Tao Kai, Zhang Yide, Yi Yuanwen, and Dai Qing (1989) reveal the development of the Great Debate on the Criterion of Truth. The questions in the

minds of the intellectuals such as Ma Beiwen about the future of China right after the downfall of the Gang of Four were as such: How could this "two whatever" be dealt with indirectly? What theoretical weapon could be used to fight with this "two whatever?" The report of an interview with Hu Fuming describes the process of how Hu Fuming generated the draft for the *Guangmingribao* (the Enlightenment Daily) editorial. The fatal flaw in the "two whatever" identified by Hu Fuming, a professor of political science in Nanjing University, was that it was contradictory to Marx's epistemology. During the period between June and July 1977, Hu Fuming, excited about what he found, drafted an article entitled "Practice is the criterion for truth," which later became the *Guangmingribao* editorial, used for the Great Debate on the Criterion of Truth. Elite scholars, such as Ma Biewen and Wu Jiang, who were inspired by Deng Xiaoping's speech arguing that Mao Zedong thought should be understood comprehensively and applied correctly, participated in the revising and finalizing of Hu's article. Hu Yaobang, the deputy president of the Party School of the Central Committee at that time, confirmed the finalization of the article. Later scholars in *Renminribao* (People's Daily) and *Jiefangjunribao* (PLA Daily), also actively supported the Guangming Ribao editorial. At the end of 1978, the Third Plenary Session of the Eleventh Central Committee highly evaluated this debate and proclaimed "seeking truth from fact." See Tao Kai et al. *Zou Hu Xiandai Mixin* (Out of Modern Superstition: the Great Debate on the Criterion for Truth).

31. EDITOR'S NOTE: A powerful depiction of the 1989 "democracy movement" and the occupation of Tianenmen Square appears in the 1995 documentary film "The Gates of Heavenly Peace," directed by Carma Hinton and Richard Gordon. Among the active, non-student participants were intellectuals involved in "the Cultural Fever," including Liu Xiaobo.

32. EDITOR'S NOTE: It is useful to remember these attacks on "bourgeois liberalization" when multinational corporations wax poetically about the opening of the Chinese market, and when we contemplate the 1997 reunification of Hong Kong with the People's Republic of China.

REFERENCES

Bao Zunxin (1988). *Cong jiuqimeng dao xinqimeng: dui wusi de fan si* (From the Old Enlightenment to the New Enlightenment: A Reintrospection of the May Fourth Movement). *Daluzhongguo* (Mainland China) 28(2):13–23.

Barme, Geremie and John Minford, Eds. (1986). *Seeds of Fire: Chinese Voices of Conscience*. Hong Kong: Far Eastern Economic Review, Ltd.

Barme, Geremie (1989). The Chinese Velvet Prison: Culture in the "New Age," 1976–1989. *Issues and Studies* 25(8):54–79.
— (1990). Liu Xiaobo and the Protest Movement of 1989. In George Hicks, Ed. *The Broken Mirror: China After Tiananmen*. United Kingdom: Longman Current Affairs, pp. 52–99.
Benton, Gregor, Ed. (1982). *Wild Lilies, Poisonous Weeds: Dissident Voices from People's China*. London: Pluto Press.
Befu, Harumi (1987). Nihonjinron in Anthropological Perspective. Paper presented at the Conference on Nihonjinron, May 4–5, Paris, France.
Bloch, Marc (1961). *Feudal Society*. Translated by L.A. Manyon. Chicago: University of Chicago Press.
Brugger, Bill and David Kelly (1990). *Chinese Marxism in the Post-Mao Era*. Stanford: Stanford University Press.
Cai Zhenchang (1988). *Heshang de zhenhan yu shifei* (The Shock, Right, and Wrong of Heshang). *Daluzhongguo* (Mainland China) 21(10) (October): 48–52.
Chen Yang (1989). *Wuannian Mao Zedong yu wenhua dageming* (Mao Zedong's Late Years and the Cultural Revolution). In Xiao Yanzhong, Ed. *Wuannian Mao Zedong* (The Late Years of Mao Zedong). Beijing: Chuanqiu Press, pp. 201–219.
Chen Xiaoya and Li Qin (1988). Underground Hot Spring. *Hainan jishi* (The Hainan Report) 1:49–58.
Chow Tse-tsung (1960). *The May Fourth Movement: Intellectuals in Modern China*. Cambridge: Harvard University Press.
Fudan University History Department (l987a). *Zhongguo chuantong wenhua zaijiantao shangpian: zhongguo chuantong wenhua de tezheng* (Reevaluations of Chinese Traditional Culture. Volume 1: Characteristics of Chinese Traditional Culture). Hong Kong: Shangwu Press, Hong Kong Branch.
— (1987b). *Zhongguo chuantong wenhua zaijiantao, xiapian: xifang wenha yu dangdai sichao* (Reevaluations of Chinese Traditional Cultures. Volume 2: Western Culture and Thought in Contemporary Chinese History). Hong Kong: Shangwu Press, Hong Kong Branch.
Goldman, Merle (1981). *China's Intellectuals: Advise and Dissent*. Cambridge: Harvard University Press.
Helmut, Martin (1982). *Cult and Canon: The Origins and Development of the State of Maoism*. Armonk: M.E. Sharp, Inc.
Holm, David (1991). *Art and Ideology in Revolutionary China*. Oxford: Clarendon Press.
Huntington, Samuel P. and Clement Henry Moor (1970). *Authoritarian Politics in Modern Society*. New York: Basic Books.

Jin Guantao (1989). *Rujia wenhua de shenceng jiegou dui makesi zhuyi zhongguohua de yingxiang* (The Influence of the Deep Structure of Confucian Culture on the Sinicized Marxism in China). *Xinqimeng* (New Enlightenment) 2:22–36.

Jin Guantao and Liu Qingfeng (1983). *Xingsheng yu weiji* (Prosperity and Crisis: On the Ultra-Stable Structure of China's Feudalist Society). China: Hunan People's Press.

Jin Zhong (1988). *Wentan heima fangwen ji* (An Interview with the "Black Horse" of the Literary World). *Emancipation Monthly* 22.

Kelly, David (1985). Wang Ruoshui: Writings on Humanism, Alienation, and Philosophy. (A special issue on Chinese studies). *Philosophy* 16(3).

— (1990). Chinese Intellectuals in the 1989 Democracy Movement. In George Hicks, Ed. *The Broken Mirror: China After Tiananmen*. United Kingdom: Longman Current Affairs, pp. 24–51.

Kraus, Richard Curt (1991). *Brushes with Power: Modern Politics and the Chinese Art of Calligraphy*. Berkeley: University of California Press.

— (1989). *Pianos and Politics in China: Middle-Class Ambitions and the Struggle over Western Music*. New York: Oxford University Press.

Kwok, D.W.Y. (1989a). Protesting Tradition and Tradition of Protest. In D.W.Y. Kwok, Ed. *Protest in the Chinese Tradition*. Center for Chinese Studies at the University of Hawaii Occasional Papers 2, pp. 1–8.

— (1989b). *The Chinese Tradition: An Essay*. Center for Chinese Studies at the University of Hawaii Occasional Papers 3.

Larson, Wendy (1989). Realism, Modernism, and the "Anti-Spiritual Pollution Campaign" in China. *Modern China* 15(1):37–71.

Li Ming (1988). *Sandairen de wenhua yu dangdai zhongguo wenhua jianshe de kunjing* (The Culture of the Three Generations and the Difficult Situation of Cultural Construction in Contemporary China). *Zhongguo qingnian bao* (China Youth Daily) (September 11).

Li Ruihuan (1989). *Dangqian xuanchuan sixiang gong zuo de jinpo renwu* (The Current Pressing Tasks of Propaganda). *Research on Political Propaganda* 9.

Li-Yi-Zhe (1982). On Socialist Democracy and Rule of Law. In *Minzhu zhongguo* (Democratic China: Collected Papers of the Captured of the Mainland China Democratic Movement). Compiled and edited by the Hong Kong Chinese Student Association. Hong Kong: Far Eastern Review Press, pp. 53–82.

Li Zehou (1989a). 1949–1976: *Zhongguo yishi xingtai de fansi* (1949–1976: Reflections on the Ideology of China). In Xiao Yanzhong, Ed. *Wuannian Mao Zedong* (The Late Years of Mao Zedong) Beijing: Chuanqiu Press, pp. 183–200.

— (1989b). *Zhongguo dalu wenhua yanjiu de fazhan qushi* (The Trend of Research on Cultural Construction in Mainland China). *Daluzhongguo* (Mainland China) 25(8) (January):73–80.

— (1985). *Zhongguo gudai sixiang shilun* (On the History of Ancient Chinese Philosophies). Beijing: People's Press.

— (1979). *Zhongguo xiandai sixiang shilun* (On the History of Modern Chinese Philosophies). Beijing: People's Press.

Lin Yanwen (1989). *Xinquanwei zhuyi shuping* (On New Authoritarianism). *Daluzhongguo* (Mainland China) 22(5): 56–61.

Link, Perry (1987). The Limits of Cultural Reform in Deng Xiaoping's China. *Modern China* 13(2):115–176.

Link, Perry, Richard Madsen, and Paul G. Pickowicz, Eds. (1989) *Unofficial China: Popular Culture and Thought in the People's Republic of China*. Boulder: Westview Press.

Liu Bai (1983). *Cultural Policy in the People's Republic of China: Letting a Hundred Flowers Bloom*. Paris: UNESCO.

Liu Wei (1986). *Zhongguo xueshujie de yige xin wenhua rechao* (A New Cultural Wave in China's Academic Circle). *Liaowang* (Overview) (February): 24–25.

Liu Xiaobo (1989a). *Xuanze de pipan* (Selected Criticism: A Dialogue with a Thinking Elite). Taipei: Fongyun Shidai Press.

— (1989b). *Qimeng de beiju: wusi yundong pipan* (The Tragedy of the Enlightenment: A Criticism of the May Fourth Movement). *Ming Pao* 269 (May): 37–45.

Liu Zaifu and Lin Gang (1988). *Chuantong yu zhongguoren* (Tradition and the Chinese: Rethinking and Recriticizing the Main Issues of the May Fourth New Cultural Movement). Beijing: Joint Publishing.

Liu Zehua, Wang Maohe, and Wang Lanzhong (1988). *Zhuanzhi quanli yu zhongguo shehui* (Despotic Power and Chinese Society). Hong Kong: Zhonghua Press, Inc.

Lu Xun (1956). A Madman's Diary. In *Selected Works of Lu Xun*. Vol. 1. Beijing: Foreign Language Press.

Mao Zedong (1952). *Lun zhongguo geming yu zhongguo gongchandang* (On the Chinese Revolution and the Chinese Communist Party). In *Mao Zedong xuanji* (Selected Works of Mao Zedong). Vol. 2. Beijing: People's Press, pp. 529–559.

Ogden, Suzanne (1989). *Chinese Unresolved Issues: Politics, Development and Culture*. New Jersey: Prentice Hall.

Pang Pu (1988a). Cultural Traditions and Democratization. Paper prepared for International Conference on Democracy and Social Justice, August 25–29, in Honolulu.

— (1988b). *Liangxiuji* (Collected Papers on Chinese Culture and Philosophy). Shanghai: Shanghai People's Press.

Rosen, Stanley (1985). Guangzhou's Democracy Movement in Cultural Revolution Perspective. *China Quarterly* 101:1–31.

Shi Zhongquan (1989). *Mao Zedong dui makesi zichanjieji quanli gainian de wujie* (Mao Zedong's Misunderstanding of Marx's Concept of "the Right of the Bourgeois"). In Xiao Yanzhong, Ed. *Wuannian Mao Zedong* (The Late Years of Mao Zedong). Beijing: Chuanqiu Press, pp. 3–14.

Shih Chihyu (1995). *State and Society in China's Political Economy: The Cultural Dynamics of Socialist Reform*. Boulder: Lynne Rienner.

Shu Zhan (1988). *Quanpan xihua yu quanpan suhua* (Total Westernization and Total Sovietization). *Xinqimeng* (New Enlightenment) 4:108–114.

Sun Kaitai (1986). *Zhongguo de kongzi taolunhui* (Conferences on Confucius in China). *Liaowang* (Overview) (February):32–33.

Tan Zhongji (1989). *Ping "wuyiliu tongzhi"* (On the "May Sixteenth Circular"). In Xiao Yanzhong, Ed. *Wuannian Mao Zedong* (The Late Years of Mao Zedong). Beijing: Chuanqiu Press, pp. 15–32.

Tang Yijie (1987). *Zhongguo wenhua de xiandaihua yu guojihua* (The Modernization and the Internationalization of the Chinese Culture). Beijing: International Cultural Press.

Tao Kai, Zhang Yide, and Dai Qing (1989). *Zhenli biaozhun taolun shimo* (The Process of the Debate on the Criterion for the Truth). In Tao Kai, Zhang Yide, and Dai Qing, Eds. *Zouchu xiandai mixin* (Out of the Modern Superstition: The Great Debate on the Criterion of Truth). Hong Kong: Joint Publishing (H.K.) Co., Ltd, pp. 1–101.

Tu Wei-ming (1991). Cultural China: The Periphery as the Center. *Daedalus* (Spring):1–32.

Turnley, David, Peter Turnley, and Melinda Liu (1989). *Beijing Spring*. New York: Stewart, Tabori, and Chang.

Wang He (1986). Traditional Culture and Modernization: A Review of the General Situation of Cultural Studies in China in the Recent Years. *Social Sciences in China* 4:9–30.

Wang Lulin (1989). *"Wuqi zhishi" chutan* (On the May Seventh Instruction). In Xiao Yanzhong, Ed. *Wuannian Mao Zedong* (The Late Years of Mao Zedong). Beijing: Chuanqiu Press, pp. 101–112.

Wang Runsheng (1989). *Dui dangjing zhongguo daode shenghuo de sikao* (Reflections on the Current Moral Life in China). *Zhonggou qingnian bao* (China Youth Daily) (February 11).

Wang Ruoshui (1989). *Zhihui de tongku* (The Pain of Wisdom). Hong Kong: Joint Publishing (H.K.) Co., Ltd.

Wang Shubai (1987). *Mao Zedong sixiang yu zhongguo wenhua chuantong* (Mao

Zedong Thought and Chinese Cultural Tradition). Xiamen: Xiamen University Press.

Wang Ruowang (1989). *Tiandi you zhengqi* (Ambience in Heaven and on Earth: Collected Essays and Prose of Wang Ruowang). Hong Kong: Pai Shing Cultural Enterprise, Ltd.

Wang Yihua (1989). *Dui dangjin zhongguo "wenhuare" de sikao* (Reflections on the Current Cultural Fever). *Ming pao yeuk kan* (Ming Pao Monthly) 280 (April):35–39.

Wang Yuanhua (1989). *Wei wusi jingshen yibian* (The Debate on the May Fourth Spirit). *Xinqimen* (New Enlightenment) 1:9–31.

Wanger, Rudolf G. (1987). The Chinese Writer in His Own Mirror: Writer, State, and the Society—the Literary Evidence. In Merle Goldman, Timothy Cheek, and Coral Lee Hamrin, Eds. *China's Intellectuals and the State: In Search of a New Relationship.* Cambridge: Harvard University Press.

Watson, James (1989). Rites or Beliefs? The Construction of an Unified Culture in Late Imperial and Modern China. Discussion paper for the Workshop on the Construction of Chinese Cultural Identity, Institute of Culture and Communication, East-West Center, Honolulu.

Whyte, Martin (1989). Evolutionary Changes in Chinese Culture. In Charles Morrison and Robert Dernberger, Eds. *Asia-Pacific Report. Focus: China in the Reform Era.* East-West Center, Honolulu, pp. 93–101.

Wu, David, Geoffrey White, Elizabeth Buck, and Larry Smith (1989). Cultural Construction and National Identity. Discussion Working Paper, Culture Studies Symposium, May 22–24. Institute of Culture and Communication, East-West Center, Honolulu.

Wu Jiaxiang (1989). *Xinquanweizhuyi shuping* (A Review of New Authoritarianism). *Shijie jingji dao bao* (World Economic Herald) (January 1).

Xiao Gongqin and Zhu Wei (1989). *Tongku de liangnan xuanze* (A Painful Dilemma: A Discussion on New Authoritarianism). *Wenhuibao* (Wenhui Daily) (January 17).

Xiao Yianzhong (1989). *Huashidai beiju de paoxi yu lijie* (The Analysis of an Epoch Making Tragedy: a Review of Mao's Political and Philosophical Thinking in his Late Years). In Xiao Yanzhong, Ed. *Wuannian Mao Zedong* (The Late Years of Mao Zedong). Beijing: Chuanqiu Press, pp. 253–266.

Xie Tianyou (1989). *Zhuanzhizhuyi zhidu tongzhixia de chenmin xingli* (The Psychology of Officials and Civilians under the Rule of Despotism). Hong Kong: Zhonghua Press, Inc.

Xiong Fu (1989). *Huida "zichanjieji ziyouhua" de yige tiaozhan* (The Answer to One of the Challenges of "Bourgeois Liberalization"). *Renmingribao* (People's Daily) (August 14).

Yan Jiaqi (1988). *Wo de sixiang zizhuan* (An Autobiography of My Thoughts). Hong Kong: Joint Publishing (H.K.) Co., Ltd.

Yi Jiayan (1989). *Heshang daodi yao shuo shenme?* (What Does Heshang Advocate?") *Renmingribao* (People's Daily) (July 17).

Yi Yuanwen (1989). *Cong mixin dao kexue, cong kongxiang dao xianshi* (From Superstition to Science, from Dream to Reality: An Interview with Ma Beiwen). In Tao Kai, Zhang Yide, and Dai Qing, Eds. *Zouchu xiandai mixin* (Out of the Modern Superstition: The Great Debate on the Criterion of Truth). Hong Kong: Joint Publishing (H.K.) Co., Ltd, pp. 194–208.

Yu Lina (1989). *Heshang dao di xiang shuo shenmo: zuotanhui* (What Does Heshang Intend to Say? A Report on the Seminar on Heshang). *Daluzhongguo* (Mainland China) 27(9) (February):6–21.

Yuan Yi (1989). *Daozhi dongluan de sixiang genyuan* (The Theoretical Origins of the Turmoil). *Beijingqingnianbao* (Beijing Youth Daily) (July 7).

Zha Jianying (1995). *China Pop: How Soap Operas, Tabloids, and Best Sellers are Transforming a Culture*. New York: New Press.

Zhang Jianxin (1989). *Ping "makesizhuyi shi yige xuepai"* (On "Marxism Is a School"). *Guangmingribao* (Enlightenment Daily) (July 31).

Zhang Weiguo (1989). *Fenyun zhongshuo xinquanwei zhuyi* (Different Views in Evaluating New Authoritarianism). *Shijie jinji dao bao* (World Economic Herald) (March 13).

Zhang Yide (1989). *Jianchi shijian biaozhun, chongxin renshi shehuizhuyi*. (Persisting in Using "Practice as the Criterion for Truth," Reevaluating Socialism: An Interview with Hu Fuming). In Tao Kai, Zhang Yide, and Dai Qing, Eds. *Zouchu xiandai mixin* (Out of the Modern Superstition: The Great Debate on the Criterion of Truth). Hong Kong: Joint Publishing (H.K.) Co., Ltd, pp. 208–215.

Zhou Yan (1988). *Women neng zouchu wenhua digu ma?* (Can We Go Out of the Cultural Lowland?) *Dushu* (Reading) 4:5–10.

Zi Zhongyun (1987). The Relationship of Chinese Traditional Culture to the Modernization of China. *Asian Survey* 26(4):442–458.

10

The Cultural Mission of the Chinese Intelligentsia: A Second Look at Cultural Fever

David Y.H. Wu

Yang's chapter describes chronologically the discourse of "Cultural Fever" (wenhuare) in a subjective, neutral way. It tells of a nationalistic movement in the 1980s that involved university scholars in the fields of philosophy, Marxist ideology, history, and literature as well as official journalists and leading writers. Most of them, as Yang has summarized, joined the debate in the assessment of the virtue and evil of Chinese civilization, finding faults with traditional Chinese culture and recursive cultural practices today and making suggestions for national reform, economic development, and modernization. During the decade (from 1980 to 1989), few participating Chinese intellectuals, however, could step outside of the event and offer a critical analysis of China's socialist culture and current sociopolitical reality, or a meaningful culturally relevant explanation for why the event occurred.

A POLITICAL MOVEMENT IN THE GUISE OF CULTURE

To understand *wenhuare* or, literally, "culture hot (cultural fever, cultural craze, cultural mania, or cultural frenzy)," this second look offers a deconstructed view of the context, background, and cultural meanings of the event from an outsider's point of view. The discussion shall be focused on the question of why it was the intellectuals who, at this juncture, launched such a discourse of culture. We shall seek to understand the cultural meanings behind the reasons, motives, and purposes of Cultural Fever within the broader context of China's modern intellectual history as well as the cultural policy of the Chinese socialist system. The main thesis in this discussion of this seemingly cultural event is that this was a movement of the disempowered Chinese intelligentsia who acted within the cultural tradition of intellectual soul-searching but also within the new tradition of class struggle for recognition in a socialist system. Put in this context, we will see "wenhuare or cultural fever" not as a cultural movement. It was a political movement in the guise of "culture" emerging at a time of perceived economic and political crisis and created by elite intellectuals who served certain factions of those with political authority, state-employed scholars, and official writers. These intellectuals wrote in newspapers, popular magazines, and academic journals in an attempt to wake up a collective consciousness among the Chinese people that would recognize the crises and search for a better course for the nation.

The event was both familiar and strange. It was new in socialist China in the sense that it was not an official campaign, not an officially initiated discourse; yet, at the end, it communicated and educated the (educated) masses with fresh thoughts and unorthodox ideas that departed from the familiar, rigid "official-speak." This is why Haiou Yang in her chapter points out that "from the beginning to the end, this cultural discourse had been partially confirmed and supported by factions of the top officials. However, this cultural discourse was also frequently interrupted by the official force... In the later stage of the Cultural Fever, the discourse was further extended to the general public."

On the other hand, put in a broad historical and cultural context in China, it is also familiar in two regards. The intelligentsia has acted in a similar way before in history, and the familiar pattern of "reform discourse" has occurred several times in the past century (the reform discourse at the end of the nineteenth century, the revolution of 1911, the May Fourth [new literature] movement of 1919, the Nationalist New Life Movement of 1934, and the communist revolution of 1949) (see Yang 1988). Each time, culture (*wenhua*) became the new discursive subject, "and no less than a total cultural transformation was prescribed as the key to the survival of China" (Yang 1988:422). The language and mentality of the discourse of the cultural fever are also familiar, conforming to a more recently established (since 1949) Maoist style in the socialist culture in China. The discourse and the manner in which it took place reflect traditional Chinese patterns of a collective sense of mission and the anxiety of the intelligentsia in the context of a modern socialist nation-state. Intellectuals voiced their deep concern for the "culture" in an attempt to influence the political course of the state. Despite the rhetoric in some of the texts of cultural fever towards the end of the movement emphasizing liberty, freedom, individual rights, democracy, modernity, and Westernization, the motivations and goals of the intellectuals, in my view, were basically ethnocentric, subjective, and authoritarian. In other words, it was Chinese culture-bound.

CHINA'S CULTURAL POLICY AND POLITICAL DISCOURSE

Haiou Yang's paper does not discuss the main theme of the present volume, which is cultural policy, and actually contributes significantly to the life of a seemingly cultural but actually political discourse. I shall begin by pointing out what cultural policy has to do with the emergence of Cultural Fever.

China indeed has a cultural policy. Among modern nations, China is one of the few that has a clear official policy of culture, which was established during the Communist revolution in the 1940s. The policy governs high culture and popular culture: literature, art, journalism, drama, dance, folklore, and films. It defines for cultural workers what is morally and politically correct to write, paint, and perform, and for the audience—the masses of Chinese people—what is morally and politically correct to read, listen to, and watch. Even today in China, officials of culture continue to invoke the guiding principles of cultural policy that originated in Mao Zedong's canonized speeches at the 1942 Yanan Literature and Art Forum (Mao 1953). Mao set down the explicit rules that literature and art must serve the masses, especially the peasants, workers, and soldiers. To translate Mao's slogan into action, this means that cultural products—literature, performing arts, and fine arts—must be used as the chief propaganda tools to attract the Chinese masses of people (the majority of them peasants) to join the Communist revolution and class struggle. Since 1942 all writers, journalists, dancers, playwrights, film makers, and artists have had to create work under the guiding ideology approved by the cultural authorities. A wholesale and overarching effect of the Mao speech was to establish, standardize, and monopolize the style and content of all texts of speech and writing, which included all political speeches, policy documents, history, academic research publications, news and media reports, literature, fiction, poems, dance, and arts; hence, the "Mao wenti" (The Mao style of writing or Maospeak). Thereafter, each time a cultural worker (anyone who writes concerning literature and the arts in the broadest sense) raised a question about the guiding principle of the cultural policy, it would signal the start of a political movement, which usually ended in the purge of certain political figures, high officials of culture, and certain groups of intellectuals. The best example is the official criticism of the script of a historical play, *Hai Rui Baguan* (Hairei Resigned from Officialdom), which marked the beginning of the ten-year (1966–1976) Great Proletarian Cultural Revolution. No cultural workers, as in fact no citizens of China, could escape the control or domination of Mao's hegemonic cultural policy and style of writing, thinking, speaking, and living. "Each person in the population comes to think and speak in the vocabulary of official discourse" (Yang 1988:413). No wonder the writers during the Cultural Fever basically exhibited Maospeak and created among themselves a new wave of authoritarian speak: e.g., China must apply the essence of the good traditional culture in modern, Western science and technology; getting rid of Confucianism is the only way to save China; to modernize, Chinese culture must be completely Westernized; education in China has no value and intellectuals are hypocrites. Mao's cultural policy was militant in order to fight the class enemy in a nonstop revolution. So was the Cultural Fever discourse, as the intellectuals had been submissive to a collective under the influence of political authorities (Wang 1989, Pye 1992).

Interesting enough, the event of "Cultural Fever" had nothing to do with culture under the official definition, be it high culture or folklore. During the 1980s, for instance, there was an official campaign in the entire country to collect cultural materials or, in the Western notion, local folklore investigations (Tuohy 1991). These kinds of cultural activities never interested members of the Cultural Fever discourse. Cultural Fever involved mostly elite intellectuals. As mentioned, it was unprecedented in socialist China because it was not an official movement; it came into being gradually, and by the end became a voice of challenge although it was, in part, endorsed by factions of political authorities holding alternative ideas about the future course of China's economic and social reform. It was the first time in Chinese communist history that debates among intellectuals on "culture" became a nation-wide, spontaneous occurrence, ending on June 4th, 1989, in the government crackdown on the mass demonstration at Tianenmen Square in Beijing. The authorities eventually blamed those intellectuals who had participated in cultural debates for inciting the student demonstration and causing social disorder centered at Tianenmen. That is why, in the aftermath, the authorities had to launch an official campaign to attack the prevalent "Bourgeois Liberalization."

Judging by the content of the discourse and published articles, writings of the Cultural Fever had little to do with the cultural policy that the authorities had always targeted for control and monopoly; neither high culture (literature and art) nor popular culture (folklore, custom, or religion) was the focus of this discourse. It was a political discourse, although the rhetoric of "wenhua or culture" played on the center stage of the debates. The argument, proposal, or attack was only to a small degree about the cultural life of the Chinese people; it was more on the philosophy of the ethics, moral character, and imagined (national) psychological characteristics of the Chinese people in the context of the old (feudal) socio-political order in imperial China (i.e., the main theme in the 1988 nationally televised TV program, Heshang or River Elegy). It attributed China's failure to modernize to traditional Chinese philosophies of social order and polity. This familiar pattern of attacking or blaming the cultural past reproduced a discursive practice common among Chinese intellectuals not only in recent years, but also in the long history of the political system.

The superficial, iconoclastic rhetoric served deeper psychological and political purposes among individual participants. As we shall discuss further later, the thought of the intellectuals reflected a strong, emotional, and collective consciousness of nationalism. The fundamental argument in this event centered on economic and political reform and evinced concern about China's future status in global politics.

One may ask, then, why in the name of "culture"? Why not directly talk about politics, philosophy, or ideology? One answer rests on the tradition among intellectuals of viewing China as a persistent, unified, great Chinese people and culture, and the idea that intellectuals carry the heavy (psychological) burden of ensuring the survival of this unified, everlasting Chinese people/culture—*zhonghua minzu* (Wu 1991). Some may consider this desire for homogeneity and unification to be derived from the Confucian worldview, differentiating the Huaxia (the civilized Han Chinese in today's term) from the *yidi* (uncivilized peoples surrounding the middle kingdom) (see Wu 1991; Wang 1989:37–38). The ultimate anxieties of the Chinese intellectuals are to see Chinese culture lose its superiority, the Chinese people not be bound by unified thoughts and action, and China invaded by barbarians or, more recently, to see the Chinese state lose respect in international politics and diplomacy. This explains what is behind Yang's analysis of the fear of "cultural anomie." Furthermore, the success of a socialist Mao-style culture in China requires every individual to conform to the unified thoughts and action. This adds another layer to the Chinese mentality of desire for homogeneity. There is only one authoritarian answer to any question regarding every aspect of China, the Chinese people, Chinese society, Chinese culture, and Chinese life. Whether challenging the official version of the route to economic reform or advocating a new ideology (such as democracy), there shall be only one correct, standard, and most authoritative answer.

Not only do Chinese people identify and feel at home with

the thought of unification, but Chinese intellectuals are also too familiar with the consequences of directly challenging political elites, be it in historical times or now. Writing by using subterfuge, hints, projection, or innuendos has been, for millennia in Chinese politics, a strategy of scholars who intend to offer policy suggestions or to criticize authorities in power. Therefore, attacking Chinese culture represents both a genuine sense of intellectual worry and a warning to the political elite. Chinese politicians and intellectuals are both familiar with the skills described in popular proverbs such as *Zhisang Mahuai* (pointing to the mulberry tree but meaning to curse the willows) and *Yigu fengjin* (manipulating the past to attack the present) (see Barme 1989:5). Barme (1989:6) cites Hungarian novelist Haraszti's book, *The Velvet Prison: Artists Under State Socialism*, to explain the Chinese situation and to draw parallels to the European Communist states in creating a "civilization between the lines." Even writing to discredit the cultural tradition, the past, or the psychological characteristics of a presumed Chinese personality, most of the writers active during the Cultural Fever (including the playwright of Heshang) could not escape being accused of, or prosecuted for, polluting the people, or being anti-government and anti-socialist. They were never accused of committing the crime of being against Chinese culture. Today most of the well known writers or commentators (those cited in Yang's chapter) have been either imprisoned or exiled.

To understand the events surrounding the cultural fever, one needs to look deeper, beyond the rhetoric or surface phenomena, to gain a contextualized understanding of Chinese political tradition and the intelligentsia—the actors, the players, the engineers, the stars, the pawns, the followers, the victims, and eventually the criminals of China's politics of culture. We need to understand the Chinese intelligentsia's motives, struggles, frustrations, and failures as manifested in Chinese history, society, and culture.

COLLECTIVE FRUSTRATION, BURDEN, AND MISSION

Overseas Chinese involvement in the Cultural Fever discourse is as important a source for insights into the event as are the writings in China for, as an intellectual movement both inside and outside China, they share a common emotional, cultural, and historical tradition. At the height of cultural fever debates, Chinese intellectuals in the periphery (in Hong Kong, Taiwan, and the United States) were able to offer some deconstructed views about the movement because Chinese intellectuals shared an ethnocentric, subjective understanding of the Chinese intelligentsia and their ideals. The following two analytical articles which came out of a symposium in Taiwan at the end of 1988 exemplified the notion that a shared concern for China's fate is the intellectuals' burden.

A Taiwanese historian teaching in Hong Kong, Li Hongqi, maintained (1989:201) that one must discuss the role of Chinese intellectuals in order to understand the interrelated phenomena in China in the eighties of the emerging discourse of "Cultural Fever" (*wenhuare*), "consciousness of collective worries and sufferance" (*youhuan yishi*), and "education is worthless" (*dushu wuyong lun*). Li attributes the Chinese intelligentsia's sense of losing its traditional place in society to the dramatic social change under the Communist revolution which eliminated the traditional intelligentsia class and, with it, the economic basis of autonomy or independent voice. He points out how Mao Zedong despised intellectuals and how China placed a low priority on education, as demonstrated by the meager national budget for education (only 2.56% of GNP). As is well known, Chinese intellectuals suffered systematic purges during the anti-right campaigns in the late 1950s and during the ten years of the Cultural Revolution. These facts gave ample grounds for intellectual frustration in the socialist system.

Li suggests that since China's leaders set economic reform

and modernization as national goals in the early 1980s, intellectuals served a utilitarian function. The more the intellectuals and technocrats served the government the more they felt frustrated, because they were unable to participate in real decision making (see Pye 1992:42–46). Li further attributes the intellectuals' frustration to their real loss of income in day-to-day life. When economic modernization produced new social phenomena such as profit seeking and conspicuous consumption, resulting in serious inflation in the late 1980s, teachers and university professors faced dwindling incomes while people in other (traditionally lower) occupations became wealthy. This reinforced the intellectuals' traditional sense of frustration as well as "sufferance" in longing for a future (prosperous) society. The student protest and demonstration in Beijing in May of 1989 in part reflected the economic frustration of the intellectuals and demonstrated the intellectuals' traditional role in carrying the national burden of seeking change to alleviate national suffering (especially in the spirit of Beijing University's leadership of the May Fourth movement).

Li cites both Fang Lizhi's and Jin Guantao's words to show the tradition among intellectuals of having a sense of "mission." When Fang was interviewed by a Hong Kong reporter a year after he was stripped of his Party membership, he said: "I felt down, but I am not giving up yet. I insist that the intellectual is an independent force, providing the guidance of social development and the energy of (social, political, and economic) advancement" (Li 1989:210). Jin, considered a leading thinker and an idol of college students, was cited on Chinese intellectuals' "sense of a mission." Jin urged intellectuals not to remain satisfied merely to do a good job in academics: Intellectuals should "seek to understand the sufferance and challenge facing the Chinese people and Chinese culture and (seek) to reconstruct Chinese culture amidst the tide of the modern world in a holistic and creative way" (cited in an article Jin wrote in the Chinese Youth Paper, January 29, 1988).

Another Taiwanese historian, Huang Jun-jei (1989), commenting on Li's analysis of Cultural Fever, remarked that Chinese intellectuals' frustration syndrome has a long history dating back to Confucian times. The scholars felt they possessed the know-how to govern the country and improve the livelihood of the people, but they were never valued by the rulers and could never gain real power. Even though the Confucian scholars had enjoyed high status since the Han dynasty (second century B.C.), they nevertheless began to fall under the domination of the rulers. This, according to Huang (1989), created what Wilhelm (1957) called the "scholar's frustration." The Neo-Confucian scholars of the Song Dynasty further developed the "sense of a great mission" in serving the lord to better the lives of the people. Chinese students in the past were taught to memorize the idealistic quotation of a Song scholar/official, Fan Zhongan: "to worry before all others begin to worry; to enjoy (a good life) only after all others have enjoyed." Whereas the Communists are accused of being anti-intellectual, authorities in China, nevertheless, have often quoted Fan's sayings in newspaper columns and in speeches in order to teach the ideal behavior of a Party member—to sacrifice oneself in serving the people or the nation. Today, Fan's poem (*Yueyanglou Ji* or A Note on the Hall of Yueyang by the Dongting Lake), which contains the above description of an ideal scholar, continues to be included in school textbooks in China and Taiwan. The phrase was once selected in the mid-1980s as the title for a national entrance examination for colleges in the subject of Chinese composition (Wang 1992). Under this title of "suffer before all others and enjoy after all others," students would be tested not only on their writing skill in Chinese but also on their sense of patriotism and sacrifice for the good of the nation.

It has been an old tradition among Chinese learned persons that they possess both the sense of a great mission to save the country and the people and a frustration in not being able to fully participate in politics. The reality of Chinese scholars has been that they play a supportive and subordinate role to the rulers (or politicians today) and are in a position no better than servants or court jesters. Huang and Li, commentators on Cultural Fever, along with China's participants in the political discourse before 1989, could not escape the subjective (or ethnocentric) predicament of being Chinese intellectuals in begging for liberty, an independent voice, or eventually political power. They expressed a longing for a future civil society where Chinese intellectuals would be allowed freedom of expression, liberated from the irony of historical sufferance, and could accomplish the historical mission of becoming an independent voice in working out a way to serve a strong and wealthy country.

The collective anxiety of the Chinese intellectuals—worry that the nation is not going to prosper and be strong—has both a psychological and a historical basis. Chinese scholars were socialized from childhood to expect to endure adverse conditions and make self-sacrifices in serving the country. This sense of mission or intellectual burden became especially strong in the early part of the twentieth century as Social Darwinism in the context of foreign invasion, economic exploitation, and demonstrations of Western technical superiority dominated the minds of scholars. Fighting to restore a national self-esteem in view of *Guoqi* (national disgrace) and *wairu* (external humiliation) was a forceful and popular idea among those who considered themselves intellectuals.

The unification of China, in a homogeneous racial, cultural, and political sense, was one of the most important political agendas favored by intellectuals after Dr. Sun Yat-sen's revolution and the founding of the Republic of China. The construction of a modern unified Chinese people/culture in a wealthy, powerful nation has preoccupied the collective consciousness of Chinese intellectuals. By the 1980s, in the aftermath of the Cultural Revolution and at a crossroads of national reform, Chinese intellectuals' deep concern for the national crises as well as their historical mission impeded another national debate on the transformation of culture as the best course to save China. One can predict that as long as the sense of sufferance and burden of mission continues within the intellectual tradition of Chinese culture, "Cultural Fever" will not be the last political discourse on culture in China.

REFERENCES

Barme, Geremie (1989). The Chinese Velvet Prison: Culture in the "New Age," 1976–1989. Paper presented at the Department of Far Eastern History, Australian National University, Canberra.

Li Hong-qi (1989). *Canyu yishi de cuozhe* (The Frustration of Participation Consciousness). *China Tribune* 319:200–211.

Huang Jun-jie (1989). *Pinglun* (Comment). *China Tribune* 319: 212–216.

Mao Zedong (1953). "Introduction," May 2, 1942, Speech delivered at the Yenan Wenyi Seminar. In *Selected Essays of Mao Zedong* (Vol. 3). Beijing: Renmin.

Pye, Lucian W. (1992). *The Spirit of Chinese Politics*. Cambridge, Mass.: Harvard University Press.

Tuohy, Sue (1991). Cultural Metaphors and Reasoning: Folklore Scholarship and Ideology in Contemporary China. *Asian Folklore Studies* (Nagoya) 50(1):189–220.

Yang, Mayfair M.H. (1988). The Modernity of Power in the Chinese Socialist Order. *Cultural Anthropology* 3(4):408–427.

Wang Penglin (1992). personal communication.

Wang, Yihua (1989). *Dui Dangjin Zhongguo wenhuare de sikao* (Reflections on Current China's "Cultural Fever"). *Mingbao Monthly* 1989, April (280):35–39.

Wilhelm, Hellmut (1957). "Scholar's Frustration" : Notes on a Type of "Fu." In John K. Fairbanks, Ed. *Chinese Thought and Institutions*. Chicago: University of Chicago Press, pp. 310–319.

Wu, David Y.H. (1991). The Construction of Chinese and Non-Chinese Identities. *Daedalus* 120(2):159–179.

PART V
Japan

11

Hegemony of Homogeneity in the Politics of Identity in Japan

Harumi Befu

> Even if the models are biased and erroneous, the very bias and types of errors are a part of the facts under study and probably rank among the most significant ones (Levi-Strauss 1953:527).

This paper is about Japanese identity, the question of who Japanese are in a cultural sense.[1] What makes this topic particularly germane is that the Japanese themselves manifest consuming interest in this topic, so much so that discourse on Japanese identity may even be called a minor national pastime. Numerous writers have articulated the nature of this cultural and national identity in voluminous publications. This discourse constitutes a well recognized genre, with its own appellations. *Nihon bunkaron*, *Nihonjinron*, *Nihon shakairon*, and *Nihonron* are some of the commonly used terms to refer to it. Any one of these terms is equally appropriate, but we shall adopt *Nihonjinron* if only because it is used most commonly in English parlance.

While there is serious, scholarly *Nihonjinron* research, carried out by erudite scholars in the ivory tower to identify the essence of Japanese culture and society, the vast majority of discourse glossed under *Nihonjinron* is for popular consumption. In this paper we shall focus on the latter type of *Nihonjinron* because our interest is in examining popular notions of cultural identity—what men and women on the street think about their cultural identity, not what an obscure scholar might write for a small audience of fellow scholars. Accordingly analysis of *Nihonjinron* carried out in this paper is based on popular books and articles in popular magazines, most of which sell in tens and sometimes hundreds of thousands of copies.

What is common in *Nihonjinron* writings is their singular objective to identify and demonstrate unique qualities in Japanese culture, society, and national character as a whole. This is an endeavor in cultural construction of identity, that is to say, a construction of identity which is perceived by the Japanese to be unique. Whether objectively, and in fact, the constructed identity is unique in the world is not the issue, or is only indirectly at issue in considering whether the constructed identity "fits" the reality, which is another matter all together. Rather it is the belief on the part of the Japanese in the uniqueness of their identity which is crucial.

As such, little or no attention is given in this genre to intracultural variations, whether along the line of region, class, gender, rural-urban differences, or any other criterion. Broad generalizations—stereotypes, if you like—about Japanese culture as a whole, Japanese social structure as a whole, or the national character of all Japanese abound in this genre.

NIHONJINRON AS A CULTURAL MODEL

Nihonjinron is a cultural model as anthropologists use the term, referring to conceptualization of a culture as a model (Caw 1974; Geertz 1973; Holy and Stuchlik 1981; Ward 1985). More specifically, the model I wish to discuss is the native or folk model, in which creators of the model are themselves Japanese. They are part of the model being created. The model is a self-portrait, as it were.

But even among Japanese, the cultural model of Japan which they carry in their heads is obviously not the same for everyone. Each *Nihonjinron* writer presents a different, albeit only slightly different, model from others. Moreover, each reader who absorbs ideas in various *Nihonjinron* writings creates a unique model in his or her own mind, though inarticulate and perhaps inchoate.

This multiplicity of models is demonstrated in the questionnaire survey Manabe Kazufumi of Kwansei Gakuin University and I undertook in 1987 in the city of Nishinomiya to investigate various aspects of *Nihonjinron*, in which rather wide ranging responses were received on all questions.[2] For example, some respondents "strongly believe" in the *Nihonjinron* proposition that Japanese "blood" is essential for competence in Japanese language, while others do "not at all" believe in this proposition. Moreover, obviously as the individual Japanese is exposed to a variety of experiences which affect this cultural model, the model will necessarily be reformulated from time to time. This reformulation is an ongoing process in a feed-back loop from experience to formulation of the model, back to experience and then to reformulation of the model, *ad infinitum*. The most prevalent source of knowledge in the formulation and reformulation of this model is the literature of *Nihonjinron*, wherein authors have articulated and elaborated on its tenets and propositions.

THE LITERATURE

A word should be said about the popularity of *Nihonjinron*. One indication of the popularity is seen in the number of titles on *Nihonjinron* being published. A 1978 compilation by the Nomura Research Institute (Nomura Sogo Kenkyujo ed. 1978) of a bibliography of monographs in this genre published since the end of the Second World War—the only more or less comprehensive bibliography on the subject—contains 698 titles published in the thirty-three year period. The list is by no means complete. Judging from my own bibliography, another ten percent can be easily added to the list. With more than ten years passing since the compilation of this bibliography, by now the list would far exceed 1,000 titles. In March of 1990 I counted about 280 titles in a section devoted to *Nihonjinron* at one of the large bookstores in Tokyo, featuring more recent and popular titles. This attests to the continued interest in the subject by Japanese. If magazine articles in this genre are included, the count of titles would easily double or even triple. Thus, on the basis of the volume of publication alone, it is not far from the mark to claim *Nihonjinron* is a national pastime.

The popularity of *Nihonjinron* can also be gauged by the number of copies of books sold in this genre. Unfortunately the volume of sales is a trade secret and is not easily divulged by publishers. The number of reprintings a book goes through, however, is public information. The large numbers of reprintings the more popular books in *Nihonjinron* go through are truly phenomenal. Let me cite a few examples. Doi Takeo's *Amae no Kozo* (1971a, 1971b), the Japanese version of *Anatomy of Dependence* (1973), which has had a major impact in the field of *Nihonjinron*, was reprinted in hardcover 67 times in the first four years of its publication, and has been reprinted in softcover 147 times since its initial publication in 1971. Another book that has played an enormously important role in shaping *Nihonjinron* is Nakane Chie's *Tate Shakai no Ningen Kankei*

(1967). This book, available in English as *The Japanese Society* (1970), has been reprinted 79 times. Both these books were last reprinted in 1989, demonstrating their continued popularity.

Books which have been reprinted more than ten times in this genre are legion. Many of them are so well sold immediately upon publication that they are reprinted at the clip of about once a month for the first six or seven months. For example, Higuchi Kiyoyuki's *Umeboshi to Nihonto* (The prune and the Japanese sword, 1974) is subtitled "the History of the Wisdom and Creativity of the Japanese" (my own translation) and extols the genius of Japanese culture as expressed in the variety of efficacies claimed of the Japanese dried prune and the technology and beauty of the Japanese sword. This book was so popular that it was reprinted 96 times in the first four years of publication. Similarly, Tsuda Masumi's *Nihonteki Keiei no Ronri* (Logic of the Japanese style management, 1977) was reprinted 11 times in the first six months of publication. Murai Jun's *Nihonjin no Ryoshin* (The conscience of the Japanese, 1988) was reprinted 18 times in the first four months of its publication.

In addition to *Nihonjinron* books authored by Japanese writers, a large volume of *Nihonjinron* literature is produced by foreigners, providing outsiders' views of Japanese. Indeed, it was Ruth Benedict's *Kiku to Katana* (1948), the Japanese translation of *Chrysanthemum and the Sword* (1946), that ushered in the post war era of *Nihonjinron*. Many notable foreigners have followed her example, including such illustrious figures as Brzezinski (1972; English edition 1972), Edwin O. Reishauer (1979; English edition 1977), and Ezra Vogel (1979; English edition 1979). Because of the close communication and the free flowing of ideas between Japanese and foreign writers, where both sides borrow ideas from each other, a good deal of in formational transfer and transfusion transpires in the *Nihonjinron* construction by Japanese. As a result, a Japanese model is likely to show an infusion of foreign views. For this reason, while this paper will focus on the *Nihonjinron* literature written in Japanese, it is well to remember that this literature includes foreigners' *Nihonjinron* writings in translation and that *Nihonjinron* authored by Japanese are "contaminated" by foreigners' views in varying degrees.

CONTENTS

Arguments have been advanced to demonstrate Japan's unique qualities by literally scores of writers in virtually all fields, natural sciences not excepted, and topics in *Nihonjinron* run the whole gamut of cultural catalogue. Individual views and approaches, of course, vary. Because of space limitations, I present here a distilled and composite version of a complex picture.

ECOLOGY

The view that Japan is a resource-poor nation subject to frequent typhoons, droughts, floods, landslides, earthquakes, and other natural calamities has been popular for many generations. Credit no doubt goes to Watsuji Tetsuro, professor of philosophy at Kyoto University, for systematizing this view, which is laid out in his long-running best-seller *Fudo* (1935), (*A Climate*, 1961). This book is still reprinted on the average of once a year some sixty years since its publication.

For Watsuji, as well as for his followers, the important point is the impact of climate upon culture. The warm and wet air from the south and the bitterly cold arctic wind blown across Siberia and the Japan Sea onto Japan provide Watsuji with ingredients for explaining everything from Japan's wet rice cultivation and conformity-ridden community organization, through patriarchal family structure and animistic religious orientation, to persevering national character and nature-loving ethos. This argument has been adopted and repeated in various forms by many of his followers (Chiba ed. 1980; Misawa 1979;

Miyamoto 1967; Sabata 1974; Sekiguchi 1983; Suzuki 1975; Yamada 1978).

SUBSISTENCE ECONOMY AS A CAUSAL FACTOR

That wet rice cultivation necessitated the formation of corporate communities is an argument maintained by so many writers, following Watsuji's example, that it is generally accepted as a truism (Tamaki 1978; Sabata 1972; Tsukuba 1969). The need for cooperation in maintaining irrigation systems, rice-transplanting, and harvesting supposedly created a tightly knit, perhaps even oppressively tyrannical, corporate community which did not allow members to express individuality and assert their rights (Tamaki 1978). The same force of wet rice cultivation requiring corporate effort, it is argued, has also created *amae*—the Japanese propensity for mutual psychological dependence—and fundamental kinship units of Japanese society (Sabata 1964:134).

Attempts to characterize Japan by contrasting its rice subsistence economy with other types of subsistence economies is a common exercise among *Nihonjinron* writers. For example, Ishida Eiichiro, one of the leading anthropologists of the past generation, has contrasted Japan's wet rice economy with the "pastoral economy" of Europe in his *Nihon Bunkaron* (1968; English edition 1974), which has undergone 16 reprints in the last 20 years and is still being reprinted. Ishida is referring to the subsistence economy of the traditional Middle East, whence Western civilization was born. According to Ishida, this pastoral economy is responsible for the monotheism expressed not only in Christianity but also in Judaism and Islam, all of which arose in a pastoral context. Drawing on Watsuji's ideas, he contrasts this monotheism to Japan's animism (1968:150 152). A similar contrast between Japan's agrarian economy and the West's pastoral economy is made by Araki (1973:23–25), Iwasaki (1980) and many others, deriving therefrom a basis of

Japanese group orientation as against the individualism of the West.

SOCIAL STRUCTURE

The special character of Japanese social structure emphasized by most *Nihonjinron* protagonists has to do with its group orientation. For some, this corporate agrarian social structure presumably has been transferred to urban settings and re-created among urban populations (Tamaki 1978:197, 204–207). Others similarly argue for the group orientation of Japanese, but without deriving it from rural community structure (Hamaguchi 1977; Hamaguchi ed. 1982; Inuta 1977; Kawamoto 1982; Nakane 1967).

Most *Nihonjinron* theses on social structure argue that Japanese are oriented toward group goals, group welfare, and group activity. This "group" is supposed to be characterized by particularistic and functionally diffused human relationships that are peculiar to Japanese. In short, the group characterized here is of a *gemeinschaft* sort, even though it may be found in a *gesellschaft* organization like a business firm.

PSYCHOLOGY

Doi (1971a), Minami (1953, 1983), and Miyagi (1972) are perhaps among the best-known *Nihonjinron* writers from the psychological perspective. Minami's earlier work, published in 1953, reprinted 44 times and still in print, characterizes Japanese personality largely in terms of such qualities as sadness, melancholy, fatalism, unhappiness, and loneliness. Doi, on the other hand, has built a whole theory of the Japanese national character on the basis of the one concept of *amae*, which denotes mutual psychological dependency among primary group members, starting in the family with the child's dependence upon parents, but later extending this relationship to other social contexts. A similar view is expressed by Kimura (1973) in a work which has seen fifteen reprintings. According to Minami (1983), Japanese lack self-conception and self-identity, which in turn bring about dependence on others and on the group to which they belong, echoing Doi's well-known thesis.

As a way of developing a conception of unique Japanese personality, Okonogi conceives of the "Ajase complex" (1978–79, 1982), which contrasts with the Oedipus complex, the Freudian foundation of the Western personality. In the Ajase complex—unlike the Oedipus complex, in which sexuality is the central theme—mutual love and the son's longing for the mother are the focal concepts, along with the sense of unity, reciprocity (or mutuality), resentment, masochism, forgiveness, and guilt between mother and child.

LANGUAGE

The view that language contains the secret of the speaker's world view, thought process, and so on is an old one. Use of Japanese language to reveal the uniqueness of Japanese culture is particularly a fond pasttime for Japanese. The view that the language uniquely expresses Japanese thought and even the primordial essence of Japanese ethnicity is corroborated in the minds of many Japanese by their belief that no one, other than ethnic Japanese, can speak Japanese properly. Since, in addition, there is supposedly a perfect isomorphism between speakers of the Japanese language and bearers of Japanese culture, whatever is unique about the language is also unique to the people and culture. Claims of the uniqueness of the Japanese derived from the language are of several kinds.

Thought Process   Because isomorphism between Japanese language and Japanese people is assumed in *Nihonjinron*, a claim is easily made that their language uniquely expresses Japanese thought (Kakehi 1985). On this ground, much ink has been spilled to elaborate on the uniqueness and untranslatability of Japanese expressions (Toyama 1976). The supposed uniqueness of Japanese linguistic categories is illustrated in everything from linguistic particles like *ga*, *wa*, and *no* (Oide 1965:135–201) to cultural concepts like *amae* (Doi 1971), *ki* (Doi 1971:108–116; Itasaka 1978:129–137), and *iki* (Kuki 1930). *Nihonjinron* claims of uniqueness based on language, such as this, are truly rampant.

Social structure   Since the Japanese language requires predicate endings expressing relative status difference between the speaker and the listener, Japanese are said to be highly sensitive to relative social status in face-to-face interaction. Use of honorifics of varying degrees to indicate the specific status relationship between the speaker and the listener is presumably another way to show the uniquely Japanese linguistic behavior (Kindaichi 1957:141–159; Yamashita 1979:157–222).

Linguistic determinism has been given a scientific validation of late by Tsunoda Tadanobu (1978), a medical doctor who found differences in hemispheric functions of speech between Japanese and Western language speakers. According to Tsunoda, whereas European speakers process independent vowels in the right hemisphere along with non-linguistic sounds from machines, nature, and emotions, Japanese process both independent vowels and non-linguistic sounds—except those of machines and musical instruments—in the left hemisphere. Since the left hemisphere performs logical and mathematical functions as well, in the Japanese brain, "logos" and "pathos" are, as it were, integrated, in contradistinction to the European thought process where logic and emotion are contrasted and opposed (Cf. *Gengo*, 1978).

Tsunoda's view has received wide publicity, as one would imagine. His book, reprinted thirty-one times in the past eleven years, for some, has given a stamp of scientific demonstration for the impressionistic social-science and humanistic *Nihonjinron* arguments. This view, however, is not entirely accepted by the scientific profession due to the paucity of the sample and substandard scientific procedure.

ETHOS

The unique *geist* of the Japanese is argued in innumerable treatises, including those on the thought process of Japanese mentioned above. The abstract, speculative nature of these concepts encourages all to join the chorus. *Yamato damashii* (spirit of Japan) (Saito 1972), *kokoro* (heart) of Japanese (Sera 1965), and *Nihon seishin* (Japanese spirit) (Aizawa 1975) are some of the favorite concepts used in *Nihonjinron* to demonstrate the unique Japanese *geist*.

A subcategory under the heading of "ethos" is a class of paired cultural concepts the Japanese often invoke to demonstrate the uniqueness of Japanese culture, such as *giri/ninjo* (social obligation vs. human feelings) (Minamoto 1969; Doi 1971:29), *tatemae/honne* (public propriety vs. private thought) (Nieda 1973; Minami ed. 1980:60–72), *oyake/watakushi* (public vs. private) (Yasunaga 1976; Mito 1976; Minami ed. 1980:122–133). One can go on elaborating these themes and adding more, but the above should be sufficient to give the reader a glimpse of the range of *Nihonjinron* propositions.

ETHNOCENTRISM

One property of contemporary *Nihonjinron* is its inherent ethnocentrism. *Nihonjinron* is formulated by comparing Japan with other cultures in arriving at what is presumably unique to Japan. But this comparison is not objective: value judgements often accompany *Nihonjinron* propositions, either explicitly or implicitly. Praising one's own culture need not lead automatically to disparaging other cultures or result from it. However, evaluative comparisons are quite common in *Nihonjinron* where Japanese culture is not only judged good, but is regarded better than others. In the wake of unprecedented economic success in recent years, Japanese are all the more in the mood for congratulating themselves and disparaging others who cannot achieve the same economic goals as Japan. This orientation is widely reflected in *Nihonjinron*.

It is well to remember that the national identity of any country is impacted, not to say determined, by its status in the international arena and perceptions thereof by the people of that country. Thus the current ethnocentric *Nihonjinron* is underpinned by Japan's place in the international marketplace as one of the wealthiest nations in the world. Forty years ago, when Japan was barely coming out of the ashes of atom bombs, its self-identity hardly bore any resemblance to what we see now (Befu n.d.).

Higuchi Kiyoyuki, mentioned above, perhaps epitomizes this contemporary ethnocentric trend; his *Nihonjinron* writings unabashedly congratulate the Japanese for how smart, how creative, and how ingenious they are. Higuchi continues to write along the same vein with unrelenting zeal, breaking his own publication record of over 120 books almost every year. He could easily put Ezra Vogel, who could only write one book (1979) to praise Japanese, to shame. Along the same line, Nakagawa (1978, English version 1979) claims that Japan is a "welfare superstate" and a paradise for workers, far surpassing Western countries.

PREMISES OF *NIHONJINRON*

HOMOGENEITY

Behind these specific uniquenesses claimed in social, cultural, psychological and other aspects lie certain assumed premises. First is the assumption that Japan is culturally homogeneous (*toshitsu* or *doshitsu*). Anthropologist Masuda Yoshio (1967) of Tokyo University has argued that in spite of the diffusion and inundation of foreign culture into Japan from prehistoric times, the purity of Japanese culture has been maintained for millennia. Anthropologist Ishida Eiichiro (1968:154), mentioned above, likewise has insisted that Japan maintains "surprising homogeneity" in comparison with European cultures. Nakane's aforementioned book on the Japanese group is subtitled *Tan'itsu Shakai no Riron* (a theory of a homogeneous society).

According to linguist Suzuki Takao of Keio University (1980), Japan's homogeneity has several components. The first is racial homogeneity, which he qualifies as "perceived homogeneity;" that is, a belief in homogeneity, regardless of how heterogeneous the reality of Japanese racial makeup may be. This acknowledgement that ultimately *Nihonjinron* has to do with perception and belief, or to put it in contemporary terms, "cultural construction," is important.

Suzuki does not consider heterogeneous elements in Japan a problem for the homogeneity thesis. For example, the Ainu, for Suzuki, are too few in number—indeed there probably are no more than a few thousand Ainu left—to be of any consequence. Koreans, he believes, are not an ethnic problem because the majority of Koreans "are culturally and linguistically indistinguishable from Japanese." This summary dismissal of the existence of ethnic minorities in Japan is an explicit stance, a conscious decision made by *Nihonjinron* writers like Suzuki to ignore ethnic variation in Japan. In short, racial and ethnic homogeneity in Japan is not an objective fact, but instead a construct of those who are motivated to promote a certain cultural conception of Japan.

Suzuki also refers to homogeneity in language as well as in religion and life style. What is important about this assumption of homogeneity is that it enables *Nihonjinron* authors to apply generalizations across the board to all Japanese. It assumes that local, class, gender, and other variations within Japan are not important enough to violate the essential sameness throughout Japanese culture and all Japanese.

This is not to say that Japanese are not aware of internal

variations or that research on them is lacking. The popular accounts abound with stereotyped differences among Japanese of different regions, occupations, classes, etc. Tokyoites are supposed to be spend-thrifts; Osaka people are supposedly obsessed with making money and eating well; and Kyoto people are self-appointed aristocrats who look down on all others as country bumpkins. Regional variations in social structure have been a subject of research for numerous scholars (Izumi and Gamo 1952; *Jinrui Kagaku* 1963–1964; NHK Hoso Yoron Chosajo ed. 1979; Nagashima and Tomoeda 1984). The neglect of internal variations along class, gender, and regional lines as manifested in *Nihonjinron* is, therefore, not due to lack of information. Instead, to repeat, the neglect of such variations is based on a deliberate decision on the part of *Nihonjinron* writers to represent a homogeneous image of Japan.

LAND=PEOPLE=CULTURE=LANGUAGE

The second assumption behind *Nihonjinron*, already alluded to, asserts isomorphism of geography, race, language, and culture. This is a set of interrelated propositions, namely

(1) that Japanese culture, its "carrier," and native speakers of Japanese alike exist coterminously with the Japanese archipelago, extending throughout the islands but not beyond its bounds, with minor exceptions, such as recent immigrants to North and South America;

(2) that all those practicing Japanese culture speak the Japanese language natively and that all speakers of Japanese are practitioners of Japanese culture;

(3) that carriers of Japanese culture and therefore speakers of the Japanese language all share "blood" and have done so for thousands of years; and

(4) that no significant amount of new blood has been infused into this "pure" Japanese race.

In short, a claim is made for equivalency and mutual implications among land, people (i.e., race), culture, and language, such that those and only those who practice the culture also speak the language and have inherited Japanese "blood" from their forebears, who have always lived on the Japanese archipelago and that no other person speaks the language natively and practices the culture.

There is in this argument an implicit genetic determinism (Hayashida 1976) which is manifested in various ways. For example, no foreigner, with rare exceptions to prove the rule, is supposedly capable of full competence in the Japanese language (Miller 1982, Ch.8).

NIHONJINRON AS A HEGEMONIC MODEL

It is well to remember that a declarative statement in Japanese, as in European languages, when put in idealized form as *Nihonjinron* propositions generally are, often carries normative implications. *Nihonjinron*, on the face of it, seems to be a purely descriptive cultural model. For example, Japanese are said to achieve harmony by belonging to a hierarchically organized group in which human relations are based on particularism, functional diffuseness, and trust, as expounded by *Nihonjinron* protagonists like Nakane. Doi describes how Japanese thrive on the affective diet of *amae*. Kyogoku (1983:251–253) tells us that Japanese politicians deal with their constituencies with parental thoughtfulness. Tsuda (1977:206–207) describes the Japanese labor union in terms of the "enterprise unionism," where all workers of a given company, no matter what the occupational specialty is, belong to one union. Other seemingly descriptive statements abound in *Nihonjinron*.

It is noteworthy that these statements are all made in declarative, and not imperative sentences. But if these descriptive models describe an idealized state and carry positive valence, then it behooves the Japanese to act and think as described so as to achieve the idealized state of affairs, i.e., to treat the descriptive model as a prescriptive one. In short, the *is* in *Nihonjinron* propositions is exchanged with *should*. Declarative propositions then become moral and hegemonic imperatives. Not to behave as prescribed is not only unusual and strange, but is "un-Japanese" and against the normative standards of the society. Only a thin line here separates a descriptive model from a normative model, as normative elements are deceptively disguised in declarative, seemingly descriptive statements of the cultural model. It is probably all the more effective, though more insidious perhaps, to slip imperative implications into descriptive statements. This way, people are led, or misled as the case may be, subliminally from approval of descriptive statements to espousal of imperative commands. *Nihonjinron* as a model *of* behavior thus becomes a model *for* behavior.

There is another covert process through which *Nihonjinron* serves as a moral imperative. Propositions of *Nihonjinron* are often stated in universal terms or at least imply that all normal Japanese are or do things as claimed in *Nihonjinron*. Precisely because such statements sound perfectly objective and nonjudgmental, their hegemonic role is all the more effective.

However, our survey data from Nishinomiya demonstrate that a significant minority, and sometimes even a majority, disclaim belief in one or another *Nihonjinron* proposition (Namabe, Befu, McConnell 1989). For example, only 35.7% of the sample "strongly" or "somewhat" support the claim that no foreigner can master the Japanese language. Yet this claim is advanced often and by noted scholars teaching at prestigious universities, such as linguist Suzuki Takao. Such a claim, discussed *ad nauseam* by Roy Andrew Miller in his *Japan's Modern Myth—Language and Beyond* (1982), is persuasive because of the positive valence of *Nihonjinron* and because of the credentials of the claimers. Not to accept *Nihonjinron* propositions and not to act according to its dictates would make one feel un-Japanese. Moreover, it is significant that claims contradicting *Nihonjinron* propositions, such as regarding foreigners' linguistic competence, are seldom if ever voiced. *Nihonjinron* as a hegemonic prescription seems to have effectively silenced contrary views. Intellectual and moral hegemony thus is an important dimension of the imperative nature of *Nihonjinron*. One might say *Nihonjinron* writings serve as a modern moral textbook, and are all the more effective because they are not textbooks in the ordinary sense, but are promoted as sources for Japanese cultural and national identity.

NIHONJINRON AS AN ESTABLISHMENT IDEOLOGY

In considering *Nihonjinron* as an ideology, it is highly instructive to analyze the contents of the report submitted to the former Prime Minister Ohira. This report, entitled *Bunka no Jidai* (The age of culture) (Bunka no Jidai Kenkyu Group 1980), was prepared by a committee appointed by Ohira, consisting of *Nihonjinron* advocates. The Committee was chaired by Yamamoto Shichihei, the suspected though unadmitted author of a three-million-copy *Nihonjinron* best seller, *Nihonjin to Yudayajin* (the Japanese and the Jew), and included other well known *Nihonjinron* writers, such as Tokyo University professor Kumon Shumpei, one of the co-authors, along with two other Tokyo University professors, of *Bummei to shite no Ie Shakai* (Ie-based society as a civilization) (Murakami, Kumon and Sato 1973), an erudite *Nihonjinron* treatise which argues for the familistic basis of Japanese society. In itself not a popular book for mass consumption, the book nonetheless established a scholarly foundation for popular *Nihonjinron* views. Another notable member of the Committee was Komatsu Sakyo, one of the best known science fiction and mystery writers and author of *Nihon Bunka no Shikaku* (a perspective on Japanese culture) (1977).

This report hails Japanese culture for its emphasis on harmonious human relations (rather than on self-centered individualism as in the West), on members of society knowing their station in life, and on Japanese tradition in general. This report is subtitled "Reports of the Policy Group of Prime Minister Ohira—Number One." As Kawamura (1982:Chapter 4) observes, the government saw fit to endorse *Nihonjinron* as an officially sanctioned ideology, and appropriated it from the private popular sector to which it had hitherto belonged. *Nihonjinron* thus entered politics and became a tool of the political establishment.

The government exercises power to shape Japanese national identity through its dominant role in education. To name but one example, all textbooks in Japanese public schools at the primary and secondary levels must be approved by the government. The Ministry of Education, Culture, and Science inspects all textbooks proposed by private publishers and "recommends" revisions for both form (grammar, etc.) and content. In a notorious case, the government objected to the unfavorable characterization of the Japanese invasion of China in the 1930s and suggested changes. A publisher must follow government suggestions in order to receive government approval.

In the private sector, endorsement of various *Nihonjinron* propositions by the business establishment, especially those dealing with group orientation and interpersonal harmony, is widely prevalent. One sees this in the New Year's statements made by corporate executives, speeches by company presidents at induction ceremonies of new recruits held in April, and in company mottos, usually called *shakun* or *shaze*. These and many other means of moral exhortation emphasize, among others, cooperation and harmony among workers, loyalty to the company, hard work and dedication, and contribution to the society through the workplace, which are all tenets derivable from *Nihonjinron*.

Thus intellectuals write *Nihonjinron* as if it were a descriptive model, whereupon it becomes a hegemonic imperative for behavior. Government turns this into a political agenda. And the corporate establishment disseminates it among industrial workers.

NIHONJINRON AND CULTURAL POLICY

It should come as no surprise that the hegemonic ideology of *Nihonjinron* is maintained and supported by the state in many and varied forms. One is the annual awards of cultural medals that are given by the government to those who excel in plastic, graphic and performing arts in traditional fields. Another is designation by the government of those in the arts as "human cultural treasures" in recognition of ultimate achievement. These medals and designations are given to only a handful of individuals each year. As they are given in fields of traditional arts and crafts, these awards indicate state recognition of traditional Japanese aesthetic values incorporated in *Nihonjinron*.

National museums and monuments also serve to reinforce the sense of cultural and national identity, as these edifices often attempt to assert a sense of cultural uniqueness. Among such edifices are state-run museums. The Historical and Folklore Museum (Rekishi Minzoku Hakubutsukan) is a good example of this sort of cultural expression. It helps to assert Japan's unique identity by housing artifacts unique to Japan. The National Museums of Art, in Tokyo and Kyoto, accomplish the same objective.

These museums may be contrasted with the National Museum of Ethnology in Osaka. Designed by Kurokawa Kisho, one of the top Japanese architects, and built only recently, it is a beautiful blend of Japanese and Western aesthetics and utilizes the latest electronic technology in research, curating, and display. Displays cover all major ethnographic areas of the world. The Museum, in other words, faithfully reflects the raison d'etre of this nation as an economic power. Thus the Historical and Folklore Museum and the Art Museums, on the one hand, and the Ethnology Museum, on the other, give different, though not inconsistent, messages. The former impresses upon visitors that which is unique to Japanese culture and history—the very essence of *Nihonjinron*. The latter symbolizes and impresses upon visitors, though only implicitly, Japan's worldwide economic success, without which the existence of this museum would not have been possible.

The Japanese government has taken upon itself to promote and propagate the official *Nihonjinron* concept overseas. This overseas propagation of *Nihonjinron* should be seen as an integral part of the *Nihonjinron* phenomenon, for it is due in large part to Japan's expansion abroad that *Nihonjinron* has become a burning issue among Japanese. I have explicated earlier (1983) the relationship between *Nihonjinron* and the internationalization of Japan. Briefly, as Japan internationalizes, it accepts foreigners and adopts foreign culture on Japanese soil, while going abroad and establishing Japanese economic investments overseas. Japanese increasingly confront cultures different from their own, and thus become aware of the need to define themselves and their culture. *Nihonjinron* fulfills this need. But this self-definition serves as self-definition only when it is accepted by outsiders. To have outsiders accept their definition of themselves is to have them accept *Nihonjinron*. It is thus that the Japanese government expends much energy on propagating *Nihonjinron* abroad.

This takes the form, for example, of government financing of the English translation and publication of some of the *Nihonjinron* classics (Mouer and Sugimoto 1986:177–178). Nakamura Hajime's *The Way of Thinking of Eastern Peoples* (1960) and Watsuji Tetsuro's *The Climate* (1962) are results of such government effort. This effort reached a new, heightened level when the Japanese government took it upon itself to print *Human Relations in Japan* (1972), a government version, as it were, of Nakane Chie's *Japanese Society* (1970); thousands of copies were distributed free of charge throughout the world.

The Japan Foundation, established during the term of Premier Tanaka, has done perhaps more than any other single government institution in disseminating tenets and premises of *Nihonjinron* throughout the world. From its inception, it has sent scholars abroad to show how unique Japan is. It has also sent artists of traditional Japanese art forms, such as Kabuki, Noh, Bunraku, and calligraphy, all of which needless to say, demonstrated the uniqueness of Japanese culture.

More recently, in 1988, an International Center for Japanese Studies was established by the government as a result of Prime Minister Nakasone's interest in promoting cooperative international research on Japanese culture. As soon as the Center came into being, it was widely rumored that the Center's hidden agenda was to validate, disseminate, and propagate *Nihonjinron*. Though I personally believe this fear is baseless, both the popularity of *Nihonjinron* and the widespread participation of scholars producing it in the activities of the International Center make this suspicion quite plausible.

CONCLUSION

Benedict Anderson (1983) argued the importance of language in the formation of nationalism, in creating—along with what he ingeniously called "print capitalism"—a sense of "community" among those who spoke the same language and read the same print. This sense of community advocates exclusiveness when the language is spoken natively only by the ethnic group and no one else.

The Japanese language is a case in point, contrasting with English, which is spoken natively by peoples of many lands, nations, and cultures. English thus ends up creating a sense of community, à la Anderson, among Britons, Canadians, Australians, and others, and does not aid in fomenting nationalism. In fact, to the extent that Anglophones perceive cultural unity deriving from linguistic homogeneity—without denying regional variations—it may be a counter to nationalism. Hebrew, Danish, Finnish, and Korean are other examples, like Japanese, where the language is largely spoken natively only within the boundary of the nation and its emigrant communities. The importance of language in creating an identity stems not only from the fact of speaking a common tongue but, as we saw, also from the unique connotations, meanings, and values implied in the expressions of the language.

What can be said about language in relation to ethnic identity can be repeated for religion. A religion that is unique to a given ethnic group can help define the identity of the group in a way a religion such as Christianity or Islam would have difficulty doing. It would be difficult, for example, for French to use Catholicism as a basis of defining French uniqueness.

In contrast, all Japanese have to do is to point to Shintoism as an attribute of Japan's uniqueness, since Shintoism happens to be a unique, indigenous religion. Elevating it from folk belief to state religion, and placing the emperor as its centerpiece, the Japanese state managed to create a unique religious basis for its nationalism. Buddhism, since it is shared among many Asian nations, cannot readily serve as a basis of nationalism. Nichiren, however, managed to give it a unique nationalistic interpretation. The Nichiren sect became the militantly nationalistic protector of Japan at the time of the Mongols' attempted invasions in the thirteenth century.

Most modern nation-states consist of multiple ethnic groups. This is true of the United States, Russia and most postcolonial states, and it certainly is true of Japan, in spite of the claim of homogeneity by *Nihonjinron* protagonists. Japan has three quarters of a million Koreans living within its boundaries. The Ainu, though small in number, are conspicuous as an ethnic minority because of their divergent culture and its long history. Chinese, southeast Asians, Americans and Europeans also are present in increasing numbers. When Japan's national identity is based on primordial sentiments held by ethnic Japanese, such an identity automatically excludes other ethnic groups from citizenship in a cultural sense. But because the ethnic Japanese are not only numerically but politically dominant, they are able to impose their own ethnicity as the official identity of the nation, ignoring claims of legitimacy by ethnic minorities with divergent identities.

But no modern state can base its citizenship purely on ethnic primordial sentiments. Japan is no exception. Its government has introduced civic sentiments calling forth universal values such as political freedom, democracy, civil rights, human dignity, equality, and so forth, which can presumably be shared equally by all groups, majority and minority. But the problem is that these civic sentiments are only superficially overlaid on more deeply seated primordial sentiments spelled out in *Nihonjinron*. This definition of the Japanese, based as it is on Japanese ethnic primordiality, excludes Koreans and other minorities from being part of the fold, precisely as Tamils are excluded from Sri Lankan "cultural citizenship" and Arabs living in Israel proper (not in the occupied territories of the Gaza Strip or the West Bank) are excluded from full membership in the Israeli nation by the Jewish majority. To be culturally Sri Lankan means to be a Sinhalese and to be culturally Israeli is to be a Jew. In the same sense, to be culturally Japanese means to be Japanese-Japanese, not Korean-Japanese. Where primordial and civic sentiments contradict each other, civic sentiments yield to primordial ethnic definitions of Japanese nationality. Koreans in Japan who insist on their civil rights are thus refused their rights because they are not ethnically Japanese.

A vast majority of the so-called nation-states in the world today are no longer, if they ever were, mono nation-states. They are multi-nationality or multi-ethnic states: Iraq with Kurds, Turkey with Kurds and Armenians, Sri Lanka with Tamils, Germany with Turkish *gastarbeiters*, France with Algerians, Australia with different immigrant groups and the aborigines,

Russia with innumerable nationalities, China with scores of declared ethnic groups, similarly the U.S. with immigrant groups and Native Americans. The list is endless.

In virtually every single one of these multi-nation-states, however, the national identity is defined solely on the basis of the cultural values invoked by the dominant nationality. What this implies is subordination and submission of minorities to majority values and to the hegemony of majority politics. Minority views are either ignored or merely (or perhaps "barely" is a more appropriate term) tolerated. They are neither integrated into the discourse of national identity nor incorporated into its symbols. Do Koreans feature in *Nihonjinron*, for example? Are Arabs represented in Israeli national symbols, even though more than 10% of the Israeli population are Arabs (not counting those in the occupied territories)? Do Sri Lankan myths portray Tamil in anything but an unfavorable light (Kapferer 1988)? Does the U.S. flag recognize the first peoples of the land, such as Native Americans and Polynesians?

Herein lies the root problem: the need to accommodate ethnic minorities in the discursive and symbolic identity of the states which have so far defined themselves in terms of the dominant group. These dominant groups have at times championed or at least acquiesced to the cause and ideology of equality. Yet practice lags behind, notably in the definition of what the state is supposed to stand for. National identity around the world is facing a critical point. It is crying out for revision and redefinition in order to bring ethnic minorities into the fold, without whom ubiquitous ethnic strife will not only continue but will no doubt even escalate in the 21st century.

NOTES

1. This paper is based upon research supported by the National Endowment for the Humanities, the Fulbright Program, the National Humanities Center, the Center for East Asian Studies of Stanford University, to each of which a grateful acknowledgement is made.

2. Japanese personal names are written with the family name first, followed by the given name.

REFERENCES

Aizawa, Shizuo (1975). *Nihon Bunka to Seishin Kozo* (Japanese Culture and Its Spiritual Structure). Tokyo: Taiyo Shuppan.
Anderson, Benedict (1983). *Imagined Communities*. London: Verso.
Araki, Hiroyuki (1973). *Nihonjin no Kodo Yoshiki* (Behavior Patterns of the Japanese). Tokyo: Kodansha.
Befu, Harumi (1983). Internationalization of Japan and Nihon Bunkaron. In Hiroshi Mannari and Harumi Befu, Eds. *The Challenge of Japan's Internationalization: Organization and Culture*. Nishinomiya: Kwansei Gakuin University, and Tokyo: Kodansha International, pp. 232–266.
— n.d. Swings of Japan's identity. (ms)
Ben-Dasan, Isaiah (1970). *Nihonjin to Yudayajin* (The Japanese and the Jews). Tokyo: Yamamoto Shoten.
Benedict, Ruth (1946). *Chrysanthemum and the Sword*. Boston: Houghton Mifflin.
— (1948). *Kiku to Katana* (Chrysanthemum and the Sword). Tokyo: Shakai Shisosha.
Brzezinski, Zbigniew (1972). *The Fragile Blossom: Crisis and Change in Japan*. New York: Harper.
— (1972). *Hiyowana Hana: Nihon*. Tokyo: Simul Press.
Bunka no Jidai Kenkyu Group (1980). *Bunka no Jidai* (The Age of Culture). Ministry of Finance Printing Bureau.
Caw, Peter (1974). Operational, Representational and Explanatory Models. *American Anthropologist* 76:1–10.
Chiba, Tokuji, Ed. (1980). *Nihon Minzoku Fudo-Ron* (Environmental Determinants of the Japanese People). Tokyo: Kobundo.
Doi, Takeo (1971a). *Amae no Kozo* (Anatomy of Dependence) (hardcover). Tokyo: Kobundo.
— (1971b). *Amae no Kozo* (Anatomy of Dependence) (softcover). Tokyo: Kobundo.
— (1973). *Anatomy of Dependence*. Tokyo: Kodansha.
Geertz, Clifford (1963). The Integrative Revolution: Primordial Sentiments and Civic Politics in the New States. In Clifford Geertz, Ed. *Old Societies and New States*. New York: Free Press, pp. 105–157.
— (1973). *Interpretation of Cultures*. New York: Basic Books.
Gengo (1978). *Nihonjin no No*. (The Brain of the Japanese). Vol. 7, No. 10. (Special issue).

Hamaguchi, Esyun (1977). *"Nihon Rashisa" no Saihakken* (Rediscovery of "Japanliness"). Tokyo: Nihon Keizai Shinbunsha.
Hamaguchi, Esyun, Ed. (1982). *Nihonjin no Aidagara* (Human Relations among Japanese). Gendai no Esprit, No. 178. Tokyo: Shibundo.
Hayashida, Cullen T. (1976). *Identity, Race and the Blood Ideology of Japan.* University of Washington doctoral dissertation.
Higuchi, Kiyoyuki (1974). *Umeboshi to Nihonto* (Pickled Plum and the Japanese Sword). Tokyo: Shodensha.
Holy, Ladislav and Milan Stuchlik (1981). The Structure of Folk Models. In L. Holy and M. Stuchlik, Eds. *The Structure of Folk Models.* New York: Academic Press, pp. 1–34.
Inuta, Mitsuru (1977). *Shudan Shugi no Kozo* (The Structure of Groupism). Tokyo: Sangyo Noritsu Tanki Daigaku Shuppanbu.
Ishida, Eiichiro (1968). *Nihon Bunkaron* (Nihonjinron). Tokyo: Chikuma Shobo.
— (1974). *Japanese Culture: A Study of Origins and Characteristics.* Tokyo: Tokyo University Press.
Itasaka, Gen (1978). *Nihongo no Hyojo* (Expression of Japanese). Tokyo: Kodansha.
Iwasaki, Takaharu (1980). Warera no Uchi Naru "Mure Bito" (The "group" within us). In Esyun Hamaguchi, Ed. *Shudan Shugi* (Groupism). Tokyo: Shibundo, pp. 31–41.
Izumi, Seiichi and Masao Gamo (1952). Nihon Shakai no Chiikisei (Regionalism in Japanese Society). In *Nihon Chiri Shin Taikei* (New Handbook on Japanese Geography), Vol. 2. Tokyo: Kawade Shobo, pp. 37–73.
Jinrui Kagaku (1963–64). *Nihon no Chiikisei* (Regionalism in Japan). No. 15 (1963), No. 16 (1964) (Special issue).
Kakehi, Yasuhiko (1984). *Nihongo to Nihonjin no Hasso* (Japanese Language and Thought Process of the Japanese). Tokyo: Nihon Kyobunsha.
Kapferer, Bruce (1988). *Legends of People, Myths of State: Violence, Intolerance, and Political Culture in Sri Lanka and Australia.* Washington, D.C.: Smithsonian Institution.
Kawamoto, Akira (1982). *Nihonjin to Shudanshugi: Tochi to Chi* (Japanese Groupism: Soil and Blood). Tamagawa University Press.
Kawamura, Nozomu (1982). *Nihon Bunkaron no Shuhen.* Tokyo: Ningen no Kagakusha.
Kawashima, Takenori (1950). *Nihon Shakai no Kazoku-Teki Kosei* (The Familial Structure of the Japanese Society). Tokyo: Nihon Hyoron Shinsha.
— (1957). *Ideorogii Toshite no Kazoku Seido* (Family System as an Ideology). Tokyo: Iwanami.

Kimura, Bin (1973). *Hito to Hito to no Aida: Seishin Byorigaku-Teki Nihonron* (Relationship between Persons: "Theory" of Japan from the Point of View of Psychopathology). Tokyo: Kobundo.

Kindaichi, Haruhiko (1957). *Nihongo* (Japanese Language). Tokyo: Iwanami Shoten.

Kuki, Shuzo (1930). *"Iki" no Kenkyu* (A Study of Iki). Tokyo: Iwanami Shoten.

Kyogoku, Jun'ichi (1983). *Nihon no Seiji* (Politics in Japan). Tokyo: Tokyo University Press.

Levi-Strauss, Claude (1953). Social Structure. In Alfred L. Kroeber, Ed. *Anthropology Today*. Chicago: University of Chicago Press, pp. 524–553.

Manabe, Kazufumi, Harumi Befu, and David McConnell (1989). An Empirical Investigation of Nihonjinron: The Degree of Exposure of Japanese to Nihonjinron Propositions and the Functions these Propositions Serve. *Kwansei Gakuin University Annual Studies* 38:35–62.

Masuda Yoshiro (1967). *Junsui Bunka no Joken* (Conditions of a Pure Culture). Tokyo: Kodansha.

Miller, Roy Andrew (1982). *Japan's Modern Myth: The Language and Beyond*. Tokyo: Weatherhill.

Minami, Hiroshi (1953). *Nihonjin no Shinri* (The Psychology of the Japanese). Tokyo: Iwanami Shoten.

— (1983). *Nihon-Teki Jiga* (The Japanese Concept of Self). Tokyo: Iwanami Shoten.

Minamoto, Ryoen (1969). *Giri to Ninjo—Nihon-Teki Shinri no Ichi Kosatsu* (Giri and Ninjo—Considerations of the Japanese Psychology). Tokyo: Chuo Koronsha.

Misawa, Katsue (1979). *Fudoron* (The Climate). Tokyo: Misuzu Shobo.

Miyagi, Otoya (1972). *Nihonjin Towa Nanika* (What is "Japanese"?). Tokyo: Asahi Shinbunsha.

Miyamoto (1967). *Fudo to Bunka* (The Climate and Culture). Tokyo: Miraisha.

Mouer, Ross and Yoshio Sugimoto (1986). *Images of Japanese Society*. London: Kegan Paul International.

Murai, Jun (1981). *Nihonjin no Ryoshin* (Conscience of the Japanese). Tokyo: Zenponsha.

Murakami, Yasusuke, Shumpei Kumon, and Seizaburo Sato (1973). *Bummei to Shite no Ie Shakai* (Ie Society as Civilization). Tokyo: Chuo Koronsha.

Nagashima, Nobuhiro and Hiroyasu Tomoeda (1984). Regional Differences in Japanese Rural Culture. *Senri Ethnological Studies*, No. 14.

Nakagawa, Yatsuhiro (1978). Nihon Koso Sekai Ichi no Fukushi Chodaikoku Da (Japan Is the Welfare Superstate). *Chuokoron* 98.8.86–103.

— (1979). Japan, the Welfare Superstate. *Journal of Japanese Studies* 5(1):5–51.

Nakamura, Hajime (1949). *Toyojin no Shii Hoho* (Ways of Thinking of Eastern Peoples). Tokyo: Misuzu Shobo. 2v.
— (1960). *Ways of Thinking of Eastern Peoples*. Honolulu: University of Hawaii Press.
Nakane, Chie (1967). *Tate Shakai no Ningen Kankei: Tan'itsu Shakai no Riron* (Human Relations in a Vertical Society: A Theory of a Homogeneous Society). Tokyo: Kodansha.
— (1970). *Japanese Society*. Berkeley and Los Angeles: University of California Press.
— (1972). *Human Relations in Japan*. Tokyo: Ministry of Foreign Affairs.
NHK Hoso Yoron Chosajo, Ed. (1979). *Nihonjin no Kemmin-Sei* (Prefectural Characteristics of the Japanese). Tokyo: Nihon Hoso Shuppan Kyokai.
Nieda, Rokusaburo (1973). *Tatemae to Honne* (Tatemae and Honne). Tokyo: Daiamondo-sha.
Nomura Sogo Kenkyujo, Ed. (1978). *Nihonjinron* (NRI Reference No. 2). Nomura Sogo Kenkyujo.
Oide, Akira (1965). *Nihongo to Ronri* (Japanese and Logic). Tokyo: Kodansha.
Okonogi, Keigo (1978–79). The Ajase Complex of the Japanese—The Depth Psychology of the Moratorium People. *Japan Echo* 5(1978) (4):88–105; 6(1979)(1):104–118.
— (1982). *Nihonjin no Ajase Kompurekkusu* (The Ajase Complex of the Japanese). Tokyo: Chuo Koronsha.
Reischauer, Edwin O. (1977). *The Japanese*. Cambridge: Harvard University Press.
— (1979). *Za Japanniizu*. Tokyo: Bungei Shunjusha.
Sabata, Toyoyuki (1964). *Nihon o Minaosu* (Re-examining Japan). Tokyo: Kodansha.
— (1972). *Bummei no Joken* (Determinants of Civilization). Tokyo: Kodansha.
— (1974). *Bummei to Fudo* (Civilization and the Climate). Tokyo: Nihon Keizai Shimbunsha.
Saito, Shoji (1972). *"Yamatodamashii" no Bunka-Shi* (A Cultural History of the Japanese Spirit). Tokyo: Kodansha.
Sekiguchi, Takeshi (1983). *Kisho to Bunka* (Climate and Culture). Tokyo: Toyo Keizai Shimposha.
Sera, Tadatoshi (1965). *Nihonjin no Kokoro* (The Heart of the Japanese). Tokyo: Nihon Hoso Shuppan Kyokai.
Suzuki, Hideo (1975). *Fudo no Kozo* (The Structure of the Environment). Tokyo: Daimeido.
Suzuki, Takao (1980). Gengo Seikatsu (Language Life). In Hiroshi Minami, Ed. *Nihonjin no Ningen Kankei Jiten* (Dictionary of Japanese Human Relations). Tokyo: Kodansha, pp. 346–364.

Tamaki, Akira (1978). *Inasaku Bunka to Nihonjin* (Rice Culture and the Japanese). Tokyo: Gendai Hyoronsha.

Toyama, Shigehiko (1976). *Nihongo no Kosei* (Distinctive Characters of Japanese). Tokyo: Chuo Koronsha.

Tsuda, Masumi (1977). *Nihonteki Keiei no Riron* (Theory of Japanese Style Management). Tokyo: Chuo Keizaisha.

Tsukuba, Joji (1969). *Beishoku no Bummei Nikushoku no Bummei* (Civilization of Rice Diet, Civilization of Meat Diet). Tokyo: Nihon Hoso Shuppan Kyokai.

Tunoda, Tadanobu (1978). *Nihonjin no No* (The Brain of the Japanese). Tokyo: Taishukan Shoten.

Vogel, Ezra (1979). *Japan as Number One*. Cambridge: Harvard University Press.

— (1979). *Japan azu Namba Wan*. Tokyo: TBS Britanika.

Ward, Barbara E. (1985). *Through Other Eyes: Essays in Understanding "Conscious Models"—Mostly in Hong Kong*. Boulder: Westview Press.

Watsuji, Tetsuro (1935). *Fudo* (Climate). Tokyo: Iwanami Shoten.

— (1962). *A Climate: A Philosophical Study*. Tokyo: Ministry of Finance Printing Bureau.

Yamada, Hideyo (1978). *Fudoron Josetsu* (Introduction to Environmental Theory). Tokyo: Tosho Kankokai.

Yamashita, Hideo (1979). *Nihon no Kotoba to Kokoro* (The Language and the Heart of the Japanese). Tokyo: Kodansha.

12

A Second Look: Anatomy of Misinterpretation

Darrell William Davis

> We needed Iraqi hordes to replace the Evil Empire, and now we need the Invading Japanese to replace the camel jockeys. And even more than the marketable gulf war, Japan bashing—born of our consuming lives—is ad-ready.... The fun-in-the-fury is expressed in the very word bash as in both the "attack" and "throw a big bash" senses. Bashing is the only fun we get these days. (Leslie Savan, "Bash and Cash," *The Village Voice*).

Savan's "Op Ad" column nicely captures the perverse glee surrounding the clamor over unfair Japanese trade practices, along with images of sclerotic congressmen smashing up small appliances on the capitol steps. The "bashing" phenomenon is close kin to the tantrum, the fit, and the rave, and it is no wonder that the media have been irresistibly drawn to its melodramatic excesses. Melodrama aside, bashing is an important cultural strategy of self-definition that simultaneously demonizes the other while exonerating the self. By pushing the rhetoric of a fairly circumscribed dispute ("dumping" of computer chips, say) out onto the grandstand of national and racial caricature, the "fighting words" used by politicians and commentators produce a distraction and (even better) a scapegoat for the intractable problems of international relations.

In Japan, there is a domestic, self-congratulatory complement to bashing that obsessively analyzes the national self even as it covertly condescends to other nationalities. *Nihonjinron* ("Japanese-people-discussion") is, according to Harumi Befu, an official orthodoxy of Japanese identity, carefully packaged and disseminated abroad for consumption by Westerners eager for clues to the Japanese economic miracle. In practice, it is a genre of expository writing out to prove the uniqueness, and superiority, of Japanese national identity. Although it did not start out that way, *Nihonjinron* is a colossal publishing, PR, and media venture that finds an even more ravenous appetite for its product inside Japan than abroad. This makes its arguments suspect, because it smacks of hegemony, an ideology propagated by the powerful down upon unsuspecting citizens and out into international currency. But Befu's useful primer of *Nihonjinron* subjects and premises is compromised by his tendency to overextend the concept to make it apply to virtually any study that purports to explain how Japanese society and culture works. By failing to adequately circumscribe *Nihonjinron*, Befu diffuses its associations into spheres that do not accommodate the nationalistic and hegemonic intentions of *Nihonjinron*.

In his epigraph Befu, an anthropologist, quotes Levi-Strauss on the significance of "bias and types of errors" in the models used to study culture, which are deemed to be as important as the facts to be explained by the model. Befu aligns himself with a symptomatic method which never takes native pronouncements about culture at face value, but instead looks for the structural functions these pronouncements serve in the mythological system taken as a whole unto itself. Levi-Strauss, for instance, emphasized the role of formal, socialized attitudes toward kinship (as opposed to individual psychological attitudes) in smoothing over the wrinkles and deficiencies of kinship terminology: "These attitudes, far from automatically reflecting the nomenclature, often appear as secondary elaborations, which serve to resolve the contradictions and overcome the deficiencies inherent in the terminological system" (Levi-Strauss 1963:38). Levi-Strauss is sensitive to areas of cultural contestation and how myth functions to ease those tensions. Likewise, Befu's procedure is symptomatic in its emphasis on the structural contours of *Nihonjinron* cultural models, how they maintain the beliefs and attitudes of average Japanese men and women without regard to the outlandish claims made by those models. Although he takes great plains to avoid a hermeneutic of suspicion, Befu cannot help but practice what he does not preach, and what Nietzsche preaches so well: "When we are confronted with any manifestation which someone has permitted us to see, we may ask: what is it meant to conceal? what is it meant to draw our attention from? what prejudice does it seek to raise? and again, how far does the subtlety of the dissimulation go? and in what respect is the man mistaken?" (quoted in Bordwell 1989:72).

Put another way, Befu subscribes to a cultural relativism which is more interested in the contents of Japanese perceptions of cultural identity than in the validity of those perceptions. "Whether objectively, and in fact, the constructed identity is unique in the world is not the issue, or is only indirectly at issue in considering whether the constructed identity 'fits' the reality, which is another matter all together," writes Befu. "Rather it is the belief on the part of the Japanese in it the uniqueness of their identity which is crucial" (p. 264; emphasis added). The question of uniqueness is a question of perception, not fact, insists Befu, for if individual Japanese absorb the ideology of uniqueness, harmony, homogeneity, and industriousness that is prescribed for them, they will be more willing participants in the programs mapped out by Japan, Inc.

As an introduction to the basic tenets of *Nihonjinron*, Befu is brief and to-the-point. He surveys the remarkably eclectic terrain in which Japanese uniqueness is found by *Nihonjinron* writers, from ecology (Watsuji Tetsuro), subsistence economy, social structure (Nakane Chie), to psychology (Doi Takeo, et al.) and especially language (Tsunoda Tadanobu). A valuable contribution of Befu's article is the schematization of *Nihonjinron* themes and their correlation with authors working in similar areas. Despite the notoriously intricate tissue of intertextual references in this literature, Befu gives no indication of any internecine discussion, synthesis or debate between these writers, leading to his not-unexpected conclusion on the themes of ethnocentrism, homogeneity, and hegemony. It would not do to have much internal dissension among Japanese writers whose stock-in-trade is the hegemonic propagation of an ideology of homogeneous conformity, but it is hard to believe that with a literally-journalistic genre so huge and lively that more controversy does not arise.

Instead, Befu casts his net far and wide—so far, in fact, that he runs together a number of important distinctions. To show that *Nihonjinron* runs the gamut of various authors and audiences, Befu makes little distinction between scholarly and popular renditions of *Nihonjinron* concepts. The eminent Kyoto philosopher Watsuji Tetsuro is bedfellow with Morita psychotherapy, Tsunoda's linguistic hypotheses on Japanese cortical differences, and government think thanks summarizing

A Second Look: Japan

Japanese cultural policy. This is not just interdisciplinary border crossing; the flippant and the frivolous are also, and especially, fair game in the *Nihonjinron* hunt. There is nothing in Befu's description of *Nihonjinron* to exclude from consideration Kenmochi Takehiko's speculations on Japanese nosepicking or Aida Yuji's connections between excrement and national identity (Dale 1986:23, n. 10). If one can overlook his pugnacious style, Peter Dale's book, *The Myth of Japanese Uniqueness*, is an entertaining and very through exposé of *Nihonjinron* and has been curiously neglected by professional Japanologists. Dale takes the arguments of *Nihonjinron* seriously, rather than viewing them symptomatically, which accounts for his combative tone. This, in turn, could itself be construed as Japan-bashing and may explain why this book has been virtually ignored.

There is, however, a different distinction from that between scholarly and popular, which Befu similarly runs together: legitimate vs. specious inquiries into Japanese national characteristics. Befu would be the first to renounce any necessary correspondence between scholarly intent and legitimate results. Given his symptomatic method, the more ridiculous the example the better, because this gives grist for the mill of structural mythology. It is in these terms, not empirical or textual analysis, that Befu wishes to scrutinize *Nihonjinron*. When questioned in person about the conflation of scholarly and popular, specious and legitimate investigations, Befu maintains there are no justifiable grounds for "quarantining" especially suspect *Nihonjinron* (lectures at East-West Center Symposium, August 1990 and Center for Japanese Studies seminar, February 1992). If the work concerns Japanese national identity, then perforce it is *Nihonjinron*. And it is all equally suspect when the analyst is checking perceptions, not reality.

Since Befu does not lay out criteria of verifiability, consistency, correspondence, or logical coherence, there is no reason to try to separate the *Nihonjinron* sheep from the goats. But unless we want to consign a good portion of established scholarship on Japanese culture to the *Nihonjinron* rubric, we need to hold out for criteria that will allow us to balance the utility of the *Nihonjinron* concept with the necessity for distinguishing good and bad scholarship. Moreover, Japanese scholarship (specious or otherwise) on the peculiarities of Japanese culture has been going on for a very long time and it is necessary to distinguish between classic, modern and contemporary instances of *Nihonjinron*, if that is really what we want to call it. The combination of the term's pejorative associations with Professor Befu's unwillingness to carefully define the extension of its use is unnecessarily confusing, conceptually and historically.

For instance, *Kokugaku* (national learning) scholarship was an early school of classical Japanese textual and lyric exegesis, beginning in the early 17th century. *Kokugaku* confronted the primarily Confucian orientation of medieval Japanese education and scholarship, and represented a desire to recover an indigenous Japanese ethos and aesthetic. During the Tokugawa era, an ideological aspect to *kokugaku* emerged, forging connections with political upheavals in the *bakufu*. *Kokugaku* thus became caught in the crossfire in which loyalties for and against the Shogun's authority were played out. The stakes in defining an authentic/authoritative national identity were tightly bound to the power struggles waged for the retention or abolition of the Shogunate. In the name of true Japaneseness, scholars like Motoori Norinaga and Hirata Atsutane criticized the bureaucratic moralism of Confucian scholarship that was used to prop up the tottering Shogunal structure. But the political utility of this scholarship does not automatically negate its value as scholarship. The political utility and intrinsic validity of national identity discourses needs to be distinguished at the risk of neutering standards of textual and historical scholarship.

Despite his desire to maintain a symptomatic anthropological detachment, Professor Befu cannot help but note his disapproval of the misleading claims of say, Higuchi Kiyoyuki, who earns some anthropological sarcasm for writings which "unabashedly congratulate Japanese for how smart, how creative, and how ingenious they are" (Befu, p. 274). With "unrelenting zeal," Higuchi turns out over 120 books every year, putting Ezra Vogel to shame, who wrote only one book unabashedly praising the Japanese (Vogel 1979). Compared with Peter Dale, however, Befu is indulgent. Dale does not mince any words:

> Reading the *Nihonjinron* is an exact task. The unflagging productivity of the genre, the extremely broad parameters of its cultural references, its mingling of trite opinion with obscure erudition, and particularly the way one text plays off another, accepting a silly idea thrown into the ring of debate only to modify it with a further twist of absurdity, make inordinate demands even on those prepared to wade and sift through what is in good part merely the intellectual fast food of consumer nationalism (Dale 1986:16).

Understandably Befu does not wish to enter this sort of diatribe, but it seems familiarity with *Nihonjinron* inevitably breeds contempt, even among those who wish to bracket its truth claims. Dale's indignation is directly proportional to his appreciation of its empirical shortcomings, shoddy logic, and sloppy research, its "anatomy of misinterpretation whose consistency of deception betrays in turn an inadvertent kind of self disclosure" (Dale 1986:15). Befu, in contrast, professes to be indifferent to its truth claims, but still finds something disturbing about its hegemonic appropriations. However, what gives hegemony theory its bite is its vigilance toward appropriation of scholarly research for ideological purposes; this gives it a meta-empirical importance that keeps asking questions after questions of empirical validity are settled. If questions of empirical validity are never asked to begin with, hegemony theory is just another conspiracy theory.

Though Befu pretends to be uninterested in serious scrutiny and testing of *Nihonjinron* propositions, he is not uninterested in empirical testing of its success as hegemony. Given the preposterousness of *Nihonjinron* propositions, one could expect that their effects in Japanese society are far from salutary. But at last, Befu reports some good news: the saturation of *Nihonjinron* among ordinary Japanese is far from complete. In a survey designed and run in Nishinomiya, Befu found significant disagreement in responses to typical *Nihonjinron* doctrines, such as the claim that no foreigner can master the Japanese language (Befu, p. 278). A point of *Nihonjinron* hegemony that so badly clashes with evidence to the contrary (television's *gaijin tarento*, foreign entertainers, being only the most obvious) has pitifully little chance of widespread acceptance. Perhaps even more heartening, many Nishinomiya respondents communicated very little awareness, and even comprehension, of some *Nihonjinron* propositions that were put to them, and also showed little knowledge of supposedly famous authors who had written the endlessly reprinted canons of *Nihonjinron* texts (Befu, Center for Japanese Studies seminar, February 1992). Befu has statistical evidence, then, that *Nihonjinron* is far less pervasive than its ubiquitousness in media, in education, and in government would lead one to think. A conspiracy to propagate Japanese uniqueness is out there, but when the Japanese themselves are questioned about their uniqueness, they don't believe it. *Nihonjinron* appears to be a conspiracy with no takers.

But we must except certain foreigners, including a number of professional Japanologists, who take *Nihonjinron* seriously. Although Befu's refusal to be drawn into a fray over Japanese uniqueness is slightly disingenuous, his implication that *Nihonjinron* has been taken far too seriously by oversensitive Westerners is correct and necessary. The sheer size of the publishing and media output of the genre is not a reliable indication of its influence, at least according to Befu's survey results. The validity of Befu's empirical findings could be questioned on grounds of representativeness, research design, statistical significance and so on. But I suspect that the real reason for Befu's focus on Japanese perceptions of *Nihonjinron* ideas is his desire to sidestep the inflamed arena of Japan-America bashing, and try to discover what the Japanese themselves think of all this. This means he does not wish to scrutinize the claims of *Nihonjinron* in a substantive way, but in avoiding such scrutiny Befu actually reproduces those claims in the realm of perception and belief, even if he finds little assent, or even comprehension. The result, oddly enough, is a diffusion or perhaps displacement of Japanese uniqueness onto the inchoate opinion of the average, randomly selected person, rather than a containment of an ideology that nearly everyone knows should be taken with a large pinch of salt.

REFERENCES

Levi-Strauss, Claude (1963). *Structural Anthropology*. Translated by Claire Jacobson and Brooke Grundfest Schoepf. New York: Basic Books.

Bordwell, David (1989). *Making Meaning: Inference and Rhetoric in the Interpretation of Cinema*. Cambridge: Harvard University Press.

Dale, Peter (1986). *The Myth of Japanese Uniqueness*. New York: St. Martins Press.

Vogel, Ezra (1979). *Japan as Number One*. Cambridge: Harvard University Press.

PART VI
Thailand

13

Buddhist Cultural Tradition and the Politics of National Identity in Thailand

Yos Santasombat

Central to the renewed quests for identity which constitute so much of the socio-cultural and political ferment today is the necessity of reconciling traditional and newly created definitions of self, community, and nation. This is what comprises the problem of identity, for these definitions are being forged out of situations where tradition and modernity make conflicting appeals—tradition providing a surge of pride in one's heritage and modernity providing the determination to benefit from the opportunities provided by the modern technological/consumeristic world. Always at the heart of identity is what it means to be a person, a community, or a nation: the perception of an overall coherence and a conscious, but not wholly conscious, commitment to a particular manner of comprehending and managing one's own self based on religious, social, political, or ethnic grounds. More often than not, the problems of identity are significantly religious and political to the degree that they take seriously those other aspects of selfhood (i.e. personal, national and cultural roots) but also fail to bestow ultimate status upon them. The notion of what authentically religious quests for identity entail is not foreign to ancient or modern man. These quests, indeed, prompt society to engage in self-criticism. Their role is thus as much that of *agent provocateur* as it is that of agent of continuity, disturber of peace and provider of assurances (Smith 1976:4).

In today's modern world, every society is confronted with the problem of providing relatively consistent cultural bases for individual identity and societal authority. Every society also contains a potential contradiction between the cultural traditions, ideas and values by which individuals identify themselves and act on their acquired meanings, and those by which the state legitimizes the exercises of its power. Every society has the potential to develop differences between the symbols and ideas which, on the one hand, support the authority of the society and its institutions and, on the other, provide a basis for individual identity. Under the impact of state patronage and charismatic personalities, there may be a "temporary" synthesis between the ideology of the state and the beliefs which organize and give meanings to individuals, as Nash (1971:106) demonstrated in the case of U Nu in Burma during the 1950s. The possibility that two systems of action will develop—the one oriented to providing the individual with a stable and meaningful identity, the other oriented to legitimizing the authority of the state—is a distinct possibility in both modern and Third World countries. Geertz (1973:142–144) notes that a contradiction of this kind produced overwhelming strains in the life of Indonesian people (as demonstrated in the case of the Javanese funeral) and Bell (1973), in speaking of American society, notes the development of an "adversary culture" which provided a basis for individual identity and life-style quite apart from the system of action (i.e. knowledge) which provided guidance for decision-making by government and its organizations (see Fenn 1980:121).

With this in mind, the thrust of this essay is to underscore three aspects of the problem of identity, each constituting a significant part of the interplay between religious cultural traditions and socio-political changes in Thailand. The first thread to follow through the essay is the historical construction of the "national identity" concept in Thailand (the relationships between Buddhist cultural traditions, national identity and nationalism). Attempts will also be made to examine the national cultural policies designed and implemented by the state and the ethnic and religious conflicts and confrontations resulting from such policy implementations. Secondly, the essay is an attempt to examine the emergence of large-scale religious movements in Thailand, the process of differentiation between personal and collective identity, and the contradiction between the two systems of action (that is, between the ideas, values and rules by which group members identify themselves and act on their acquired meanings, and those by which the state legitimizes the exercise of its authority). And finally, the third theme which runs through the essay concerns how the state and elite groups use Buddhist cultural traditions to capture or influence power and secure gains that are never permanently won. How does the state maintain, claim, and reclaim its position as the "legitimate interpreter" of cultural traditions?

It is in this realm, this paper argues, that one becomes particularly aware of social conflict as legitimacy is sought and resisted, cultural traditions interpreted and re-interpreted, and dilemmas which result from culture changes and power shifts potentially lead to the intensification of group rivalries and identity crises. This problem will be illustrated in empirical detail by discussing the case of the long-standing controversy surrounding the unorthodox Santi Asoke Buddhist sect and the attempt of the Ecclesiastical Council to defrock Phra Potirak, leader of the Santi Asoke movement, for his alleged rebellion against the mainstream monastic order. As will be shown, the case of Santi Asoke is representative of "social dramas" in which the political and symbolic orders interpenetrate and affect each other. For the participants in this social drama, the political struggle becomes not merely something external but also a crisis of personal and national identity.

THE HISTORY OF BUDDHISM, NATIONAL IDEOLOGY AND THE STATE (TO 1932)

Ever since the tacit adoption of Buddhism as the state religion in the fourteenth century, "the strain to identify the Buddhist religion with the polity and the Buddhist polity with the society were deep structure tendencies in the Buddhist kingdoms of Southeast Asia" (Tambiah 1978:112), and they are more intact in Thailand today than in any other Southeast Asian Buddhist country (see Tambiah 1976; Somboon 1976; Spiro 1982; Murashima 1988). Buddhism forged a grand conception of the polity as ordered through kingship and imbued with certain Buddhist values. The Buddhist genesis myth, *Agganna Suttanta*, espouses the twinship of *bhikku* (Buddhist monk) and king, of religion and the state. The ideal relation between Buddhism and the state is one of complementarity: the monarch is the man of highest merit and virtues, the patron and protector of religion, and in turn religion is the special treasure of the polity and the fountainhead of its legitimacy. But this ideal relation of complementarity, as Tambiah (1978:115) has noted, is ambiguous and holds within itself the germ of a problem. On one hand, the *Sangha* (the church-like organizational body of Buddhist monks) and the state were separate domains. But on the other hand, the king was authorized to intervene in extreme circumstances both to protect and purify the religion. This implies the penetration of the state into the "disciplinary" aspect of the Sangha and even into matters of doctrinal orthodoxy.

In normal situations, the state and the Sangha were decentralized constellations. But in abnormal circumstances, their relation changed in two directions:

> When a particular king did come to exercise strong power and his kingdom expanded and waxed strong, when he won wars, booty, and prisoners, and when he made attempts at a greater centralization of power, under such a king the Sangha too was built up as an ecclesiastical hierarchy and enjoyed royal liberality. But this resulted in the paradox that the Sangha that was organizationally strengthened was also thereby politically regulated. Conversely, when a king was weak and his rule crumbling, this erosion of political authority meant also the loss of political protection and supervision of the monasteries, resulting in their decline. Witness the revival of *upasampada* ordination at the beginning of many a reign after a period of political collapse (Tambiah 1978:115).[1]

The impact of colonialism and the challenge of the encroaching Western powers in the mid-nineteenth century forced the Thai kings to introduce many features of central and provincial administrative restructuring in order to achieve a greater national integration and to maintain independence. Even though Thailand was never directly colonized, the Bowring Treaty of 1855 (Ingram 1971) by which Thailand's doors were opened to free trade led to an expansion of the economy, largely from increased rice exports and the growth of commerce. As the national economy expanded, so did the scope of power to be exercised. During the reigns of King Mongkut (Rama IV, 1851–1868) and his successor, King Chulalongkorn (Rama V, 1868–1910), Thailand underwent a process of increased bureaucratization and centralization combined with enlarged royal absolutism and, correspondingly, the ritual elaboration of the kingship also took place (see Wyatt 1969; Chula Chakrabongse 1960).

This process of political stabilization and the transformation of the Thai polity in the nineteenth and early twentieth centuries had two important effects on Buddhism and its organization and practices. First, it resulted in periodic purifications of Buddhism and the Sangha. Secondly, it instituted a hierarchical and politically regulated system of ecclesiastical organization paralleling the governmental bureaucracy (see Tambiah 1978:118–119; Suwanna 1986:16–18; Keyes 1989:6–12).

However, the process of political stabilization and augmentation of the Thai polity had not been without serious problems. Thai political history since the beginning of the twentieth century has been punctuated by a succession of efforts by various groups who have sought to reshape the polity by reinterpreting Buddhist cultural traditions and reinstituting an order in line with their interpretations. In 1901–1902, *phu-mi-bun* (person-having-merit) movements (Varunee 1989:399–405) led by charismatic personalities began to persuade villagers in various parts of the northeastern region that an apocalypse was about to occur. Villagers were attracted to the millennial belief in *Maitreya*, the Buddha-to-come, partly because their world had been rapidly disrupted by governmental reforms and the restructuring of provincial administration. The process of economic development had resulted in considerable hardship for villagers because of increased taxes and the commercialization of agriculture (which threatened the security of peasants' landholdings). Droughts and harsh weather also wreaked agricultural havoc for two successive years and threatened the peasants' subsistence security. The local elites also suffered a substantial reduction in income and were required to pay land taxes along with the peasants (see Ishii 1975; Keyes 1977; Chattip 1984 and Varunee 1989).

In order to extricate themselves from the chaos into which the central government had plunged the social order, the leaders and proponents of the movements spread the word that those who performed certain rituals would be spared from cataclysm and would prosper under a new king who would rule according to *dhamma* (Buddhist morality) (Keyes 1989:12). Manipulated from the inside by these leaders, the villagers were led to believe that the king was not the only "person-having-merit," and that the local elites were also quite capable of performing miraculous acts. These leaders, therefore, became "symbols" of merit (*phu-mi-bun*) and led the villagers to challenge the established social order.

To a large extent, the peasant uprising channeled villagers' energy for resistance into religious expressiveness. The millennial belief was perhaps the only possible form of resistance which allowed the peasants to become fully aware (for the first time) of those who were exploiting them. It reflected reasoned judgment and an interpretation which followed paths of Buddhist beliefs. The uprising represented an effort to sift and filter values through various forms of Buddhist beliefs and mythologies to meet new needs and requirements.

Nevertheless, the government was able to swiftly suppress this uprising through the use of greater force and through efforts to discredit the legitimacy of the leaders by calling them *phi-bun* instead of *phu-mi-bun*.[2] In so doing, the government was able to justify its suppression of the uprising with reference to the same traditional cosmological perspective that made the millennial movements legitimate in the eyes of the villagers. And even though the government was able to reclaim its position as the "legitimate interpreter" (Eisenstadt 1966) of Buddhist cultural tradition, the peasant uprising prompted the government to realize that its legitimacy must be continuously reclaimed and reproduced through various symbolic forms and strategies, especially at times of rapid change.

In this light, it is hardly surprising to find that the *phu-mi-bun* uprising in northeastern Thailand coincided with the promulgation by King Chulalongkorn of the Sangha Act of 1902, even though it has never been made clear whether or not these two events are causally linked. According to the Sangha Act, a more centralized hierarchical ecclesiastical structure, with positions such as ecclesiastical governor generals, provincial governors and district governors, was to be established. The appointment of major abbotships in the capital's royal temples was made by King Chulalongkorn himself, while the appointment of other positions issued by the ecclesiastical officers was subject to approval by the king's civil officials in the provinces and districts. Through this Act, the Sangha, now controlled and supervised from the center and encompassing all the provinces, was made more conducive to greater national integration (Tambiah 1978:119). The reform of the ecclesiastical order was also an attempt at ironing out sub-cultural and dialectical differences existing in the kingdom by a policy of homogenization. Thereby, the variant traditions of Theravada Buddhism previously existing in various provinces were incorporated into the mainstream monastic order under a national umbrella.[3]

To a great extent, the homogenization of the Sangha resulting from the Sangha Act of 1902 was a paragon of success. The drafting of the Sangha Act of 1902, moreover, coincided with the forging of a tighter central and provincial administration, and the establishment of the Departments of Interior, Justice, Finance, and so forth. It also coincided with the spread of primary education on a nation-wide basis via local monastic schools.

With a better grip on the provincial administration and tighter control of the Sangha, the government succeeded in implementing a new national ideology among the peasants, although it took more than thirty years before this goal was accomplished. This new ideology—conveyed to villagers through primary school texts emphasizing the connections between Buddhism and the monarchy, through the Sangha and local temples, and through rituals in which symbols of the king and the Buddha are linked—focuses on the idea that the only "person-having-merit" who has the power to share and distribute the benefit of this merit with others is the king, the legitimate interpreter of Buddhism.

By the early years of the twentieth century, the bureaucracy and the Sangha were both centralized and politically regulated. The state exercised effective influence over Sangha policy and procedures at the higher administrative level while the hierarchically organized administration of the Sangha extended from the national level into villages and was controlled and supervised by the government (Somboon 1976). Through this pattern the Sangha was kept in line with governmental policy and seemed to be effectively incorporated into the governmental structure at various administrative levels. The centralized hierarchy of the Sangha was designed to insure that the Sangha was loyal to the government and provided the best apparatus for extension of governmental policies.

The seeds of "national ideology" planted by King Chulalongkorn were to bear potent fruit a decade later during the reign of King Vajiravudh (1910–1925). Under his rule, the concept of "nationhood" and a firm state ideology based on national political traditions were fully developed to counter the influx of Western liberalism (Murashima 1988:80). According to this ideology, "nation" is closely identified with "religion" and "monarchy," both of which are fundamental elements in the Buddhist cultural traditions. The monarch is regarded as elected by a gathering of all loyal subjects and should reign justly according to the law of *dhamma* (see Murashima 1988; Vella 1978; Dhani Nivat 1947).

In a real sense, the official Thai state ideology was a product of the continuity of King Vajiravudh's fundamental political ideas with those of his predecessors, especially the "national ideology" constructed during the reigns of King Mongkut and King Chulalongkorn. The "nation," in the sense of a national political community, became a popular word in the Thai vocabulary during the reign of King Chulalongkorn when Thailand was facing a most critical threat to its independence. It was during this time that the concept of nationhood was incorporated into the traditional Buddhist theory of kingship, thereby linking "nation" with "king" and "Buddhism." King Vajiravudh inherited these political ideas from his father and formulated them as the official state ideology in an effort to counter the influx of Western liberalism. Like his father, King Vajiravudh denied Western liberal political principles on the grounds that the Thai people had their own unique political principles based on Buddhist cultural tradition. He accused advocates of Western liberalism of believing in a cult of imitation and insisted that the Thai had to build a modern nation that was distinctly Thai and not a corrupted imitation fabricated from Western political traditions (Murashima 1988:95–96).

The construction of a "national ideology" based on the triumvirate of nation, religion, and king and aimed at countering Western liberalism during the reigns of King Chulalongkorn and King Vajiravudh did not go without serious challenge. In January 1885, eleven princes and high-ranking officials who had been educated abroad submitted to King Chulalongkorn a proposal advocating the adoption of Western political principles. The proposal requested that the government of the country be changed to a constitutional monarchy, and that a constitution and equality under the law be promoted (see Chai-anan and Kattiya 1975:59; Saneh 1985:49–50). The proposal also stated that these political principles had become the standard of practice among civilized nations and needed to be adopted in order to preserve Thai national independence and to turn Thailand into a modern nation-state. King Chulalongkorn chose neither to accept the proposal nor to treat it as evidence of treason. In his reply (see Murashima 1988:83–86; Wyatt 1969:89–92; Chula Chakrabongse 1960:261–265), he acknowledged that he agreed with many ideas expressed in the proposal, especially those regarding the international situation, but he did not agree that the borrowing of Western political and administrative institutions would solve the difficulties facing the nation. In fact, King Chulalongkorn strongly objected to the introduction of Western political institutions which would limit his power and hamper and corrupt the reforms he was implementing.

SECULAR DEMOCRATIC POLITY AND NATIONALISM (1932–1957)

Even though the proposal advocated by these petitioners was rejected by King Chulalongkorn, the seeds of Western liberalism they planted were to bear potent fruit four decades later when a group of young Western-educated civilian and military officials launched the revolution of June 24, 1932, which toppled the royal government of King Prajadhipok and moved to establish a secular democratic polity (see Wilson 1962; Thawatt 1972; Sombat 1978; Morell & Chai-anan 1981; Batson 1984; Yos 1985). While the 1932 revolution appeared to be an ideological rebellion against an anachronistic system of personal rule, no attempts had been made by the revolutionaries to develop a broad base of popular support for their ideological causes. Nor were there attempts to establish a new belief system or a new political culture and ideology which would give meaning and significance to the newly established system of parliamentary democracy.

The revolutionary leaders claimed that they were attempting to transfer the power of the monarch to broader segments of the society. But the establishment of an elected representative legislature, the key principle of democracy, in fact violated the cultural orientations of the Thai people, who viewed authority as coming from above, not as being based upon popular sovereignty. With the attempted destruction of the system of traditional political beliefs, the arena of politics was abruptly transformed from the realm of the "sacred" to that of the "profane." Since power was legitimized neither by religious beliefs nor by popular consent, and since there was no basis for legitimacy and no individual in whom sovereignty could be said to rest, the abrupt end of absolute monarchy, as Wilson (1962:16) has noted, left something of a void. There was neither a unanimity of opinion about who should have power nor agreement on the proper method for getting and exercising power. As such, legitimacy became a serious challenge facing these Western-educated revolutionary leaders in their attempt to establish a secular democratic polity.

With their secular vision of the Thai political order, the revolutionaries not only relegated King Prajadhipok (Rama VII) to a marginal role, but they were also disdainful of Buddhist cultural tradition. These new elites discontinued sponsorship of state ceremonies and elaborate rites which had previously been sponsored by the court, moved to secularize education by replacing monks with lay teachers in government schools, changed the calendar so that the Buddhist Sabbath was no longer an official or school holiday, and passed laws which circumscribed the independence of the Sangha to establish new monasteries and to use revenue from monastic properties (Keyes 1989:14).

To a great extent, the problem of legitimacy prompted the revolutionary leaders to attempt to deconstruct the triumvirate of nation, religion and king. Since Buddhism was seen as closely identified with the concept of kingship, the idea of "nationhood" devoid of Buddhist tradition became more desirable. Henceforth, the term "culture" was used as a substitute for Buddhism. The word "culture" (*Wattanadham*), devoid of its Buddhist tradition, was promptly placed within the First Provisional Constitution promulgated in 1932, which stated: "The state shall support and maintain national culture." Given the way culture was singled out as a key consideration in connection with the state and social change, it is interesting to note that the meaning of culture was obfuscated, not to say emasculated, by the tacit consensual adoption by the new elite of modern statehood and the development paradigm—secularized and distinctively modern/Western. And since the meaning of culture was secularized and devoid of Buddhist tradition, one can hardly be surprised to see that when the first "National Culture Act" was promulgated in 1937, the term culture was defined as having four essential attributes: modernization, cleanliness, harmony and morality, all of which made little sense in terms of Buddhist cultural tradition.

In 1938, Field Marshal Phibun Songkhram, a military leader and one of the promoters of the 1932 revolution, became prime minister. An admirer of the Japanese militaristic ethos, Phibun pursued a policy of aggressive nationalism which eventually led Thailand into World War II, and he embarked on a campaign of military encroachment into neighboring countries. With regard to domestic affairs, Phibun was ruthless; he got rid of his opponents, arrested those who were plotting to oust him from power, and declared that all Thais must "follow the leader" (Yos 1985:92; see Terwiel 1980). However, Phibun was not simply a military leader, but also a revolutionary with a vision of creating a new social order—a secular nationalistic polity.

Though the political system in Phibun's term had taken a turn towards military authoritarianism, it is interesting to note that the Sangha Act of 1941 promulgated during his era (Tambiah 1978:121) created a democratic structure within the Sangha paralleling the structure of the cabinet system and the legislative assembly in the political realm. Through this Sangha Act, the Sangha had under the leadership of the Supreme Patriarch its own cabinet, assembly and judicial institutions paralleling the three divisions of the government. Despite these liberalizing measures, however, the Sangha continued to be linked to political authority and closely regulated (as evidenced by the fact that the appointments made by the Supreme Patriarch had to be countersigned by the Minister of Education upon approval by the Department of Religious Affairs within the Ministry of Education).

Even though the Sangha was still politically regulated, Phibun paid no particular attention to the Buddhist and monarchical conceptions of social order but, rather, made conscious efforts to undermine them. When he first came to power, Phibun strongly advocated the conception of a new "nation" which would include not only Thai-speaking peoples in Thailand but also those living in the neighboring Shan State of Burma, Laos and southern China, many of whom were not Buddhist. On May 8, 1939, "Siam" (the former, official name of the Thai state) was changed to "Thai"-land.[4] In 1939, the "unitary" view of "Thai"-land and "Thai" society was thus established. For Phibun, Thai identity was rooted not in Buddhist cultural tradition, but in a "civic identity" predicated on the cultural heritage all Thais shared. Phibun embarked on a campaign to establish a nationalist ideology based on "racial theories which were Western in derivation" (Keyes 1989:14). The defeat of Japan, however, discredited Phibun's nationalistic ideology, and he was replaced by civilian leaders immediately after the war.

The secular vision of the Thai political order did not end with the failure of Phibun's nationalism. Civilian leaders who replaced Phibun after the war sought to reestablish the secular democratic polity which had been the original ideal of the 1932 revolution. Their attempts, however, were in vain. The government's inability to cope with a severe economic crisis resulting from the war, and especially its ineptitude in handling the investigation of the mysterious death of King Ananda (Rama VIII), provided a pretext for another military take-over in 1947 which brought Phibun back to power.

Upon returning to the prime minister's office, Phibun sought to reestablish a secular nationalistic polity. In 1951, a "Ministry of Culture" was set up to serve as the central organization handling national cultural policies and strategies. The main emphasis given to the cultural policy during this period was an attempt to instill a strong sense of national identity—modeled after the Western ideal—in the public consciousness. Western styles of clothing and manners were adopted as national cultural policy (e.g. all Thais were required to wear shirts and hats in public places) while beetlenut chewing and other so called "primitive habits" were outlawed.

While Phibun's nationalistic cultural policy aroused a great deal of public discontent, it was the new generation of military leaders (most of whom were not Western-educated) which was most intolerant of Phibun's secular nationalistic view of the Thai political order. Phibun himself recognized the growing discontent and attempted to institute another polity, one centered on Buddhist cultural tradition (Nakarin 1989:256). As 1957 (the 2500th anniversary of Lord Buddha's death) approached, Phibun began to act more and more like a traditional monarch whose support for Buddhism and acts of alms-giving to the Sangha could be regarded as indicative of possessing great merit. Phibun took a leading role in many state ceremonies associated with the 2500th Buddhist era celebration— a role which should have more appropriately been taken by King Bhumibol (Rama IX), King Ananda's brother and successor (Keyes 1989:15). However, Phibun's attempts to establish his legitimacy and reinstitute a Buddhist polity were not successful. Another coup d'etat was staged by Field Marshal Sarit Thanarat in late 1957 and Phibun was forced into exile.

THE RETURN OF A BUDDHIST POLITY AND ITS AFTERMATH (1957–PRESENT)

When Sarit came to power, the national ideology based on the triumvirate of nation, religion and king was readily revived. As Morell and Chai-anan (1981:65) have noted, Sarit saw the opportunity to gain enhanced legitimacy and status for his own rule by providing the king with a more active role in the nation's affairs. Sarit and his regime, whose concern was with national development and national integration, acknowledged that Buddhism and the monarchy were important traditional institutions that would enhance the achievement of his political aims. Sarit's policy of creating a strong and loyal Sangha went hand in hand with his active promotion of the ceremonial role of kingship as a vehicle for promoting national pride, unity and identity. The secular vision of the political order brought about by the 1932 revolution was thus put to an end.

With this change in political climate, traditional state ceremonies were revived. The king now presided over the Oath of Allegiance ceremony, transformed to express loyalty to the king and the nation, and his role as the patron of Buddhism was recreated. The Sangha, too, once again was politically regulated. The Sangha Act of 1963 constituted a denial of the democratic provisions of the 1941 Act (Tambiah 1978:121). The power was now concentrated in the Supreme Patriarch and the cabinet system; the assembly and the judicial divisions were abolished. The Sangha once again resumed its function as a "tool of the state" and served to provide identity, morale and meaning for the body politic. The governments of Sarit and Thanom Kittikachorn, Sarit's successor, had also laid down the ground work for the politicization of the Sangha by establishing programs whereby Buddhist monks would assist in promoting government policies. The most important of these programs was called *Thammathut* (Dhammic Ambassador), whereby a number of monks were sent into communist-infiltrated areas and took active roles in promoting anti-communist and community development objectives. Another important program, called *Thammacarik* (wandering dhamma), was designed to convert tribal peoples in north and northeastern Thailand to Buddhism (Keyes 1989:18; see Tambiah 1976; Somboon 1981). These programs are illustrative of Sarit's national policy of homogenization whereby the Sangha became reasonably supportive of government initiatives and directives, especially in promoting religious and cultural unity among ethnically distinct subgroups. Conversely, any high-ranking monk who was construed as a political threat to the military authority was dismissed. The defrocking of Phra Phimolatham, the abbot of Wat Mahathad (Tambiah 1978:121) is a case in point.

Following 1957, modern industrialization and development programs were launched by the government. Military leaders saw industrialization and modernization as a means to attain economic growth, while the non-economic aspects of development programs such as education, culture and communication were used as a means to achieve political goals rather than to achieve real developmental purposes. The educational institutions, Western-imported culture, technological advancement and widespread communication networks existed primarily in Bangkok—the primary city—which reflects the development bias toward the elite class and urban sectors. Furthermore, Buddhist tradition and socio-cultural concerns were accompanied by the enduring overgrowth of political and bureaucratic authoritarianism which, in Thailand, had hitherto put its imprint on the practice of development. The ruling elite invariably required a supportive—or perhaps passive—nation, complete with a homogeneous national culture and reasonably supportive of government initiatives and directives in the tradition of patron-client relationships. In this unitary view of Thai society and culture passed on from Phibun's nationalism, there was no room for diversity, neither ethnically nor culturally. There was no concern for cultural dynamics and the congruity between culture and the development/modernization paradigm.

To a great extent, the polity initiated by Sarit holds within itself the germ of the problem (Thak 1979:152 170; Sanch 1985: 242–283). On one hand, Sarit's military authoritarianism identified itself with, and derived its legitimacy from, the triumvirate of nation, religion and king. But, on the other hand, the modernization/development programs initiated by the government resulted in the expansion of the economy. And as the economy grew significantly after the late 1950s, an increasing number of people were educated in universities and other institutes of higher learning set up to meet the growing needs and requirements of national development. As time went by, both the students and the urban middle class felt more and more excluded from the decision-making process. The spread of social awareness coupled with internal conflicts within the military led to the unprecedented uprising of October 14, 1973, which forced the ruling junta and the military to relinquish the power they had held for several decades.

During 1974–1976, leftist groups, including the Communist Party of Thailand (CPT), gained tremendous support among university students through their various campaigns. The continuing activities of the left in both urban and rural areas alarmed many conservatives who viewed student militancy and peasant and labor activism, and their corresponding support for a radical secular view of the political order, as the major causes of political unrest and the sharp decline in foreign investment. Successive communist victories in Vietnam and Cambodia in 1975, as well as the abdication of the Laos king several months later, sent a spasm of fear through the military establishment and the conservative groups (Girling 1981:207–209). Consequently, they began to fight back: propaganda was launched about the threat of communism, right-wing terrorist organizations were formed, and leftists became the targets of intimidation and widespread assassinations. As the national atmosphere grew increasingly tense, Kittivuddho Bhikku, an outspoken right-wing monk, openly advocated his view that to kill communists incurred no demerit (Keyes 1978), thus fueling more violence and conflict between the two camps. On October 6, 1976, Thammasat University became the target of a ferocious attack as militant groups and police stormed the campus, spraying the assembled students with gunfire from heavy weapons. That evening another coup d'etat was staged in order to "preserve the nation, religion and monarchy from communism."

By 1978, however, the radical view of the political order had been abandoned by most of its proponents. The new government led by General Kriangsak Chamanan began an amnesty program which over the next few years succeeded in attracting out of the jungle many former students who had previously joined the CPT. The amnesty program also attracted mass defections of CPT members, thereby bringing communist insurgency in Thailand close to a virtual standstill. Henceforth, the radical secular view of the political order was no longer a serious threat to the state ideology centering on the nation, religion and king.

To a great extent, the Buddhist view of socio-political order based on the triumvirate of nation, religion and king has prevailed and still remains dominant today. While this view remains elitist, the Thai elite now includes not only the military and bureaucratic officials but also the intellectuals and business elite who have begun to play an increasingly decisive role in shaping the economic and political life of the nation (Yos 1989:98–99). In their present manifestation, these power groups now operate on pragmatic assumptions and secular views of the world, but they "still derive their legitimacy from the monarch and thus must attend periodically to demonstrating in ritual and ceremonial events their acceptance of the king's moral superiority" (Keyes 1989:17). Since the 1960s, the monarchy has played an increasingly important role in modern Thai society. The power of this institution has, therefore, not only increased but also been strengthened and institutionalized.

This is due mainly to the charismatic personality of King Bhumipol himself. Ever since the beginning of his reign (1946), and especially from the Sarit era to the present, the king has taken a genuine interest in almost every aspect of life in the kingdom. The king has established residences and built palaces in every region, and has spent much of his time outside Bangkok. He has shown special interest in various development programs, especially in the poverty-stricken rural areas. He has set up an experimental farm, a co-operative system, and many other projects designed to raise the living standards of the peasants. His frequent visits to various military stations in the border areas and his concern with virtually every aspect of the nation's affairs have all contributed to a very benign fatherly image of the king as the final refuge of his subjects. In the past three decades, the king has been able to establish popular support in almost every sector of the populace, and to that extent has been able to restore the public's faith and confidence in the royal authority (Yos 1989:99–102). Given the importance of the monarchy as the symbol of unity and the binding force of society, the question of royal succession—of changes in personality and leadership style—is likely to be one of the key factors affecting the state ideology in the near future.

Furthermore, the process of industrialization, modernization and urbanization which has taken place in Thailand since the 1950s has resulted in a great deal of changes not only in terms of life-styles but also with regard to religious beliefs, values, and ways of thinking. The values of an urban consumer society, promulgated by the mass media as well as personal contacts, radiated from the urban centers which, in turn, were heavily influenced by the international metropoles of the United States and Europe. The tastes and mores of the economically affluent, Western-oriented, and materialistic urbanites of Bangkok now set the ideals. Wealth and power—measured in secular terms—have increasingly become the indicators of success in life.

Perhaps stability and continuity in personal and collective identities based on Buddhist cultural tradition was possible in the past, but it is clearly increasingly difficult to achieve this in the rapidly changing contemporary Thai society. The primary question, however, is not whether Thai society lacks a set of common beliefs and values. It is whether Buddhist cultural tradition provides the symbols around which the society, as a collective actor, legitimizes its authority and defines its identity and meaning.

MODERN THAI SOCIETY AND THE QUEST FOR IDENTITY

During the past three decades, observers and students of Thai society have all agreed that Buddhism plays a crucial role in the making and development of Thai society, culture and personality. A great deal of attention has been given to the relationship between Buddhist belief in merit and traditional Thai social order (Hanks 1962; Kirsch 1973); between Buddhism and the state (Tambiah 1976; Somboon 1976; Ishii 1986); between Buddhism and social values embedded in the Thai personality (Phillips 1965; Piker 1964); and between Buddhism and other aspects of Thai social life. Buddhism was, and to a great extent still is, the keystone of Thai culture. Buddhist beliefs influence the form of governmental structure, rituals and almost all social activities. Indeed, it has often been asserted that "Buddhism is Thai" and vice versa (Suwanna 1987:33). Buddhism offers a framework of beliefs, expressive symbols and values with which the Thai people define their world, identify their lives, express their feelings and make their judgments. It provides special legitimacy and validity to Thai experiences and offers a model which has persisted through time and contributed to the stability of Thai society. However, the processes of industrialization of institutional structures and the modernization/Westernization of culture have, in recent years, produced an emphasis on wealth, competition, mobility and achievement that have sharply reduced the salience and significance of Buddhism as anchor points for personal meaning, fulfillment, and identity.

Within the development paradigm, the expansion of markets and trade leads to the incorporation of local and regional economies into national and international economies and, concomitantly, there arises the need to develop a larger pool of capital, resources, and skilled labor and to compete successfully for access to it. The sheer scope of this economic development requires new methods of production and management. It thus becomes necessary for private sectors to be outward-looking and future-oriented, and to plan ahead as never before. The pressures for new styles of rational procedures and administration are not confined only to commercial and industrial enterprises. For instance, a great many of the organizational and institutional systems of Thai society are undergoing expansion and differentiation. The mass media, scientific and academic societies, labor unions, entertainment circles, religious bodies and agencies of government all have experienced the same processes of growth in size and complexity and in the rationalization of their operations.

As Thai society becomes more internally complex, the bases of personal identity become more distinct from the symbolic and ideological bases of the society. Sources of authority may use one set of values to express its identity, while private organizations and individuals will use others; not even the Sangha or the state can guarantee much overlap between the two. Inevitably, pluralism in religious culture and in social norms and values emerges; it provides the conditions in which personal types of religious culture express the differentiation and separateness of the individual from the larger society. The emergence of the Wat Thammakai and Santi Asoke movements (to be discussed below) are two cases in point.

Despite the increasing complexity and differentiation of social systems and religious culture, a unitary view of Thai society as a more or less integrated system of action, with Buddhism as its binding force, is still firmly held by the state. This elitist, unitary view of Thai society was clearly expressed by Dr. Bunsom Martin, Head of the Thai Delegation at the second World Conference on Cultural Policies in 1982, when he stated:

Thailand has, by tradition, pursued liberal policies regarding cultural promotion and cultural cooperation. Thailand's governmental agencies, individual scholars and artists as well as the private sector, have in general been free to combine traditions with modernity in carrying out their cultural programs and activities *so long as those activities do not infringe upon the nation's peace and solidarity and basic values* (Ministry of Education 1982:53; emphasis added).

A similar view was also expressed at the same conference by Mr. Banchong Chusakulchati, Chairman of the Culture Committee, Ministry of Education:

The issue of cultural identity is certainly one of the most important issues in cultural policy, planning and development, in any society. There is no denying that the cultural identity of all peoples must be respected and properly promoted. Yet it is also very important that in the promotion of respect and preservation of cultural identity in any country, *the national goals which are of prime consideration are national harmony, national solidarity, national security and nation-building.* These goals are most imperative for the growth and stability of all countries and must therefore never be lost sight of.... The Thai government has been making all efforts to promote the cultural identity and cultural rights of all groups of people taking into consideration the different needs of the various cultural regions of the country, such as the North, the Northeast, the South and the Central. These efforts are best exemplified in our new educational curricula in which all the geographical and cultural needs and aspirations of the people living in different regions are incorporated. It is therefore through education, both in school and out of school, that the Thai government implements its policy for the promotion of cultural identity and cultural right of all people, while preserving the harmony, solidarity and secrerity [sic] of the nation as an entity (Ministry of Education 1982:56–57; emphasis added).

In this unitary view of Thai society firmly held by the state and elite groups, special emphasis is given to national solidarity, security and nation-building, while cultural, religious and ethnic diversity are largely undermined. This unitary view of Thai society is further illustrated by the cultural policies and strategies designed and implemented by the state, and also by the state's continuous attempts to resist religious pluralism and reclaim its position as the "legitimate interpreter" of Buddhism. In these last sections of the paper, I will address the national cultural policies designed and implemented by the state and the conflicts and confrontations resulting from such policy implementations. I will end with the problems of religious pluralism and the crisis of Buddhist identity in contemporary Thai society.

NATIONAL CULTURE POLICIES AND MOMENTS OF CONFRONTATION

In 1979, a Committee on National Culture and the Office of National Culture Commission were established within the Ministry of Education to handle national cultural affairs and cultural policies. Since then, three sets of national cultural policies were issued in 1981, 1984 and 1985, respectively. In these policies, culture has been defined as (1) patterns of life which are deemed good, desirable and appropriate for the Thai people, (2) a tool which serves to correct all social ills, to bring about peace, security, harmony and prosperity for the nation and (3) national identity, a symbol of national trait and character. The Thai "national identity" is further defined as "a sense of being Thai" which stems largely from utmost loyalty to the monarchy, the family roots and the Thai cultural heritage and traditions (National Identity Promotion Office 1983:19–23) and, correspondingly, the "national ideology" is defined as the system of thought which all Thais share in order to promote and maintain the nation, religion, monarchy, and democracy (National Identity Promotion Office 1984:19, 131). Furthermore, the objectives of cultural development are divided into 10 major areas: (1) public health and cleanliness, (2) recreation and sports, (3) work and occupation, (4) language, literature and communication, (5) family relations and foreign affairs, (6) education and academic growth, (7) religion, philosophy, ethics and customs, (8) politics, ideology and national security, (9) cultural heritage, and (10) Thai images and honor.

These policies and policy objectives look vague not only on paper; they have never actually been implemented and there have never been feasible strategies designed to achieve these stated objectives. To a great extent, these cultural policies are the outcome of the Thai government's responses to the "World Conference on Cultural Policies" organized by UNESCO in 1970 and 1982 respectively. As such, these policies are based exclusively on servile imitation of the cultural policies of Western countries, while Thai cultural heritage is entirely different. Policy planners—mostly urbanites, political elites, professionals, and technocrats under the socializing impact of modern Western-oriented education and training—have come to believe that progress depends only on the economic aspects of life. Concerns for cultural diversity and cultural change stemming therefrom have never been thought of, planned for, or carefully implemented.

When implemented, however, cultural policies designed by the state tend to create conflicts and confrontations rather than promote peaceful co-existence among distinct sub groups. For example, in early 1985 the National Cultural Committee and the National Primary Education Committee created a national policy to install Buddha images in all schools in Thailand, purportedly to promote moral education and to serve as a tribute to His Majesty the King. Within a few months, however, a controversy erupted in the Southern provinces where the majority of the populace were Muslims. This policy met with strong resistance from Muslim leaders who maintained that the policy violated their religious beliefs, as it was a grave sin for a Muslim to join in any worship ritual paying respect to a Buddha image. They also warned that the policy would lead to conflict and misunderstanding between Buddhists and Muslims, and that the problem might escalate if the policy were not reviewed. The conflict grew increasingly tense in October, 1985, when some local officials in Satun province encouraged Buddhists in Kuan Kalong district to rise up against the Muslims (who had staged a demonstration at Kuan Doan school to protest against this policy a month earlier). In November, 1985, over a hundred Muslims from the Southern provinces rallied at the Ministry of Education to protest the policy. It was only when the Ministry of Education gradually backed down that the confrontation began to subside.

This controversy is by no means an isolated incident. In 1987, another confrontation erupted in Yala province over the wearing of *hijab* (traditional Islamic clothing for women, including a blouse with long sleeves, an ankle length skirt and a head covering). On December 11, 1987, a group of female Muslim students at Yala Teachers' Training College conveyed to the College administration their intention to dress in accordance with Islamic teachings. For them, wearing *hijab* was not only a matter of conforming to the Islamic dress code, it was also an indicator of their Islamic identity. These students met with strong disapproval from the College administrators, who sternly pointed out that *hijab* was not in keeping with the College uniforms and regulations.

The issue of Islamic dress soon became a crisis as Muslim students (who were barred from attending classes and from using the College library) rallied to protest against the College administration. Mr. Marut Bunnag, the Minister of Education, quickly issued an order asking the Teachers' Training

Department to accommodate Muslim students' demands. This only led to another protest, however, staged by non-Muslim students who rallied against the Minister's order. These non-Muslim students began to wear Thai classical dresses and demanded that uniform regulations be applied to all students without exception.

As months went by, protests by both camps became a daily occurrence and a solution to this problem was nowhere in sight. Further, the *hijab* crisis generated a public debate between those who supported the rights of Muslim students to wear *hijab* and those who were against it. The nature of the debate and the details of the *hijab* crisis (see Chaiwat 1989) are far too complex to describe here in detail. The key point for this essay, however, is that the controversy over installing Buddha images in public schools and the *hijab* crisis are not single isolated cases. Rather, these incidents raise the perplexing and continuing problem of the relationship between a dominant religious group and a religious minority.

These incidents not only reflect the inadequacy of national cultural policies in handling the problem of religious diversity and the insensitivity of the state with regard to cultural issues. They also illustrate the unitary view of the Thai social order still firmly held by the elite. According to this view, any challenge to the national cultural policy and the Buddhist symbolism engineered by the state is a challenge to the established social order. In a real sense, the incident which took place in Yala could stand as a microcosm of Thai society: Muslim students constituting a minority cultural identity in a college governed by administrators armed to the teeth with rigid regulations. The basic question is whether these regulations were formulated to take into account the peaceful co-existence among distinct subgroups (Chaiwat 1989:18–19) or formulated instead with a rigid, unitary view of "Thai" society, devoid of ethnic and cultural diversity.

The incidents which took place in southern Thailand are not peculiar to the Muslims. Similar problems have arisen with

Christian and Catholic religious minority groups (see Cohen 1987), the rural poor, and the disadvantaged from the outlying provinces. The process of modernization which has taken place in Thailand during the past few decades has provoked a massive geographical dislocation of people, especially in terms of rural-urban migration, and a profound disorientation in their ways of thinking and leading their lives. The values of an urban consumer society now set the standards for the rural folks; the urbanite elite culture patterns have overshadowed most other cultural identities from rural sectors. And since political, economic and social mobility for the rural folks depends largely on conforming to or assimilating the dominant cultural patterns, large numbers of people with different cultural origins find themselves in the situation of having either to shed the traditional culture that gave their lives meaning and then proceeding into the mainstream, or receding to the periphery of Thai society.

The cultures of the rural poor and the disadvantaged tend to be disdained by the predominant elite culture. The results are self-disparagement and insecurity among ethnic groups of the subordinated cultures. Beliefs about superiority and inferiority form an important but often unacknowledged barrier to cultural development in Thailand. In fact, it can be argued further that culture has long been employed as an instrument of control by the elite. An attempt to develop a strong sense of national identity has greatly undermined local systems of knowledge, traditions, and identities and has taken away the freedom, dignity, and potential of the local people to develop themselves. A sense of personal or minority identity, of knowing who one is and what one aspires to—on one's own terms— has never been a primary concern of cultural policies designed and implemented in Thailand.

The addresses made by Dr. Bunsom Martin and his colleague at the World Conference on Cultural Policies notwithstanding, the Thai government has never made any effort to promote the cultural identity and cultural rights of all groups of people and has never taken into consideration the different needs of the various cultural regions of the country. There is no denying that the cultural identities of all peoples have not been respected and properly promoted. To the contrary, the cultural policies designed by the elite and for the elite have not come to terms with the problems of religious and cultural diversity among ethnically distinct minority groups. As long as this monolithic unitary view of Thai society is still firmly held by the state and the meaning of "Thainess" is still defined solely by the elite on an ethnic basis, crises and confrontations among these groups will reappear and the politics of national identity will continue.

THE SANTI ASOKE CONTROVERSY AND THE CRISIS OF THAI IDENTITY

Debates over the politics of identity—what is Thai and who has the legitimate right to define it—are not peculiar to religious minority groups such as the Muslims, but are currently posing a perplexing problem among the Buddhist Thais as well. During the past two decades, Thailand has witnessed the emergence of a number of activist movements, and some of these adhere to ideologies which are explicitly Buddhist. While these movements are of both the right and the left, they all share an activist orientation toward the world. Some of these movements seek to draw on Buddhism to formulate a critical stance toward the existing socio-political order and become foci for political movements, while others simply draw on Buddhism to formulate a new basis for leading a moral life in the world.[5]

Of all the religious movements which have recently emerged in Thai society, that which has generated the greatest controversy and which has had the most significant impact on the political culture of Thailand is the Santi Asoke movement led by Phra Potirak, a former television personality who was ordained a Buddhist monk in the early 1970s. Soon after his ordination, Phra Potirak began to formulate a radical critique of the mainstream monastic order. He relentlessly attacked the animism that was practiced by orthodox Buddhists, strongly criticized the ruling ecclesiastical council for its failure to administer the monastic order, and challenged the legitimate supremacy of the ecclesiastical council over all monks in the country. In 1975, the unorthodox monk established the Santi Asoke religious center in Bangkok and openly declared that his religious center was independent of the Sangha council.

Since 1975, Phra Potirak has attracted a growing number of both monk and lay followers. He has written books and circulated newsletters designed to promote the Buddhist fundamentalism of the Santi Asoke. The monk and his disciples strictly follow Buddhist principles with a strong emphasis on simplicity, hard work and self-sacrifice. They eat only one vegetarian meal a day and do not involve themselves in preaching or practicing animism. The emergence of the Santi Asoke and other fundamentalist movements which have attracted many followers, especially from the younger generations, college students and the urban middle class, clearly reflects increasing disillusionment towards the mainstream monastic order. It also reflects the inefficiency of the Sangha council in dealing with the misbehavior of monks within its domain.

By the early 1980s, it was estimated that almost a hundred people had become Santi Asoke monks after long periods undergoing strict tests, and the lay followers were believed to number tens of thousands (*The Nation*, May 29, 1989). As the Santi Asoke grew in size and in popularity, the movement became actively involved in national politics. Whether cause or effect, the increasing politicization of the Santi Asoke movement seemed to coincide with the Sangha Council's appointment of a committee of legal authorities and senior monks to investigate the legal status of the movement, whose fundamentalist teachings were said to have distorted conventional

Buddhist principles. In late 1985, the Santi Asoke became the center of national attention when Chamlong Srimuang, a recently retired major general, former member of the powerful military Young Turks (Chai-anan 1982) and devout disciple of Santi Asoke, was elected by a landslide as the new governor of Bangkok. There was no doubt that Chamlong owed his landslide victory over the candidate of the Democrat Party (which has long held a dominant place in Bangkok politics) to the tremendous support given to him by the Santi Asoke's *Yati-Dham* (disciples).

As a member of the Santi Asoke Buddhist sect, Chamlong had for many years subjected himself to the eight Buddhist "precepts" (*Sila*). In addition, Chamlong had observed strict ascetic practices which included eating one vegetarian meal a day, avoiding all sexual activity, and dressing only in simple farmer's garb. During the election campaign, Chamlong was depicted as a clean and honest man who led a simple life. One of the most famous folk-music bands, the "Carabao," even wrote a song praising Chamlong's honesty, trustworthiness, and virtues. In the eyes of the public Chamlong was seen, in essence, as a monk in lay clothing: a true believer in, and an adherent of, a fundamentalist Buddhist sect. As such, his image contrasted sharply with other money-seeking, corrupt, and power-oriented politicians. Chamlong represented an alternative to both business and military rule, a modern microcosm of traditional Dhammic (moral) rule. As Keyes has noted:

> [Chamlong] has even been viewed as a potential future Prime Minister. Despite the fact that some would dismiss Chamlong's appeal as an aberration and without any lasting significance—a close advisor to the King and the Crown Prince whom I asked about Chamlong in a meeting in October 1987 was disdainful of his behavior and dismissive of his popularity—polls have indicated that he is attracting increasingly positive attention

from people outside of Bangkok constituency which elected him mayor (Keyes 1989:2–3).

Chamlong's rising popularity and public support also won him foes and enmity. And gradually, Chamlong became a serious threat to the military-bureaucratic-business cliques that run the country. Hostility and verbal attacks directed towards him became even more widespread when, in late April, 1988, Prime Minister Prem Tinsulanonda dissolved the Parliament and Chamlong decided that the time had come to establish a new political party to run in the upcoming election scheduled for July 24, 1988. Even though Chamlong himself was not a candidate in this election, during the election campaigns he became a prime target for personal attacks, especially from political parties which had traditionally dominated Bangkok politics. While his *Palang Dhamma* (Dhammic Force) Party suffered somewhat from a scandal related to Chamlong's alleged involvement in the October 6, 1976, massacre at Thammasat University, the party still managed to win 14 seats in the Parliament.

On May 23, 1989, a committee of 150 senior Buddhist monks who had been instructed to investigate the legal status of the Santi Asoke Buddhist sect four years earlier issued a unanimous decision recommending that the ruling Ecclesiastical Council order the leader of the unorthodox Santi Asoke religious center, Phra Potirak, defrocked as punishment for his alleged rebellion against the mainstream monastic order. The committee, which was chaired by the Supreme Patriarch, ruled that Phra Potirak had violated the Sangha rules in such a way that it undermined and ridiculed Buddhism. Phra Potirak was also accused of sowing the seeds of divisiveness within the clerical circle by setting up his own religious empire outside the domain of the Ecclesiastical Council. Phra Sophonkhanaporn, secretary of the committee, said Potirak would be defrocked by the Education Ministry officials if the Council approved the recommendation but, if Potirak resisted, the Interior Ministry would be asked to take legal action against him (*The Nation*, May 24, 1989). The unanimous decision made by this committee brought the long-standing conflict between the mainstream monastic order and the Santi Asoke movement to a head.

When asked to express his opinion on this controversy, Governor Chamlong said "It is a matter to be decided among the monks. We have religious freedom, we have the individual right to follow whatever religion" (*The Nation*, May 24, 1989). But Chamlong later suggested that a ruling by the Ecclesiastical Council could have "far-reaching impact," and that the issue would not be taken lying down. "Disciples of Santi Asoke will continue to uphold their beliefs despite legal action to dissolve the sect. They can arrest Santi Asoke monks and disrobe them, but the authorities can't eliminate our beliefs and practices," Chamlong said (*The Nation*, May 29, 1989). Meanwhile, Phra Potirak vowed not to leave the monkhood whatever the Ecclesiastical Council's ruling would be. He was also reportedly contemplating the possibility of filing a lawsuit with the court.

On May 30, 1989, in a meeting chaired by the Supreme Patriarch, the Ecclesiastical Council unanimously decided to uphold the ruling made by 150 senior monks that Phra Potirak and his clerical followers be defrocked. The Council's decision was immediately challenged by Phra Potirak, who announced that he would accept the verdict only if it came from the Supreme Court. He also said that, although his interpretation of Buddhism differed from that of mainstream Buddhist monks, he should not be condemned as if he had done something wrong. Meanwhile, the Interior Ministry's Permanent Secretary, Phisan Moolasartsathorn, warned Phra Potirak that he would be arrested and put in jail if he challenged the Ecclesiastical Council's ruling (*Bangkok Post*, May 30, 1989). A number of politicians also condemned Phra Potirak and his movement. Samak Sundaravej, a Bangkok MP and leader of the Prachakornthai Party, likened Phra Potirak to a termite, arguing that Potirak was more dangerous than Acharn Suan (another much-publicized monk known for his distribution of phallic amulets to people seeking good fortune) even though he had compared Acharn Suan to an ant "which disturbs us but cannot ruin the whole house" (*The Nation*, May 30, 1989)). Minister Chalerm Yoobamrung, a Bangkok MP and a cabinet member, also declared that his special police unit attached to the Government House "is ready to arrest monks ordained under Santi Asoke Buddhist sect. If nobody dares to take action against these monks, the special forces will arrest them on charge of dressing themselves like monks" (*The Nation*, June 2, 1989).

As the controversy surrounding the Santi Asoke movement was generating heated public debate on various issues, the Police Department issued a warning to newspapers voicing sympathy for Santi Asoke and criticizing the behavior of the mainstream Buddhist monks "because such reports could jeopardize national unity" (*The Nation*, June 2, 1989). The Chief of the Bangkok Ecclesiastical Council, Phra Thammahaveeranuvat, also warned the press that they should refrain from publishing articles and political cartoons satirical of the religious body and monks. "Any slanderous criticism against the religious institution may be regarded as violation of Article 44 of the Ecclesiastical Code," the monk said. He also added that "we do not mean to confine the press freedom. Comments on the religious affairs can be made but only in appropriate contents" (*The Nation*, June 2, 1989).

On June 10, 1989, the decade-long controversy over the Santi Asoke movement seemed headed for a solution when Phra Potirak announced that he and his clerical followers would change their robes in a bid to become totally independent and avoid legal action. But Phra Potirak vowed to continue preaching and practicing his Buddhist fundamentalism. Chaipak Siriwat, Secretary to the Education Minister who was entrusted with the responsibility of persuading Phra Potirak to leave the monkhood voluntarily, said "the Santi Asoke monks will no longer call themselves 'monks' but will adopt a new uniform and become *'Samana-Pharm'* or the recluse-brahmins instead" (*Bangkok Post*, June 10, 1989).

Two days later, however, the Ecclesiastical Council ordered Phra Potirak to disrobe unconditionally in seven days or face arrest for breaking discipline and ecclesiastical laws. The Council refused to recognize any deal made between the Santi Asoke movement and the Education Ministry. In light of the Council's relentless position, Phra Potirak said he was being forced too far and vowed not to budge an inch. He said he was ready to face arrest and would not defend himself because he "did nothing wrong." He insisted that the tentative agreement to change robes did not mean he would give up the monkhood. "We do not leave the monkhood, we would just change our status to become recluse-brahmins," Potirak said (*The Nation*, June 11, 1989). The following morning, Interior Minister Pramarn Adireksarn issued a stern warning to Phra Potirak, saying the controversial Santi Asoke leader should formally leave the monkhood in seven days as demanded by the Council or police would deal with him "their own way" (*The Nation*, June 12, 1989).

On June 15, 1989, Phra Potirak triggered another controversy by applying for an identification card, sparking debate about whether that meant he had voluntarily given up his 14-year status as a monk. His move, however, failed to satisfy the mainstream Buddhist leadership and authorities who said he must "verbally" declare an end to his monkhood. Meanwhile, Santi Asoke clergymen and lay followers continued their routine religious activities at their center. Smiles on their faces belied the biggest crisis facing the movement since it was founded in 1975. A signboard at the center quoted one of Lord Buddha's most popular statements: "We have stopped (but you have not)."

On June 19, 1989, police arrested Potirak after the Education Ministry filed formal charges against him for violating the ecclesiastical laws and refusing to defrock himself as ordered by the Council. The Santi Asoke leader was asked by the police to change his dark brown robe and put on white clothing after being transferred to a detention center. Though Potirak agreed to the changing of clothes, he refused to make the disrobing vow. He had said earlier that "even if they undressed me and put me in jail, I will never make the disrobing vow." He also defended the Santi Asoke teachings of a modest life-style, saying that it would help the government solve economic problems. "Isn't that what the society wants?" he asked; "we are proud of ourselves, we are willing to sacrifice our lives in order to maintain the religious faith" (*The Nation*, June 19, 1989).

Meanwhile, the government issued an order banning television and radio news reports on the arrest of Phra Potirak. Prime Minister Chatichai Choonhavan, though denying he had issued the order, said he was concerned about the possible ill feelings that television news coverage of Potirak's arrest could create. General Panya Singhsakda, the Prime Minister's Secretary General, also denied having imposed the electronic news blackout, although he did admit to asking all television and radio stations to use "their own judgment" on how to handle the Santi Asoke controversy.[6]

On June 21, 1989, Potirak was released on bail from police custody, and the next morning he immediately returned to his routine by offering a sermon to about 200 followers (including Governor Chamlong Srimuang) at the Santi Asoke religious center. Since then, even though the controversy surrounding the Santi Asoke movement has gradually subsided, the real issue goes on unresolved and the political struggle continues.

What, then, is the real issue concerning the Santi Asoke controversy? Let me answer this question by way of making a few observations on the politics of identity in Thailand. First of all, the Santi Asoke controversy reveals the single most recurring feature of the relationship between religion and social order in Thai society, that is, the problem of personal and corporate identity. The unity of individual and communal political spheres, as Binder (1964:13) has noted, "was a characteristic of only the most perfect theocratic societies, the ancient Hebrew, the early Islamic, and perhaps the Greek city-state." In modern Thai society, the social and economic changes which lead the rising middle class to demand the reaffirmation of the independent sphere of the individual also undermine the exclusive social basis of the state. New cultural models of identity have also emerged in the form of large-scale religious movements despite the state's insistence on its unitary view of society and Buddhist legitimation. In order to reduce the complexity inherent in the multiplicity of identity models, and "official" identity model was imposed on the people of Thailand by the state, with powerful enforcement. The Santi Asoke controversy thus becomes a "drama of imposition" of an identity model. The Santi Asoke movement was charged with the crime of creating "divisiveness" and "disunity" among the Buddhist Thais. In other words, they are guilty because they maintain a distinct identity.

The Santi Asoke controversy is illustrative of "social dramas" (Turner 1957) in which the political and symbolic orders interpenetrate and affect each other. Each drama tries to effect a transformation in the psyches of the participants, conditioning their attitudes and sentiments, repetitively renewing beliefs, values and identities, and thereby creating and recreating the basic categorical imperatives on which the group depends for its existence (Cohen 1974:132). Following some breach of crucial norms, a phase of mounting crisis supervenes and, at this stage, there is a polarization of the parties, each taking its guidance from a particular set of symbols and an ideology. The symbols which define the situation for the participants of both camps are those which have strong emotional and conceptual meanings. The essence of the drama, according to Cohen (1974:134), is the struggle to achieve "communion" between potential enemies and to give a tangible expression to this communion. In the course of the drama, the struggle is internalized within the psyches of the participants. Here it becomes a struggle for the achievement of "selfhood" in terms of the symbolism of communion. The individual creates and recreates his identity by taking part in the symbolism that articulates the corporate organization of the group of which he is a member. In other words, the political struggle becomes for the participants not merely something that is happening outside of themselves; it also becomes a crisis of personal identity. To use our case, the Sangha calls its members and the public to fight for Buddhism because to be Thai is to be Buddhist. Threats to religion and social order are perceived as threats to personal identity. But, on the other hand, the public is confronted with another set of Buddhist symbols, another style of expression which has been adopted by many Buddhist Thais, some of whom have been depicted as morally good and virtuous. This is the crux of the crisis.

Even though the next phases of the social drama have not yet emerged, the Santi Asoke controversy cannot be dismissed as a transitory phenomenon without any lasting impact on the politics of identity in Thailand. On the contrary, the Santi Asoke movement has challenged the Sangha at the heart of its authority. The question asked is not simply what Buddhism is or who has the legitimate right to define it, but also what "Thai" is and what the difference is between individual and corporate identity. In other words, this is a challenge not only to dominant legitimation but also to identity formation.

According to the Sangha, there is no doubt that the emergence and persistence of the Santi Asoke movement poses a greater threat to social order than to individual freedom. But at times, this issue appears sublimated in debates and discussions of the ontological and epistemological bases of Buddhism, and it is possible to detect in these debates different commitments to order, justice and freedom, with justice occupying a middle ground between the polar conceptions of freedom and order. In arguing that the Santi Asoke movement was misinterpreting

Buddhism and misleading the Buddhist Thais about what was really "real" about Buddhism, the Sangha (and the state behind it) persistently claimed that the issue at stake was one of unity and order. But the Santi Asoke maintained that the issue was one of freedom and that the Santi Asoke members, like all Thais, must be guaranteed their individual rights to uphold their religious faith. The controversy thus reveals the real contradiction between the two systems of action, that is, between the ideas, values, and rules by which the Santi Asoke members identify themselves and act on their projects, and those by which the Sangha legitimizes the exercise of its authority and reclaims its position as the legitimate interpreter of Buddhism.

CONCLUDING REMARKS

This essay has discussed the historical development of the Thai Buddhist polity, national ideology, and nationalism, and it has examined the development of national cultural policies designed and implemented by the state, along with the ethnic and religious conflicts and confrontations resulting from such policy implementations. I have argued that the unitary view of Thai society which is still firmly held by the state—with its emphasis on national solidarity, security and nation-building—has increased problems of cultural, religious and ethnic identity and diversity. In doing so, I have touched upon the problems of religious pluralism, the processes of modernization and the emergence of large-scale religious movements, and the crisis of Buddhist identity in contemporary Thai society.

The increasing variety of religious cultures in Thai society reflects more than the process of differentiation between personal and collective identity. This differentiation also accounts for the growing disjunction between personal and social belief systems which, in turn, limits the degree to which the individual expresses his or her personal identity in symbols belonging to the larger society at the corporate level. There are clearly other sources of variation as well, though I have focused upon just a few.

In this context, religious pluralism makes it difficult for the state to use religion to legitimize its authority while claiming to act on behalf of the entire society. In other words, Buddhism no longer provides an overlapping basis for personal identity and national authority. Pluralism reinforces the separation of the state from the society but it does not prevent the state from claiming religious legitimacy for its authority. So long as the state can articulate its purposes in terms of the religious beliefs and values of persons or individuals, the possibility remains that the state will appeal to some highly generalized set of religious beliefs and values. In this way, the notion of a Buddhist, a Muslim, or a Santi Asoke people disappears from view, and in its place emerges a recognition of social order as "a process of negotiation" concerning the relative needs of the state as a corporate actor and religious individuals or groups (cf. Fenn 1980:137–139). But as long as the unitary view of a "Buddhist Thai" society is still firmly held by the state and Buddhism still serves to obscure the separation between the values and purposes of the state and those of the individuals, then, legitimacy will continue to be sought and resisted, cultural traditions interpreted and reinterpreted, and group rivalries and identity crises maintained or even exacerbated.

NOTES

1. The purification and reform of Buddhism at the beginning of the reign of King Rama I, the founder of the Chakkri Dynasty in 1782, is a case in point here (Butt 1978:43–46; Keyes 1989:6). It is suggestive that as the first of a new line of kings Rama I was conscious of the propriety of being an orthodox Buddhist king. On one hand, the purification of the Sangha helped to inaugurate and legitimize his position as king and protector of Buddhism and, on the other hand, the king's regulation of the Sangha and ensuring of its loyalty were a political necessity.

During the first two years after his ascension to the throne Rama I issued seven decrees concerning the Buddhist monks in Thailand. Their purpose was to raise the moral level of this class and to restore its prestige and authority. Additional laws were passed in 1789, 1794 and 1801. The last law, the tenth, expelled 128 monks from the Buddhist clergy and condemned them to hard labor for "they had been guilty of all kinds of ignoble behavior, namely drinking, wandering about at night, rubbing shoulders with women, using improper language, buying silly things from Chinese junks" (Wenk 1968:39). Under the Chakkri dynasty, the kingdom became steadily stronger and larger and its political authority expanded. Correspondingly, the Sangha became more centralized, hierarchical, and politically regulated than ever before.

2. As Keyes has noted: "Within the cosmological framework of traditional Buddhism, the term *phi-bun* is an oxymoron since 'spirits' (*phi*) occupy the place on the moral hierarchy because they lack, rather than 'have' merit (*bun*). Thus, a *phi bun* is one who falsely claims to have a positive moral heritage which would legitimate a claim to power" (Keyes 1989:12).

3. It is interesting to note here that in the 1920s and 1930s the policy of homogenization of the Sangha was seriously challenged by a powerful movement centered around Khruba Srivijaya, a monk seen in the *Yuan* (northern Thai) Buddhist tradition as a man of great merit and virtues and who was acclaimed a "saint" (*nakbun*) by a large part of the northern Thai populace. Khruba Srivijaya and Khruba Kaopii, one of Khruba Srivijaya's disciples, openly resisted many of the reforms instigated by the central government and sought to maintain the distinctive northern Thai Buddhist tradition. Although he came close to accomplishing this goal, Khruba Srivijaya backed away from advocating an open rebellion and the government, in turn, refrained from defrocking and jailing him (an act which would have turned him into a martyr and fueled anger among the northern Thais). The conflict came to a peaceful end when Khruba Srivijaya accepted the authority of the ecclesiastical order and, in turn, the ecclesiastical order tacitly permitted northern Thai monks to carry on many of their *Yuan* practices as long as they were confined within their local communities (see Ishii 1986).

4. In subsequent years, myths of Thai origin were constructed whereby the ancestors of the present-day Thai people were believed to have been pushed by Chinese forces to migrate from southern China. The historical construction of "Thai" identity was thus inexorably linked with anti-Chinese and ethnic fervor.

5. These religious movements were by no means a new development. There have existed in Thailand since the dawn of its history a number of "forest

monasteries" founded by highly respected hermit-monks and meditation masters. The most famous of these "Buddhist saints of the forest" (Tambiah 1984) in the twentieth century was Acharn Man Bhuridatta, who actively promoted a highly critical stance toward the material world and soon became a model of Buddhist meditation and practices outside the mainstream monastic order.

The following is a brief summary of some of the more significant political and non-political Buddhist movements of the last thirty years. In the 1950s Phra Phimolatham, then a high-ranking ecclesiastical official of the monastic order, began to promote the popular practice of Burmese-style meditation and attracted a great deal of followers. His disagreements with other high-ranking monks and especially his conspicuous travels abroad, including trips to Communist countries, brought him to the attention of Field Marshal Sarit Thanarat. In 1960, Phra Phimolatham was removed from his ecclesiastical office. A few years later he was formally charged with being a Communist and defrocked. Even though Phra Phimolatham was cleared of all charges against him and returned to monkhood in 1966, the incident apparently sent a message to all activists both within and outside the Sangha that a radical critique of, and deviation from, the social order would not be tolerated.

Nevertheless, during the period between 1973 and 1976 a number of monks began to play increasingly active roles in Thai politics. The most controversial of the political activists during this period was Kittivuddho Bhikku, a right-wing Buddhist monk and founder of Cittabhavan College, a Buddhist College which provided training programs designed to prepare monks and novices to take active roles in society. Kittivuddho became an outspoken leader of an anti-Communist movement and strongly advocated militant political action against the student, labor and peasant movements to safeguard Buddhism and the monarchy.

Another religious-cum-political movement which attracted substantial numbers of followers, including some high-ranking military officers, during the 1970s was Samnak Pu Sawan (The Adobe of the Heavenly Grandfather), which later became Huppha Sawan (The Heavenly Valley). Suchat Kosonkittiwong, the leader of this movement, was a poorly-educated Sino-Thai of humble origin. Suchat began as a small-scale medium but later acquired a large following when he was reputed to be the spokesman for the great spirits, including a number of Buddhist saints and Supreme Patriarchs of former times, Jesus Christ and prophets of other religions. Suchat also cultivated international connections and began to claim that his Huppha Sawan would soon become the Center for World Religions. But in the early 1980s, when Suchat began styling himself a religious prince and offered unsolicited advice to the king on the basis of his symbolic claim that he was situated on the moral hierarchy on a par with the monarch, his movement was no longer tolerated (Keyes 1989:13; Yagi 1988). The government moved to condemn Huppha Sawan arguing that the movement was illegal and a threat to the national security. All of its headquarters were raided and condemned, thus bringing an end to this movement.

Aside from the religious leaders who became foci for political movements, there also emerged a number of religious leaders whose this-worldly interpretations of Buddhism have been influential in contemporary Thai society. Buddhadasa Bhikku, unquestionably the most beloved and respected monk and scholar of Buddhism, has been an influential teacher in recent times. His interpretation of Buddhist *dhamma* situates the quest for enlightenment within the world rather than in a rejection of the world. Many of his disciples have also been actively promoting his teaching in every region of the kingdom. Another highly-respected monk, Phra Rajavaramuni, has also been influential in providing a *dhamma* for leading a moral life in the world. The new interpretations of Buddhism advocated in the writings and teachings of these Buddhist scholars not only have a great deal of impact on the new generations of Thai intellectuals, but they also provide an inspiration to the human rights groups, social activists and volunteers, community workers and other non-government organizations which have proliferated in Thailand during the past two decades.

Another Buddhist movement which has attracted a great number of followers, especially among the college students and urban middle class in Bangkok and surrounding areas, was Wat Thammakai. Following a new meditation method developed by a famous monk, Luang Pho Wat Paknam, two of his disciples, Phra Thammachayo and Phra Thattachiwo have been actively promoting a distinctive method of meditation by concentrating on a crystal ball to achieve a visual image which is interpreted as signalling a realization of the *dhamma*. Once attaining this vision of *dhamma*, it is claimed that the practitioners will be able to live and act in this hectic world with serenity and harmony. In recent years, Wat Thammakai has become a popular place of retreat for students and the urban middle class who take on the strict discipline, as signified by their donning of white robes, and practice the new method of meditation for a period of time. Even though Wat Thammakai has suffered somewhat from a scandal relating to land disputes between the Wat and local residents and farmers in Pathumthani where the Thammakai headquarters is located, the movement can still draw over tens of thousands

of followers on special occasions and major religious festivities which means, in effect, that the movement has great potential to play a significant political role in the near future. This fact has recently brought the Wat Thammakai movement to the attention of the state and the Sangha, as shown in a statement made by a senior ecclesiastical official who cautioned during a newspaper interview that the Sangha is now "keeping an eye on the Thammakai movement" (*The Bangkok Post*, May 31, 1989).
6. As it turned out, all of these elites quite miraculously came to the same conclusion, namely, that any more news coverage of the issue would not serve the public interest. This conclusion was rather strange, as two weeks earlier government television and radio stations had spent several hours replaying tapes recording vehement attacks on Potirak by senior monks in a grand ceremony organized by the Sangha to denounce and excommunicate Potirak and his movement.

REFERENCES

Batson, B.A. (1984). *The End of Absolute Monarchy in Siam*. Singapore: Oxford University Press.
Bell, Daniel (1975). *The Coming of Post-Industrial Society: A Venture in Social Forecasting*. New York: Basic Books.
Binder, Leonard (1964). *The Ideological Revolution in the Middle East*. New York: Wiley.
Chai-anan Samudavanija (1982). *The Thai Young Turks*. Singapore: Institute of Southeast Asian Studies.
Chai-anan Samudavanija and Kattiya Kannasutr, Eds. (1975). *Documents Concerning Thai Politics and Administration*. Bangkok: Text Book in Social Science and Humanities Project.
Chaiwat Satha-anand (1989). Hijab and Moments of Legitimation: Islamic Resurgence in Thai Society. A paper presented at the Communities in Question Conference, organized by the Social Science Research Council and the American Council of Learned Societies, May 4–8, Hua Hin, Thailand.
Chattip Nartsupha (1984). The Ideology of "Holy Men" Revolts in Northeast Thailand. In Andrew Turton and Shigeharn Tanabe, Eds. *Historical and Peasant Consciousness in Southeast Asia*. Osaka: National Museum of Ethnology.
Chula Chakrabongse (1960). *Lords of Life: A History of the Kings of Thailand*. London: Alvin Redman.

Cohen, Abner (1974). *Two Dimensional Man: An Essay on the Anthropology of Power and Symbolism in Complex Society*. Berkeley: University of California Press.

Cohen, Erik (1987). Christianity and Buddhism in Thailand: The Battle of the Axes and the Contest of Power. Unpublished manuscript.

Dhani Nivat, Prince (1947). The Old Siamese Conception of the Monarchy. *Journal of the Siam Society* 36.2.

Eisenstadt, S.N. (1966). Sociological Aspects of Political Development. In I. Wallerstein, Ed. *Social Change: The Colonial Situation*. New York: John Wiley.

Fenn, Richard K. (1980). Religion, Identity and Authority in the Secular Society. In *Identity and Authority: Explorations in the Theory of Society*. Oxford: Basic Blackwell.

Geertz, Clifford (1973). *The Interpretation of Cultures*. New York: Basic Books.

Girling, J.L.S. (1981). *Thailand: Society and Politics*. Ithaca, New York: Cornell University Press.

Hanks, Lucien M. (1962). Merit and Power in Thai Social Order. *American Anthropologist* 64:1247–1261.

Ingram, James C. (1971). *Economic Change in Thailand, 1850–1970*. Palo Alto: Stanford University Press.

Ishii, Yoneo (1975). A Note on Buddhistic Millenarian Revolts in Northeastern Siam. *Journal of Southeast Asian Studies* 6(2):121–126.

— (1986). *Sangha, State, and Society: Thai Buddhism in History*. Peter Hawkes, trans. Honolulu: University of Hawaii Press.

Keyes, Charles F. (1977). Millenialism, Theravada Buddhism and Thai Society. *Journal of Asian Studies* 36(2):283–302.

— (1978). Political Crisis and Militant Buddhism in Contemporary Thailand. In Bardwell L. Smith, Ed. *Religion and Legitimation of Power in Thailand, Laos, and Burma*. Chambersburg, PA: Anima Books.

— (1989). Buddhist Politics and Their Revolutionary Origins in Thailand. A paper presented at the Communities in Question Conference, organized by the Social Science Research Council and the American Council of Learned Societies. May 4–8, 1989. Hua Hin, Thailand.

Kirsch, Thomas (1973). The Thai Buddhist Quest for Merit. In John T. McAlister, Ed. *Southeast Asia: The Politics of National Integration*. New York: Random House.

Ministry of Education, Office of the Permanent Secretary (1982). *World Conference on Cultural Policies: Report of the Thai Delegation*. Bangkok: Ministry of Education.

Murashima, Eiji (1988). The Origin of Modern Official State Ideology in Thailand. *Journal of Southeast Asian Studies*, XIX. 1.

Morell, David and Chai-anan Samudavanija (1981). *Political Conflict in Thailand: Reform, Reaction and Revolution*. Cambridge: Oelgeschlager, Gunn and Hain.
Nakarin Mektrairat (1989). Field Marshal Phibun Songkhram's Statism: The Formation of Political Thoughts and Meaning. *Journal of Political Science* (Thammasat University) 14(3):228–274.
Nash, Manning (1971). Buddhist Revitalization in the Nation States: The Burmese Experience. In *Religion and Change in Contemporary Asia*. Minneapolis: University of Minnesota Press.
National Identity Promotion Office (1983). *National Identity*. Bangkok: Prime Minister's Office.
— (1984). *National Ideology*. Bangkok: Prime Minister's Office.
Office of the National Culture Commission (1986). *National Culture Policy*. Bangkok: Ministry of Education.
Phillips, Herbert P. (1965). *Thai Peasant Personality*. Berkeley: University of California Press.
Piker, Steven (1964). *Character and Socialization in a Thai Peasant Community*. Unpublished Ph.D. Dissertation, University of Washington.
Rabinow, Paul (1975). *Symbolic Domination: Cultural Form and Historical Change in Morocco*. Chicago: University of Chicago Press.
Saneh Chammarik (1985). *Thai Politics and the Development of the Constitution*. Bangkok: Text Book Project Foundation and Thai Khadi Research Institute.
Smith, Bardwell L., Ed. (1976). *Religion and Social Conflict in South Asia*. Leiden: E.J. Brill.
Sombat Chantornvong (1978). Cosmological Basis of Thai Bureaucratic Behavior: A Missing Link. *Social Science Review (1978)*. Bangkok: Social Science Association of Thailand.
— 1989. Religion and Politics: A Preliminary Observation on Ideology and Policies of King Rama I. *Journal of Political Science* (Thammasat University) 14(3):22–127.
Somboon Suksamran (1976). *Political Buddhism in Southeast Asia: The Role of the Sangha in the Modernization of Thailand*. New York: St. Martin's Press.
Spiro, Melford E. (1982). *Buddhism and Society: A Great Tradition and Its Burmese Vicissitudes*. Berkeley: University of California Press.
Suwanna Wongwaisayawan (1985). Merit and Power: Trilak and Laksana Thai. In Sombat Chantornvong and Chaiwat Satha-anand, Eds. *Yuu Muang Thai: A Collection of Essays in Honour of Professor Saneh Chamarik*. Bangkok: Thammasat University Press.
— (1986). *Buddha-Dhamma in Thai State*. Bangkok: Thai Khadi Research Institute.

Tambiah, Stanley J. (1976). *World Conqueror and World Renouncer: A Study of Buddhism and Polity against a Historical Background*. Cambridge: Cambridge University Press.

— (1978). Sangha and Polity in Modern Thailand: An Overview. In B.L. Smith, Ed. *Religion and Legitimation of Power in Thailand, Laos and Burma*. Chambersburg, PA: Anima Books.

— (1984). *The Buddhist Saints of the Forest and the Cult of Amulets: A Study in Charisma, Hagiography, Sectarianism and Millennial Buddhism*. Cambridge: Cambridge University Press.

Terwiel, B.J. (1980) *Field Marshal Plaek Phibun Songkhram*. Queensland: University of Queensland Press.

Thak Chaloemtiarana (1979). *Thailand: The Politics of Despotic Paternalism*. Bangkok: Social Science Association of Thailand and Thai Khadi Research Institute.

Turner, Victor (1957). *Schism and Continuity in an African Society*. Manchester: Manchester University Press.

Varunee Osatharom (1989). A Comprehensive study of Thai Peasant Rebellion: Themes, Methodologies and Changes. *Journal of Political Science* (Thammasat University) 14(1):341–409.

Vella, Walter F. (1978). *Chai Yo! King Vajiravudh and the Development of Thai Nationalism*. Honolulu: University Press of Hawaii.

Wenk, Klaus (1968). *The Restoration of Thailand under Rama I, 1782–1809*. Arizona: University of Arizona Press.

Wilson, David A. (1962). *Politics in Thailand*. Ithaca, New York: Cornell University Press.

Wyatt, David K. (1969). *The Politics of Reform in Thailand: Education and the Reign of King Chulalongkorn*. New Haven: Yale University Press.

Yagi, Shusuke (1988). *Samnak Puu Sawan: Rise and Oppression of a New Religious Movement in Thailand*. Unpublished Ph.D. Dissertation, University of Washington.

Yos Santasombat (1985). *Power and Personality: An Anthropological Study of the Thai Political Elite*. Unpublished Ph.D. Dissertation. University of California. Berkeley.

— (1989). Leadership and Security in Modern Thai Politics. In Mohammed Ayoob and Chai-anan Samudavanija, Eds. *Leadership Perceptions and National Security*. Singapore: Institute of Southeast Asian Studies.

14

The Politics of Cultural Citizenship[1] : A Second Look at "Buddhist Cultural Tradition and the Politics of National Identity in Thailand"

Chaiwat Satha-Anand

In "Buddhist Cultural Tradition and the Politics of National Identity in Thailand," Yos Santasombat maintains that the development of national cultural policies designed and implemented by the state while informed by the unitary view of Thai society has greatly undermined the problems of cultural, religious and ethnic diversity. Moreover, he argues that the context of religious pluralism makes it more difficult for the state to use religion to legitimize its authority while claiming to act on behalf of the entire society. Categorically, he states that "Buddhism no longer provides an overlapping basis for personal identity and national authority" (Yos 1992:12). Yos suggests that such a discrepancy is primarily a result of the fact that

Thai society "becomes more internally complex" because of processes of industrialization of institutional structures and the modernization/Westernization of culture, among other things (Yos 1992:1–2).

This paper is an attempt to take a second look at the politics of national identity by arguing that such a "discrepancy" is also a result of a national cultural policy which determined to politically construct a new type of citizen for the emerging Thailand. I will first trace the reasons given for the adherence to the unitary view Yos pointed out back to a critical time in modern Thai history when a strong cultural policy was formulated almost half a century before the Thai delegations expressed their views at the second World Conference on Cultural Policies in 1982 (Yos 1992:2).[2] Then, its impact on the Muslim religio-ethnic group, the Chinese ethnic group and some Buddhists themselves will be addressed. Contemporary efforts to define an integrative Thai identity based upon the resurgence of Buddhism will also be discussed in connection with the prominent role during the May 1992 uprising of Maj. Gen. Chamlong Srimuang, a national politician who is also a member of the Santi Asoke Buddhist group. Finally, the Thai state's perspective on different groups of citizens, especially the Buddhists and the Muslims, will be critically appraised.

PHIBUN'S CULTURAL POLICY AND 1939

Before 1939 the name of the country that is known all over the world today as "Thailand" was "Siam." The name change which took place in 1939 was a manifestation of Field Marshal Phibun Songkhram's cultural policy which first ruled the country from 1938 to 1944. While the name change can be seen as a response to "nationalistic aspirations" and the concepts of "nationhood" at the time (Reynolds 1991:5), the fact that the then cabinet spent only ten minutes making such a historic decision on May 8, 1939, mainly discussing legalistic effects of their action, means that the government was using state power to legalize tradition (Chai-anan 1991:62–63). In other words, the name change was a legal decision backed by state power which dictated the cultural direction as well as the identity perimeter of the citizens in the country.

The name change from Siam to Thailand was promulgated in the first Cultural Mandate issued on June 24, 1932 (Reynolds 1991:6). It is interesting to note that this political act of historic significance took shape under the term of "cultural mandate." In addition, the mandate was promulgated on the seventh anniversary of the revolution which put an end to absolute monarchy in Thailand. If the revolution of 1932 is seen as an effort by the official class who captured state power and put an end to the ancient regime (Chai-anan 1991:61), then the emerging regime faced a new type of problem: to secure popular loyalty to a centralized state without the support of the special feature of absolute monarchy through which the loyalty of the subjects can be much more personalized and focused, not to mention the long traditional ground which legitimized the institution. In an attempt to create a new type of loyalty in the emerging state, a new form of citizenship needed to be created. I would argue that the Thai state in 1939 then devised the "cultural mandate" mainly as a vehicle for this purpose.

After issuing the name change in the first Cultural Mandate, the Thai state negatively defined Thai identity by identifying the perimeter of "un-Thai" in the second Cultural Mandate. Activities such as revealing information to foreigners that might jeopardize national interests or acting against them by working as foreign agents were considered "un-Thai" or "anti-Thai." Then the fourth Cultural Mandate of August 2, 1939, discouraged the use of the terms Northern Thais, Northeastern Thais, Southern Thais or Islamic Thais (sic) in favor of "the Thais"

(Reynolds 1991:6). The new loyalties were channeled through newly constructed national symbols such as the flag and the national anthem. Other Mandates which continued until 1942 encouraged national growth, unity through hard work, use of the national language, prescriptions for proper dress, and motivating people to engage in healthy activities in their daily lives, among others (Reynolds 1991:6).

The promulgation of these Cultural Mandates can be attributed to the personal inclination of Field Marshal Phibun Songkhram whose dictatorial orientation is widely known. According to a prominent Thai social critic, the Field Marshal made himself the leader, "the Fuhrer," and expanded the earlier version of nationalism espoused by King Rama VI while encouraging suspicion of the Chinese in favor of the Thai race as well as glorifying the Thai empire in a manner not unlike that of Nazi Germany (Sulak 1991:47). But taken together, I would argue that these "cultural" mandates sought to create a new Thailand with a new type of citizen through cultural policies. These policies would effectively link national identity and national security (Reynolds 1991:6) because forsaking or jeopardizing national interests had become an act of betrayal of one's identity as a Thai. In addition, the regional self-understandings which in themselves were informed by local traditions and historical legacies were all but denied under the term "Thai." In the process of undermining local realities by discouraging local languages and histories— though encouraging some behaviors such as husbands kissing their wives before going to work and women wearing hats and gloves (Likhit 1988:94)— a new exclusivistic sense of national identity was created through purposeful cultural policies. The impact of these cultural policies on different ethnic groups, especially the Malay Muslims and the Chinese, can now be discussed. These two groups are chosen because while the former can be considered an ongoing concern of the Thai establishment (as evident in the opinion expressed by the commander of the Fourth Regional Army responsible for security in the South, quoted in Wijeyewardene 1991:179–180), the latter is widely regarded as a story of success.

THE IMPACT OF CULTURAL POLICIES ON DIFFERENT ETHNIC GROUPS

Thai society is not homogeneous (Chavivun and Chaiwat 1985). Due to the Muslims' everyday practices and images, they are perhaps the most visible religio-ethnic group. But the Muslims themselves are also heterogeneous. There are Persian, Arab, Indian, Cambodian, Chinese and Malay Muslims in the country; some came to what is now Thailand in the Ayudhaya period during the seventeenth century (Chaiwat 1991:96–97). Due to a combination of factors which include the demographic concentration of the Malay Muslims in the area, the geographical proximity to Malaysia, and the separatist movements, they have been perceived as a unique religio-ethnic group by the Thai government. Their distinct character is a result of their ethnicity, religion, and history. The ethnic Malays who constitute the majority in the four southernmost provinces of Thailand share a commonality of religious beliefs, language, a series of customs, styles, rituals and appearance more with peoples in the Malay cultural world of Southeast Asia than with their fellow citizens in the rest of the country. Historically, their homeland was incorporated into the modern Thai nation-state after the policy of administrative centralization introduced by King Rama V (1868–1910) in 1906. With the Anglo-Siamese Treaty signed in March 1909, the present Malaysia-Thailand border was established and Malay Muslims became citizens of the new Thai nation-state (Che Man 1990:35).

As a people whose manifestation of ethnicity is possible mainly by means of cultural forms that give the impression that they are inherent as a particular category, their ethnic identity (as a relational construct) would not mean much without the existence of "Malay Muslims" as an ethnic group and category (Roosens 1989:19). In this sense, the Cultural Mandate promulgated by the new Thai state affected them most in the process of clashing over existing local cultural expressions. For example, in the 1941 royal decree, "Prescribing Customs for the Thai People," improper dress and decorum were defined. Certain kinds of clothing, including sarongs (common clothing among the Malay Muslims in the South), were deemed to be damaging to the prestige of the country (Reynolds 1991:7). The process of creating a new type of citizen out of the Malay Muslims using cultural policies gained impetus with the government's integrative strategies and methods, using numerous social programs including government policies on *pondok* education (Muslim traditional religious school) and youth programs as well as economic policy aiming at their dependency on the Thai economic system. In fact, a Thai scholar asserts that in Southern Thailand, the key thing for the success of the government's political integration policy is "to erase the Malay ethnicity of the Malay Muslims according to which potential integration will be successful at the point when most Malay Muslims identify themselves as Thais (who profess Islam) or Thai Muslims, not as Malay Muslims" (Panomporn 1984:34–35).

It is wise to view the chance of success of such a governmental policy cautiously. The process of erasing a portion of ethnic identity of a people is especially difficult given Islam and Malay nationalisms which have always been unified and nurtured by the Malay language and transmitted through the family. The success of modern media such as television and radio notwithstanding, differences between the Malay Muslims and other Thai citizens are likely to continue. When such differences are situated in a turbulent political history of involuntary incorporation into a modern nation-state which is considered foreign to the Malay Muslims (Chaiwat 1992:13–14), conflict arising out of the state's effort to construct a new type of citizenship (with a standardized culture out of such a tightly-knit religio-ethnic group) will not easily disappear. The same, however, cannot be said about the Chinese ethnic group in Thai society although in the beginning the story was not much different.

With the passing of the Cultural Mandates, the identity perimeter was set. As a result, any name or surname which denoted "un-Thai" origin, notably Chinese, had to be changed. Educational opportunities for the "un-Thai," especially in the military field, were severely curtailed because only "pure Thai" could join the naval or military academy. Those who wished to join these academies had to prove that their grandfathers were pure Thai and not of Chinese extraction (Sulak 1991:49–50). In fact, trades involving the sale of ecclesiastical objects for the monkhood were preserved for the Thais and the "foreign" Chinese were prohibited from engaging in them (Sulak 1991: 50).

In the eyes of the emerging Thai state, the Chinese were discriminated against not because of any direct or immediate political threat but because their economic success could develop into a potent political force. Thus, their opportunity to do so needed to be curtailed. As a result, the Chinese who were marginalized had to resort to underground associations or develop political links with the Kuomintang or the communists. These political relationships were considered subversive to the Thai state and therefore illegal. In effect, the state successfully contained the Chinese influence by providing them with economic space while externalizing them as political forces through the process of identifying them as "alien" or "un-Thai" (Chai-anan 1991:70). With the perceived rise of the communist threat in the 1940s and 1950s, the Chinese were forced to abandon their identity on two levels. First, culturally "they had to prove that they recognized, accepted and were willing to socialize under dictates of the state which established a set of criteria for its citizenry." Second, no political option was open to them (Chai-anan 1991:74). In other words, the Thai state attempted to construct a new type of citizenship for the Chinese by limiting their Chinese identity space to such a degree that, at the cultural-political nexus, its meaning is all but vanished. This again begins to change when the Chinese were positively perceived as good for economic development in Thailand in the 1970s (Chai-anan 1991:75). But then it can be argued that the Chinese were given an opportunity to become "good" Thai citizens. With the decline of the communist threat in the late 1980s, the expanding democratic space of the Thai polity and the rise of the middle class, many of whom were Chinese descendants, these citizens of the new Thai state began to reassert their cultural identity.

In the latter part of 1992, there was a popular television series which generated a lively debate on the Chinese in Thailand. The show is called "Lodd Lai Mungkorn," or "'Through the Dragon's Design." It is the story of a poor Chinese immigrant who successfully built a business empire in Thailand after years of hard work, Confucian business ethics and keen business sense. There are two important points about this television show. First, it is a story that is no different from the humble beginning of many a Chinese family's real life in Bangkok. Second, it can be seen as a rebellion against the traditional way of representing the Chinese in mainstream Thai media. This is because in the past the image of the Chinese in cinema or on television has always been negative. They were portrayed as cruel villains or funny rural coffee shop owners who are almost always unable to speak Thai correctly. Their accents had become a constant source of laughter in Thai cinemas. To make the main characters of the drama Chinese while retaining most Chinese characteristics was, in effect, revolutionary (Kasian 1992:107). It was revolutionary both because of its realist form and its accurate portrayal of the rise of bourgeoisie in Thailand who have primarily been Chinese. What is interesting is that this revitalized cultural politics of Chinese identity should take place at this time. It goes without saying that Thailand's economic success (in terms of its growth rate), with the Chinese-Thai at the front line, has been a major contributing factor. But the success of the show as well as the debate it was able to generate suggest a move away from the phase when their citizenship was primarily imposed by the emerging nation-state and they had to compromise their identity (Seksan 1992:120). The imposed citizenship was not able to erase their cultural traits completely. Now that they are more secure in the cultural political space as Thai citizens, their Chinese culture can be expressed.

In comparative terms, the Chinese began to express their Chineseness publicly because the new state was able to respond to their economic needs and provide them with operative political space, while the Malay Muslims continue to express theirs perhaps because the citizenship platform suggested by the new Thai state has not been quite compatible with their cultural citizenship. In the Malay Muslims' case, their assertion of cultural citizenship is informed by both cultural practices and history. Many of their cultural practices are incompatible with mainstream Thai culture, perhaps most notably in the area of food. In addition, their history is not a history of immigrants, as is the case with the Chinese, but a history of inhabitants of a land involuntarily incorporated into the new Thai state. Moreover, the role of religion in legitimizing their cultural citizenship is also significant. For the Malay ethnic group, being a Malay is almost synonymous with being a Muslim. Islam in this sense serves as an additional factor rendering the imposition of national citizenship more difficult. But for the Chinese, it seems that Buddhism has long been accepted in the way it is being practiced in Thai society. In fact, the Thai state has more problems with other Buddhist movements than with the Chinese who are Buddhists. This becomes quite clear when viewed through the May 1992 uprising.

VIEWING THE CULTURAL POLITICS OF THE MAY 1992 UPRISING

The issue of Thailand's emerging Buddhist movements has recently been widely addressed (Suwanna 1990; Yos 1992; Apinya 1993; Taylor 1993). Here I choose to discuss the politics of Buddhism by focusing on the May 1992 uprising and the role played by Maj. General Chamlong Srimuang.[3]

At the risk of oversimplification, the May 1992 event was a response to the military attempt to perpetuate its power in national politics after the successful coup of February 1991. General Suchinda Kraprayoon, one of the major February coup leaders, became the unelected Prime Minister after the March 1992 national election. Chamlong, an opposition party leader, led a large group of people in a campaign against the unelected Prime Minister. The campaign was mainly nonviolent, but then on May 18 Chamlong was arrested and the troops opened fire on unarmed demonstrators. The scene shocked the world, given Thailand's reputation as a society informed by Buddhist culture. Then with the intervention of the King, among other things, the military returned to the barracks and General Suchinda resigned. Thailand had another national election on September 13, 1992, and a fully elected government led by the Democrat Party was installed (Chaiwat 1993).

What is relevant in the context of this discussion is the way Chamlong was portrayed by the State-controlled media. Chamlong is a follower of the Santi Asoke group. As a strict vegetarian, he normally eats one meal a day and abstains from indulging in worldly luxuries and pleasures. His ascetic lifestyle has always been a subject of criticism by many Thai Buddhists. In a television interview, M. R. Kukrit Pramoj, a former Prime Minister and one of the most influential columnists in Thai society, said that Chamlong's lifestyle could be a threat to all mainstream Buddhists in Thailand and lead to a religious war (*The Nation*, May 11, 1992). In fact, Suchinda seized on this fear of religious conflict and told the Thai parliament on

May 7, 1992, that one of the reasons he accepted the premiership was that a large number of Buddhists requested him to "stop a certain political leader from setting up a new religion." On May 8, amidst the heat of the campaign against him, Suchinda was called on at the Government House by a group of Buddhists to thank him for "defending Buddhism." They also asked him to make Buddhism a state religion (*The Nation*, May 11, 1992). Then on May 10, there was a special conversation on television between two "experts" on anti-communist psychological warfare and Buddhism. Essentially, while ridiculing Chamlong's practice of Buddhism as a Santi Asoke style which is shunned by the Sangha, they accused him of mixing politics with religion, something which they claimed was against the Buddha's teaching of the search for enlightenment. The religious "expert" said that Chamlong's activity could start a "religious war" and that "True Buddhists wouldn't approve of such a rally" (*The Nation*, May 11, 1992).

A prominent Buddhist monk wrote that two main qualities of a Buddhist include being born in a Buddhist country and in a Buddhist family (Phra Raj Dhamnithet 1990:(4)). Then he pointed out that to be a cultural person in practice a person should "obey the laws of the land unconditionally even though he/she might disagree with some laws, but they are inviolable" (Ibid.: 3). Seen in this light, Chamlong's action was considered unbecoming for a "Thai Buddhist."

It can be argued that Chamlong, as a politician who is a devout Buddhist with a strong moral stance, brings Buddhism and the Thai state into a closer relationship which makes the already tenuous distinction between secular and religious affairs even more difficult to uphold. Chamlong represents the "possibility of the political imposition of fundamentalist ethical restrictions on individual behavior, based on religious ethics and justified in terms of promoting the national good and socio-economic development" (Jackson 1989:189). In this sense, Chamlong's inclusion of Buddhism in his politics can be seen as a competing endeavor in the accepted definition of Thainess.

His action and leadership in the May event were a political threat not only to the Suchinda regime, but also to the way in which Buddhism associates itself with the Thai state. They also amounted to a questioning of the practices of Thai citizens who are Buddhists.

CONCLUSION: THE THAI STATE'S PERSPECTIVE ON CITIZENSHIP

Taken together, I would argue that the emerging Thailand needs to construct a new type of citizenship which would fit the new national construct. The new Thai, directed first by Cultural Mandates in the beginning and later by cultural policies both implicit and explicit, should adopt the cultural style espoused by the State. Those whose identity bases are not conspicuously incompatible with this new type of citizenship will be accepted as full fledged citizens when they are considered a political threat, as has been the case with the Chinese. For those with a somewhat incompatible identity basis, as in the case of the Muslims, the state can be elastic enough to accommodate their cultural differences. This is perhaps because, due to their historical position vis-a-vis Thai society, the Malay Muslims realize the fact that their cultural citizenship belongs elsewhere. As a result, they can choose to accept the Thai state without questioning "Thainess." On the other hand, some Buddhists, especially the Santi Asoke and public figures such as Chamlong, are a threat to the foundation of Thainess. Since the basis of their identity is also Buddhism, they pose a formidable challenge to the unifying definition of the new citizens who are Buddhists and Thais. In reconnecting their cultural citizenship to Buddhism through practices and sometimes direct engagement in politics, they seriously challenge the unified political citizenship informed by cultural policies.

NOTES

1. I was first introduced to the idea of "cultural citizenship" by the distinguished Stanford University anthropologist, Professor Renato Rosaldo, in a Social Science Research Council Workshop in Honolulu in 1993.
2. Yos is fully aware of the beginning of the first Culture Act of 1937 which he considers as an extension of the 1932 revolution (Yos 1992:13, fn. 4). 1.1.
3. A learned discussion of Chamlong's political idea, especially his exposition of the linkage between "Thainess" and his style of Buddhism, can be found in McCargo (1993).

REFERENCES

Apinya Fuengfusakul (1993). Empire of Crystal and Utopian Commune: Two Types of Contemporary Theravada Reform in Thailand. *Sojourn* 8(1):153–183.

Chai-anan Samudavanija (1991). State-Identity Creation, State-Building and Civil Society. In Craig J. Reynolds, Ed. *National Identity and Its Defenders: Thailand, 1939–1989*. Clayton, Victoria: Monash Papers on Southeast Asia-No. 25, pp. 59–85.

Chaiwat Satha-Anand (1993). Nonviolent Practices, Professional Class and Democracy: The Bangkok May 1992 Case. A paper presented at the Program on Nonviolent Sanctions in Conflict and Defense, Center for International Affairs, Harvard University, March 17, 1993.

— (1992). Pattani in the Eighties: Academic Literature and Political Stories. *Sojourn* 7(1):1–38.

— (1991). Bangkok Muslims and the Tourist Trade. In Mohamed Ariff, Ed. *The Muslim Private Sector in Southeast Asia*. Singapore: Institute of Southeast Asian Studies, pp. 89–121.

Chavivun Prachuabmoh and Chaiwat Satha-Anand (1985). Thailand: A Mosaic of Ethnic Tensions under Control. *Ethnic Studies Report* 3(1).

Che Man, W.K. (1990). *Muslim Separatism: The Moros of Southern Philippines and the Malays of Southern Thailand*. Singapore: Oxford University Press.

Jackson, Peter A. (1989). *Buddhism, Legitimation, and Conflict: The Political Functions of Urban Thai Buddhism*. Singapore: Institute of Southeast Asian Studies.

Kasian Tejapira (1992). *Lae Lodd Lai Mungkorn* (Looking through the Dragon's Design). *Journal of Political Science* (Thammasat University) 18(2):104–108.

Likhit Dhiravegin (1988). Nationalism and State in Thailand. In K.M. de Silva et al., Eds. *Ethnic Conflicts in Buddhist Societies: Sri Lanka, Thailand and Burma*. London: Pinter Publishers, pp. 92–106.

McCargo, Duncan (1993). Towards Chamlong Srimuang's Political Philosophy. *Asian Review 1996*. Institute of Asian Studies, Chulalongkorn University, pp. 171–208.

Nation, The (1992). No Dharma in the Pro-Suchinda Propaganda. May 11, 1992.

Panomporn, Anurugsa (1984). Political Integration Policy in Thailand: The Case of the Malay Muslim Minority. Ph.D. Dissertation, University of Texas at Austin.

Phra Raj Dhammnithet (1993). *Su Suksant*. Bangkok: Buddhism Sustaining Center.

Reynolds, Craig J., Ed. (1991). *National Identity and Its Defenders: Thailand, 1939–1989*. Clayton, Victoria: Monash Papers on Southeast Asia, No. 25.

Roosens, Eugeen (1989). *Creating Ethnicity: The Process of Ethnogenesis*. Newbury Park, CA: Sage Publications.

Seskan, Prasertkul (1992). *Chuachart, Chonchun Iac Prachathipatai* (Races, Classes, and Democracy). *Journal of Political Science* (Thammasat University) 18(2):118–121.

Sulak Sivaraksa (1991). The Crisis of Siamese identity. In Craig J. Reynolds, Ed. *National Identity and its Defenders: Thailand, 1939–1989*. Clayton, Victoria: Monash Papers on Southeast Asia, No. 25, pp. 41–58.

Suwanna Satha-Anand (1990). Religious Movements in Thailand. *Asian Survey* 30(4):395–408.

Taylor, Jim (1993). Buddhist Revitalization, Modernization, and Social Change in Contemporary Thailand. *Sojourn* 8(1):62–91.

Wijeyewardene, Gehan (1991). The Frontiers of Thailand. In Craig J. Reynolds, Ed. *National Identity and Its Defenders: Thailand, 1939–1989*. Clayton, Victoria: Monash Papers on Southeast Asia, No. 25, pp. 157–190.

Yos Santasombat (1992). Buddhist Cultural Tradition and the Politics of National Identity in Thailand. *Culture & Communication Working Papers, No. 4*. Honolulu, Hawaii: Institute of Culture and Communication, East-West Center.

ABOUT THE CONTRIBUTORS

Harumi Befu is currently a Professor emeritus at Stanford and a Professor of Anthropology at Kyoto Bunkyo University in Japan. His current research interest is ethnicity and nationalism. His major publications include *Japan: An Anthropological Introduction* (1971), *The Challenge of Japan's Internationalization* (coeditor, 1984), and numerous journal papers.

Chua Beng-Huat, is currently Associate Professor, Department of Sociology, National University of Singapore and a co-editor of *Southeast Asian Journal of Social Science* published by the Department of Sociology. His research interests include local issues of public housing and urban planning. He has published in *Journal for the Theory of Social Behavior, American Sociologist, Philosophy and Social Criticism, Asian Studies Review, The International Journal of Urban and Regional Research*, and *Contemporary Southeast Asia*.

Allen J. Chun has been a research fellow at the Institute of Ethnology, Academia Sinica (Taiwan) since 1983. In 1993, he joined the Research School of Pacific Studies, Australian National University, as a research fellow jointly in the Anthropology Department and Contemporary China Centre. His current research interests include socio-cultural theory, historical anthropology, postcolonial formations, and Chinese society. His recent publications include articles in *The Journal of Historical Sociology, Dialectical Anthropology, The Australian Journal of Chinese Affairs*, and *History and Anthropology*.

Darrell William Davis is Director of the Asia Program at the Yamagata International Documentary Film Festival. He has published articles on Asian and American Cinema in a number of journals, and his essay "Genroku Chushingura and the Primacy of Perception" appears in the anthology *Cinematic Landscapes: Observations on the Visual Arts and Cinema in China and Japan* (University of Texas Press, 1994). Currently, he lives and teaches in Kobe, Japan.

Virginia R. Domínguez is Professor of Anthropology and Co-Director of the International Forum for U.S. Studies at the University of Iowa. Her research interests include public discourse(s) and the histories and politics of collective classifications. She has published *People as Subject, People as Object: Selfhood and Peoplehood in Contemporary Israel* (Madison: University of Wisconsin Press, 1989), *White by Definition: Social Classification in Creole Louisiana* (New Brunswick: Rutgers University Press, 1986), and (with Jorge I. Domínguez) *The Caribbean and Its Implications for the United States* (New York: Foreign Policy Association, 1981).

Wari Iamo is currently the Director of the Papua New Guinea National Research Institute and a senior lecturer in the Department of Anthropology and Sociology at the University of Papua New Guinea. His current work focuses on reforms in the local level government system of Papua New Guinea.

Eddie C. Y. Kuo is Professor and founding Dean of the School of Communication Studies at Nanyang Technological University, Singapore, and Director of the Mass Communication Programme at the National University of Singapore. His research areas include sociology of language and communication, communication policy and planning, information technology and information society, and Singapore as a plural society. He is the author of *Language and Society in Singapore* (1980), *Communication Policy and Planning in Singapore* (1983), *Information Technology and Singapore Society* (1990), and *Mirror on the Wall: Media in a Singapore Election* (1993).

Lamont Lindstrom is Professor of Anthropology at the University of Tulsa. His research interests include the refitting and reconceptualizing of Pacific island cultures within nationalist and other discourses of identity. His publications include *Kwamera Dictionary* (1986); *The Pacific Theater: Island Representations of World War II* (1989); *Island Encounters: Black and White Memories of the Pacific War* (1990, 1st ed. edited by and 2nd ed. written with Geoffrey M. White); *Drugs in Western Pacific Societies* (1987); *Kava: The Pacific Drug* (1992, with Vincent Lebot and Mark Merlin); *Knowledge and Power in a South Pacific Society* (1990); and *Cargo Cult: Strange Stories of Desire from Melanesia and Beyond* (1993).

Yos Santasombat is Professor of Anthropology, Faculty of Social Science at Chiang Mai University and serves as the Director of Research at the Local Development Institute, Thailand. His current research interests include community-based natural resource management, biodiversity and indigenous knowledge, women and sexual regulations, and consumerism and modern society. He is the author of *Power, Personality and the Thai Political Elite* (1990) and *The Commoditisation of Female Sexuality in Thailand* (1992) and co-editor of *Community Forestry in Thailand: Development Perspective* (1993).

Chaiwat Satha-Anand is the President of the Social Science Association of Thailand and serves as the Director of the Peace

Information Center, Foundation for Democracy and Development Studies, and convenor of the Nonviolence Study Group with the International Peace Research Association (IPRA). He has written, edited, and co-edited books in both Thai and English. Most recently, he has published *The Nonviolent Crescent: Two Essays on Islam and Nonviolence* (Alkmaar, The Netherlands: International Fellowship of Reconciliation, 1996) and *Thailand's Military Budget 1982–1991: Vision and Policy Thoughts* (Bangkok: Thailand Research Fund and Kobfai, 1996), and co-edited *Islam and Violence* (Matsunaga Peace Institute, University of Hawaii).

Jacob Simet is currently the Executive Director of the Papua New Guinea National Cultural Commission. His research interests include cultural activities and cultural and national identity in Papua New Guinea. In addition to Dr. Simet's publications with the Institute of Papua New Guinea Studies (IPNGS) and in anthropological journals, he has also had short stories, poems, and legends published in Papua New Guinea and international magazines and books.

Sasha Su-Ling Welland is currently pursuing her PhD in anthropology and is working on *From All This Journey*, a dual biography of two sisters who came of age during the May Fourth Era in China and subsequently emigrated to England and America, forthcoming from the University of Iowa Press.

David Y. H. Wu is Professor and Chair of the Department of Anthropology at the Chinese University of Hong Kong. His most recent publications include *Preschool in Three Cultures: Japan, China, and the U.S.* (1989, with J. Tobin and D. Davidson), *Chinese Culture and Mental Health* (1985, ed. with Wenshing Tseng), and *A Study of the Southeast Asian Chinese Society* (1985, in Chinese, with Y. Y. Li, W. T. Shu, W. L. Wang and J. Hsieh), as well as numerous journal articles.

Haiou Yang is currently a Research Associate at the Center for Occupational and Environmental Health at the University of California, Irvine. Her research areas include the political culture of China and social and cultural issues related to the family, the elderly, and persons with disabilities in the U.S. and Asian and Pacific regions.

INDEX

Acharn Suan 337
Adorno, T.W. 96
Africans, an influx 193
AIDS 163
Aizawa, S. 273
Ajase complex 271
Aksilly, L. 178
Aldrich, B.C. 53
Algerians 285
Aloha Friday 173
Altar of Heaven in Beijing 117
America 52, 276
Americans 284
  native 286
Ananda, King 318
  his brother 319
anatomy of misinterpretation 293ff.
Anderson, B. 9, 12, 25, 80, 139
Anglo-American societies 21
Anti-Bourgeois Liberalism
    Campaign 224, 230
Anti-Spiritual Pollution
    Campaign 230
Apinya, F. 362
Apisai Enos 154
Appadurai, A. 20, 21
Arabs 285, 286
Araki, H. 269
Armenians 285
Art Museums 281
Asia-Pacific regional system 105
Asian, capitalism 62
  culture 52, 62, 63
  population 36, 61
  South and Southeast 193, 284

values 3, 52, 59, 60, 61
  revitalization of 59
Asian-ness 62
Atlantic axis 7
Atsutane, Hirata 298
Australia 24, 52, 142, 285
Australian(s) 149, 283
  colonialism 147
  government 199
  grant 196

Badu, N. 198
bakufu 298
Bangkok 324, 335
  uprising in 19
Bank of Papua New Guinea 171
Bank of Taiwan 117
Barme, G. 254
Basch, L. 21
Battle of the Indigenous Literature 125
Befu, H. 10, 143, 233, 263, 294, 295, 299,
    300, 301
Beijing 252
Beijing Friendship Store 1
Beijing University 256
Bell, D. 59, 306
Benedict, Ruth 267
Bengi, M. 152
hensheng 102
Beona, G. 163, 171, 172, 174
bhikku (Buddhist monk) 308
Kittivuddho 322
Bhumibol, King 319, 323
Biblical text 99
blacks 149

373

Boisen High School 156
boongs 149
borders 2
Bordwell, D. 295
Boroko shopping district 162
Bosavi, Mt. 158
 area 158
 traditions 158
Bosnia 180
Bougainville 149, 197
 Island 177
 Republican (or Revolutionary) Army 167, 180
boundedness 3, 78
 ideologies of 78
 of Hong Kong 20
 of Republic of China 100
 technologies of 9
Bourgeois liberalization 231, 252
 liberalism 224
Bowring Treaty 309
British/Britons 161, 283
 colonial trading post 35
 colonialism 147
British High Commission 161
Brzezinski, Z. 267
Buck, E.B. 126
Buddha, images 16, 329
Buddha's death 319
Buddhism 284, 310, 325, 342
 and social values 325
 as the state religion 308
 history, national ideology and the state 308
 is Thai 325
 Theravada 312
Buddhist, beliefs 325
 cultural tradition 305ff.
  a second look 353ff.
 family 363
 fundamentalism of the Santi Asoke 334
 identity 328
 kingdoms 308
 monks 308, 336, 337, 338, 362
 morality 311
 movements 361
 polity 308
  return of, and its aftermath 319
 principles 333

Sabbath 316
Thais 333, 341, 342, 343, 344
tradition 316
values 308
view of socio-political order 323
Bulmer, R. 191
bunka no Jidai 279
Bunraku 283
Bureau of Culture, Cultural Works (Taiwan) 95, 125
Burma 306

CMIO 48
Cai Shangxi 208
Cai Zhenchan 225
Cambodia 322
Campaign of Criticizing Lin Biao and Confucius 228
Canada 24
Canadians 283
cannibalism 159
capitalist internationalism 24
Caribbean countries 193
Catholic minority groups 332
Catholicism 284
Caw, P. 265
Central Provident Fund (Singapore) 57
Center for Creative Arts (Papua New Guinea) 200
Center for Japanese Studies 283, 297, 300
Centurion, D. 147
Chai-anan, S. 314, 315, 319, 355, 359, 360
Chaiwat Satha-Anand 16, 19, 358, 362
Chakrabongse, Chula 310, 314
Chalmers, I. 46
Chamanan, General Kriangsak 323
Chamlong Srimuang 335, 337, 363
Chan, H.C 46
Chattip, N. 310
Chen Chi-lu 127, 137
Chen Kaige 2
Chen Xiaoya 226
Chen Yang 220
Chiang Ching-kuo 93, 97, 105, 127
Chiang Gong 124
Chiang Kai-shek 87, 97, 100, 124

Index

his reformism 102
memorial hall 117
Chiba, T. 268
Chie, Nakane 282, 296
Chimbu 160, 161
China, PRC 2, 5, 9, 23, 24, 26, 100, 205ff., 286
  citizens of 79
  cultural fever 6
  mainland 19, 100
  Marxism 219
  modern 78
  modernity of 77
  Republic of 115, 122
China-Taiwanese independence political spectrum 105
China Youth Corps 90
China's, post-Mao era 14, 207ff.
  cultural policy and political discourse 250
Chinese 35, 48, 62, 79, 128, 284
  children 60
  civilization 84, 94, 115, 247
  composition 257
  cultural renaissance movement 87, 88
  cultural traditions 209
  culture (see culture)
    in Taiwan 85
  ethnic group 359
  ethnic nationalism 73
  ethnicity 16
  feudalism 216
  folk customs 119
  government 231
  hegemony 97
  history 254
  humanism 211, 212
  intellectuals 255
  intelligentsia 248, 255
    the cultural mission 247ff.
  language 98
  life 253
  majority 36, 43
  medicine 94
  monarchism 211, 212
  nation-state 16
  national character 207, 213
  national consciousness 84
  national identity 136

  nationalism 136
  people 253
  political tradition 254
  polity 80
  population 44
  rendition of nationalism 79
  Republic 116
  rites 211
  scholars 211, 213
  socialist system 248
  society 216, 253
  state 43
  to Taiwanese 123
  traditional culture (see culture)
  traditional identity 85
  traditional value systems 217
  traditions 134
    psychology of 220
Chinese Communist Party (CCP) 208
Chinese Cultural Renaissance Movement 124, 125
Chinese Culture Study Society 227, 229
Ch'ing imperial dynasty 79
Chong, K.C. 54
Choonhavan, Chatichai, prime minister 340
Chowning, A. 149, 166
Christian, campaign 158
  religious minority groups 332
  missions 198
  principles 151
Christianity 135, 146, 153, 158, 164, 269, 284
  fundamentalist 158
  Melanesian 146
Chua Beng-Huat 33ff., 144, 170
Chulalongkorn, King 309, 311, 312, 313, 314
Chun, A. 14, 69ff., 77ff., 115, 133ff., 143
Chusakulchati, Banchong 327
Citizenship Advisory Committee (Papua New Guinea) 152
Clammer, J. 81
Cohen, A. 341
Cohn, B.S. 81
Cold War 97, 99, 100
collective frustration, burden, and mission 255

colonial, experience   190
　regime   50
　rule   190
colonialism   147
　and cultural awareness   190
　Australian   147
　British   147
　Dutch   147
　German   147
　Indonesian   147
Committee for Cultural
　Reconstruction (Taiwan)   93, 94
Committee for Cultural
　Renaissance (Thailand)   93
Committee on National Culture
　(Thailand)   328
Communist, era   84
　national polity   81
　Party   6, 231
　regime   99
　revolution   250
Communist Party of Thailand   322
Confucian, ethical legitamacy   97
　ethics   60
　　and praxis   115
　flavor   92
　gentleman   73
　ideology   92
　scholarship   298
　schools of learning   92
　system   14, 216
　times   257
　tradition   92
　world view   253
Confucianism   62, 91, 92, 136, 220, 228
Confucius   88, 228
　worship of   125
contested collective identity   116
coolie   36
Council for the Education of Muslim
　Children (Mendaki)   45
Crocombe, R.   189
Crawford, A.L.   151, 158, 172, 173
creeping individualism   58
Criterion of Truth   229
cultural, authority   78
　awareness   190
　centers   200
　consciousness   102

construction   123
development   42
difference   2
discourse   52, 63, 87, 207ff.
distinctiveness   2, 3
diversity   197
　and identity   189
　through education   198
elements   224
extinction   4
fever   207
hegemony   208, 209
identity   2, 3, 4, 20
institutions   200
mandates   359, 364
mission   247
plan   163
policies   4, 26, 172
politics   4, 362
promotion   97
reconstruction   97
renaissance   86, 121, 123
　as social movement   82, 87, 91, 93
resistance   4
revolution   86
survival   4
traditions   170, 209, 307
uniqueness   2
unity   192
values   151
Western   163
Cultural Development Program
　3, 172
Cultural Fever   207ff.
　a second look   247ff.
　factors contributing to its
　　emergence   225
　main dimensions of the cultural
　　discourse during   209
Cultural Revolution   208, 221, 228,
　255, 258
cultural(ist)
　articulations of nationalist
　　stakes   1ff.
　discourse in PNG   179, 180
　policies   5, 6, 7, 10, 17
　politics   4,
　　in Europe   4
　representation   8

Index 377

culturalization 4
culture(s) 12, 17, 143, 151, 171, 202,
   208, 209, 224, 231, 316
   as identity 145
   Asian 52, 62, 63
   -asserting 3
   blue 225
   categorized 98
   commodified 98
   Confucianizing of 98
   -crossing 3
   Chinese (traditional) 15, 78, 81, 82,
      84, 89, 90, 92, 94, 98, 115, 120,
      135, 207, 208, 210, 211, 217, 221,
      223, 228, 229, 247, 253
      examination of 210
      scapegoating 211
   Christian 158
   contests 26
   ethnic 60
   fever 5, 14, 19
   global 2
   industry 94, 96
      as national enterprise 77ff.
   Japanese 264, 267, 273, 276, 279, 283
   Melanesian 202
   national 63
   official 93
   PNG 144, 160
   Papua New Guinean 202
   popular 2
   preservation of 72
   racial 43, 61, 63
   secularizing of 98
   Singaporean 5, 70
   Taiwanese 16, 98, 123, 137
   totalized 98
   Western 14, 210, 214, 223, 229
   writing of 98
   yellow 225

Dale, Peter 297, 299
dungwui 102
Daniel, V. 20
Danish 284
Davis, D.W. 11, 293ff.
democracy 224
   ethnicity and tradition in Taiwan's
      national future 99

Democracy Wall Movement 226
Democrat Party 335, 362
Democratic Progressive Party 16, 101
Deng Xiaoping 229, 230
Deng's blueprint 227
Department of Culture and Tourism
   (Papua New Guinea) 168, 174, 201
Departments of Interior, Justice and
   Finance (Thailand) 312
Department of Religious Affairs
   (Thailand) 318
Devan, J. 55
Deyo 47
dhamma 311, 313
Dhani Nivat 313
Dhammic, force 336
   (moral) rule 335
Dibela, Sir Kingsford 167
Doi, T. 270, 272
Dominguez, Virginia R. 1ff.
Drysdale, J. 37, 41
Dumont's monad 73
Dutch colonialism 147

East Asia 8
East Asian 23
East-West Center 3, 7
   scholars 5
   Symposium 297
Eastern Europe 180
   dissolution of 100
Eastern European Countries 4
Ecclesiastical Council 308, 337
ecology 268
Economic Reform 233
Eiichiro, Ishida 269, 275
Elegy, river 208, 217, 224, 225, 252
Enga 173
English 51, 148, 283
   as *lingua franca* of society 51, 70
enlightened colonialism 81
Eoc, S.M. 171
ethnic, consciousness 72
   culture and identity 60
   groups 79
   harmony 72
   identity 73
   nationalism 73
Ethnology Museum (Japan) 282
Europe 52, 118

European(s) 23, 164, 284
  colonization 8
  colonialism 4
  colonialists 141
  settler colonies 18, 23
  global culture 2 (see also culture)
evaluating culture 153
evaluation of Marxism and Mao
  Zedong Thought 217
Evangelical Church of Papua 158
evil empire 293
excesses of success 56
excessive, individualism 57
  material consumption 57

Fan Zhonggan 257
Fang Lizhi 219, 227, 256
Fiji 190, 191
Filer, C. 157, 162, 163, 170, 175, 197,
Finney, B.R. 156
Finnish 284
Five Year Cultural Development
  Plan (Papua New Guinea) 171, 201
Foster, R.J. 189
Foucault, M. 73
Foucaultian terminology 71
Four Modernizations 227
Fox, R. 21, 90
France 285
Free China Journal 95
Free China Review 94, 95
freedom 224
French uniqueness 284
Freud, Sigmond 230
Fudan University 228

Gakuin University 265
Gam, G.S. 158
Gamo, M. 276
Gates, H. 122
Gaza strip 285
Geertz, C. 81, 265, 306
Gellner, E. 25, 80
German colonialism 147
Germany 26, 285
Ghai, Y. 150
Gillroy, P. 25
Girling, J.L.S. 322
global culturalism 24
Gogodala 158

Goh, K.S. 46, 54
Goialas 195
graduate mother policy 55
Gramscian sense 136
grassroots 170
Great Debate 229
Great Wall 84
Griffin, J. 198
Guam's Chamorros 153
Guanggong Province 128
Guise, J. 148, 192
guobao 84
Guoqi 258

Haiou Yang 7, 249
Hajime, Nakamura 282
Hall of Yueyang 257
Hamaguchi, E. 270
Han Dynasties 220
Handler, R. 9
Hanks, L.M. 325
Hannet, L. 191
Hanson, A. 8
Harding, T. 194
Haraszti 254
Haus Tambaran 159
Hawaii 173
Hawker, B. 160
Hayashida, C.T. 277
Hebrew 284
hegemony of homogeneity 263
Heng, G. 55
Heshang 208, 217, 224, 227
Hiambohn, W. 163
Highlanders 149
hijab 17, 330
  crisis 331
Hiri Motu 147, 148
Hiri trade 195
Historical and Folklore Museum 281
Ho, K.L. 59
Holy, L. 265
Hobsbawm, E. 8, 25, 81
Hong Kong 1, 20, 23, 40, 255
Horkheimer, M. 96
House of Assembly 192
Howard, M.C. 189
Hsia dynasty 79
Hsu, Ching-yun 126
hua-hsia 99

Index 379

Huang Jun-jei 257
Huang Wuangsheng 217
huaxia 79, 85, 86, 253
Hughes, L. 194
Human Genome Diversity Project 2
human rights 24
humanism 24
humanized 224

IPNGS Annual Report 192
Iamo, W. 168, 189ff.
Ishii, Y. 310, 325
imagined community 70
Indian(s) 48, 63, 70
Indonesian(s) 149
  colonialism 147
  life of the people 306
Institute of Papua New Guinea
    Studies 172, 200
  founding Director of 193
instituting cultural diversity 198
Internal Security Act 44, 144
International Conference on Chinese
    Traditional Culture 228
International Center 283
Inuta, M. 270
Invention of Taiwanese 115ff.
  A second look 115ff.
  rejoinder 133ff.
Iraq 285
Islam 269, 284
Islamic dress 16
Israel 285
Israeli 285
Itasaka, G. 272
Iwasaki, T. 269
Izumi, S. 276

Jackson, P.A. 363
James, P. 80
Jameson, F. 82, 99
Japan 9, 23, 26, 40, 128, 261ff.
  a second look 293
  -bashing 11
  politics of identity 263
Japan Foundation 283
Japan's, *Nihonjinron* 6
  ecology 268
  homogeneity 274
  national identity 284

pastoral economy 269
post-Meiji era 117
social structure 272
Japanese 135, 263, 264, 279, 285
  colloquial 86
  colonization 6
  culture (see culture)
  cultural sentiment 136
  expressions
  ethnicity 271
  ethos 273
  geist 273
  -Greek architectural style 117
  identity 263, 264
  invasion of China 279
  language 271, 272, 276, 283
  legacy: official amnesia and
    collective nostalgia 119
  linguistic categories 271
  materialism 135
  perceptions 295
  psychology 270
  race 276
  social structure 264, 270
  sword 267
  thought 271
Japanologists 297, 300
Jau Shao-kang 106
Javanese funeral 306
Jawodimbari, A. 168, 169, 172,
    175, 191
Jew 279
Jewish majority 285
Jin Guantao 210, 216, 227, 256
Jinrui Kagaku 276
Judaism 269

K2 Meri 164
Kabuki 283
Kadiba, J. 158
Kakehi, Y. 271
kokoro 273
Kamod, P. 151, 170
Kapferer, D. 286
Kasaipwalova, J. 191
Kasian, T. 360
kastom 5, 13
Katiya, K. 314
Kawamoto, A. 270
Kawamura, N. 280

Kazufumi, M. 265
Keesing, R. 8, 81, 148, 150, 166, 170, 172, 175, 189
Keio University 275
Kelly, D. 227
Kemba, B. 159
Keyes, C.F. 310, 322, 323
Kili, P. 161
Kimura, B. 270
Kirsch, T. 325
Kittikachorn, Thanom 320
Kittivuddho Bhikku 322
Kiyoyuki, Higuchi 267, 299
KMT (Kuomintang) 6, 84, 92, 100, 108
  authoritarianism 104
  government 15, 84
  legislators 106
  model 16
  monopolistic practices 107
  new alliance 107
  old guard 101
  post-war cultural policies 134
  public citizen 73
  riots 104
  totalitarianism 134
  world view 91
Koitas 195
kokugaku 298
Kolia, J. 152, 168
Kong-Yan moral quality 214
kongyan renge 214
Koreans 275, 284, 285, 286
Kraprayoon, Suchinda, General 36, 37
Kros, P. 146, 158
Kuan Kalong 330
Kuki, S. 272
Kula ring 195
Kumon, S. 279
Kundiawa 147
Kuo, Eddie, C.Y. 35ff., 143, 144, 170
Kurds 285
Kuro, R. 179
Kyogoku, J. 277
Kyoto City, Cultural Museum 116
Kyoto University 268

Lakatoi 178
Larmour, P. 141, 149, 150, 180

Lasch, C. 59
  narcissistic individual 73
Latukefu, S. 146, 150, 151, 158, 162, 173, 176
Lee Kuan Yew 37, 55
  People's Action Party 40
Lee Teng-hui 105
Lenin 218
Levi-Strauss, C. 263, 295
Levine, H.B. 8
Lhasa 1
Li Honglin 218, 230
Li Hongqi 255, 256
Li Qin 226
Li Ruihuan 231
Li, Yih-yuan 126, 127, 137
Li-Yi-Zhe 226
Li Zehou 210, 220, 221, 223
Lim, C.Y. 56
Lin Biao 228
Lin, Ching-chieh 126
Lindstrom, L. 12, 16, 20, 154, 189, 190, 197, 199
  report 15
Linnekin, J. 8, 153, 175
Lisse, Y. 164
Liu Xiaobo 210, 213, 214, 219, 220, 230
Liu Zaifu 215, 216
Liu Zehua 210, 212
local traditions, decentralized 78
Lodd Lai Mungkorn 360
Loiskandl, H. 189
Lu Xun 84, 211, 213, 215

Madang 195
Mahathir Mohammed, Malaysian Prime Minister 3
Mailu 195
Maitreya 310
making of a new economic order 46, 49
making of a new nation 35ff.
  a second look 69ff.
making of a new state 42
Malay(s) 35, 48, 50, 55, 63, 70
  as indigenous population 44
  cultural world 16
  majority 44
  Muslims 16, 17, 53
  party 44

Index

Malayo-Polyesian 128
Malaysia 23, 40
Malaysian model 43
Malinowski, B. 195
Malu-Aroma trade 195
Manchu long gowns 124
Mandarin 62, 118, 128
Mannan, M.A. 147
Mao Zedong 213, 233, 250, 255
  death 229
  -style culture 253
  Thought 14, 210, 217, 218, 220, 221, 229, 230, 231, 232
Mao's, Cultural Revolution 5, 221, 222
  cultural system 221
  hegemonic cultural policy 251
  theoretical framework 221
  theories 218
Mao wenti 251
Maoism 21
Martin, Bunsom 326, 332
Martyr's Day 89
Marxism 207, 210, 218, 221, 222, 226, 228, 232
  and Chinese traditional culture 221
  and Mao Zedong Thought 217, 218
  in China 220
  true 218
Marxist, concept of alienation and humanism 219
  framework 222
  system 218, 220
  theories 218
Masumi, Tsuda 267
materialism, the cult of 59
May, R.J. 197, 198
May Fourth Movement of 1919 211, 213, 215, 223, 249, 256
Mekeo 195
Melanesian(s) 149, 154
  Big-Man system 194
  Christianity 146
  countries 144
  cultures 202
  kastom 13
  nationalism 191
  nations 190
  socialism 13
  village 169

Voice 191
Way 13, 167, 168, 176, 191, 194
Merimba, I. 161
Metropolitan Museum of Art 3
Miller, R.A. 277, 278
Minami, H. 270
minben sixiang 214
Ming emperors 84
Minister of Culture and Tourism (Papua New Guinea, Thailand) 170, 318
Minister of Education (Thailand) 318
Ministry of Community Development (Singapore) 55
Ministry of Education (Japan, Thailand) 280, 327, 328, 330
  Chairman of Culture Committee (Thailand) 327
Ministry of Education, Culture and Science (Japan) 280
Minol, B. 167
minority groups 44
minzu yishi 80, 83
minzu zhuyi 79
Misawa, K. 268
Miszlivetz, F. 101
Miyagi, O. 270
Miyamoto 269
modern Thai society and the quest for identity 325
Mongkut, King 309
Mongol invasion 84
Moolasartsathorn, Phisan 337
Moral Education Report 62
Morel, D. 315, 319
Morita psychotherapy 296
mother tongue 52
Motu sailing canoe 178
Motuan language 148
Mouer, R. 282
Muke, J. 146, 159
multi-ethnic settings 77
multiculturalism 43, 144
multiracialism 43, 44, 48
Murakami, Y. 279
Murashima, E. 308, 313, 314
Muslim(s) 330, 341
  children 45
  identity 17
  Malay 356, 364

Malay girls 17
students 331

Nagashima, N. 276
Nakane, C. 277
Nakarin, M. 319
Nale, A. 152
Namabe 278
Namaliu, former Prime Minister 171, 173, 179
Nanyang University 73
 Chinese language stream 73
Narokobi, B. 146, 149, 154, 156, 159, 162, 163, 164, 167, 169, 171, 176, 191
North Solomons province 167, 197
Nakane, C. 270
Nakasone, prime minister 283
nation-ness 17
national, consciousness 73
 cultural identity 190
 culture 78
 culture policies and moments of confrontation 328
 identity 73, 102, 193, 307
 ideologies 63
 solidarity 102
 treasures 2, 84
 unity 192
National Arts School 172
National Collection 171
National Cultural Council 172, 173, 198, 200
National Cultural Committee 329
National Cultural Development Act 200, 201
National Cultural Development Service 200
National Culture Act 317
National Culture Service 201
National Identity Promotion Office 329
National Memorial 117
National Museum 171, 200
National Museum of Ethnology in Osaka 281
National Palace Museum 2, 84, 117
National Primary Education Committee 329
National Trade Union Congress 47

National Theater 117
National Theater Company 200
National Tourism Corporation 201
National University of Singapore 73
National English stream 73
National Wage Council 47
nationalism 283, 284
 crisis of 78
nationalist, government 99
 politics 101
 stakes 17
Nationalist New Life Movement 249
nationalistic rituals 50
Neo-Confucian scholars 257
Negritude 194
Nelson, H. 198
New Authoritarianism 229
New Authoritarianists 217
New Caledonia 191
New Guinea 155
New Guinean(s) 198
 society 197
new national system 50
News Agency 95
News of the World 160
neo-Marxists 59
NGOs 2
Nichiren 284
Nietzche, Friedrich 230
Nishinomiya 265
Nihon bunkaron 264, 269
Nihon seishin 273
Nihon shakairon 264
Nihonjinron 5, 7, 10, 233, 264, 266-268, 273, 275, 277, 284, 285, 294-301
 and cultural policy 281
 as a cultural model 265
 as a hegemonic model 277
 as an establishment ideology 277
 classics 281
 ethnocentrism 273
 literature 267
 phenomenon 282
 premises of 274
 proposition 265
 theses 270
 writers 269, 270
 writings 265, 268
nihonron 264
Nilkare, J. 161

Index 383

Noga, B.G.   164
Noh   283
Nomura Research Institute   266
Nomura Sogo Kenkyujo   266
non-Marxist Western culture   231
Norinaga, Motoori   298
North Atlantic perspective   22

O'Rourke, D.   159
Oala Oala Rurua   192
Oath of Allegiance ceremony   320
Oedipus complex   271
Offe   41
Office of National Culture Commission   328
official culture and mass consumption   93
Oide, A.   272
Okonogi, K.   271
Osaka people   276

Pacific, axis   7
  nations   190
  region   8, 173
Pacific Sogo of Japan   118
Palang Dhamma   336
Pang, C.L.   43
Pang Pu   208, 210
Panomporn   358
PAP government   42, 56, 72
PNG identity   171
PNG's, National Constitution   199
  new Governor-General   177
  North Solomon's Province   167
  security forces   197
Papua New Guinea (PNG)   3, 9, 12, 15, 16, 24, 26, 139ff., 189ff.
  as the epitome of the primitive   159
  Bank of   171
  cultural diversity and identity   189ff.
    a second look   189
  cultural policies   6
  culture and nationalism in   141ff.
    (see also culture)
  Department of Culture and Tourism   152
  government   20
  lingua franca, Tok Pisin   143
  multiculturalism in   24
  multiracialism in   24

national identity   145
post-colonial   156
provincial government   172
Papuans   149, 198
Pasin Tumbuna   141ff.
Patriot   162
Peiping Opera   117
Peninsular Malaya   40
peoplehood in policy and practice   82
People's Action Party   15
perestrioka   72
Philibert, J.-M.   175
Phimolatham, Phra   321
Phra Potirak   308, 333, 336, 337, 338
Phra Sophonkhanaporn   336
Phra Thammahaveeranuvat   338
plural society   36
Podolefsky, A.   163
Pokawin, P.S.   158
political independence   42
political movement in the guise of culture   248
politics of cultural citizenship   353ff.
Polynesians   286
pondok   38
Poor Student   157
popular culture   2   (see also culture)
Port Moresby   141, 150, 177, 178, 202
  Chimbu residents   161
Post-Chiang Ching-kuo Era   116
Post-Courier   156, 160, 191, 199
Post-Mao era   208, 231, 232
postcolonial experience   190
Potirak, Phra   308, 333, 336
Powell, G.   175
Prachakornthai Party   337
Prajadhipok, King   315, 316
Pramarn Adireksarn   339
Pramoj, M.R. Kukrit   362
Pye, L.W.   251, 256

Qin walls   84
Qing dynasty   89, 121, 124
Qiu Chuiliang   213
Quah, S.   41
Quebec   9

Rabaul   156
racial, chauvinism   61
  communities   44

culture 43, 61, 63 (see also culture)
  identities 61
  statements 149
  terms 149
  tolerance 43
racialism 43
Rajaratnam, S. 42, 59
Rama IV 309
Rama V 309
Rama VIII 318
Rama IX 320
Ranger, T. 8, 81
Raun Raun Theatre 200
Reishauer, E.O. 267
restructuring, community 52
  education 49
  the family 54
Revolution of 1911 79
Reynolds, C.J. 354, 355
Richardson, P. 158
River Elegy 208, 217, 224, 225, 252
Robinson, D.C. 126
Rodan, G. 40, 45
Rodman, M. 175
Rong Jian 217
Rural Advancement Foundation
  International 1
Russia 286

Sabata, T. 269
Sabeh 40
Said, E. 25
Saito, S. 273
Samana, U. 150, 167, 169
Samana-Pharm 339
Samarai Island Observer 157
Sandhu, K.S. 41
Saneh, C. 314
sangang wuchang 211
sangha 308, 310, 326, 342
Sangha Act 311, 312, 317, 320
Santasombat, Y 20, 305ff., 353
Santi Asoke, Buddhist sect 308, 333,
    335, 336, 338, 364
  controversy 333, 342
  movement 7, 308, 333
Sarawak 40, 326
sarong 358
Sartre, Jean Paul 230
Sato, S. 279

Savan, Leslie 293
second look at Taiwan's cultural
  policy 115ff.
  rejoinder 133ff.
secular democratic polity and
  nationalism 315
Sedi, J. 162
Sekiguchi, T. 269
Seksan, P. 361
Seligman, C.G. 195
Senge, F. 161
Sera, T. 272
Shan State of Burma 318
Shared Values 63
Shichihei, Yamamoto 279
Shintoism 284
Shogunal structure 298
Shu Zhan 223, 224
Shumpei, Kumon 279
Siam 318
Siddique, 48
Simet, J. 189ff.
Singapore 9, 26, 33ff., 144, 145
  cultural construction and national
    identity 35ff.
  cultural discourse in 52
  culture 71, 74
  multiculturalism in 24
  multiracialism in 24
  National University 73
  New 74
  politics 72
Singaporean(s) 20, 36, 47, 56, 73, 142
  culture 5, 12, 36, 37, 70
    construction of 70
    genealogy of 39
  government 13
  identity, history of 39
  national identity 37, 69
  nationhood 12
  peoplehood 12
  state 17
  ugly 58
  Westernization of 59
Singhsakda, Panya, General 340
singsins 177
Sinhalese 285
Sinorama 94, 95
Siriwat, Chaipak 338
Sissons, J. 144

Skul Bilong Wokim Piksa 200
Smith, B.L. 306
Social Development Unit 55
social engineering 49
Socialist Road 231
socio-politico-economic order 71
Solomon, A. 3
Solomon Islands 144, 146, 148, 190, 191
Somalia 180
Somare, Michael 192, 199
Sombat, C. 315
Somboon, S. 308, 313, 325
Song Dynasties 220, 257
Songkhram, Phibun, Field Marshall 317, 319, 354
Sophonkhanaporn, Phra 336
South Americans 193
South Asia 8
South Korea 40
South Pacific State, PNG 141
southeast Asians 284
Southern Massim 195
Soviet Union, breakup 101
Sowei, E. 158
Speak Mandarin Campaign 62
spiritual escapism 216
Spiro, M.E.
Spriggs, M. 197
Sri Lanka 285
Sri Lankan Tamil refugees 20
Srimuang, Chamlong 335, 340, 354, 362
Stalin 218
State political control and domination 228
Stone Age in the Space Age 159
Strathern, A. 151, 171, 172
Stuchlik, M. 265
Su Shaozhi 218, 219, 230
subsistence economy as a causal factor 269
Suchinda regime 364
Sugimoto, Y. 282
Sun Yat-sen 80, 84, 124, 258
Sundaravej, Samak 337
Suwanna, W. 310, 325< #^@
Suzuki, H. 269

Tadanobu, Tsunoda 272, 296
Taipei city 116, 118

presidential hall 116, 117
presidential office 116
Taiwan 15, 19, 23, 26, 40, 75ff., 255
 contemporary 77ff.
  politics of heritage 77ff.
 cultural policy and national
  identity 115ff.
  a second look 115ff.
 cultural uniqueness 103
 expulsion from United Nations 100
 identity 107
 independent status in the United
  nations 103
 is China 123
 Land Bank 117
 national culture 97
 national independence 101
 nationalist government 15, 78, 82
 political climate 99
 postwar nationalist 78, 81, 135
 province of China 129
 unofficial status 103
Taiwan Government-General of
 Imperial Japan 117
Taiwanese 20, 118, 128
 colloquial 86
 culture (see culture)
 ethnic 101
 ethnic consciousness 85
 ethnic nationalism 102, 134
 folk culture 16 (see culture)
 government 25
 independence movement 108
 invention of 115ff.
  a second look 115ff
  rejoinder to second look 133ff.
 music 1
 nation-state 16, 103
 national independence 105
 nationalism 101, 102
 students 2
Takao, Suzuki 275, 278
Takehiko, Kenmouchi 297
Takeo, D. 296
Talyaga, K. 169
Tamaki, A. 269, 270
Tambiah, S.J. 308, 309, 310, 320, 321
Tamil(s) 285
 nationalism 20
 refugees 20

Tan 46
Tanaka, prime minister 283
Tang Yijie 210
Tannos, J. 177
Taoism 209
Tawali, K. 191
Taylor, J. 362
Taylor, L. 173
Terweil, B.J. 317
Tetsuro, Watsuji 268, 269, 282, 296
Thai 20
  citizens 361
  classical dresses 331
  cultural heritage 329
  culture 325
  Delegation 326
  essayist 20
  identity, crisis of 333
  is to be Buddhist 342
  Islamic 355
  national identity 20
  northeastern 355
  northern 355
  people, and their customs 356
  personality 325
  political history 310
  polity 310
  society 324, 326, 361
  southern 355
  traditional social order 325
  vocabulary 313
Thai Buddhist, country 19
  cultural identity 20
  polity 343
Thai-ness 364
  foundation of 364
Thai State's perspective on citizenship 364
Thailand 26, 303ff.
  Buddhist cultural tradition in 305ff.
  Buddhists in 362
  political citizenship 19
political culture of 333
  politics of national identity in 305ff.
    a second look 353ff.
  uprising in 311
Thailand's *Santi Asoke* 6
Thak, C. 321
Thammacarik 320
Thammasat University 322, 336

Thammathut 320
Thanarat, Sarit, Field Marshall 319, 320, 321
  his military authoritarianism 321
  his national policy 320
Third Plenary Session of the Eleventh Central Committee of CCP 208, 228
Third World nations 77, 122, 194
Thomas, N. 81
Thumboo, E. 58
tian ren heyi 214
Tiananmen Square 116 , 252
  incident 100
Tinsulanonda, Prem, prime minister 336
Toana Day 173, 199
Toilman, Mathias 192
Tok Pisin (Pidgin English) 143, 147, 148
Tokyo University 274, 279
Tokyoites 276
Tolai people 174
Tomoeda, H. 276
Tonkinson, R. 81, 166
Toro, A., filmmaker 168
Tourism Corporation 201
Tourism Development Act 201
Toyama, S. 271
Trobriand Islands 195
traditional culture 16, 82, 83
  (see also culture)
  Chinese 6, 82, 83
Traditional Mangi of Hagen 174
Trompf, G.W. 146
True National 178
Tsukuba, J. 269
Tu Wei-ming 225
Tuohy, S. 251
Turkey 285
Turkish *gastarbeiters* 285
Turner, V. 341

U Nu 306
U.S.A. 26, 118, 180, 255, 286
U.S. Cultural Studies 4
U.S. National Academy of Sciences 2
USSR 101, 136, 180
UNESCO 4, 329
Umetrifo's poem 175

Index

underground hot spring 226
United Nations 25
  expulsion of Taiwan 100
  independent status for Taiwan 103
United Party 192
unity in (cultural) diversity
  6, 144, 166, 167
University of Papua New Guinea 191
upasampada 309

Vajiravudh, King 313
Vanuatu 23, 144, 146, 148, 154i7, 190, 191
Varunee, O. 310
Vella, W.F. 313
Verdery, K. 18
Vietnam 322
Vogel, Ezra 267, 299

Waiko, J. 146, 169, 191
wairu 258
waisheng 102
Wang Chien-hsiun 106
Wang, G. 35, 126
Wang He 212
Wang Penglin 257
Wang Ruoshui 218, 219, 220, 227, 230
Wang Ruowang 230
Wang Shubai 220, 221
Wang, Yihua 251, 253
wantok system 147, 162
Ward, B.E. 265
Wari, K.R. 152, 173
Washington, D.C. 1
Wat Mahathad, abbott of 320
Wat Thammakai 326
Watson, L. 192
Wei Jingsheng 226, 228
Welland, Sasha Su-Ling 1
wenhua 249, 252
wenhua fuxing yundong 87
wenhua jiaoyu 209
wenhua yishi 209
wenhua zhongxin 93
wenhuare 247, 248, 255
West Bank 285
Western, civilization 175
  cultural elements 36, 224

cultural traditions 209
culture 52, 222, 223
  discussion 222
  democracy 36
  European Countries 4
  ideas 222, 232
  imperialism 83
  language, superimposed 52
  perversions 164
  westernization 51, 52, 61, 224
  westernized 224
  women 175
Wheatly, P. 41
White, G. 12, 190, 201
whites 149
Wilhelm, H. 257
Willmott, W. 40
Wilson, D.A. 316
Wilson, H.E. 49, 50
Wingti, Paias 164
Wolfers, E.P. 149, 166, 177
Wong, A. 55
World civilization 224
World Conference on Cultural
  Policies 326, 329, 332, 354
World War II 86, 120, 317
Wu, D. 5, 14, 19, 115ff., 133, 136, 137, 226, 247ff.
Wu, E. 120
Wu Jiaxiang 217
Wyatt, D.K. 310, 314

Xiao Gongqin 217
Xiao Yanzhong 220
xiaoguan 90

Yala Province 330
Yamada, H. 269
Yamashita, H. 272
Yamato damashii 273
Yan Jiaqi 224, 227, 228
Yanan Literature 250
Yang, H 14, 19, 207ff.
Yang M.M.H. 251
Yati Dham 335
Yellow River 235
  valley 79
Yew, Lee Kuan 37, 55

Yigu fengjin 254
Yokohama Mama 178
Yoobamrung, Chalerm, minister 338
Yos, S. 317, 323, 324, 353, 362
Yoshio, Masuda 274
Youhuan yishi 14, 255
Yu Haocheng 217
Yu Lina 225
Yue Fei 89
Yugoslavia 136
 breakup 101
Yuji, Aida 297

Zhang Jianxin 231
Zhang Weigo 217
Zhang Yimou 21
Zhao Ziyang 217, 229
Zhisang Mahuai 254
zhong yong 223
zhonghua minzu 79, 253
zhongguo 79
zhongguo jie 127
zhongguo ren 79
Zhu Wei 217
Zimmer-Tamakoshi, L. 175, 176